S0-DTB-851

Harry B. Smith

FORGOTTEN STARS OF THE MUSICAL THEATRE

Kurt Gänzl, Series Editor

Lydia Thompson BY KURT GÄNZL

Leslie Stuart BY ANDREW LAMB

William B. Gill BY KURT GÄNZL

David Braham BY JOHN FRANCESCHINA

Alice May BY ADRIENNE SIMPSON

Harry B. Smith BY JOHN FRANCESCHINA

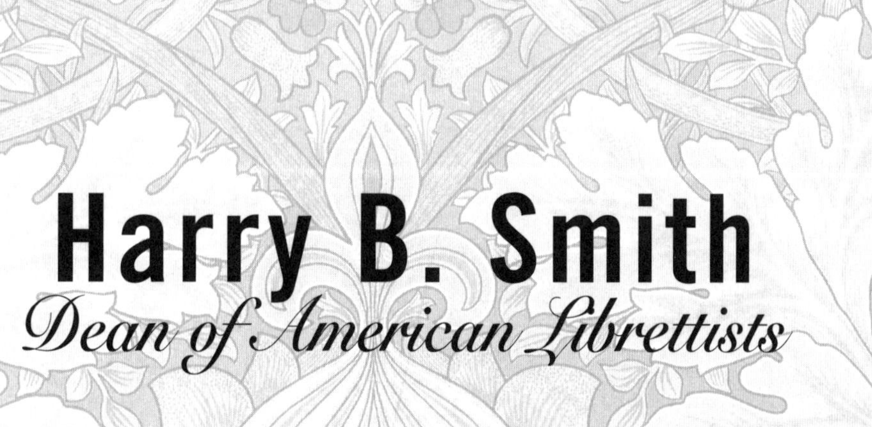

Harry B. Smith

Dean of American Librettists

John Franceschina

FORGOTTEN STARS OF THE MUSICAL THEATRE

Kurt Gänzl, Series Editor

ROUTLEDGE
NEW YORK AND LONDON

Published in 2003 by
Routledge
29 West 35th Street
New York, NY 10001
routledge-ny.com

Published in Great Britain by
Routledge
11 New Fetter Lane
London EC4P 4EE
routledge.co.uk

Routledge is an imprint of the Taylor & Francis Group.
Printed in the United States of America on acid-free paper.

All photos are from the author's collection.

10 9 8 7 6 5 4 3 2 1

Library of Congress Cataloging-in-Publication Data

Franceschina, John Charles, 1947–
Harry B. Smith : dean of American librettists / John Franceschina.
p. cm. – (Forgotten stars of the musical theatre)
Includes index.
ISBN 0-415-93862-7 (hardcover : alk. paper)
1. Smith, Harry Bache, 1860–1936. 2. Librettists—United States—Biography. I. Title.
II. Series: Forgotten stars of the musical theatre.

ML423.S6 F7 2003
782.1'092—dc21

2002153869

Contents

Acknowledgments vii

Series Introduction ix

Chapter One

FROM BUFFALO TO BURLESQUE 1

Chapter Two

BURLESQUE TO BROADWAY 23

Chapter Three

"COME TO SHERWOOD; JOIN OUR JOLLY CREW" 49

Chapter Four

"AM I A WIZ?" 85

Chapter Five
"I'D LIKE TO HAVE A PHOTOGRAPH OF THAT" 121

Chapter Six
"IF I ONLY HAD A THEATRE ON BROADWAY" 157

Chapter Seven
FOLLIES OF THE YEAR 183

Chapter Eight
GERMAN IMPORTS 205

Chapter Nine
JEROME KERN AND IRVING BERLIN 231

Chapter Ten
"HARRY-B-SMITHING" 251

Chapter Eleven
"A LONG WALK UPHILL AGAINST THE WIND" 275

APPENDIX 285

INDEX 291

Acknowledgments

Special thanks to David Boynton, for meticulous research; Marty Jacobs, Associate Theater Curator for Collections and Research Services at the Museum of the City of New York, for providing access to the Harry B. Smith Collection; Susan C. Pyzynski, Librarian for ILS Development and Special Collections, Brandeis University Libraries, for documenting correspondence between Reginald de Koven and Harry B. Smith; Dieter Ullrich, Special Collections and University Archives, Helen A. Ganser Library, Millersville University of Pennsylvania, for providing copies of sheet music; Janet West, Sinclair Lewis Collection at the Port Washington (New York) Public Library, for accessing correspondence regarding *Hobohemia*; and Barb Woods, Interlibrary Loan at the Pattee-Paterno Library, The Pennsylvania State University, for supplying hard-to-find scores and manuscripts. Thanks also to librarians at the Library of Congress, the Rare Book, Manuscript, and Special Collections Library at Duke University, the Harry Ransom Humanities Research Center at the University of Texas at Austin, and the Film Music Archives, Special Collections and Manuscripts, Harold B. Lee Library, Brigham Young University, who provided quick and expert help in this study.

Series Introduction

"Sic transit gloria spectaculi"

Some Famous but Forgotten Figures of the Musical Theatre

Over the past few years, I have spent most of my time researching, writing, and otherwise putting together the vast quantity of text involved in the second edition of my now three-volumed *Encyclopedia of the Musical Theatre.* And, as the Lord Chancellor in *Iolanthe* exhaustedly sings, "thank goodness they're both of them over!" Part of this extremely extended extending exercise involved my compiling bibliographies of biographical works for the hundreds (or was it thousands?) of people whose careers in the musical theatre warranted an entry in the *Encyclopedia.* As I duly compiled, however, I became surprisedly aware of just how many outstanding figures of the historical stage have never, ever been made the subject of even a monograph-sized "life and works." Time and time again, I found that the articles that I have researched (from scratch, not only by choice but quite simply because no-one has ever, it seems, done it before) and written for the *Encyclopedia* are the largest pieces of biographical copy up till now put together on this or that person or personality. And I do not mean nobodies: I mean some of the most important and most fascinating theatrical figures of the nineteenth and early twentieth century theatres.

This series of short biographies is intended to take the first small step towards rectifying that situation. To bring back to notice and, perhaps, even to their rightful place in the history of the international theatre, a few of the people whose names have—for all but the scholar and the specialist—drifted into the darkness of the past, leaving too little trace.

This is a very personal project and one very dear to my heart. And because it is so personal, even though the majority of the volumes in the series are written by my closest colleagues in the theatre-books world, rather than by myself, you will find that they have me stamped on them in some ways. And I take full responsibility for that.

These books are not intended to be university theses. You will not find them dotted with a dozen footnotes per page, and hung with vast appendices of sources. I am sure that that is a perfectly legitimate way of writing biography, but it's a way that has never appealed to me and, because I am being allowed to "do it my way" in this series, the paraphernalia of the thesis, of the learned pamphlet, has here been kept to a minimum. My care, in these biographies, is not to be "learned"; it is to tell the story of Lydia, or Willie or Alice, of Tom or Harry or of Dave, of her or his career in the theatre and (as much as is possible at a century's distance) on the other side of the footlights as well: to relate what they did and what they achieved, what they wrote or what they sang, where they went and with whom, what happened to them and what became of them. Because these people had fascinating lives—well, they fascinate me, and I hope they will fascinate you too—and just to tell their stories, free of any decoration, any theorizing, any generalities, any "significance" (oh! that word)—seems to me to be thoroughly justified.

The decoration, the theorizing, the generalities, and an exaggerated search for (shudder) significance will all be missing. Perhaps because I've spent so much of my life as a writer of reference works and encyclopedias, I am a thorough devotee of fact, and these books are intended to be made up wholly of fact. Not for me even the "educated guess." Not unless one admits it's just a guess, anyhow.

So, what you will get from us are quite a lot of dates and places, facts and figures, quite a lot of theatre-bills reproduced word for word from the originals, quite a lot of songwords from the songwriters and singers, of text from the playwrights and actors and, where we have been able to dig it up, as much autograph material from the hands of our subjects as is humanly possible.

What you won't get any more than can be helped is the "he must have felt that . . ." (must he, who says?), or the "perhaps she. . . ." There will be no invented conversations. No "Marie Antoinette turned to Toulouse-Lautrec and said 'you haven't telephoned Richard the Lionheart this week . . .'" Direct speech in a biography of a pre-recording-age subject seems to me to be an absolute denial of the first principle of biography: the writing down of the content and actions of someone's life. Indeed, there will be nothing invented at all. My theory of biography, as I say, is that it is facts. And if the facts of someone's life are not colorful and interesting enough in themselves to make up a worthwhile book, then—well, I've chosen the wrong people to biographize.

Choosing those people to whom to devote these first six volumes was actually not as difficult as I'd thought it might be. When Richard, my editor, asked me for a first list of "possibles" I wrote it down—a dozen names—in about five minutes. It started, of course, with all my own particular "pets": the special little group of a half-dozen oldtime theatre folk who, through my twenty years and more working in this field, have particularly grabbed my interest, and provoked me to want to learn more and more and indeed everything about them. The only trouble was . . . I was supposed to be editing this series, not writing the whole jolly thing. And there was no way that I was handing over any of my special pets to someone else—not even Andrew, Adrienne, or John—so I had to choose. Just two.

Lydia Thompson, to me, was the most obvious candidate of all. How on earth theatre literature has got to its present state without someone (even for all the wrong reasons) turning out a book on Lydia, when there are three or four books on Miss Blurbleurble and two or three on Miss Nyngnyng, I cannot imagine. Lydia chose herself. Having picked myself this "plum," I then decided that I really ought to be a bit tougher on myself with my second pick. Certainly, I could take it easy and perhaps pot the incomplete but already over-one-million-word biography of the other great international star of Lydia's era, Emily Soldene, which is hidden bulgingly under my desk, into a convenient package. But then . . .why not have a crack at a really tough nut?

When I said I was going to "do" Willie Gill, almost everyone—even the most knowledgeable of my friends and colleagues—said "who?" Which seems to me to be a very good reason for putting down on paper the tale of the life and works of the man who wrote Broadway's biggest hit musical of his era. Tough it has been and tough it is, tracking him and his down, but what satisfaction to drag from the marshes of the past something which seemed so wholly forgotten. A full-scale biography of a man about whom *nothing* was known!

Having realized that these two choices were pinned to the fact that it was I who was going to be writing about them, I then also realized that I ought to be considering my other choices not from own "pet" list, but to suit the other authors who were going to take part in the series. First catch your author.

Well, I caught three. The fourth, pretexting age, overuse, and retirement, got away. But I got the other three—my three (since the fourth is retired) favorite and most respected writer colleagues in the theatre-books business. Enter Andrew, Adrienne, and John: one from England, one from New Zealand, and one from America. A very judicious geographical spread. And the subjects for the four final volumes were, of course, chosen in function of what enthused them.

For Andrew, the not-so-very-forgotten English songwriter Leslie Stuart, whose *Florodora* songs stunned Broadway, and the rest of the world, in the earliest years of this century. For Adrienne, the mysterious Alice May, whose career ranged from Australia and New Zealand to the West End and Broadway and who has gone down in history—when anyone reads that bit of history—as Gilbert and Sullivan's first (full-length) prima donna. For John, two very different American writers: the musician Dave Braham who, while his wordsmith Ned Harrigan has attracted repeated attention down through the years, has been himself left puzzlingly in the shade, and the prolific, ebullient Harry B. Smith, the writer who flooded Broadway with over two hundred musicals in an amazing and amazingly successful career.

I feel bad about the ones who have got left on the cutting-room floor . . . but, maybe later? If we all survive what I've discovered with some apprehension is the intensive work needed to extract from the past the life and works of someone long gone, and largely forgotten.

But it has been worth it. Worth all the work. I've enjoyed it enormously. I know my colleagues have enjoyed it, and are still enjoying it. And I hope those of you who read the stories of Lydia, Willie, and Alice, of Dave, Harry, and Tom, will enjoy them too. And that you will remember these people. Because I really do reckon that they deserve better than to be forgotten.

Kurt Gänzl

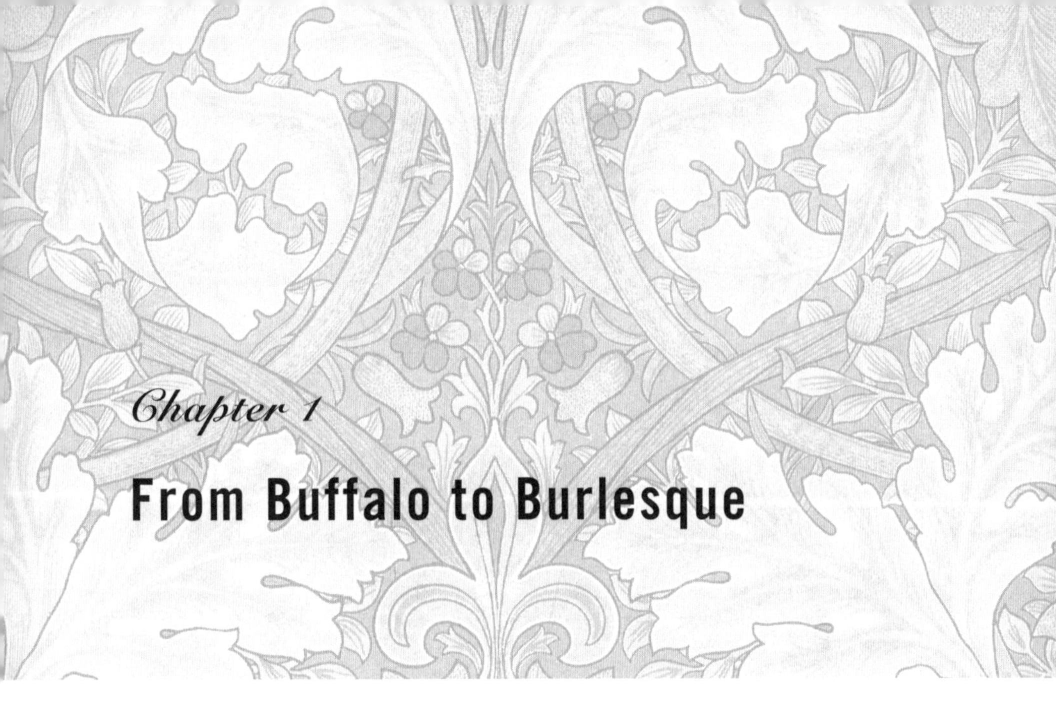

Chapter 1

From Buffalo to Burlesque

So long as Harry Smith writes the librettos I care not who looks after the orchestra.

And it looks as though I was going to have my wish.

If the choirs of angels and Gabriel, the trumpeter, came down to earth looking for an opera that would make a hit they would rush off to Harry Smith's libretto factory.

They say he writes them two at a time, one with each hand, and numbers the pages with his feet as he throws them to the floor to avoid confusion. —THE MATINEE GIRL

Throughout a career that spanned fifty years writing dialogue and lyrics for the American musical theater, Harry Bache Smith was plagued by two contradictory myths. The first suggested that he was a *wunderkind*, a kind of *über*-librettist capable of manufacturing musicals at the speed of light, with superhuman craftsmanship and wit provided by Thalia herself. Many of Smith's friends and colleagues did much to

Harry B. Smith

advance this myth, relating stories of how he would dash off an ingeniously rhymed lyric in ten minutes' time without breaking a sweat. To the purveyors of the second myth—that Smith was little more than a hack—his facility resulted in work that was essentially facile, mass-producing recycled plots and antique jokes for popular consumption. Proponents of the first myth speak glowingly about Smith's vastly eclectic knowledge of literature, history, and current events, while advocates of the second theory argue that his work relies too slavishly on literary models and history, rendering him devoid of any real originality. When the first group hear his name, it conjures up positive images of popular comic operas, bright, sassy, slangy musical comedies, and easily digestible translations and adaptations of European operettas. The others reduce his name to a verb form, "Harry-B-Smithed," inferring a lack of wit, pretentious lyrics, and all that is wrong with dramatic construction.

Those who denigrate Smith and his achievements have also put forward a related theory about the author. It has been said that Smith aspired to be the "John D. Rockefeller of light opera"—that he wrote for the theater to make money not art. This myth is the easiest to dispense with because it is true. Smith had few illusions about creating art, and he did make a lot of money writing librettos. In the 1911–12 season alone, he collected royalties from eleven shows either on Broadway or out on tour—and that does not take into account revivals of older comic operas. But it does not necessarily follow that, in making a comfortable living, he did not succeed occasionally in making art. As he often said, "I think it is possible to write comic opera that shall be at the same time artistic and popular. I don't do it often myself, for I am merely in the business of filling orders, but it can be done."

Filling orders for producers, stars, and popular consumption—his words seem to lead him straight to the Harry-B-Smithed camp. And yet, what good would be his almost inexhaustible supply, if there were no demand? Alone, or in collaboration, Smith produced the words for three hundred shows, and the lyrics to six thousand songs. Impressive as that sounds—and it remains the world record—even more astounding is that almost half of his prodigious output was staged in his lifetime, and most of that was in New York City.

Harry B. Smith was born to Josiah and Elizabeth Smith on December 28, 1860, in a residential suburb of Buffalo, New York. Although he was named after his uncle Henry Tisdale Smith, he was always called Harry as a child and, since the nickname seemed to fit his personality better than his given name, it stuck with him for the rest of his life. The middle initial "B" for "Bache" represented his mother's maiden name, Bach, with an added "e" to accommodate the way it had always been pronounced by family friends. Although he was ever anxious to claim a lineage with the German Bach family of composers, Harry admitted that he was of Welsh rather than German descent. However, his maternal grandfather, James Brown Bach, was an accomplished musician and book collector, described by Smith as "a man of versatile mind, a linguist, very musical, and with a cultivated taste in literature." He married Mary Van Nostrand, a descendant of one of the earliest Dutch families to live in Brooklyn, whose name (minus the "Van") still is in evidence today as Nostrand Avenue, one of the major thoroughfares of the borough. From Grandpa Bach, Harry inherited a love for books, literature, and language, as well as an appreciation for music.

The Smith family were simple farmers hailing from Litchfield County, Connecticut. Litchfield was also the home of Reuben and Abigail Smith, parents of Elihu H. Smith, the librettist of *Edwin and Angelina* (1797), one of the first original musical theater works to have been written by an American. Given the prevalence of Smiths in Litchfield County during the eighteenth century, it is not unlikely that Harry B. is related—if only distantly—to Elihu H. About 1820, the Smith family moved from Connecticut to Buffalo, New York, where Harry's father, Josiah Bailey Smith, was born in 1837, the youngest of seven children.

The Smith household belonged to the quintessential New England stereotype, from the patchwork quilts, to the gingerbread home, to the antiquated square piano that provided simple entertainment after a hard day's work on the land. In the late 1850s, just around the time Josiah married Elizabeth Bach, he built a house on Franklin Street where Harry would spend his early days playing pirate with the Bettinger boys who lived across the street. Because he was only four or five years old, "not of full piratical age," Harry was admitted to the confraternity of pirates as a cabin boy, assigned (because of his mother's well-stocked pantry) to search for food and drink. When he returned, loaded with jars of preserves and bottles of "raspberry shrub," his mother's special soft drink, he was immediately promoted to full membership and proclaimed the most valuable member of the pirate crew. Harry's celebrity was short-lived, however. His mother quickly discovered the depletion of her pantry and immediately put a stop to the marauding, dealing a deathblow to her son's reputation among the pirates.

Harry did not have to struggle to save face with the pirates because, soon after the humiliating incident, his family moved from Buffalo to Chicago at the request of two of his uncles whose state-of-the-art reaper factory had gone bust. While his father was helping his uncles start another business, Harry was off to school where his first lessons were taught mostly in German by a red-haired headmistress named Fräulein Heinrichs. This early exposure to the German language would later become a significant benefit to Smith in his career as an adapter and translator of foreign musicals. In these early days at school, Harry discovered a fondness for reciting speeches and poems (many of them in German), and an instinct for things theatrical, inherited from his parents, who were especially fond of going to the theater.

Smith's first recollection of seeing a play dates to 1866–67 when he attended an amateur production of *The Mistletoe Bough*, a play about a bride who, on a lark, hides in a chest on her wedding night. The leading lady of the piece was a Mrs. Houghteling, a great local beauty, whose youngest daughter, Laura, would become Harry's first (though secret) love. Other visits to the theater exposed Smith to the Carl Anschutz Opera Company and its German-language production of Gounod's opera *Faust*, and to some of the major celebrities of the American theater: Edwin Booth in *Romeo and Juliet* and *The Taming of the Shrew;* Louis Mestayer and W. J. Florence in *The Field of the Cloth of Gold;* Charlotte Cushman in *Meg Merrilees* (Henry Leslie's version of *Guy Mannering*); and Lotta Crabtree in *Little Nell.* In 1869, Smith saw his first musical comedy, a production of *Sindbad* at the Crosby Opera House produced by the Lydia Thompson Burlesque Company. Here, the nine-year-old Smith was introduced to ridiculously clever puns delivered by "frisky" women in tights, whose morals were continually being called into question by puritanical critics and jealous wives.

Later in life, writing his autobiography, *First Nights and First Editions*, Smith expressed great admiration for Thompson and her company, defending them valiantly against charges of indecency: "*O tempora!* O morons! There is a greater prejudice against tights now than there was sixty years ago. Indeed it is considered mid-Victorian to wear any." He also recalls attending a performance of Goldsmith's comedy *She Stoops to Conquer*, in London on June 6, 1898, that paints another picture of the "shocking" Lydia Thompson:

> I attended the first night of a play in London and applauded the performance of an actress named Zeffie Tilbury. During the intermission my companion remarked that Miss Tilbury was clever and charming, and I agreed. Whereupon a little old lady seated beside me exclaimed! "Oh, *do* you think so? I'm so glad. She's my daughter." We congratulated the proud mother, and the little old lady said, "I used to be an actress too. Perhaps you have heard of me—Lydia Thompson?"

A few months before Harry turned eleven, he was enrolled in a college preparatory school where his studies in French, Latin, and classical literature—and his prospects of going to college—were abruptly terminated by the great Chicago fire on October 9, 1871, which devastated most of the city. Like hundreds of other families, the Smiths (now including three daughters, Bessie, Gertrude, and Mary) found themselves looking for new living quarters. After searching for a few weeks for suitable accommodations, they settled on a house on West Monroe Street, a few doors away from the Leonard family, whose daughter Nellie (soon to become Lillian Russell, the "queen of comic opera") attended the same public school as the Smith children. Evidently the new house did not suit the family, because the following year the Smiths moved out to Fullerton Avenue, close to the northern boundary of Chicago. A year later, they were back in their old neighborhood when Harry's father bought a house on La Salle Avenue, just blocks away from their pre-fire address. Harry admits to having become stage struck during these years because of his success as an elocutionist at school, where he recited melodramatic monologues with such blood and thunder that students were brought from neighboring school districts to hear him.

After the move to La Salle Avenue, Smith attended Ogden High School, where elocutionary studies again drew his attention. Although he managed to impress the headmaster, George Heath, by correctly spelling the name of the king who was conquered by Pizarro—Atahuallpa (a detail he acquired when reading Prescott's *Conquests of Peru* a few days before)—Harry was disinclined to a liberal education. Instead, he invested his time in everything that pertained to the theater, including producing musical plays in the barn behind his house for a paying audience. Although the entertainment was clearly sophomoric, the ticket prices were reasonable at five cents. More than thirty years later, in an interview with the *New York Herald* (May 8, 1904), Smith remembered his early theatrics with great fondness:

> I suppose I must have lived in the Paleolithic age as a prehistoric musical comedy potentate or a comic opera swashbuckler. Be this as it may, at a very early age I felt the musical comedy impulse strong within me. At an age when most bad boys are in the reform school, I roamed untrammeled and got up minstrel shows in the stable, tickets being purchasable for any marketable produce—marbles, tops, foreign postage stamps or any coin of the boys' realm.

What free time was left was spent singing in the glee club, editing and printing a gossip newspaper called *The Weekly Sieve*, and attending lectures by the likes of Henry Ward Beecher and Mark Twain.

In 1875, as Harry was starting high school, his brother, Robert, was born. The event had little immediate impact on the teenager, who could not know the extent to which the pair would collaborate in their professional careers. For now, Robert was a doll-baby, better seen and not heard, especially in the evening hours when Harry was up late reading—a habit he had acquired nearly a decade before when he discovered Charles Dickens, Washington Irving, and James Fenimore Cooper among the treasures on the shelves in his grandparents' house in Buffalo. His affinity for reading did not always benefit him, however. After his first year of high school, Smith took a job in a real estate office to earn train fare to go to the Philadelphia Centennial Exposition in July. Because he was the entire office staff (minus the owner of the establishment, who was out showing real estate much of the time), Harry spent his time reading Gothic novels and hand-copying piano music that he had borrowed from his friends. After two months at the real estate business, Harry was fired for making a copy of Beethoven's *Sonata Pathetique* during business hours. His dismissal conveniently saved him the trouble of having to quit the job because he had already saved enough money for the trip to Philadelphia. The level of piano music that Smith had been copying indicates that, even as a teenager, Harry was an accomplished pianist, a characteristic often noted by the many composers with whom he worked during his professional career.

Fifteen-year-old Harry B. Smith stayed in Philadelphia for two weeks, during which time he attended a concert conducted by Jacques Offenbach, the celebrated French *opéra-bouffe* composer, the only event in any way connected with musical comedy he witnessed during the Exposition. Leaving Philadelphia, the teenager took a train to New York City to visit his aunt Emily Bach, who lived in Gramercy Park, and to experience the theatrical life in the big city. If Harry arrived in New York a stagestruck youth, his first trip to the great metropolis did nothing but deepen his love affair with the stage. Theaters he had only heard of—the Academy of Music, Wallack's, the Union Square, the New Fifth Avenue Theatre—he finally got to see, filled with enough plays and stars to make an impression to last a lifetime. Resolved to quit school and pursue a dramatic career, young Harry B. Smith returned to Chicago, where his father, after patiently listening to his son's plans for the future, calmly decided that if school was out of the question, Harry must immediately find lucrative employment. Because the younger Smith had no theatrical experience, lucrative theater work was impossible, so he took a job as bill clerk in a wholesale hardware business.

What made the hardware store tolerable was the fact that it looked out on the Tremont House, a popular actors' residence in Chicago, and from his desk, Harry was able to catch glimpses of performers going to and coming from the theater. One day, John McCullough, who was appearing as Virginius in the tragedy by James Sheridan Knowles, entered the store, asking, in a dramatically booming voice, for a pocketknife. Awestruck in the presence of one of Chicago's favorite actors, Harry tried to explain that this was a wholesale, not a retail store in as stentorian a tone as he could muster, and the tragedian made a hasty exit. Suddenly Harry realized that seeing a tragic actor on the stage and standing beside him in real life were altogether different things, and feeling dwarfed by McCullough's stature convinced the lad that his physical appearance was most unsuitable for a career in tragedy. Undaunted, Harry turned his attention to comedy, a choice he never regretted, particularly when he learned, some time after, that McCullough went insane and had to be confined to a sanitarium.

Several months later, Harry was promoted to city buyer, which required him to be driven to other wholesale houses to replenish the stock of his own firm. The extra income enabled the boy to take lessons in playing the banjo and clog dancing, mostly during working hours, while his wagon driver assumed the responsibilities of city buyer. As in past employment, Smith's extracurricular activities proved to be his undoing. When business was slow, the boy took to practicing his dancing. One day, in the middle of a jig step, Harry sensed that he was being watched, and his staunchly Puritanical employer stepped from behind a pile of packing cases. When asked for an explanation for his acitivities, Smith boasted that he was destined to become a famous comic actor, so he had to practice his routines. While such devotion to the art might be applauded in schools designed to foster performance, it found no support with the deeply religious Puritan, who urged Harry to give up the theater, or lose his present job. Not inclined to give up his dreams, Harry B. Smith once again found himself among the unemployed.

Josiah and Elizabeth Smith were less than pleased with their son's inability to sustain a regular job, but Harry managed to make the most of his unemployment. He wrote the music for a comic opera, with his friend Walter Roloson providing the libretto. The pair decided to transform Shakespeare's *Othello* into the tongue-in-cheek *O'Thello*, a comedy with songs, in which the Moorish title character spoke with an Irish brogue, and Desdemona ends up smothering O'Thello, satirically inverting Shakespeare's original ending. Fifty years later in his memoirs, Harry B. Smith sardonically recalled that his talents as a composer and Roloson's as a librettist were "about equal," and that the satire in *O'Thello*, although based on a real-life, Irish-born bootblack, was "evidently too subtle for the neighborhood audience that attended its performance by amateurs."

Undaunted, Harry continued to pursue his theatrical ambitions. While in the employment of a publisher of religious literature where he contributed verses to such aptly named publications as *The Little Christian at Home*, an opportunity presented itself. His employer was a good-natured alcoholic who often invited Harry along on his binges, hoping the boy might stay sober enough to carry him home. During one of these outings, Harry learned that the Dickie Lingard Company was looking for actors to perform burlesques at the Olympic Theatre in Chicago and on tour. English Dickie Lingard had made her American debut on February 1, 1869, when she appeared with her sister, Alice Dunning, and her brother-in-law, William Horace Lingard, in *Pluto*, a burlesque written by Henry B. Farnie with music by David Braham. Her husband, Davison Dalziel, a British newspaper man, was convinced that Dickie was a bankable name on the burlesque touring circuit, and he assembled a company that included theater veterans like Roland Reed, once the principal comic actor with the McVicker Stock Company, Fanny Wright, a popular English comedienne, and her illegitimate daughter, Alice, a soubrette, as well as novices the likes of seventeen-year-old Harry B. Smith, who ran away from home to join the troupe and sing in the chorus.

After two months of playing to lackluster audiences in unfriendly cities, with a repertoire that included Lydia Thompson's burlesques *Robinson Crusoe* and *Oxygen*, an adaptation of Jules Verne's "Dr. Ox's Experiment," the tour finally disbanded in Philadelphia. Because business had been so bad, no one in the company received the salaries that were promised, some receiving no pay at all, and little cash was available to send the actors back to their homes in New York or Chicago. Harry would have had to walk back to Chicago had it not been for a Philadelphia relative of his mother who offered him money and a railroad ticket back home. In an interview with the *New York Dramatic Mirror* (June 13, 1896), Smith recalled his early theatrical experiences without regret: "I was not especially desirous of achieving fame as an operatic baritone. I cherished a latent desire to write librettos, and my apprenticeship behind the scenes made me thoroughly familiar with the practical and mechanical possibilities of scenic effects. I learned to do everything in the line of stage setting from a grip up."

What Harry did not know how to do was act. So, when he asked the celebrated actor-manager James H. McVicker for a job in his company, he was sent for training to Harry Pearson, a skilled old comedian who had performed with Samuel Phelps at Sadler Wells in London. McVicker claimed that the best way to prepare for a career in the theater—whether as a performer or writer—was to study acting. Smith auditioned for Pearson with Hamlet's "To be or not to be" soliloquy and was accepted as a student and a member of The Chicago Dramatic Club, an organization founded by Pearson to showcase his students. Harry soon found himself cast as Rodrigo in the single-performance student production of *Othello*, and he was determined to play the role as a comic turn, speaking the lines with the "falsetto chuckle and squeak" typified by Stuart Robson, the actor who epitomized Harry's comic ideal. In addition, Smith chose to wear blue tights and a blond wig—both several sizes too large—that brought the audience to convulsive laughter during his death scene. Years later, Smith recalled that "no characterization of Roderigo ever got more laughs than mine, not only from the audience but from my fellow players." Although Smith was severely reprimanded by Pearson for his performance, and not permitted to reprise the role in a revival of the production, he maintained a positive attitude and accepted the criticism with a congeniality that would become a trademark in his later career.

Not long after Smith's debut with The Chicago Dramatic Club, his teacher was hired to direct an amateur operetta called *The Rival*

Cantineers, written by wealthy Chicago socialite Mrs. Alexander Kirkland, with music composed by a local voice teacher named James Gill. Smith was relegated to the menial role of a Corporal, but he made the most of it, blue tights, blond wig, and all. As in *Othello,* Harry's performance was remarkable for its inappropriateness and, immediately after opening night, he was fired from the production. The experience was a significant one for the twenty-year-old actor, because it taught him that, although burlesque-like clowning is highly inappropriate in a disciplined company, audiences do like to laugh. And their laughter would continue to ring in Harry's ears for years to come as he tried to balance his burlesque leanings with the responsibilities attendant to his becoming a legitimate librettist. In addition, the production marked his first association with Jessie Bartlett, a young contralto from Morris, Illinois, who would later find international celebrity as Jessie Bartlett Davis, a concert singer and comic opera star (often in musicals written by Smith).

The incident also ruptured the relationship between Harry and his teacher, whose alcoholic tendencies were severely exacerbated by Smith's theatrical shenanigans. Unable to find a theater in Chicago that would hire him, Harry set out to write a burlesque extravaganza like the ones he performed during his brief tenure with the Dickie Lingard Company. He created libretto, music, costumes, and scenic designs, and took the entire package to one William J. Davis, a manager associated with J. H. ("Jack") Haverly, a Chicago minstrel promoter and entrepreneur who managed Haverly's Fifth Avenue Theatre, the Fourteenth Street Theatre, and Niblo's Garden in New York City. Davis pronounced the work "hopeless," and Smith stuffed it into a drawer until 1885, when he offered it to Henry E. Dixey, then performing the title role in *Adonis,* Broadway's longest-running musical to date. Although Dixey never produced the work, he did hold on to Smith's drawings and sketches, a detail fondly remembered by the author, even though, in an interview with the *Green Book Magazine* (September 1912), he could not recall the name of the show.

Not long after Davis rejected his script, Smith auditioned for him again, seeking employment with a new touring company Davis had organized, called the Chicago Church Choir Opera Company. This time Harry was accepted on the strength of his baritone voice and hired for chorus work and supernumerary roles in three Gilbert and Sullivan comic operas, *H.M.S. Pinafore, The Sorcerer,* and *Patience,* as well as the Notary in Robert Planquette's *The Chimes of Normandy,* and Sergeant Steipan in Franz von Suppé's *Fatinitza.* The company had been established in the

Jessie Bartlett (Davis)

summer of 1879 to tour a comic opera repertory throughout the West and Southwest in an attempt to capitalize on the *Pinafore* craze that erupted throughout America after its Broadway premiere on January 15, 1879. Among the roster of top-flight concert singers, the cast included Jessie Bartlett, who would marry manager Davis at the end of the tour.

Although cast in minor roles, Smith learned a great deal about comic opera in its English, French, and Viennese incarnations on the tour. In addition, because he was a quick study and knew all the roles in all of the shows, Smith was thrust into the limelight from time to time due to the incapacitations—or, rather, infatuations—of the actor-manager of the company, Herbert Cripps, whose amorous adventures, legendary among theater folk, resulted in his missing a number of performances. Covering for Cripps as Bunthorne, an "aesthetic" poet, in *Patience* and Sir Joseph Porter, the admiral of the Queen's navy, in *Pinafore*, Harry found himself unable to restrain his burlesque instincts, attempting to replace the original blocking with new and imaginative stage business, designed to evoke laughter from both audience and cast, but also enraging producers and critics. When the company found itself in Texas, however, where a local vigilante actually killed an actor because he did not appreciate his performance, and where audience members bearing guns demanded free tickets to the shows, Harry's waggishness was the least of their concerns. As Smith recalls in his autobiography:

> A Chicago Church Choir Company's performance of "Patience" was not an appropriate attraction for Texas in the earliest Eighties. Derisive comments greeted the lady-like poets, *Bunthorne* and *Grosvenor;* but the climax of disorder was reached when the three military officers entered as aesthetes gazing enrapt at sunflowers. At the moment, prospects looked promising for a lynching. Public sentiment in Texas was against that kind of folks.

The Midwest generally proved to be more amenable to Gilbert and Sullivan than the Wild West, and a stop in Minneapolis occasioned the first meeting between Harry B. Smith and the twenty-four-year-old Reginald de Koven, a Connecticut-born, Oxford-educated musician, who would marry a Chicago socialite in May 1884. De Koven had traveled to Minneapolis to meet with producer William Davis to play the score of a two-act operetta he had written and composed called *Cupid,*

Hymen and Company. Impressed with what he heard, Davis promised to produce the work with his company, which turned Smith green with envy. Meeting the composer, Harry confided in him that his secret ambition was to write librettos for comic operas, and de Koven responded encouragingly, agreeing to collaborate with him if he came up with a workable text. Although it would take several years for the partnership to become a reality, the hope of a collaboration buoyed Harry's spirits as the tour came to an end in March 1880, and he returned to Chicago, once again, in search of gainful employment.

The homecoming was not an especially pleasant one. Harry's parents were concerned about the "lunacy" of their son's interest in the theatrical profession, and Harry was hard-pressed to defend it. This time, his father insisted that he find a good job and made him promise never to go on stage again, a promise Harry happily kept, with rare exceptions, for the remainder of his life. He found a good job as well, through the intervention of a old school chum who helped him secure a position as a publicist with the Slayton Lyceum Bureau of Chicago, a booking agency for concerts and lecture series, located at 33 Central Music Hall, the same building that housed the Chicago Musical College, established in the 1860s by Dr. Florenz Ziegfeld, a music teacher and one-time bandleader in his native Germany. Dr. Ziegfeld took an immediate interest in Harry's well-crafted publicity notices, and hired him to become the press representative for the college. It was in this capacity that Harry first met Florenz Ziegfeld Jr., then a fifteen-year-old student at Harry's old *alma mater*, Ogden High School, and soon to become one of America's most celebrated impresarios.

So successful was Smith's work publicizing concerts for Dr. Ziegfeld that other area musicians sought him out for similar work. One of these was an idiosyncratic composer named Silas G. Pratt, the "Wagner of America," who had written and composed an opera entitled *Zenobia*, one of the earliest full-scale operas by an American composer to be performed. Smith was hired to do publicity for the work, scheduled for production in June 1882. During the rehearsal period, Harry's job was upgraded to business manager, and he quickly found himself having to function like a producer rather than a publicist, antagonizing the composer, who began to lament in an overly melodramatic tone that Smith was neglecting him, dooming his opera to failure. No matter how much Harry did, it was not enough for Pratt. Ultimately, *Zenobia* did fail, but not because it was underpublicized.

Perhaps it was his treatment at the hands of actor-managers, producers, and temperamental composers that led Smith to become a critic in his own right for a variety of local newspapers; perhaps he was simply more literate and articulate than others interested in writing about theater and music. But as his career as a publicist flourished, so did his career as a journalist. Beginning with Davison Dalziel's *Chicago News Letter*, a somewhat shady enterprise established by Dickie Lingard's husband after he gave up trying to be a theatrical producer, Smith moved on to the western edition of the *New York Dramatic News*, and when both of these papers folded, to a literary weekly called *The Current*, which published many of Smith's early attempts at poetry and short stories. Harry would dramatize one of the stories—about a composer who allows his opera to be stolen so that the woman he loves can have a chance at stardom—in 1904 as *The Second Fiddle*, a vehicle for the comic actor Louis Mann. After assisting a young lady who admitted to knowing almost nothing about music write a concert review for the *Chicago Daily News*, he began a long association with that paper, first as a humorous columnist, then as a reporter, and finally as its official music critic, a position that afforded him hours of pleasure, attending concerts and operas, and meeting many of the most celebrated performers of the day.

Well into the 1890s, Harry B. Smith continued working for Chicago newspapers, adding the *Tribune*, *Journal*, and *Herald* to his long list of credits. His creative writing, however, was hardly relegated to a constant flow of press releases, music and theater reviews, entertainment gossip, and humorous stories and verse. In between deadlines and certainly in most of his free time, Harry wrote librettos for the musical stage. The earliest of his efforts to see an actual production was a pastoral comic opera, of the "Watteau Shepherdess order," entitled *Amaryllis; or, Mammon and Gammon*. Smith composed it while still a teenager, during his touring chorus-boy days; the music was supplied by Henry Thiele, the musical director of the tour, who later became the resident musical director for McVicker's Theatre in Chicago.

The plot of *Amaryllis* evokes the eighteenth-century French pastoral opéras-comique of Rousseau, Dalayrac, and Monsigny, with a pinch of the satirical burlesque tradition, and a heavy dose of William Schwenck Gilbert. On the Hudson River estate of a rich and practical widower named Geoffrey Grosgrain, "an American aristocrat to whom money is no object," his sentimental daughter, Amaryllis, and her friends, tired of high society, dress up like shepherdesses from various Watteau paintings and luxuriate in the country surroundings. This peaceful tableau—somewhat reminiscent of "Twenty Love-Sick Maidens We" from *Patience*—is disturbed by the arrival of Felix and Leander, twin brothers from a nearby college, who immediately fall in love with Amaryllis. The heroine, in turn, is in love with a bashful farmer by the quintessentially rustic name of Colin, who is betrothed (at his father's behest) to a feisty country wench named Dorothy. The farmer, of course, must spurn Amaryllis's advances, much to the delight of Lord Vivian Vere de Vere, a "Fortunus Hunter," who wants the Grosgrain heiress for her money.

Disappointed in her suit with Colin, Amaryllis decides to marry whichever twin can amass a fortune in a week's time, to which end Leander and Felix buy lottery tickets, hoping to win the jackpot. When 999 is announced as the winning number, Leander tries to claim victory, inverting his own ticket (number 666) so that it reads 999 (a plot detail straight out of Offenbach's *Le "66"*). Sensing foul play, his brother challenges Leander to a duel, but because the twins are both cowards, neither appears on the field of honor at the appointed time. It turns out that Colin holds the winning ticket (having spent much of the act believing his number to be 666), and he serendipitously discovers oil on his farm. No longer feeling the need to marry Dorothy (or obey his father, for that matter), he proposes to Amaryllis, whose father, in turn, decides to marry the suddenly fiancé-less Dorothy. The twins find amorous substitutes for Amaryllis among her society friends, and the villain of the piece, Vere de Vere, is revealed to be a grafter and impostor by "an emissary of Nemesis, unpopularly known as a detective," named McNab.

Though Smith's work could scarcely be called original, it had sufficient merit to be produced in Milwaukee by an amateur theatrical ensemble called The Arlington Quartette in the spring of 1884. What's more, the local reviewers praised the libretto and music and singled out Smith's performance as Detective McNab as a highlight of the evening. The young authors, believing they had struck gold, published their maiden effort and immediately set to work on a follow-up piece. Where their first collaboration borrowed from the bucolic meadows of *Patience*, their second work anticipated the comic opera orientalism popularized internationally by Gilbert and Sullivan's *The Mikado*. Moreover, the musical was to receive a professional production. Manager Jacob Litt was in the audience for *Amaryllis* and was impressed by what he saw, so he negotiated for the new work to be performed as part of the first summer season at the Schlitz Park Theatre, specially designed to provide Milwaukeeans with three months of opera, burlesque, and comedy. Smith and Thiele's second effort, *Prince Chow Chow*, opened on June 11, 1884, and provided the citizens of Milwaukee with none of those things. The correspondent for the *New York Mirror* (June 21, 1884) spoke for the critics at large when he complained: "with the exception of *On Guard* [by W. S. Gilbert, *Prince Chow Chow*] was the worse I ever saw. A lot of rubbish set to old airs, and no plot to support it at all. We are a little surprised to think that Manager Litt should risk damaging the reputation of his theatre by putting it on." The public evidently also agreed with the critics, because the week *Prince Chow Chow* was on the boards produced the poorest attendance records of the summer at the theater. At the end of June, the *New York Mirror*'s correspondent (June 28, 1884) appropriately called the show "a flat failure," and Smith and Thiele parted as collaborators, both destined for greater things.

Somewhat more successful was Smith's early collaboration with a pianist and composer named George Schleiffarth, whom Harry met serendipitously one day while soliciting advertisements for a concert he was publicizing. As Smith recalls in his autobiography:

> On a subsequent visit to his studio he played his latest waltz and asked me if I could write a lyric for it. He had the inspired title "Who Will Buy My Roses Red," and so great was his confidence in the melody and the title that he was willing to pay a goodly sum for a suitable lyric; maybe as much as five dollars; or he would share the royalties equally if the writer of the words felt inclined to gamble on the chances of success. I decided to play a sure thing and take the five dollars. I stayed at the office that evening and completed my first lyrical masterpiece. The composer was satisfied with it and paid me the five dollars on the spot.
>
> Incredible as it may seem, people actually bought this song and its pictorial title-page was liberally displayed in the windows of music shops. Three months after its publication, the composer jubilantly informed me that he had received over four hundred dollars in royalties and the sales continued active. Eventually he made several thousand dollars out of this vocal

gem, and when I reflected that I might have been a sharer in this gold mine, I cursed the cowardice that had prevented my taking a gamble with the composer. Afterward we wrote several songs, in which, warned by experience, I retained my half interest. Some of these were slightly profitable; but there were others that I should have sold in advance for five dollars.

The experience with Schleiffarth appeared to change Harry B. Smith's desire for a career in the theater; having discovered that the personal satisfaction of hearing one's work performed could also be financially remunerative, his performative goals became literary.

His histrionic ambitions behind him, Smith (abetted by his new collaborator, Schleiffarth) set out to write a comic opera. The product of about a month's work was *Rosita; or, Cupid and Cupidity*, a Chile-flavored operetta full of disguise, transvestitism, brigands, and dancing girls, part Offenbach's *La Périchole*, part Gilbert and Sullivan's *The Pirates of Penzance*. The plot, set in the outskirts of Valparaiso, Chile, in 1784, involves Walter Edgerton, an American officer traveling in South America, who finds himself in hot water because he kissed his partner while dancing the bolero at a village festival. He takes refuge in the garden of Señor Encinal, a prosperous citizen with enough daughters to make up an operetta chorus, one of whom happens to be Rosita, the very girl Walter kissed at the dance. The villagers rush into the garden calling for vengeance when, propitiously, Rosita appears from Encinal's house and quiets the crowd. She is desperately in love with Walter (who is a very good dancer), but cannot follow her heart because her father has promised her hand to Don Miguel de Mantilla, a "miserly jeweler" who has already had seven wives (the sixth of whom is rumored to be yet alive). Walter comes up with a scheme to break off the engagement: he will disguise himself as the Alcalde before whom Rosita and Don Miguel were betrothed, and his servant will cross-dress as wife number six, the appearance of whom will cause the old roué no end of embarrassment and prompt the faux-Alcalde into calling off the wedding. Before the plan can be put into effect, a gang of masked brigands, led by the good-natured Carlos, crosses over the wall and kidnaps all of Encinal's daughters, taking them to the brigand's lair.

Act two opens in the bandits' hideaway, where Carlos, "more sanguine than sanguinary," displays his love for Rosita. As he falls more and more under her spell, he agrees to trap Don Miguel into confessing that he is the leader of the brigand gang and revealing where all the loot is stored. In addition he cajoles Mantilla into signing a paper transferring all of his accumulated wealth "to the man that marries Rosita." Don Miguel, of course, imagining that man to be himself, signs the deed and gives it to the faux-Alcalde, demanding that he carry out its provisions to the letter. Suddenly, the real wife number six appears, and she forces Don Miguel to confess his brigand past. Encinal appears to bless the union between Rosita and Walter, who now legally owns all of Don Miguel's possessions, Mantilla and his sixth wife are woefully reconciled, and each of the bandits pairs up with one of Encinal's daughters as the curtain falls on "unexampled connubial felicity."

Again, there is little that is original in the work. The plot of parents blocking love marriages because of financial considerations is as old as Menander, and the parallels with Smith's earlier comic opera, *Amaryllis,* are obvious. Still, there was sufficient vitality in the writing to interest John Templeton, then managing the career of his teenage daughter, Fay, and her touring opera company. Templeton had once been the editor of the *Tammany Times* in New York City, and was generally viewed as a savvy and meticulous theater manager. Fay's mother, who also traveled with the company, was former comic opera prima donna Alice Vane. Smith presented the show *gratis* to Templeton on the condition that he produce the work with his daughter in the title role. Like most of the young men in Chicago, Harry was in love with Fay Templeton, and he was not beyond giving away his (and his composer's) royalties to hear her speak his lines and sing his lyrics. Given the unusually generous terms of the contract, Templeton accepted the work and put it into rehearsal.

On April 1, 1884, *Rosita* opened at the Criterion Theatre in Chicago, playing four performances with Fay Templeton in the title role and her mother in the britches part of a brigand lieutenant, Beppo. On April 12, 1884, the critic for the *New York Mirror* was cautiously complimentary: "The new opera, *Cupid and Cupidity*, proved a success. The predominance of the farcical element led the performers to verge closely on burlesque, but the music was really bright and meritorious." In addition, Walter's song, "Kisses Are like Witches' Spells," Rosita's "Beware Faces Fair," and Don Miguel's topical song, "We Draw the Line at That," were singled out as having made "the best impression." The local critics agreed but found that the many topical allusions in the text—although quite humorous—were inappropriate to events occurring in eighteenth-century Chile. The tendency toward topical humor and satirical burlesque would remain with Smith for the rest of his career, and reviews such as these would continue to haunt him, constantly reaffirming the conviction he expressed in his opening night speech for *The Serenade* (March 16, 1897) that "when a comic opera succeeds the people say: 'What beautiful music!' and when it fails: 'What a bad book!'" In any event, the critics seemed to agree that the audiences found the comic opera entertaining and that both of the writers demonstrated a great deal of promise—a far cry from the scolding *Prince Chow Chow* would receive two months later.

Manager Templeton was also satisfied with the production. One night, when he was counting the box-office receipts after a performance, he took money from the cash box and handed it to Smith, remarking, "There! You can't say now that you didn't get any money out of your damned old opera." As Smith recounted the story in various interviews over the years, the amount handed him varied from five to twenty dollars. Neither amount is princely nor anywhere close to the royalty for a comic opera that was to become part of a touring repertory. Still, Templeton was under no obligation to pay Smith anything, and the playwright appreciated the gesture, as he indicated in an interview with the *New York Dramatic Mirror* (June 13, 1896): "I've kept that twenty dollar gold piece as a memento, and it would take a very strong inducement to make me part with it."

On April 30, 1884, *Rosita* was given a matinee performance at the Park Theatre in Brooklyn, the first of Smith's original librettos to appear in the New York metropolitan area. Fay Templeton kept the opera as part of her repertoire for the rest of the season, after which the title fades from the theater bills, only to reappear in printed form in 1887 when it was published by Bowen and Schleiffarth as *Rosita; or, Boston and Banditi*, with a book attributed to Matthew C. Woodward (large print), lyrics by Harry B. Smith (much smaller print and in parentheses), and music by George Schleiffarth (large print again). While the printed text differs in the names and occupations of characters, the plot remains intact, though much of the overtly burlesque business and topical humor appears to have been subdued or jettisoned entirely. The only vestige of a topical song is a single stage direction in the second act that reads: "Topical Song may be introduced here."

During his journeyman years as a librettist, Harry B. Smith also claimed to have translated comic operas from both the French and

Viennese schools for touring opera companies he encountered while he worked as a publicity agent at the Slayton Lyceum Bureau. That established opera companies would employ a neophyte such as Smith comes as no surprise. Smith was quickly making a name for himself as a newspaper humorist and poet. His work was articulate, witty, and accessible. And, most importantly, as a newspaper man, he knew how to deliver his work on time. More than once in his career, Smith noted that learning how to meet a deadline—the bane of every writer—was the most important lesson he ever learned. Finally, Smith was inexpensive. He still had an idealistic view of working in the theater, and was willing to translate librettos for the experience and the promise of future employment.

For C. D. Hess's Acme Opera Company, he adapted Edmond Gondinet's text for *Le roi l'a dit*, with music by Leo Delibes, and for James C. Duff, he provided an English version of Friedrich Zell (Camillo Walzel) and Richard Genée's *Eine Nacht in Venedig*, with music by Johann Strauss II. Neither adaptation was particularly successful, and, not unsurprisingly, Smith received no further commissions from either opera company. He was unconcerned, however, because no sooner had he dashed off the comic opera librettos, he was busy writing for a new artistic journal, and developing a strong and collaborative working relationship with an up-and-coming young American composer named Reginald de Koven.

Chapter 2

Burlesque to Broadway

On March 29, 1884, the first issue of *The Rambler: A Journal of Men, Manners and Things* appeared in Chicago. The weekly publication, modeled after the topical British literary magazine *Truth* and costing the less-than-princely sum of five cents, was the brainchild of Ian Lewis, an architect, and Reginald de Koven, a classically trained composer withering away in the employ of the J. V. Farwell Company, a dry-goods wholesale business owned by his fiancée's family. The promised production of *Cupid, Hymen and Company* had never come to pass, and de Koven had followed his father's advice and given up the hope of making music his career, but the wholesale business was providing too slender an outlet for the art that was calling to him. As his wife, Anna, recalled in her memoir, *A Musician and His Wife*:

> I have in my mind's eye a picture of my perplexed young husband, sunk in a deep blue armchair, who, at my question as to his profound despondency, announced that he was convinced he had done very wrong to heed his father's advice to give up

> music as a career. That talent will find some way of expressing itself, and will try all sorts of experiments, was shown by my husband's attempts to found a weekly paper.

Harry B. Smith, already an experienced critic and publicity agent, was hired in the fall of 1884 to write theater reviews and to talk local merchants into buying advertising space; by October, Smith's name was listed on the masthead alongside those of Lewis and de Koven as co-editor and part proprietor of the journal. By the summer of 1885, the original funding for the operation had been withdrawn and Smith had taken over the weekly on his own. Paying what he described as "nothing or almost nothing" for the name, a subscription list, and the "good will" of the paper, Harry set up a small office in the Central Music Hall Building where he functioned as "the proprietor, the business manager and the literary staff." Assisted only by a young artist named J. H. Smith, hired to do a number of drawings each week (and who helped to create the illusion that, like W. S. Gilbert in the *Bab Ballads*, H. B. Smith was both literary giant and artist as well), Harry managed to keep *The Rambler* afloat for several months without running into debt. This was because he was working day and night at the *News* and the *Tribune*, and putting most of his earnings into *The Rambler*.

Then, suddenly, the bottom dropped from under him. The editors of the two Chicago daily newspapers discovered that Smith was "leading a double life—journalistically," and fired him. Even though Melville Stone, the editor of the *News*, relented and subsequently rehired Smith, the experience seemed to sound the death knell for *The Rambler*. It was difficult enough paying expenses with two salaries; it was an impossibility to manage on one. Just when the magazine seemed lost, a young man named Elliot Flower appeared to save the day. As Smith tells the story:

> I had about decided to let *The Rambler* ramble out of existence when one day a young man, who had occasionally brought in contributions, came into the office with the startling announcement that, if I would take him as a partner, his father would invest five thousand dollars to start him in a congenial business. This was manna in the wilderness. Sure enough, my new partner appeared next day with a check for five thousand. As we now regarded ourselves as plutocrats, my partner and I played at being editor until the money was gone. Both of us

Reginald de Koven

aspired to be literary and neither wanted to waste his talents on such sordid details as getting subscriptions and advertisements.

By the time the money ran out in January 1887, *The Rambler* had earned its place among the best of the weekly humorous journals, even rivaling New York magazines in its trenchant satire and sparkling wit. Again, Smith's predilection for the burlesque tradition found fertile ground as pun after pun leapt out from the page, especially in a regular feature called the "Follies of the Day," a title that would have particular resonance in Harry's future, under the management of Florenz Ziegfeld Jr.

Although Reginald de Koven left the magazine in the summer of 1885, he was by no means a stranger to Smith. The two men were from profoundly different social classes and education, yet their love for theater and music—especially their fondness for amateur theatricals—drew them together. In the winter of 1886, when Smith and de Koven were appearing with a socially prominent amateur theater troupe with "professional connections," the pair decided to try their hand at a collaboration, a West Point–inspired satire of military life and girls' boarding schools entitled *Fort Caramel* (or "Fort Something-or-other" as Smith would call it in later years). According to Harry, the team offered their burlesque opera to W. T. Carleton in the hope that he would include it in the repertoire of his touring opera company, but the manager was uninterested. Because no complete score or libretto for the project exists, it is unknown whether Smith and de Koven had even completed the work, or simply presented to Carleton a kind of "backers' audition" with an outline of the plot fleshed out with key scenes and musical numbers. Evidently de Koven lost interest in the project, and he was replaced by Henry Thiele (*Amaryllis*, *Prince Chow Chow*) as composer. The completed *Fort Caramel* was finally produced in Milwaukee at the New Academy on April 13, 1888, where Smith's "bright and witty" libretto was favorably received by both audiences and critics.

The team of Smith and de Koven was undaunted by Carleton's rejection and turned its attention to another idea, a "Hindoo" comic opera, capitalizing on the popularity of Gilbert and Sullivan's *The Mikado*, called *The Begum*. The complicated burlesque-like plot involves an east-Indian princess (the Begum of Oude) with a connubial fixation. She is in the habit of marrying her general-in-chief and then, after the honeymoon, sending him off to war and certain death (an efficient alternative to divorce) so that she can marry his successor. The prime minister, Howja-

Dhu, has managed to climb the political ladder by sending Klahm-Chowdee, a menial private in the army, to do his fighting for him and taking credit for Chowdee's military prowess. When the Begum decides to promote Howja-Dhu to general-in-chief and marry him (much to the distress of the young private, who actually deserves the promotion and who really loves the princess), the prime minister decides to fake his demise so that he can marry the woman he really loves, a Nautch dancer named Damaynti. Thinking that Howja-Dhu is dead, the Begum decides to marry his son, Pooteh-Wehl, ruining his engagement to Aminah, the daughter of the court astrologer, Myhnt-Jhuleep. In addition, until her matrimonial bed is filled, the Princess forbids her four nieces, Tafeh, Kahra-Mel, Nougat, and Bon Bon, from marrying the army officers they love. Howja-Dhu is convinced that the easiest way to save his skin is to return from the dead and exchange military stripes and status with Klahm-Chowdee, who, now a general-in-chief, can marry the Princess he loves. The Begum, in turn, realizing that she is loved for herself and not her position, calls off the war, and settles down to a long life with her new husband.

It took about a year for the collaborators to complete *The Begum*, most of the work being done at nights and on weekends at the home of de Koven's father-in-law, Senator Charles B. Farwell. The opera had been finished for some time when Colonel John McCaull, a former Confederate Army officer and "grand panjandrum" of the comic opera circuit, happened to be in Chicago with his opera company in the spring of 1887. Through De Wolf Hopper, one of the leading performers in McCaull's company for whom de Koven had written a song, the composer managed an introduction to the colonel, who was subsequently invited to the senator's house for dinner. Treated to an impeccable meal, in sumptuous surroundings, McCaull agreed to produce the show, although not without asking for certain financial guarantees. As Mrs. de Koven recalls in her memoir:

> My husband had vainly sought for a manager, when one day Colonel McCaull visited Chicago and came to my father's house at my husband's invitation. His leading actress and singer, the very brilliant Austrian called Mathilde Cottrelly, told me that after my doubtless naïve and probably amusing plea to him "to please put on my husband's opera, even if we did not really need to have him do it," he said: "I believe I will

put on the opera. I would like to, because that young woman asked me." However this unusual plea might have evoked his fancy, he was not fanciful enough to forego a guaranty [sic] for part of the production, which fortunately we were able to furnish. The important, the all-important object was attained, for under the best, the only real manager of the time, this first opera of my husband was destined to be well performed.

Although Colonel McCaull later quipped that after the dinner at Senator Farwell's home he would have produced *The Begum* whether it were any good or not, Smith's work must have impressed him because, later that summer, he wrote to the librettist—back at his job at the *News*—asking how much he would charge to adapt the book and lyrics of Franz von Suppé's *Boccaccio*, originally written in German by Friedrich Zell and Richard Genée. McCaull was not asking for a simple translation; he wanted Harry to alter the libretto "to suit the personalities of the players." Eager to comply with the request, but wary of receiving the same kind of treatment he had tolerated with the Hess and Duff tours, Smith replied that he would require a year contract at no less than fifteen dollars per week. Two weeks passed without a reply from the manager. Finally, at the end of July, Smith received a letter commissioning him to write the lyrics for a topical song to be sung by De Wolf Hopper and interpolated into *Bellman*, another of Suppé's comic operas fresh from Vienna that the colonel wanted to produce a month later.

Not untypically, Smith already had an idea for such a lyric in mind and, barely two hours after receiving McCaull's letter, Harry telegraphed him saying that the song, entitled "Do You Catch the Idea," was already in the mail. McCaull was appropriately impressed by the rapidity with which the lyricist was able to work and, not long after, Smith received a note from Ben Stevens, the colonel's business manager, agreeing to pay him fifteen dollars a week for a year. On August 22, 1887, McCaull's Opera Company produced *Bellman* at Wallack's Theatre in New York City, and the critics were unanimous in their praise for the new song, some even finding it superior to Hopper's performance. Happily, Smith was able to escape the barbs directed against the English adaptation of the libretto, which was described as "witless, stupid, and mixed up at every point" and "one of the worse books that has come within the range of our somewhat extensive experience." Irrespective of the quality of the libretto, and due in great measure to the success of Smith's original song, *Bellman* continued performances for nearly another two months, lasting to the end of the summer opera season on October 8, 1887.

A month earlier, Smith had been sent a letter informing him that he was expected to attend rehearsals of *The Begum* in New York beginning immediately after the close of the opera season in October. He had already sold his interest in the production to the composer as a kind of advance royalty to fund his upcoming nuptials. His bride-to-be was a dark-eyed blonde by the name of Lena Reed, whom Harry met some months earlier while on assignment for the *News*. She was sufficiently beautiful, high-spirited, and witty to make Harry forget that he was ever in love with the likes of Laura Houghteling and Fay Templeton and, finally earning a guaranteed income from his writing, Smith got up the nerve to propose marriage. The plan was to wed early in the month and then travel to New York as a combined honeymoon and "triumphal eastward tour as a playwright." In his autobiography, Smith merrily recalled the clever ways in which he financed the journey:

> Instead of asking for leave of absence, I represented to Mr. Melville Stone that it would be greatly to the advantage of the Chicago *News* if he would continue my salary and have me interview prominent politicians and other celebrities in the East. As I magnanimously offered to pay my own expenses, he thought this a bright idea. The General Passenger Agent of the Michigan Central Railroad was Mr. O. W. Ruggles, who was always on the lookout for novel ideas in the way of advertising. With the motive of getting free railway transportation I wrote a story about *Don Quixote* and *Sancho Panza* taking a trip from Chicago to New York on the Michigan Central; their experiences in sleeping cars and dining cars, and their visit to Niagara Falls. . . . This won the approval of Mr. Ruggles, who published the story in book form with clever illustrations and paid me five hundred dollars in railroad tickets.

After less than a month of rehearsal in New York City, McCaull's company headed to the Chestnut Street Opera House in Philadelphia, where *The Begum* would be given its world premiere performance early in

November. With diva Mathilde Cottrelly as the Begum, and De Wolf Hopper and Digby Bell, two of the leading funnymen in comic opera, playing Howja-Dhu and Myhnt-Jhuleep, success seemed destined for Smith and de Koven. The opera appeared to please the audience in every way, but, in spite of popular approval, the critics were mixed in their praise. Smith's libretto was called clever and "better than average," with crisp and humorous dialogue, notwithstanding the author's "tendency toward punning." The lyrical numbers in the score were commended but de Koven's chorus work and orchestrations were considered weak, with all the best material in the first act. The correspondent for the *New York Mirror* (November 19, 1887) summed up the critical view: "The opera was mounted in beautiful style and had the advantage of an excellent cast. It may meet with considerable success upon the road, but it would be unsafe to venture it for a long run."

From Philadelphia, *The Begum* returned to New York, where it opened on November 21 at the Fifth Avenue Theatre. Due in no small part to the social prominence of the composer, an audience rather more fashionable than normally seen at comic opera openings was in attendance. The boys in the balcony did their best to applaud vociferously at every opportunity and, if the number of flowers pelted upon the stage was a measure of success, then the opening night in New York City was a triumph. Once again, the critics were mixed in their opinions, most preferring Smith's work to de Koven's. The *New York Times* (November 22, 1887) was especially complimentary to the librettist, calling his lyrics "extremely clever" and "worth more careful examination than the hearing of an initial performance permits." Even though the similarity of Smith's work to that of W. S. Gilbert was openly acknowledged, the reviewer pointed out that *The Begum* was not a slavish imitation of the Englishman's work, but simply reminiscent of his style, and predicted that Smith would have an "exceedingly promising" future.

The *Spirit of the Times* (November 26, 1887), likewise noting the parallels to Gilbert and Sullivan, complained that the performances of the low comics, De Wolf Hopper, Digby Bell, Jefferson de Angelis (Jhust-Naut, the Court Jester), and Harry MacDonough (Asch-Kahrt, an Officer in the Royal Household), robbed the script of a crispness and clarity:

> On its merits, played as the author and composer intended, with its amusing little story and its jingling transcriptions of

> popular melodies, there would be a chance of success for *The Begum*. But the four low comedy conspirators are too much for it. . . . Colonel McCaull has fallen into the error that comic opera means low comedy opera. On the contrary, the higher the comedy the better for the opera. *The Begum* would be much more successful if the parts which de Angelis, Hopper, MacDonough and Bell spoil by their monkey-shines were seriously acted.

The *New York Mirror* (November 26, 1887), echoing the complaints of the *Tribune* and the *Herald* concerning the lack of originality in the work, found the dialogue "lively and frequently clever" and the music "extremely pretty," and concluded, "On the whole, *The Begum* offered an unusually large share of the good qualities demanded of an operetta, with a proportionately small percentage of its drawbacks, and may be set down, with confidence, for a run."

After a three-week run to excellent business in New York City, the McCaull Opera Company traveled to Chicago, where *The Begum* was scheduled to open the day after Christmas. Harry B. Smith, however, was in no hurry to leave Manhattan. His reluctance had less to do with his sudden celebrity as a librettist than his having discovered one of New York's greatest treasures: bookstores. Although he had always been a bibliophile, his first experience as a collector of rare books began at the "Saints and Sinners" corner of McClurg's Bookstore in Chicago, where he purchased a presentation copy of Dickens's *Pickwick Papers* for the exorbitant price of sixty dollars. Now, wandering from shop to shop, scrutinizing window displays, and browsing the bookshelves inside, collecting quickly went from being a pastime to a habit, and then to an avocation; and when George Richmond, a bookseller with Dodd, Mead and Company, tempted him with a five-volume, first-edition *Collection of the Christmas Books* by Charles Dickens, Harry succumbed, even though the price was alarmingly high. Once Smith discovered that he could obtain rare books on credit, he was hooked. It would not take long before Smith would be celebrated, not only as a comic opera librettist, but as a book collector.

Back in Chicago, the opening of *The Begum* was being treated as the social event of the season. An audience of 2,300, mostly from the upper strata of Chicago society, crowded the Chicago Opera House on December 26 to hear the music of the senator's son-in-law, the local

"Beau Brummell," and the words of the ubiquitous newspaper columnist. The *New York Mirror* (January 7, 1888) called the evening "a society event on one hand, and a newspaper advertisement on the other," and reports of "who was seen with whom wearing what" filled the tabloid columns for the rest of the week. Following the performance, the composer, librettist, and manager were called upon to give speeches, de Koven taking the opportunity to answer a journalist who announced before the premiere that he "would never give notice to a man who led Germans" (as cotillions were called in those days) or wore a monocle, for that matter. The composer glibly reminded the crowd that Wagner and Strauss had "led Germans" all their lives and he could certainly do worse than follow in their footsteps. Even if the words Smith spoke, thanking the audience for their enthusiastic applause, were "more or less facetious" as he suggests in his autobiography, an important point was raised by manager McCaull when he expressed how deeply pleased he was to have been able to produce a comic opera written by Americans. At a time when the repertoire was stuffed with European imports, *The Begum* was certainly unique.

Not untypically, the Chicago reviews emphasized the homegrown nature of the libretto and score, praising the high points and glossing over the faults. Casting a rare dissenting vote, the local correspondent to the *New York Mirror* (January 7, 1888) emphasized the comic opera's deficiencies, noting that "*The Begum* is a sample of what a liberal expenditure of cold cash will do to boom a very mediocre article." He argued that although Smith's dialogue was "bright" and after the style of W. S. Gilbert, "it is such a long way after that it is not even a good imitation." Like the *Spirit of the Times* review in New York, the critic suggested that if there was anything original in the text, it was killed by the performances, but also added that it was the performances alone that created the humor in the piece.

More significant than the (now typical) mixed reviews were published allegations of plagiarism against the composer suggesting that a German musician named Seebeck, who had once been employed as a copyist by de Koven, had actually written the score to *The Begum*. Even when Seebeck swore that he had never composed a note of the music, rumors continued to fly that de Koven's social connections managed to secure the copyist's testimony. To put a stop to the rumors, de Koven issued a statement offering to turn over all of his royalties from the opera to anyone who could actually prove that Seebeck had composed even a single note of his music. No one ever came forward to collect the cash, and the rumor gradually withered away as the new year began and *The Begum* continued its highly lucrative run in Chicago.

One night, before the McCaull Opera Company and *The Begum* returned to the East for a week's stay at the Park Theatre in Brooklyn, Smith and de Koven were given box tickets by a manager named W. A. McConnell to the opening night of William Young's *The Rajah*, then on the Chicago leg of a national tour. McConnell, once a theatrical advance agent, now the manager of a touring company, was also playing the title role, and he took every opportunity to satirize the librettist and composer's new comic opera, as well as the sartorial idiosyncrasies of the ever-monocled and impeccably attired Reginald de Koven. Smith recalls the occasion most vividly in his autobiography:

> In the scene in which the amiable idler nicknamed *The Rajah* shows unexpected nerve and defies a mob of strikers, McConnell addressed the ragged, black-bearded leader of the proletariat: "I know you well, Reginald de Koven. You needn't try to hide behind those whiskers." Later, when the ring-leader accused him of some injustice to the people, his defense was: "At least you'll admit that I did not write 'The Begum.'"

Although the experience of getting a comic opera produced was not exactly life altering for either composer or librettist, both were extremely encouraged by the modicum of success (and notoriety) they had experienced in the process. De Koven, taking to heart the critics who found fault with his orchestral skills, decided to travel to Vienna in the spring of 1888 to study with Richard Genée, a master of orchestration whose students included Franz von Suppé and Johann Strauss II. Among the projects de Koven pursued in Europe was a new Harry B. Smith libretto based on Cervantes's novel *Don Quixote*. The idea for the new work had developed during the rehearsals for *The Begum* when the composer and librettist had befriended De Wolf Hopper and Digby Bell. Watching the two comedians interact, they realized that they had the perfect casting for an adaptation of Cervantes's book: Hopper in the role of Don Quixote, the Knight of La Mancha, and Bell as his sidekick, Sancho Panza. As would be his typical practice, Smith quickly drafted an outline of the plot, then composed the lyrics for the songs so that the composer could work on the music while he was creating the dialogue and comic business.

Digby Bell and De Wolf Hopper

While de Koven was in Europe perfecting his orchestral technique and composing the score for *Don Quixote*, Smith continued working during the day at his newspaper desk, and polishing his adaptations of foreign operettas for the McCaull company at night. Smith's version of Suppé's *Boccaccio* was already in the repertoire and doing nicely on the road, and Harry was hard at work on *Fatinitza*, the next of Suppé's comic operas scheduled to enter the touring repertoire. What free time Harry had was devoted to drafting new projects, three of which were registered for copyright during the spring and summer of 1888: *The Blizzard; or, Families Supplied*, a three-act comedy, *Bambo, the King of the Tramps*, a musical farce in three acts written with J. C. Buchanan, and *The Scarecrow*, another three-act comedy with songs written with Robert Peattie, and the only one of the lot to be produced.

Although Harry was busy, he was always on the lookout for new ideas, so when Robert Peattie, a fellow member of the *Chicago Daily News* staff, approached him with a concept for a farcical comedy, Smith was happy to set off on another collaboration. No sooner had the pair begun to draft a working outline for the project when they encountered actor-manager McConnell, who claimed to have discovered a young comedienne with a great deal of talent, and even more money, who was looking for a play with which to "exploit her potential." Smith announced that he and Peattie were working on a play, and McConnell asked for a synopsis. As the collaborators recounted the plot of their comedy, both were so tickled with the humor of the piece that their laughter eventually infected the manager, who quickly became convinced that he must produce the play. A contract was immediately agreed upon, granting the authors a small advance upon the completion of each of three acts, and the promise of royalties when the play was produced.

Concerned that the lady might change her mind about funding the production, McConnell was in a hurry to see the play produced. As a result, while maintaining their day jobs at the newspaper, Smith and Peattie pumped out the comedy in ten days. Their effort, *The Scarecrow*, was scheduled for a three-week run at the Haymarket Theatre with a cast of local actors of only marginal abilities. On opening night, Peattie and his wife sat in one proscenium box while Lena and Harry Smith sat in the box across from them. Eugene Field, the celebrated poet and journalist, and colleague of the authors at the *News*, kept running from box to box during the performance, inquiring of the authors' wives which of their husbands was responsible for a "particularly tart" bit of dialogue. That neither of the authors wished to claim ownership for a single word of the play was one measure of its success. Another was the catatonic response from the audience, prompting McConnell, who was seated next to the critics, to try to convince them that the actors had gotten the script confused and were performing the third act first.

At the end of the first week, it was wisely decided that the show should close to save everyone involved further embarrassment. The authors, who had not been paid their stipulated royalties, sued the manager—a joke in itself, because McConnell was notorious for always being in the red. Although before the trial, the manager threatened to have Smith arrested for perjury if he claimed to be an author on the witness stand, there were no such outbursts during the hearing itself, and the plaintiffs were awarded damages in the amount of $365.

While Smith and Peattie were working on *The Scarecrow*, Harry accepted the position of business manager and associate editor on yet another short-lived magazine, an idealistic political journal called *America*. With essays, stories, and reviews contributed by the likes of James Russell Lowell, Theodore Roosevelt, and Frank R. Stockton, the publication had high literary standards without much popular appeal. Harry was hired to inject humor and colloquial verse into what was basically a polemical newspaper actively trying to reform government policies—but his efforts met with little success. While Smith was thus engaged, he was approached by David Henderson, a local drama critic turned impresario who offered to pay him thirty dollars weekly to act as press agent for the summer extravaganzas at the Chicago Opera House, and to rewrite the libretto for *The Crystal Slipper*, a burlesque of Cinderella, scheduled to open on June 12. Reginald de Koven had told him that, before his marriage, he was earning twenty-five dollars a week working in his uncle's bank in Chicago, so to Smith thirty dollars a week was a princely sum, particularly on top of the fifteen dollars McCaull was paying him and his regular salary at *America* and the *News*.

The previous year, David Henderson and his Imperial Burlesque Company had produced *The Arabian Nights; or, Aladdin's Wonderful Lamp* at the Opera House in an attempt to re-create in Chicago a burlesque-extravaganza inspired by Lydia Thompson's box-office successes. The format, kept alive in the English Christmas pantomime, always involved a fairy tale or familiar story, dialogue in rhymed couplets, topical satire, a preponderance of puns, plenty of low-comedy clownishness, music borrowed from the classics or popular tunes, and ample opportunity for lavish costumes, spectacular scenery, and extravagantly choreographed ballets. To ensure the success of the venture, Henderson had hired Captain Alfred Thompson, an English designer well known for his work in pantomimes in London, to write the libretto for *The Arabian Nights* and supervise the spectacle. Because Thompson was not amenable to

Henderson's brand of creative bookkeeping and demanded payment as contracted, the manager publicly condemned the author as a literary midget, incapable of pleasing the tastes of an American audience. In fact, Henderson told the newspapers that when the text of the burlesque was first presented to him, he found it to be "so bad that it could not be presented to the American public," forcing him to engage surreptitiously a number of authors (all American, of course) to render the piece unembarrassing to the cast and public alike.

When *The Arabian Nights* opened in Chicago on June 4, 1887, both the audience and critics were so enraptured by the costumes, scenery, and choreography that not even the "banalities" of the libretto could prevent the show from being an extraordinary success playing to capacity audiences throughout its fourteen-week run. In addition, the *New York Mirror* (September 3, 1887) proudly announced that "for the twelve weeks which ended with last Saturday's matinee it has enjoyed the largest receipts ever taken in twelve consecutive weeks during any season at any Chicago house." When the show left the Opera House, it moved east to New York City, where it opened at the Standard Theatre on September 12 and remained there until the end of October, a popular favorite that continued to earn substantial dividends for manager Henderson but diatribes from the critics. The worst of the lot came from the *New York Mirror* (September 17, 1887):

> Our Critic is a long-suffering and conscientious person. In the interests of art and MIRROR readers he has patiently sat through rubbish enough to fill New York harbor several times over. Dominated by a righteous feeling of duty, he has held on to his orchestra seat again and again to the bitter end of some bad, bad performance, while more fortunate spectators were gathering up their hats and fleeing away by battalions. . . . But at the Standard he found that the time had come to rebel against custom, duty, Fate and Captain Thompson's burlesque. When the first act was ended he stole silently away in search of poison or an ambulance. He drew the line at the second act and the rest of the piece, for he was a wise man, and he knew that he had had enough. . . .
>
> He saw a crowded house of presumably intelligent people soberly watching the stage. He heard a collection of stale music, very badly sung . . . , two or three clever actors, vainly opposing their skill against the dreadful trash they were called

upon to utter and the inane actions they were obliged to do. He saw a ballet of unexampled antiquity . . . garish scenery and cheap but showy dresses.

What he did not see was a pretty girl, an attractive costume, or any reason why *The Arabian Nights* should have been seen at all. What he did not hear was a pretty song, a clever line or a real burst of applause or laughter. . . . [N]o drearier burlesque, and no worse burlesque company, has ever come within our knowledge.

When it came time to begin preparations for his second summer extravaganza, and Captain Thompson turned in his draft of the Cinderella spectacle, Henderson hired the exceedingly amenable Harry B. Smith to rewrite and punch up the libretto. The Englishman was initially resistant to change, claiming that he saw the material work in London, but when the manager positively refused to produce the piece unless it was considerably rewritten, Thompson relented and accepted Smith as a collaborator. However, in a letter written to the editor of the *New York Dramatic Mirror* (March 30, 1889), Henderson argued that the revision was a less-than-collaborative effort, noting that Smith "so thoroughly discarded Thompson's book as to make his [Smith's] work practically original." What essentially remained of Thompson's contribution were his designs for the physical production.

In Smith's version, *The Crystal Slipper; or, Prince Prettywitz and Little Cinderella* opens with a prologue establishing the disagreement between She, the Witch of Selfishness, and the Fairy Graciosa over which drive is the strongest in humankind: self-interest or love. Smith not only parodies N. Rider Haggard's popular novel, *She*, in the name of the witch, but makes a pun upon the author's name in She's rhymed speech as she awakens at the beginning of the play:

Sleep at my age? What can the matter be?
(To public) You've heard of me before?
Well, I'm "She."
A haggard hag, an antiquated relic.
But once upon a time I was angelic.

To prove her point that love is the strongest drive of all, Graciosa introduces the story of Cinderella, and the scene changes to a plaza in Pretzelstadt where a fair is in progress attended by Baron Anthracite, his two ugly daughters, Angostura and Flordefuma, and the Baron's valet, Yosemite. Cinderella appears just as Prince Polydore von Prettiwitz enters with his courtiers, and the couple immediately falls in love and watches a Maypole Dance performed by the local clowns.

The second act opens on the kitchen in Anthracite Castle, where Cinderella is found frolicking with Yosemite and the castle cat. The valet and the cat solve a personal dispute by donning boxing gloves and sparring to the Marquis of Queensbury Rules, and the Baron enters and jovially acts out an inning of baseball with Yosemite. The ugly sisters enter and complete the series of anachronisms with a topical song about the Chicago social register called "We Love Sassiety." The invitations to the Prince's ball arrive, and although a Fairy Godmother appears to tell Cinderella that she shall go to the ball, Baron Anthracite insists that the girl remain at home. The next scene depicts the Elizabethan gardens of the castle, where the Fairy Godmother spectacularly transforms a pumpkin, lizards, rats, and mice into a coach-and-six. Before Cinderella departs, however, she stays to watch a ballet of nursery rhymes including "Four-and-Twenty Blackbirds," "Jack and Jill," "Little Boy Blue," and "Little Miss Muffet."

Act three presents the well-attended Prince's ball, with a "Grand Banquet Ballet," featuring dancing cutlery, plates, and dinner courses, anticipating the lavish spectacle of the *Ziegfeld Follies*, Busby Berkeley's choreography on film, and the production number "Be Our Guest" from Alan Mencken and Howard Ashman's *Beauty and the Beast*. The clock strikes twelve and Cinderella flees, leaving one of her crystal slippers behind.

Act four opens on the throne room in the palace, where the beautiful women of all nations are lined up to step into the glass shoe. Only Cinderella's foot fits properly, however, and she and Prince Polydore are finally united, an occasion marked by a spectacular transformation scene depicting the Temple of Time.

The extravaganza opened at the Chicago Opera House on June 12 to superlative notices, calling it the "most gorgeous spectacle that has ever been put on on an American stage" and an "instantaneous hit." Smith's dialogue was considered "good enough for the piece," but it was the scenery and costumes and "electrical illuminations" that drew all the focus during the exceptionally well attended twelve-week run that broke the record for gross receipts taken during fifty consecutive performances of a spectacular or burlesque production.

When *The Crystal Slipper* moved to the Boston Theatre in September, Colonel McCaull's Opera Company was in residence at

The interior of the Boston Theatre

Wallack's Theatre in New York City performing Smith's adaptation of *Boccaccio* to enthusiastic popular and critical response. Even the reviewer from the *New York Times* (September 4, 1888) was unusually lavish in his praise, calling Smith's libretto "the best of all the English versions." After six weeks in Boston, *The Crystal Slipper* moved to the Star Theatre for a month's run beginning November 26 in New York City, where the reviewers were less impressed with the spectacle and more critical of the libretto. Although the *Herald* (November 27, 1888) found cleverness in the lyrics and a "wild" humor throughout, the *Mirror* (December 1, 1888) complained that the extravaganza was typically "imbecile in text and acrobatic in performance," the authors not having treated the subject "with more wit or cleverness than their predecessors." In fact, the review continued, "if it were not for the mirth-making antics of some and the hard work of others in the company *The Crystal Slipper* would be a very flat and stupid piece indeed."

Among the noteworthy performances were Cinderella, performed by Marguerite Fish, who had joined the company in Boston, and Prince Prettywitz, acted by May Yohe, who was replaced the day after the opening by Mamie Cerbi. Yohe, who had been with the show since Chicago, was uncomfortable in the role of the Prince, and the cold she caught in Boston robbed her of the ability to give even a mediocre performance. Although she was a favorite performer in New York (cheers and flowers greeted her entrance on opening night), real celebrity would ultimately find Yohe through her extratheatrical romantic liaisons with the rich and famous. She is perhaps best known as the sometime wife of Lord Francis Hope, wearing the famous Hope Diamond, supposed to bring bad luck to those who own it.

Calling her "diminutive" and "dainty," critics found Marguerite Fish among the most artistically gifted soubrettes of the day, with an almost faultless technique in both her acting and singing. Perhaps recalling her acclaimed performance in a repertoire of German comic opera two years before at the Thalia Theatre, the *New York Mirror* (December 1, 1888) sounded the consensus of critical opinion when it suggested, "She is too good by half for such a show as *The Crystal Slipper*."

R. E. Graham was applauded for his "funny" performance as Baron Anthracite, during which he interpolated his critically acclaimed imitations of actors Henry Irving and Lawrence Barrett, and low comedian Edwin (Eddie) Foy, as Yosemite, was found to be a "versatile, whimsical, exceedingly entertaining fellow" who never stoops to vulgarity or coarseness. Foy joined Henderson's company with *The Crystal Slipper*, and for the next six years, he toured as the resident clown of the company. Foy's brand of comedy was so popular with audiences that a month after he was hired, Henderson raised his salary from $65 to $150 weekly, substantially more than Smith was earning as author of the show. Then again, Harry's reviews had not been quite as good as Foy's.

After *The Crystal Slipper* left the Star Theatre on December 22, it moved to the Amphion Academy in Williamsburgh, Brooklyn, for Christmas week before heading out on tour. McCaull's Opera Company was preparing to produce Smith's adaptation of *Fatinitza* in Philadelphia at the end of January, and back in Chicago, having signed on for a second year with the colonel—at a substantial increase in pay—Harry was hard at work on four more adaptations, the first, a version of Alfons Czibulka's newly imported comic opera, *Der Glücksritter*, retitled *The May Queen*, and scheduled to open on April 1, 1889. Set in Restoration England on the first of May, the opera turns on a plot against King Charles II by the Lord Mayor of London, Lord Middleditch, whose niece, Lady Beatrice Hamilton, is in love with a brave, but penniless, Scottish soldier of fortune named Harry Macdonald, who bears a striking resemblance to King Charles. In an attempt to help the Queen, who happens to be presiding over the Maypole festivities, Beatrice convinces Macdonald to impersonate the King and to allow himself to be captured by her uncle, who is also the leader of the Roundhead faction. After a fair amount of comedy involving Macdonald, his squire, Toby, two of the Mayor's spies secreting themselves behind pictures, and the Scotchman's decision to use the pictures for target practice, serious intrigue takes over, nearly leading the soldier of fortune to his death. At the eleventh hour, however, the true King is restored to power, the Roundhead plot is disrupted, and Harry and Beatrice are reunited in a rousing final chorus.

Because Smith was not advertised as the adapter when McCaull's production appeared at Palmer's Theatre in New York, the reviewers praising the comedy in the piece that "kept 'wreathed smiles' upon the faces of the most hardened playgoers" did not acknowledge Harry's handiwork. Both the *Times* and the *Mirror* noted the presence of far less buffoonery than usual in a production by the McCaull company, the comic business being kept "within the lines of legitimate comedy" and actually indigenous to the plot. The fact that the company comedians still managed to delight the audience with their characteristic funny business, earn critical approbation, and stay within the confines of the plot attests to Smith's highly imaginative ability to integrate actors' personalities into plots.

The next of Smith's adaptations to be produced was also the most successful, opening at Palmer's Theatre on May 8, 1889 (the day after *The May Queen* closed), and continuing on to October 5 for a total of 173 performances and unstinting critical acclaim. Based on another recent Suppé comic opera, *Die Jagd nach dem Glück*, the title, translated as *The Chase after Happiness*, was altered to *Clover* because McCaull had promised the Clover Club of Philadelphia that he would use the name of their club in his next comic opera. Even though the plot about Rudolf, a young man traveling the world in search of fame, and Stella, the lady who loves him, had nothing to do with a clover, Smith managed to integrate the title into the proceedings by creating a scene in which Stella gives Rudolf a four-leaf clover as a good luck charm before he begins his journey. It was certainly a mark of success when critics attributed the title of the work to Smith's interpolated scene, but what pleased Harry even more was the fact that Dion Boucicault, the internationally acclaimed actor, manager, and playwright, praised the adaptation, calling it the best comic opera libretto he had ever seen. The *New York Dramatic Mirror* (May 18, 1889) also found Smith's version unique in that the "unity and purpose of the original have been adhered to with more fidelity than is usual, and the comedy scenes are less interlarded with anachronistic allusions and contemporary slang."

Typically, Smith managed to capitalize on the strengths of the performers in McCaull's company, with handsome baritone Eugene Oudin and Marion Manola, an accomplished singing actress, given the romantic leads and De Wolf Hopper and Jefferson de Angelis given the low comic roles (Digby Bell and his wife having left the company when *The May Queen* closed). According to De Wolf Hopper, a second baritone named Charles W. Dungan was not well served by the script. McCaull had wanted the actor to take an unpaid "vacation" because there wasn't a role in *Clover* to showcase his talents. Under contract to the colonel for a substantial salary, Dungan decided that even a small role is better than no salary at all, so he elected to stay and was offered a walk-on part, appearing in a single act, with a single line: "My Lord, the King is dead!" (McCaull still hoped that an actor's ego would prompt Dungan to leave at such an effrontery.) Nonplussed, the actor accepted the role and performed it conscientiously throughout the run, becoming the target of practical jokes played by the rest of the cast. As Hopper recalls in his autobiography, *Once a Clown, Always a Clown:*

> The rest of us got a good deal of malicious sport out of the situation and made it as difficult for Dungan as possible. We tried every trick known to actors in an effort to break him up in the delivery of his one line. I used to tap my wooden shoes on the stage at his entrance in imitation of a galloping horse. But when he did trip at last the catastrophe was purely accidental. . . .
>
> [O]ne summer evening toward the close of the run, Dungan tripped on the scabbard of his sword as he entered and fell flat center stage with the words, "My Lord—"
>
> I have never known another such utter collapse to overtake a company. We had heckled him for weeks to no result, and now, when we had given up, he had fallen over his own sword. With one exception none of us, principals or chorus could utter a note. Marion Manola, the prima donna, became so hysterical

that she fainted. The orchestra was silent; the conductor, Adolph Nowak, had laid down his baton and buried his head on the stand.

Although the critics praised the absence of unmotivated horseplay on stage, they had nothing to say about the offstage shenanigans.

When *Clover* was starting its run at Palmer's Theatre in New York, McVicker's Theatre in Chicago was running a revival of Shakespeare's *The Tempest*, and to advertise that event, the theatre offered a fifty-dollar prize for the poem that could best summarize the play. Harry came up with an acrostic, the first letter of each line acting as an advertisement for the production when read downward, and won the prize. At the same time, manager David Henderson was preparing for his next summer extravaganza, *Bluebeard, Jr.*, scheduled to open at the Chicago Opera House on June 11. Even before rehearsals began, the project was a nightmare for the manager.

Late in 1888, Henderson had expected that Captain Thompson would collaborate with Harry on his next extravaganza, the third in the summer series. However, because he still bore a grudge against Smith for rewriting *The Crystal Slipper*, Thompson refused to work with him, suggesting instead a collaboration with a New York City newspaperman named Chrystal. When the preliminary draft of *Blue Bashaw* (then the working title of *Bluebeard, Jr.*) arrived, not only did Henderson discover that Thompson had written it without assistance, he again found it to be "utterly deficient in plot and characterization" and absolutely impossible to produce unless it were completely rewritten. Still irritated by his previous experience with Smith, the captain refused to permit anything but a light edit of his script and the addition of colloquial expressions to make the text more immediately accessible to an American audience. When the manager insisted on a complete overhaul of the material, Thompson severed all relations with Henderson and headed for New York City, where two months later, in a long diatribe published in the *New York Dramatic Mirror* (March 16, 1889), he threatened to sue the Chicago Opera House for breach of contract.

In the meantime, Henderson had approached playwright Clay M. Greene to rewrite the captain's libretto. Because of Thompson's resistance to Smith, the manager had not wished to fuel an already incendiary situation by asking Harry to do the script doctoring. By April, a new script was ready. A new designer and choreographer (William Voegtlin) was engaged to replace Captain Thompson, and rehearsals were scheduled toward a June 11 premiere. When *Bluebeard, Jr.* finally opened to the typically large and enthusiastic audience, Greene's text, a more-or-less faithful rendering of the Bluebeard myth, was completely overshadowed by spectacular production numbers, lavish scenery, and an almost magical use of electric lighting effects. *Divertissements* such as the "Ballet of Birds and Insects" and the "Glittering Grotto of Fantastic Fancy," peopled with characters from nursery rhymes, were said to surpass "anything seen on the American stage."

Henderson was acclaimed by the critics as having outdone every previous extravaganza produced in America (high praise indeed), if not even surpassing the great spectacles of Europe. The singing, the dancing, even individual members of the cast—Eddie Foy in particular—were singled out for praise. The only significant negative vote went to Greene's libretto, the *Dramatic Mirror* (June 22, 1889) complaining of the number of "old chestnuts" in the text, and concluding that the book "is mediocre, in fact it will need a good deal of rewriting to strengthen it." Taking the criticism seriously, Henderson returned to Harry B. Smith and engaged him to rewrite and revise the text (a task for which Harry would be paid but uncredited) before *Bluebeard, Jr.* was revived in Chicago in September 1890.

While *Bluebeard, Jr.* was in its second month in Chicago, Harry B. Smith and Reginald de Koven were in Boston, negotiating with an opera company for a production of *Don Quixote*, their recently completed comic opera. De Koven had returned from Vienna the previous fall with a completed, fully orchestrated score that demonstrated a marked improvement in his orchestration skills. The work had originally been offered to the McCaull Opera Company for inclusion in its touring repertoire. Convinced that the opera was an excellent vehicle for De Wolf Hopper, McCaull optioned *Don Quixote*, hoping to schedule it among his current repertoire of foreign works. Twice he planned an opening, and twice he canceled because of the popularity of the Viennese fare—a situation for which Smith must accept some of the responsibility, as he had written the adaptations for McCaull's most successful productions. As a result, Smith and de Koven were in the market for an opera company willing to produce an American work.

Harry B. Smith had known about the Boston Ideals, a comic opera company that came into prominence a decade earlier during the early days of the *Pinafore* craze, primarily because they managed to perform Gilbert and Sullivan better than anyone else. After touring for a number of years under the management of Effie Ober, who ran the Lyceum Bureau, a vocal and theatrical agency in Boston, a number of the actors—Henry Clay Barnabee, Tom Karl, and William H. MacDonald—dissatisfied with the repertoire and the machinations of what Barnabee called a "sprightly but scheming prima donna," set off on their own to create a new company: The Bostonians. The trio was strengthened artistically by the addition of George Frothingham, Jessie Bartlett Davis, her sister, Josephine Bartlett, Eugene Cowles, and Edwin Hoff, and the company's reputation soon overshadowed that of the original Ideals.

It occurred to Smith that Barnabee and Frothingham were not inappropriately suited for the characters of Don Quixote and Sancho Panza, so he and the composer approached the Bostonians with the prospect of producing the opera. Barnabee liked the music more than the libretto, but he decided to take a chance, because the standard repertoire had gotten stale, and composer and librettist's previous work, *The Begum*, showed promise artistically and was generally popular with audiences. On July 15, 1889, the Bostonians signed a contract with Smith and de Koven agreeing to perform *Don Quixote* sixty times within a year, to pay the authors 5 percent of the gross receipts for each performance, and to produce the opera in Chicago for at least one week before the termination of the contract.

After a fair amount of advance publicity, including the report that the opera had been accepted for production by the Prince of Wales Theatre in London, *Don Quixote* opened at the Boston Theatre on November 18, 1889, to what Smith described as a "merry war among the critics." The correspondent for the *Dramatic Mirror* (November 23, 1889) gushingly called the opera "bright and sparkling" and predicted that it would take "a prominent place among the favorite operettas of the day," while the *Boston Advertiser* (November 19, 1889) complained that the text was incoherent to anyone unfamiliar with Cervantes's novel. The *Boston Post* (November 19, 1889), however, complimented Smith for having written a libretto far superior to that of *The Begum*, and excused the deficiencies in the text because of the author's inexperience.

Experienced or not, Smith had cleverly consolidated the multiplicity of events in Cervantes's novel into two romantic plots interwoven with the crackbrained adventures of Don Quixote. De Koven's score aspired to operatic legitimacy, but Smith's text, although devoid of aimless buffoonery, still displayed the author's burlesque tendencies in the juxtaposition of archaic language with contemporary colloquialisms. Neither author took part in the rehearsal process, but, according to an interview with

Smith in the *Dramatic Mirror* (June 13, 1896), each was assigned a duty on opening night:

> [T]he only portion of the production that was entrusted to us was the production of a horse and donkey on the first night. Just as I was leading Sancho's donkey to the stage door I encountered De Koven [*sic*] with a broken-down nag in tow that he had selected to impersonate Rosinante [Quixote's horse]. It's a wonder that he wasn't arrested by the Society for the Prevention of Cruelty to Animals. It was the most wretched equine specimen I ever saw in my life.

Even the hoped-for incongruity of a would-be knight riding a broken-down nag failed to hit the mark and, after the advertised four performances in Boston, *Don Quixote* was withdrawn and added to The Bostonians' touring repertoire.

The following month, Smith was back in Chicago to witness the opening night (December 30) of *Captain Fracassa*, another of his adaptations for McCaull at the Chicago Opera House and featuring De Wolf Hopper in the title role. Set in sixteenth-century Venice, the complicated plot concerns a goldsmith named Oberto who falls in love with Princess Coligny, after rescuing her from an adventurer named Captain Fracassa. Through a great deal of intrigue, the two men compete for the attentions of the lady until, at the eleventh hour, when their differences are scheduled to be settled by a duel, it is discovered that the goldsmith is the son of a banished nobleman. The Princess pardons the father and marries the son, and Fracassa goes off in search of other adventure.

Although the score by the German composer Rudolph Dellinger was considered less melodic than his usual fare, the Chicago critics found the adaptation highly suited to the tastes of an American audience, if at times "static." The runaway hit of the production was the topical song Smith composed for Hopper, "Bid Me Good Bye and Go," for which both the author and performer were rewarded with high marks by critics and full houses at every performance.

The achievement of the McCaull Opera Company and Harry B. Smith in presenting foreign works to the American public cannot be emphasized enough, especially considering the speed with which the works were optioned, translated, adapted, and rehearsed. *Kapitän Fracassa* had premiered in Hamburg, Germany, on March 2, 1889. By May, Harry was working on the adaptation, and by the fall, the work was gradually integrated into the touring repertoire. Adding the fact that Smith was holding several day jobs and writing other shows with and without de Koven (a libretto for a three-act comic opera, *The Knights*, for example, was registered for copyright in September 1889) and the difficulties of maintaining a well-rehearsed touring repertoire within a fifty-week season, it is certainly surprising that the products—both in text and performance—turned out as well as they did.

While McCaull was touring Smith's adaptations, The Bostonians headed out to the West Coast, performing *Don Quixote* once or twice a week along the way. The company had little confidence in the work, and neither Barnabee (Don Quixote) or Frothingham (Sancho Panza) seemed capable of stepping into roles originally designed for De Wolf Hopper and Digby Bell. In his autobiography, Smith complained, "Barnabee was elderly and could not stand the punishment given to him by the windmill and other antagonists. On the day following a performance he would appear at rehearsal, limping, plastered and bandaged." It was no surprise when, after The Bostonians fulfilled their commitment of sixty performances and a week in Chicago, the company withdrew the opera from their regular repertoire.

Don Quixote drew large audiences for the last week of May 1890 at the Chicago Opera House. Among the rich and infamous in attendance on opening night was Smith's old nemesis, William McConnell, the defendant in the *Scarecrow* royalty case two years before. Never one to miss an opportunity to bear a grudge or crack a joke, McConnell spotted Harry in the audience with his wife and shouted: "If the audience calls for the author and you come out, so help me Heaven! I'm going to yell for Cervantes."

The reviews were no better in Chicago than they had been in Boston, although the general critical opinion, reflected by the correspondent to the *Dramatic Mirror* (May 31, 1890), was that "the music is much better than the libretto." Although the implication that the composer was "too good" for the librettist had no immediate effect on the collaboration, the seeds of dissension were planted for the future. Regardless of the fate of *Don Quixote*, and certainly unforeseen by the critics themselves, the Chicago reviews were startlingly significant to the careers of Smith and de Koven, because they advertised a "new opera . . . soon to be produced here by the same authors." The name of the opera was *Robin Hood.*

Chapter 3

"Come to Sherwood; Join Our Jolly Crew"

On July 15, 1889, the same day The Bostonians signed the contract with Smith and de Koven for *Don Quixote*, the company also agreed to produce another of the duo's collaborations, then in the planning stages, called *The Outlaw; or, Robin Hood and His Merry Men*, during their 1889–90 touring season. The agreement may have been precipitous on the part of The Bostonians, taking a chance on two untried operas, but it certainly energized the authors, prompting them to rent an office in Chicago where they could meet every day and work face to face. Smith had not enjoyed the long-distance collaboration that produced their previous effort. A musician in his own right, he wanted to have some creative input during the composition process, just as he knew a composer would appreciate the opportunity of making suggestions regarding the structure of the scenario or the lyrics. Because de Koven traveled in a very elite social circle and was the product of highly sophisticated European schooling, the middle-class Smith, without a college degree, had always felt an inherent distance between them. At least if they shared an office, leaving behind their divergent lifestyles and attitudes, he believed they might accomplish something significant.

In an interview with the *Green Book Magazine* (September 1912), Smith outlined his process for creating a libretto: "I first think of the locale—selecting one that will suggest musical color. Then I write my scenario. A good scenario is fully half the work. I write that at length, perhaps twenty-five or thirty pages. Usually I write the lyrics before I begin on the book. I do this, in order to get the composer started. Necessarily his work takes more time than mine. Afterwards I write the book." The lyrics of *Robin Hood*, imitating the structure and style of Old English ballads, were provided to the composer act by act so that, while de Koven was composing the music, Smith could be fleshing out the dialogue. Once an act was completed, it was shipped out to The Bostonians, then on tour with *Don Quixote* in their repertoire, so that the actors could begin learning the music and text. According to the authors' recollections, it took Smith three weeks to complete the libretto for *Robin Hood* (a week per act), and de Koven three months to compose and orchestrate the full score.

The familiar story was set in the medieval town of Nottingham during the May Day celebrations that always included an archery championship. King Richard, setting off for the Crusades, had placed his ward, Marian Fitzwalter (Marie Stone), in the care of the Sheriff of Nottingham (Henry Clay Barnabee), with the order that she should marry Robert, the Earl of Huntington (Edwin Hoff), when he comes into his inheritance. The Sheriff of Nottingham, however, is plotting to pass off his ward, Sir Guy of Gisborne (P. M. Lang), as the lawful heir of Huntington, and marry him to Marian. The Sheriff's duplicity sends Robert (who has won this year's archery competition) into the forest to join a band of outlaws, calling himself "Robin Hood."

Six months pass. Robin has become the leader of the outlaw gang, "merry men" except for Allan-a-Dale (Jessie Bartlett Davis), who is lovesick for the flirtatious Annabel (Carlotta Maconda), and who believes himself in competition with Robin for her attentions. The Sheriff, with Sir Guy, both disguised as tinkers, have come to the forest looking for Robin Hood, followed by Marian, who has managed to escape the Sheriff's clutches. When Allan-a-Dale hears Robin serenading Marian, he thinks it is his own Annabel betraying him, so he hands over Robin Hood to the Sheriff. When Allan discovers his mistake, he and the band of outlaws rescue Robin, but only momentarily, for Sir Guy and the King's archers quickly appear and take the outlaws to prison.

The wedding day has arrived for Marian and Sir Guy and for Annabel and the Sheriff, who first encountered her in the forest. Having been rescued by Friar Tuck (George Frothingham), Robin and his merry men appear in the nick of time to prevent the weddings and to return with the women to their hideaway. Suddenly, a messenger appears with a pardon for Robin from the King, restoring his inheritance and his title, and enabling Marian to marry the true Earl of Huntington at last.

The Bostonians did not think much of the piece initially when it arrived, act by act, in the spring of 1890. Only Henry Barnabee and William MacDonald (Little John) seemed to like their roles, the rest approaching the task of learning the opera unenthusiastically, with little faith in its success. It is not surprising that the company would react in such a way. The authors' *Don Quixote* was not a popular piece, and it appeared to many that *Robin Hood* would be even less successful. As a result, a week before the scheduled opening, the company renegotiated the royalty contract with the authors, substituting a graduated royalty scale based on cash receipts for the original 5 percent. The better the business, the higher the royalty, and if business was as poor as anticipated, the authors would share in the loss.

The Bostonians needed to produce the opera before the end of their season in Chicago to maintain the rights to it, but their lack of faith in the material prompted them to spend as little money and time as possible on the production. Although the principals involved all recall a different monetary figure—Smith claims $109.50, de Koven suggests it was two dollars less, and his wife puts the amount at $150—the fact remains that the production by any standard was slovenly. Costumes were pulled from other operas in the repertoire, and the perspicacious viewer on opening night could easily recognize that Robin Hood was wearing Manrico's costume from Verdi's *Il Trovatore.* In addition, because time was running out, rehearsals were rushed, and because the actors were resistant to learning their roles, nothing in the opera seemed to work. The musical director even refused to conduct the "Tinker's Song" in the second act because he felt that the writing was of such poor quality. Happily, the opening scheduled for June 1 was postponed due to lack of preparation.

Finally, on June 9, *Robin Hood* opened at the Chicago Opera House to a small but enthusiastic and fashionable audience. Smith's newspaper cronies and de Koven's blue-blooded supporters were clearly in evidence to support the local boys, but the general public had little immediate

Henry Clay Barnabee as the Sheriff of Nottingham

interest in the production. The cast had spent so much time learning the music that, even with an extra week of rehearsal, the text was far from memorized. As a result, the author had to serve as prompter for the entire performance, standing beneath the stage floor, text in hand, only his head being seen by the actors on stage, and hidden from the audience by means of a canvas hood. As Smith recalls in his autobiography, "It was a very hot night and after I had stood for nearly four hours close to the footlights, with my head in a canvas box, the fate of the opera was a matter of comparative indifference. As I had to read most of the dialogue to the actors, the performance, dramatically, was slow and depressing."

Not uncharacteristically, the critics were mixed in their opinions. While the Chicago papers were generally kind and predicted a bright future for the work, the correspondent to the *New York Clipper* (June 14, 1890) complained that the "efforts to make a comic opera out of the story of the outlaw of Sherwood Forest are painful at the best." Although Smith was complimented for having "done his best with the materials" at his command, the review noted a "rather ancient and musty flavor about it that did not set well with the flashy music and the approaches to modern jokes." What's more, the production "dragged terribly," and the actors (with the exception of Barnabee, Edwin Hoff playing Robin Hood, and Carlotta Maconda playing Annabel) seemed uncomfortable in their roles.

While the *Clipper* cast a generally unfavorable vote, the correspondent to the *Dramatic Mirror* (June 21, 1890) argued that the opera "made a hit and will, doubtless, become popular." In addition, the review was highly complimentary to the librettist, saying that "The book is better than anything Harry Smith has yet done," and predicted that "the piece is likely to prove the greatest success of the authors."

The reviews were positive enough to encourage attendance, and business picked up tremendously during the run, causing The Bostonians to reconsider their original assessment of the work. They certainly had no inkling of how big a hit *Robin Hood* would become, or that the company would perform it more than four thousand times. For the moment, it was enough that the opera was not a failure, and because of the sliding royalty agreement with the authors and the little money spent on scenery and costumes, the company looked forward to profiting from the production.

Shortly after the Chicago run of *Robin Hood*, de Koven was off to Europe again to study with Leo Délibes and to attempt to negotiate a

London production of *Robin Hood* with Horace Sedger of the Prince of Wales Theatre, the manager who had previously accepted *Don Quixote.* A British production of the opera must have been in the authors' minds even before the Chicago premiere, because at the end of May, Smith sold the British rights for both operas to the composer, leaving all further negotiations up to de Koven. Harry had other immediate concerns, not the least of which was the revival of *The Crystal Slipper* scheduled to open at the Chicago Opera House on June 19 with a newly revised book, cutting the original prologue and adding "many special features." These included a new ballet, "La Carte D'Amour," with music especially composed by W. H. Batchelor, who replaced Fred Eustis as musical director for the company, and a Grand Transformation Finale called "The Fleeting Seasons," ending in a spectacular tableau depicting "The Golden Age." The critics found the new production superior to the original, and Henderson's company, now called The American Extravaganza Company, kept the Opera House filled throughout the rest of the summer.

Shortly before *The Crystal Slipper* completed its "phenomenally successful" run at the Opera House to begin a national tour, the McCaull Opera Company opened its season at Hammerstein's Harlem Opera House on September 1, 1890, with Smith's adaptation of Karl Millöcker's 1887 comic opera, *The Seven Suabians.* Although the critics found the work overlong, they all were impressed with Smith's libretto, finding the dialogue "bright" and "pointed," even though the jokes seemed a little stale. The "bright and harmonious" lyrics were unanimously praised for their "taking allusions to prominent topics of the day," with two of the comedy songs, "Wait a Little Bit" and "Not Now but Later," receiving multiple encores to the hearty amusement of the audience.

While *The Seven Suabians* was merrily touring the New York area with Harry's popular topical songs, Smith received a request from Digby Bell asking for three verses for a patter song he was performing in Gilbert and Sullivan's *Iolanthe* that would mention John L. Sullivan the prizefighter, the practice of American girls marrying foreign counts, and some local Chicago gossip. He was willing to pay Smith ten dollars for the job, but he desperately needed the work the next morning. Never one to turn down easy money, Harry dashed off a lyric and tossed it into the return mail. A week later, Bell sent Smith his fee and requested another topical interpolation, this time for the role he was playing in Gilbert and Sullivan's *Patience.*

Harry kept himself occupied while de Koven was in Europe and his adaptations and extravaganzas were on the road. He and David

Henderson were collaborating on yet another spectacular production for the Chicago Opera House, *The Lost Twins; or The Babes in the Wood*, registered for copyright on September 15, 1890. This was the second team effort by the pair, the first being a three-act farce comedy called *Easy Street*, registered the previous May. Although neither work appears to have been produced, it is difficult not to be impressed by the breadth and variety of Smith's output. During the month of September 1890, three companies were touring the United States with his works: The American Extravaganza Company with a spectacle piece, McCaull's Opera Company with an adaptation of a German comic opera, and The Bostonians with an original comic opera.

At the end of September, *Robin Hood* opened for a five-week engagement at the Boston Music Hall to excellent reviews, the *Boston Herald* (September 28, 1890) proudly proclaiming that "an American composer has at last produced a highly creditable opera comique, and one that can but win fame and fortune for Messrs. De Koven and Smith on both sides of the Atlantic." Unfortunately, critical praise did not draw an audience, and The Bostonians began their United States tour still uncertain of *Robin Hood*'s commercial potential. The company only played the opera two or three times weekly, alternating it with the more standard works in their repertoire. It was only during the Detroit leg of the tour when The Bostonians began to realize the gold mine they had.

Harry B. Smith told the story several years later in the *Dramatic Mirror* (June 13, 1896):

> [T]he Bostonians were announced to appear in *Robin Hood* on Monday at Whitney's Opera House and in repertoire to fill out the week. After the performance on Monday night Manager Clark J. Whitney was so impressed with the opera and its reception that the next day he placarded Detroit from one end to the other with the announcement that nothing but *Robin Hood* would be performed throughout the week. Business went up with a bang, and *Robin Hood* has been drawing crowded houses ever since.

A return engagement in Chicago saw appreciably better business than the previous season, and Cincinnati welcomed the show enthusiastically in December with unreserved critical praise, the *Cincinnati Enquirer* (December 2, 1890) claiming, "Never since the beginning of the present craze for comic opera has a more brilliant or delightful opera been produced." At long last, The Bostonians relaxed in the knowledge that they had a hit on their hands, and they began pressing Smith and de Koven for another opera.

Shortly after the new year, Harry was hard at work on *The Tar and the Tartar*, written expressly for Digby Bell, and Reginald de Koven was in London supervising the production of *Robin Hood* scheduled to open at the Prince of Wales Theatre on February 5, 1891. With a chorus of sixty voices and an orchestra expanded to forty musicians, the London production, retitled *Maid Marian* (not to confuse the opera with the dozens of English pantomimes called *Robin Hood*), was heralded as the first comic opera written by Americans to be produced in London, and the opening night was a glittering affair. The composer and his wife shared a box with Mr. and Mrs. Waldorf Astor, and Edward, Prince of Wales, was seated with his entourage in the box below them. Even Oscar Wilde was on hand to try to upstage the proceedings with his remarkably trenchant wit.

The London version of *Robin Hood* assigned Maid Marian's second-act coloratura "Forest Song" to Annabel, replacing it with a less-demanding song for Marian. In addition, a duet for Annabel and Allan-a-Dale was substituted for the original third-act duet, "There Will Come a Time" for Robin and Marian, and a non–Harry B. Smith song, "O Promise Me" (composed by de Koven, while he was studying with Richard Genée in Vienna, to words by Clement Scott), was interpolated into the same act, to be sung by Robin Hood after he rescues Marian from an unwanted marriage to Sir Guy. Designed to emphasize the strengths of the London cast, including C. Hayden Coffin as Robin Hood, Marion Manola as Maid Marian, Attalie Claire as Annabel, and Violet Cameron in the trouser-role of Allan-a-Dale, the alterations had little effect on the overall response to the opera. As usual, the public was enthusiastic and the reviews were mixed. Noting de Koven's debt to Jacques Offenbach and Arthur Sullivan, the *Times* (February 7, 1891) concluded that if *Maid Marian* "falls greatly below the best of the Savoy operas, it is far above the level of ordinary comic opera." The *Illustrated London News* (February 14, 1891) considered Smith's book "a very fair one as such opera books go," but *Punch* (February 28, 1891), sporting a cartoon of the librettist "hammering" out the text, found the comic opera to be deficient in its comedy and overly reminiscent in its music.

Harry B. Smith was pleased with the British reception of *Robin Hood*. A run of ten weeks—sixty-five performances—was nothing to be

Harry B. Smith, caricatured by *Punch*

ashamed of, even though he knew that the piece could have run longer had it not been overproduced. The decision to enlarge the chorus to sixty voices and the orchestra to forty musicians raised production costs immensely, and the show would have needed to attract very large audiences to sustain itself. But those were de Koven's concerns, not his. What bothered Harry as he sat in Chicago was that de Koven seemed interested in advancing no one but himself in all of the press releases surrounding the event. Smith's concerns were certainly valid. De Koven had always felt superior to his librettist, and the British attitude toward Smith's libretto certainly fueled this belief. While in London, the composer made more than one attempt to convince W. S. Gilbert (then feuding with Arthur Sullivan) to employ him as the composer of his next comic opera. It was Gilbert's refusal to work with de Koven that ultimately reconciled the composer to maintaining a working relationship with Smith, and the team began a long-distance collaboration on two projects, one designed for De Wolf Hopper, called *The Dey*, and the other for the international favorite Marie Tempest, entitled *The Fencing Master.*

On April 15, Smith's latest comic opera, *The Tar and the Tartar*, opened at the Chicago Opera House, with a score by twenty-two-year-old Adam Itzel Jr., a composer and conductor with the Peabody Institute in Baltimore. The production featured Digby Bell as Muley Hassan, a sailor shipwrecked off the coast of Morocco, who exchanges places with a world-weary Sultan who subsequently pretends to be drowned so that he can enjoy the finer things in life. The real heir to the throne, Cardamon, is a Bedouin chief who is in love with a slave girl named Farina, recently given to the Sultan as a gift. Because Farina is intent on marrying a title, Cardamon coerces Muley into agreeing to rule alternately with him, an hour at a time. As a result, each man receives the affections of the slave girl while he is on the throne, and of her companion, Taffeta, when he is not.

Khartoon, the "royal purveyor of amusements," is also in love with the slave girl. When she refuses his advances, he takes advantage of the rumored conspiracies at court to denounce Farina and Taffeta (who enjoy wearing male attire) as two young princes intent upon murdering the Sultan. Having discovered that the shrewish wife he left behind him, Alpaca, is the queen of the harem comprising 400 wives and 1,313 children, Muley asks the court physician, Pajama, for a potion that would allow him to sleep for twenty-five years and wake up with all of his troubles behind him. He drinks the medicine and falls asleep, only to wake up the following day, believing that a quarter century has passed and that Farina dressed as a boy is really her son. The confusion that ensues is put to rest when the real Sultan, now tired of the better things in life, returns to the throne, uniting Farina with Cardamon, and offering Muley an admiralcy in the royal navy. Because it is forbidden for officers' wives to accompany them aboard ship, Muley happily accepts and finally escapes his wife.

The critics were unkind to the work, complaining that the performances were underrehearsed and poorly sung, that the music and libretto were "mummified," and that the work had absolutely no chance of success. Nonetheless, on May 11, the show opened at Palmer's Theatre in New York, where it received substantially better notices and remained for 152 performances. As the *Dramatic Mirror* (May 16, 1891) concluded:

> If Messrs. Itzel and Smith have not made a particularly valuable contribution to the current comic opera repertoire in *The Tar and the Tartar*, they can claim credit, at least, for composing and writing a merry, jingling, care-killing piece that in all likelihood will enjoy a larger measure of popular success than any operetta of native origin that has yet had a metropolitan hearing. The first night audience received it heartily and lengthened the representation nearly half-an-hour by demanding numerous encores.

Not suprisingly, one of Smith's characteristic topical songs, "Nothing Is Like It Used to Be," was the hit of the evening, helping to propel the piece to a full-year's run.

Barely a month later, on June 11, Smith's new extravaganza, *Sinbad; or, The Maid of Balsora*, opened at the Chicago Opera House with music by W. H. Batchelor. Advertising a cast of two hundred that included a chorus of fifty voices and a *corps de ballet* of sixty dancers, *Sinbad* was designed to surpass all of Henderson's earlier spectacles. The plot centers on Sinbad's affection for Ninetta, who has been promised by her bankrupt father to a smuggler named Snarleyow. The smuggler manages to abduct Ninetta, causing Sinbad and his cronies to follow after them. On the way, the characters sing topical songs that satirize dime novels, a liberated Ireland, female suffrage, taxation, and contemporary swimwear. In "That's What the Wild Waves Are Saying," for example, it is noted that swimming is healthy and wonderful: "But when in the waves a young girl goes to splash,/ It strikes me as being remarkably rash,/ To wear a bath suit just the width of a sash."

The search gives Sinbad and Snarleyow the excuse to visit various lands where they meet up with a variety of colorful characters including a cannibal, Count Maledetta Spaghetti, Tuesday, Wednesday, and four Neapolitan typewriter girls whose topical song "Tick-a-Tack-a-Tack" imitates the sound of a typewriter. Ultimately, Sinbad discovers the Valley of Diamonds and marries Ninetta in a kind of old-fashioned variety show, where each of the principals performs a specialty number (anticipating by eighty years the "Loveland" sequence in Sondheim's *Follies*). A grand ballet called "A Winter Carnival," depicting dancing icicles, snowflakes, toboganers, and skaters, and a final transformation sequence called "The Morning of Life" complete the spectacle portion of the production.

Although the reviews were complimentary to all the designers and most of the performers involved in the production, Smith's book was taken to task for being full of forced humor and "not remarkable for much but its shortcomings." Nonetheless, the production played the Opera House for the rest of the summer and went on tour, returning to Chicago in December for a "phenomenally successful" engagement that the *Dramatic Mirror* (December 19, 1891) predicted "could run for six months to a profitable business."

A few days after *Sinbad* opened in Chicago, Harry wrote to de Koven complaining that the composer seemed to have sided with The Bostonians against him regarding the libretto for *Robin Hood*. Evidently, de Koven had used the word "common" in reference to Smith's work, and the librettist was justifiably disturbed that his collaborator seemed to view his work in such a light, especially now that they were working on a new project for the same company. Although the recent touring season had proved remarkably successful for The Bostonians, due in great part to *Robin Hood*, there was still dissension among the company, particularly from contralto Jessie Bartlett Davis, who, as Allan-a-Dale, had no solo number until the third act. On June 19, 1891, Smith wrote to de Koven explaining the problem:

> Jessie Bartlett Davis wants a song in the second act, a dramatic aria and I think it would be well to give it to her as she will be the most attractive woman in the company next year. See if you can fix up something. She wants to sing . . . it in the second act where she thinks Annabel is playing her for a sucker.

"Oh, Promise Me" was the natural choice because it had already been used in the London production, but the contralto was resistant, insisting that the song had an oddly structured melody and was written in an uncomfortable range. Gradually the melody grew on her, but it was not until she "marked" the song during the rehearsal that its potential was finally revealed to her. Because rehearsals often require singers to repeat musical numbers over and over again, most performers choose to sing in half voice or down the octave to spare their voices. At one rehearsal, almost unconsciously, Davis started to sing "Oh, Promise Me" an octave below the written key. In that range the velvet tones of her voice began to ring, and she (and everyone else in the room) knew immediately that the song would succeed. The composer's wife recalled fondly in her memoirs that Davis "so loved it that she almost persuaded herself that she had written it herself, and directed that a copy of its adored melody should be buried in her coffin."

In August 1890, Smith contracted another agreement with The Bostonians guaranteeing a production of *Robin Hood* in New York within two years. For almost a year, the prospect seemed slim because The Bostonians, although artistically sound, were not a sound box-office investment in New York, and no manager was willing to take a risk on the usual profit-sharing terms. James Hill—who managed the Standard Theatre and had commissioned Smith and de Koven to write a vehicle for Marie Tempest (primarily to show her off in tights)—rented the theater to Henry Barnabee for five weeks at $2,000 per week.

Reginald de Koven returned from Europe in July 1891, and he and Smith went right to work on *The Fencing Master* while The Bostonians set about refurbishing the physical production of *Robin Hood*. Two months and $5,000 later, on September 28, 1891, *Robin Hood* opened at the Standard Theatre with Tom Karl and Edwin Hoff alternating performances as the title character, and the following week, it was advertised as "the only acknowledged hit of the season." The reviews ranged from the *Clipper* (October 3, 1891) calling Smith's libretto "a long way in advance of previous comic opera books by that persistent writer," but "still neither brilliant nor specially well constructed," to the *Dramatic Mirror* (October 3, 1891), which praised:

> Mr. Smith's libretto is smoothly written. His comedy lines are not particularly comic, nor is the action always sustained by the dialogue; but the lyrics are neatly turned and the flavor of the time and surroundings is excellently preserved throughout.
>
> Altogether, the book is superior to the class of librettos tacked on to the comic operas such as metropolites are familiar with. Mr. Smith is a man of letters as well as a dramatic writer, and his work, therefore, has two qualities that the products of the ordinary translators, adaptors and slangifiers do not posses, viz., merit and dignity.

Although the reviews were generally enthusiastic, the first two weeks of the run played to very small houses. Word of mouth, however, was excellent, and by the third week, every performance was crowded, pushing

Edwin Hoff as Robin Hood

box-office receipts beyond the $10,000 mark. For the first time, The Bostonians found themselves wishing they had not contracted a graduated royalty with the authors. Gross receipts began to range between $12,000 and $14,000 per week and, suddenly, Henry Barnabee was caught in an impossible situation. Smith tells the story in his autobiography:

> Then there was a merry war of words. Mr. Barnabee's argument was: "If we play to enough money, you two fellows get it *all!*" It certainly looked that way. If the gross receipts for a week reached one hundred thousand dollars, we appeared to be entitled to one hundred per cent of it. To preserve peace in the "Robin Hood" family and keep the Bostonians from thinking that they were about to become public charges, we agreed to make a new contract with a fixed rate of royalty.

As *Robin Hood* began its national tour following five weeks in New York, Smith again had three productions touring simultaneously: McCaull's Opera Company with *The Tar and the Tartar;* the American Extravaganza Company with *Sinbad;* and The Bostonians. Even though Harry had suddenly became free from financial worries (he would earn $225,000 in royalties from *Robin Hood* alone), little changed in his lifestyle. He maintained his job as a newspaperman (by now, he was with the *Morning News* and soon to become the dramatic editor of the *Chicago Tribune*), and continued to live as "retiring" and "unobtrusive" a private life as he could. Reading was still his favorite pastime, and buying books his principal vice. He enjoyed sitting in on poker games but never betting heavily, preferring a witty remark to a winning hand. And, as his friend Rennold Wolf observed, in the *Green Book Magazine* (September 1912), he conformed to the "everyday amenities with ordinary diligence" but had virtually no social ambitions and shied away from crowds.

What Harry B. Smith did enjoy was work, and by the spring of 1892, two more comic operas, *The Salem Witch* and *The Rope Dancer*, were registered for copyright, while Smith was collaborating on projects with Reginald de Koven, drafting a new extravaganza for David Henderson, and putting the finishing touches on a new comic opera for Digby Bell, scheduled to open once the phenomenally successful *The Tar and the Tartar* completed its national tour. The new work, *Jupiter; or, The King and the Cobbler*, had a score by British composer Julian Edwards. In 1888, Edwards had come to the United States to work with the James C. Duff

Opera Company, and *Jupiter*, his first original score in fifteen years, was his first of many comic operas written in America.

In the opera, Jupiter comes to earth to court Claudia, a maiden betrothed to a drunken cobbler named Spurius Cassius. To win her affections, the god decides to transform himself into the figure and personality of the cobbler, a poor decision on Jupiter's part because, as soon as the transformation is complete, he is arrested and incarcerated for a crime the cobbler committed in the past. After Jupiter has been carried away, the real cobbler appears, completely inebriated. Sergius, the god's charioteer, believing the cobbler to be the god in disguise, takes the drunken sot back to Olympus, where he wreaks havoc among the celestial beings. Just as the cobbler is beginning to enjoy being "King of the Gods," Jupiter's wife, Juno, appears and, immediately recognizing the impostor, has him evicted from Olympus. Back in Rome, Jupiter and Spurius return to their proper identities, each a little wiser from the experience, as the opera ends.

After a short run in Washington, D.C., the Digby Bell Opera Company's production of *Jupiter* opened at Palmer's Theatre in New York City on May 2, 1891. The roles of Jupiter and Spurius Cassius were acted by Digby Bell, Claudia was played by Maud Hollins (the composer's niece), Juno by her sister, Hilda Hollins, and the trouser-role of Sergius was performed by Josephine Knapp. The *Dramatic Mirror* (May 7, 1892) found the opera "one of the most genuinely funny and free from vulgar buffoonery of any that has been presented for a long time past." Edwards's score was praised as "catchy and sparkling," with encores given to a "Shoemaker's Song" and one of Smith's characteristic topical numbers. E. Forrest Jones as Marcus Coonius, Jupiter's attendant, sang a medley of minstrel songs, and Digby Bell, "in his best manner," made anachronistic jokes about baseball and interpolated the popular song "Annie Rooney."

While *Jupiter* was in the middle of its run, *Robin Hood* returned to New York for an engagement at the Garden Theatre beginning May 16, and Smith's new summer extravaganza, *Ali Baba, Jr.; or, Morgiana and the Forty Thieves*, was in rehearsal in Chicago. Smith had completed the first draft of *Ali Baba* in January so that the composer, choreographers, and designers would have ample time to prepare for a June opening. In the spring, just before rehearsals were to begin, Franklyn W. Lee and John Gilbert were brought in to provide additional lyrics for Smith's libretto.

The extravaganza begins in a public square in Bagdad [*sic*] where the entire populace of the city has gathered for the "Carnival of Bagdad." After the opening chorus and oriental ballet, Alibazan, the Caliph of

Digby Bell in *Jupiter*

Bagdad, enters, welcoming his guests to the festivities. Hackaback, leader of the Caliph's troupe of mountebanks, and Nicotine, the leading lady of the company, sing for their supper as entertainment for the guests. Following a great commotion offstage, Ali Baba and Morgiana rush in, begging for the Caliph's protection. Ali had just rescued Morgiana from a ruffian trying to abduct her when they realized that the villain was none other than Arraby Gorrah, the lieutenant of the "Band of Forty Thieves" in town sizing up houses to burglarize. The Caliph is about to sentence Gorrah for his misconduct when Ali's vagabond brother, Cassim, enters, singing a song about his situation ("When You're Flush and When You're Broke"), claiming to have information that would lead to the arrest of the Forty Thieves. Because the Caliph decides to call for the military, the "Telephone Girls" enter and do a musical number.

Abdallah, Alaska, Manitoba, Mustapha, Bismillah, and the rest of the Forty Thieves enter disguised as the military, having intercepted the telephone message. The Caliph appeals to Abdallah (who happens to be the leader of the robber band) to arrest the thieves, while Arraby (who is jealous of Abdallah and wants to lead the band himself) offers to take the bogus military to where the thieves are hidden. After the military exit, Ali reveals that he is in love with Morgiana, even though she is only a slave girl, but he fears that, since she is the last vestige of his once considerable fortune and his only valuable possession, he may have to sell her. The festivities resume with an elaborate "Umbrella Dance," and it is discovered that houses have been robbed. Amid the confusion, Arraby kidnaps Morgiana, Cassim is arrested for unpaid debts, and Abdallah and the military rush off in pursuit of the criminals as the curtain falls on act one.

Act two opens on Ali's humble home, where the boy, bereft of money and food, is comforted by his friends Genem, "the Irish Post Boy of Bagdad," and his sweetheart, Zamora, Arraby's daughter. Hackaback and Nicotine enter seeking food and shelter, followed by Cassim (who has managed to escape his creditors) and the Caliph, who suspects that Ali is in league with the Forty Thieves. A comic topical number, during which the characters attempt to eat a nonexistent supper, is followed by the entrance of Morgiana, who has just escaped from the robber band. In a private moment, she reveals the location of the thieves' cave to Ali, who vows to find it the next time he is out chopping wood. Cassim, however, has overheard Morgiana's directions, and he decides to beat his brother to the treasure. He joins the Caliph's bodyguards, and the company performs a "Burlesque Military March."

A "Grand Panorama" depicts Morgiana leading Ali to the robbers' cave. They are followed by Cassim, Nicotine, and Hackaback in a donkey cart led by a "Trick Donkey" (an actor—George Ali—dressed up to resemble a donkey), various members of the robber band, and the Caliph's comic bodyguards. The scene changes to the "Robber's Mountain Lair" with a fountain of real water flowing on stage. Moonlight changes to sunrise, and Ali and Morgiana are discovered hiding among the rocks. The donkey cart is the next to arrive, but Cassim, Nicotine, and Hackaback all run away when they hear the outlaws approaching. Abdallah and his Forty Thieves enter the cave by speaking the magic words: "Open Sesame." After they leave, Ali and Morgiana enter the cave using the same words, and remove from it as much gold as their arms can carry. They borrow the donkey cart and drive off with their treasure. Cassim and Nicotine have overheard the magic words, so, when the coast is clear, they enter the cave to gather treasure, only to be interrupted by the unexpected arrival of Arraby Gorrah and the band of thieves, who surround them. A highly melodramatic "Grand Finale Operatis" ensues, followed by a "Flower Ballet."

Act three begins at the housewarming party at Ali's mansion, built with the money he took from the cave. Because of his new wealth, Ali has been elected Caliph of Bagdad, his predecessor now forced to eke out a living as a cobbler. Cassim, having escaped from the robbers, is now an alderman and sings a topical political song satirizing the election year. Abdallah and Arraby crash the party in an attempt to discover who has stolen their treasure. The robbers recognize Cassim, and they call upon the rest of their band to seize him. A musical combat follows, during which the robbers are repulsed through the efforts of Morgiana. The scene changes to the cave, where Cassim, Ali, and others of their "political party" appear with baskets, hoping to take away more treasure to support their political campaign. They are surprised by Abdallah, Arraby, and the robbers, and a desperate struggle ensues. Again through Morgiana's manipulations, everyone manages to escape except Cassim, who is dragged away by the robbers, after which a "Ballet of Jewels" ends the act.

The final act begins with a "Tally Ho Song" performed by Ali and his upscale friends, whose festivities are marred only by the memory of Cassim, who has been drawn and quartered by the robbers, even though he is being sewn back together by the cobbler. Against Morgiana's advice, Ali is convinced by Abdallah to store "forty jars of oil" in his mansion. Because she realizes that the jars all contain a thief inside, Morgiana empties a "petrifying potion" into each jar, causing every robber to become a statue. She then stabs Arraby (though not fatally) as he tries to murder Ali Baba, and a number of weddings and reformations follow: Ali marries Morgiana, a contrite Abdallah marries Zamora, and Cassim, now whole again, marries Nicotine. Arraby recovers and reorganizes the robber band, and the curtain falls on a "Grand Transformation Scene," in which a huge silken cocoon bursts open to reveal a gigantic butterfly.

The production, opening on June 3, 1892, at the Chicago Opera House, was advertised as costing $80,000 to mount, $11,000 of which was spent on the Ballet of Jewels alone. The opening night critics praised the lavish spectacle and the performances of Bessie Cleveland (a new addition to the company) in the trouser-role of Ali Baba, Ida Mulle as Morgiana, Ada Deaves as Nicotine, Arthur Dunn as Hackaback, and Alfred Whelan, who replaced Eddie Foy in the cast that summer, as Cassim. As usual, Smith's libretto was said to be full of "old and tame" jokes and "not as bright as it ought to be." Nonetheless, on opening night, the house was sold out and the standing-room audience was six deep.

Ali Baba played for the rest of the summer in Chicago, during which time *Sinbad* followed the run of *Robin Hood* at the Garden Theatre in New York on June 30, and remained there until October 8. Although the New York critics were unimpressed with Smith's "bovine book," the *Dramatic Mirror* (July 9, 1892) reviewer spoke for the majority when he called *Sinbad* "a bizarre, dazzling, lively show, quivering with pink tights and revealing a heterogeneous display of warm color."

While The Bostonians were touring *Robin Hood*, Washingtonian William Pruette was traveling with *The Tar and the Tartar*, and Digby Bell was out with *Jupiter*. Although the Digby Bell Opera Company was a popular favorite, and the gross receipts of fourteen weeks on the road totaled more than $71,000, the *Jupiter* tour suffered from disreputable management leaving a trail of unpaid bills from Boston to Chicago. The week before Christmas, the tour opened at Hooley's Theatre in Chicago and managed $7,832.75 in box-office revenue, a record for that house at that time of the year. Still, that was not enough to keep the scenery and costumes from being attached and the company from being disbanded. The villain of the piece appeared to be Thomas W. Pryor, formerly in the employment of David Henderson in Chicago, who joined Harry Askin as producer of the tour. Not only did Pryor have insufficient capital to manage *Jupiter* (Smith had to lend him $2,500 to get the tour started), he also wanted to oust Digby Bell as star and bring in Henry E. Dixey. To that end, Pryor tried to poison Smith against Digby Bell, claiming that

Bell intended to discard *Jupiter* in favor of a new work by J. Cheever Goodwin and Julian Edwards. Bell not only managed to convince Smith that the allegations were untrue, he demonstrated his commitment to the work, securing "proper and ample backing" to obtain the sole rights to the libretto and music for *Jupiter* and to continue the national tour. Bell truly believed in the commercial potential of *Jupiter*. As he reported to the *Dramatic Mirror* (January 14, 1893):

> Considering the fact we were badly booked for several weeks; that we played sometimes to wrong prices, and sometimes in houses where it was impossible to get all the people in who wanted to see us; that we went through the Columbus celebration, the election excitement and the dull period before the holidays, and that many one-night stands were included in our route, our business was excellent.

While Digby Bell was attempting to fend off creditors from the East Coast to the Midwest, James M. Hill's Opera Company was engaged in presenting Marie Tempest in Smith and de Koven's newest collaboration, *The Fencing Master*, opening in Buffalo, New York, in the fall of 1892. The comic opera was one of a pair of projects that occupied Smith and de Koven in the aftermath of *Robin Hood*. The other was an unfinished Turkish-flavored opera called *The Dey*, proposed for De Wolf Hopper.

Jan. 14, 1893. THE NEW YORK DRAMATIC MIRROR. 3

The Digby Bell Comic Opera Company---Season 1893.

MR. DIGBY BELL

AND HIS COMIC OPERA COMPANY

PRESENTING

Harry B. Smith and Julian Edwards' Brilliantly Successful Comic Opera,

JUPITER

NEW SCENERY. NEW COSTUMES. A MAGNIFICENT PRODUCTION. BETTER THAN EVER BEFORE.

COMPANY OF 60 PEOPLE, INCLUDING

MISS BERTHA RICCI, MRS. LAURA JOYCE-BELL, MISS JOSEPHINE KNAPP, MISS HILDA HOLLINS, MISS MAUD HOLLINS, MR. H. M. IMANO, MR. JOHN BELDEN, MR. CHAS. H. JONES, MR. JOSEPH WEISNER, MR. E. FORREST JONES,

AND

MR. DIGBY BELL

Musical Director, Mr. JULIAN EDWARDS. Stage Manager, Mr. CHARLES H. JONES.

Sole Proprietor and Manager, JAMES H. PALSER.

Business Manager, J. D. LEFFINGWELL. Address this Office.

NOTE:

Managers and agents will take notice that I have acquired and own the sole rights to the book, music and rights to produce Smith and Edwards' Comic Opera, Jupiter. Managers and all persons in any manner infringing my rights will be held personally liable for so doing. Mr. James H. Palser is the only person authorized to make engagements and contracts for the production of the same. DIGBY BELL.

Advertisement for *Jupiter*

Perhaps the work was preempted by another Hopper vehicle, J. Cheever Goodwin's popular oriental musical, *Wang*, that opened in New York in May 1891. For whatever reason, Smith and de Koven abandoned the project after a few musical numbers had been composed to devote more time to *The Fencing Master*.

Marie Tempest, the star of *Dorothy* in London, had come to the United States with *The Red Hussar*, by Edward Solomon and H. P. Stevens, in August 1890. She had recently signed a contract with James Hill, who commissioned Smith and de Koven to come up with a comic opera scenario in which Miss Tempest could play a "boy part." What Smith and de Koven produced was the story of a young fifteenth-century Milanese girl, Francesca, raised as a boy by her father, a fencing master, who educated her in the finer arts of swordsmanship. She loves Fortunio, heir to the throne of Milan, but he thinks she is a boy and is in love, instead, with Countess Filippa, ward of the usurping Duke of Milan. In turn, a young widow, Marchesa Goldoni, is in love with Francesca. The Duke, being superstitious, has hired a private astrologer whose fees are so high that he has had to mortgage his palace, one room at a time, to money lenders.

Filippa has been sent to Venice to be married to Count Guido Malespina, but Fortunio plans to elope with her instead and tells Francesca his secret. Jealous, Francesca reveals Fortunio's plans to Count Guido, who foils them, and Fortunio, learning of Francesca's betrayal, challenges her to a duel. When she is wounded in the process, she reveals her true identity, only to hide it when the Duke arrests Fortunio for trying to abduct Filippa. Francesca (again in the guise of a boy) takes the blame and is led off to prison in Fortunio's place.

Francesca manages to escape from prison in women's clothing provided her by the Marchesa (still thinking she is a man), and crashes a party hosted by Filippa at which she has intended to announce her choice of husband. Wearing a mask and hooded cloak exactly like her rival's, Francesca takes Filippa's place in a conversation with Fortunio and discovers that it is really she whom Fortunio loves. With the romantic issues solved, the usurping Duke and his astrologer are easily driven from Milan, and Fortunio is restored to his rightful place on the throne of Milan, with Francesca, now acknowledged as a woman, by his side.

After Marie Tempest approved the scenario, the team went to work in earnest, readying the script and score for a fall 1892 premiere. On the day *The Fencing Master* opened in Buffalo, Smith and de Koven went to the barbershop in their hotel to be made presentable for the big night. Harry B. Smith recalls the episode with much fondness in his autobiography:

> "Are you with the troupe?" asked De Koven's [*sic*] barber; and the composer admitted that he was.
>
> "One of the actors?" was the next query.
>
> "I wrote the music," said Reginald.
>
> "Wrote the music, eh? Ever write anything else?"
>
> "Well, yes," De Koven replied. "Maybe you have heard of a piece I wrote called 'Robin Hood.'"
>
> "No," said the barber and after a few strokes of the razor, bethinking him of a song then popular, he added, "Do you mean, 'When the Robins Nest Again'?"

From Buffalo, *The Fencing Master* went to the Hollis Street Theatre in Boston, where it met with a highly enthusiastic response, mostly because of the star. As Jay Benton wrote in the *Dramatic Mirror* (November 12, 1892):

> Marie Tempest and her splendid company at the Hollis in *The Fencing Master* has captured the town. Her own acting is delicate in every way and exquisite in the extreme, and her singing is delightful. The rest of the company is more than adequate, and the whole production is finished and most attractive. The house is packed every night, and every one is happy at the great success of the piece.

A week later on November 14, the production opened at the Casino Theatre in New York City and remained there for 150 performances, closing on February 25, 1893. The *Clipper* (November 19, 1892) chirped merrily that the show was "a worthy successor to . . . 'Robin Hood'" and that Marie Tempest, who was in "admirable voice, and in most jovial mood" was welcomed back to New York as an "instant hit." Although not every critic agreed that *The Fencing Master* was as successful a comic opera as *Robin Hood*, most admitted that the work was of a very high order, full of romance, and free of the nonintegrated topical humor for which Smith had been so often criticized. In March, *The Fencing Master* began a national tour, starting with weeklong engagements at Hammerstein's Harlem Opera House, the Amphion Academy in Williamsburgh, and the Columbia Theatre in Brooklyn before moving west to Chicago.

While *The Fencing Master* was enjoying its long and profitable run at the Casino Theatre in New York, another Smith and de Koven collaboration, *The Knickerbockers*, was introduced by The Bostonians on December 5, 1892, at the Tremont Theatre in Boston. Although the work had been in rehearsal since the beginning of the season, the company chose to postpone the premiere until the tour reached Boston, where the first half of the run was devoted to the ever-successful *Robin Hood* and the last four nights given to the new show. The strategy evidently paid off, because the *Dramatic Mirror* (January 14, 1893) reported tremendous business, "the most successful" engagement in Boston ever experienced by The Bostonians.

Based on Washington Irving's *Knickerbocker's History of New York*, *The Knickerbockers* tells the story of one Miles Bradford (W. H. MacDonald), a Puritan captain, who travels to New Amsterdam to visit his sweetheart, Katrina (Camille D'Arville), the daughter of the Dutch governor, William the Testy (Henry Clay Barnabee). Because the relationship between the Dutch "Knickerbocker" and Puritan factions is badly strained, it is dangerous for Bradford to be seen in the colony, particularly after his having helped a Puritan spy escape. However, one of his friends, Hendrick Schemerhorn (Edwin Hoff), son of the Burgomaster, helps him escape wearing a dress belonging to his fiancée, Priscilla (Jessie Bartlett Davis), a Puritan girl. The plan is overheard by Antony Van Corlear (Eugene Cowles), the governor's trumpeter, who also is in love with Katrina, and he reports the plot to the governor, giving a description of the disguised Miles Bradford. When the governor's men bring back the "spy" that matches the description, it is Priscilla who has been captured in the captain's place, hiding her true identity so that Miles can safely escape.

In prison, Priscilla is dressed as a British officer, perpetuating the ruse that she is a great soldier, and causing all the women in town to fall in love with her. Among the interested women is Katrina, creating jealousy in Bradford, who has joined the governor's bodyguard to be near the woman he loves. As a Puritan army approaches to do battle with the Knickerbockers, Priscilla is drafted as the leader of the Dutch army. Before any fighting ensues, however, the four lovers, representing both sides of the conflict, confer and decide that marriage between factions is the best way of solving their differences.

Although Smith and de Koven borrowed some of their musical numbers from their unfinished opera, *The Dey*, for use in *The Knickerbockers*, the critics were impressed by the integration of music and drama in the work, with Jay Benton of the *Dramatic Mirror* (January 14, 1893) concluding: "It was evident from the applause that *The Knickerbockers* will prove a second *Robin Hood*."

The Bostonians toured with *Robin Hood* and *The Knickerbockers* throughout the spring, opening at the Garden Theatre in New York City on May 22, 1893, with the old favorite, followed on May 29 by Smith and de Koven's latest effort. The reviews noted the serious pretensions in the music and the anachronisms in the libretto, but concluded that the audience on opening night did not seem put off by either and welcomed the new work enthusiastically. Such enthusiasm was short-lived, however, for after only a week on the boards, *The Knickerbockers* was replaced, on June 5, by *Robin Hood*, celebrating its one thousandth performance on June 19, and continuing until the end of the season on July 1.

While The Bostonians were settling into a summer at the Garden Theatre, Smith's extravaganza *Ali Baba* was once more in residence at the Chicago Opera House, grossing more than $11,000 a week, during the 1893 World's Fair. Eddie Foy was back in the company as Cassim, Ali's vagabond brother, interpolating popular songs into his performance, including one of the earliest of Charles K. Harris's pre–"After the Ball" songs to be performed on the stage, and Henry S. Miller's novelty number, "The Cat Came Back." Foy recalls the production vividly in his autobiography, *Clowning through Life*:

> To many village dwellers who seldom or never saw a real play in their ordinary routine, *Ali Baba* was a life's high-water mark. And it was a beautiful and wondrous spectacle—the gorgeous Ballet of Jewels, the Monster of the Cavern, a great dragon which crawled across the stage, the waterfall of real water which cascaded down over waterproof canvas rocks, the curtain of steam rising from jets near the footlights—all these were things to be marveled at, even by city dwellers. But after more than thirty years I still meet people whose pleasantest recollection of the show seems to be that of having heard me, "during that summer of the World's Fair," sing "The Cat Came Back."

In the fall of 1893, *Sinbad* was revived and played in Chicago until the middle of November, when it began a national tour, going as far west as Salt Lake City and as far east as Philadelphia. Eddie Foy played Fresco, "an idle apprentice" who blossoms into a blackface character

CHICAGO OPERA HOUSE

(FIRE PROOF.)

DAVID HENDERSON - - - Sole Manager.

SEVENTH ANNUAL EXTRAVANZA SEASON.

Sixth Week Beginning Sunday, July 2nd, 1893:

MATINEES WEDNESDAY and SATURDAY.

AMERICAN EXTRAVAGANZA CO.

IN

ALI BABA

OR

MORGIANA AND THE FORTY THIEVES.

An Operatic Extravaganza in four acts, originated and designed by DAVID HENDERSON.

Originally Produced under the Direction of RICHARD BARKER.

CAST OF CHARACTERS.

ALI BABA, a poor wood cutter, formerly a member of Bagdad's 400, and leader of the German, but now in very hard luck..... ....Miss Louise Eissing

Morgiana, a slave girl, the only property now owned by Ali Baba, which property is in love with the owner.........................Miss Ida Mulle

Nicotine, the leading lady of the Caliph's troupe of Mountebanks, "in love with her art" ....Miss Ada Deaves

Genem, the Irish Post Boy of Bagdad. Ali Baba's intimate friend......... ....Miss Frankie M. Raymond

Zamora, daughter of Arraby Gorrah. in love with Ganem, whose suit does not fit papa.......................... Miss Edith Newton

Abdallah, Captain of the Fortv Thieves. a distingue young criminal, and a leader in kleptomaniac society..........................Miss Bessie Lynch

Hassan, his aid-de-camp, a dashing young communist, who enjoys life with his ill-gotten gains ....MissRicca Allen

Cassim, Ali Baba's brother; a vagabond, the world owes him a living, which he collects.. ....Mr. Edwin Foy

Arraby Gorrah, Chief of the Bagdad Police and Detectives; Professor of Purloining: Tutor of the Forty Thieves in Scientific Crime...... ....Mr. Henry Norman

Hackaback, brief but bold. Manager of the Caliph's private troupe of Mountebanks with a clew..........................Mr. Joseph Doner

Alibazan, the best Caliph Bagdad ever had, elected on the platform: "The Forty Thieves must go!" As the platform does not go he afterwards assumes the role of Policeman and Cobler of Bagdad ....Mr. J. L. Guilmette

Amineh, Seraphina, } Dancing girls, belonging to the Caliph's Seraglio.... { Nellie Lynch, Alice Stoddard

Ali Baba's Donkey.......................... George Ali

A Lion,.......................... Chas. Beni

Menah,..........................Miss I. Martin

Mestour	Officers of the Band	Miss Lee Easton
Veramah		Miss Bessie Pope
Backsheesh		Miss Carrie Morgan
Sequin		Miss Rose Frank
Salaam		Miss Lillie Holt
Minaret		Miss Alice Cassidy
Al Raschid		Miss Ellen Ringquist
Mustapah		Mr. F. I. McCarthy
Bismillah	Arraby Gorrah's Staff	Mr. C. Froom
Aleikum		Mr. Fred Gould
Abuben		Mr. W. Morgan
Adehm		Mr. Harrv Carter
Haroun		Mr. Geo. Martin
Aleika		Mr. G. Riversdale
Daph		Mr. C. Eyles

Playbill for *Ali Baba*

called the King of the Cannibal Isles. The pair of Foy and Jimmy Sullivan, the latter cross-dressed and in blackface as the Cannibal Queen, interpolated the popular song "Mamie, Come Kiss Yo' Honey Boy," by comedienne May Irwin, into the oriental-flavored extravaganza.

In the midst of all this national exposure, Harry B. Smith had stopped being a newspaperman who composed comic opera librettos, and had become a librettist in his own right, and the day was not far off when he would devote all of his time to writing musicals. As 1893 was drawing to a close, Smith registered two more librettos for copyright in the fall, *Captain Kidd; or, The Bride of the Buccaneers* and *The Caliph*, soon to become the first of Smith's collaborations with the Vienna-born composer Ludwig Englander. The study of English ballads and folklore in preparation for writing *Robin Hood* directed Smith to Shakespeare and his contemporary playwrights, and, after reading a great many plays and reference books on the subject, he synthesized the material into a comedy, *Will Shakespeare, Player*, published at his own expense in November 1893. Although the book received favorable notices, Smith made little effort to get the play produced until 1930, when it resurfaced as *Rogues and Vagabonds*, with music by Geoffrey O'Hara.

The celebrated manager and playwright Augustin Daly, who had asked Smith to write a play for actress Ada Rehan, was especially complimentary about a speech at the end of the first act, in which Will Shakespeare answers the question, "What is a player?" Smith recalls that much later, well into the twentieth century, a comedian named Ralph Herz asked him to suggest a monologue to perform on the vaudeville circuit. When Harry gave him Shakespeare's speech, Herz was extremely enthusiastic about it, wondering where Smith could have acquired such a treasure. Harry told him that it came from an "old play" and took back the manuscript, suggesting he look elsewhere for material. Recalling the incident, Harry noted, "Even a librettist will turn when trodden on hard enough."

The holidays arrived, and Harry and his wife had a great deal to celebrate with the birth of their son, Sydney. *Robin Hood* was still as popular as ever and about to reach its twelve hundredth performance, *Sinbad* was doing exceptional business on the road, and the Whitney Opera Company production of *The Fencing Master* was in residence at Daly's Theatre in New York City. The new year brought *The Tar and the Tartar* back to Keith's Union Square Theatre for a week in February, with Milton Aborn in the role of Muley Hassan. Never a critical success, the show continued to be a favorite with audiences in New York and on tour, the only success of the composer, Adam Itzel Jr., who had died of consumption in Baltimore the previous September at the age of twenty-four.

Harry B. Smith began the new year completing comic opera librettos, *Soldier of Fortune* and *The Minute Men*, both of which were registered for copyright in the late spring, and continuing two projects with de Koven, a Scottish opera loosely based on Walter Scott's novel *Rob Roy*, and *The Tzigane*, a vehicle for Smith's old acquaintance Lillian Russell.

Harry and Reginald had never been the best of friends—in fact, they were really never friends at all. Each tolerated the other's peculiarities because their collaboration made money, if not art. In December 1893, two months after de Koven's *The Algerian* opened in New York, with a libretto by neophyte writer Glen MacDonough, Smith sent the composer a scenario for *Rob Roy*, and by February 1894, the collaboration was under way, with Fred C. Whitney, son of the proprietor of the Detroit Opera House, scheduled as producer. De Koven was insistent that the musical numbers emerge from the action, contrary to Smith's conviction that songs should have an independent life of their own, so the librettist worked steadily to motivate the musical moments while attempting to maintain a certain autonomy in the lyrics, allowing numbers to exist apart from the dramatic context in the show. But no matter how determined each was to compromise, the fact that de Koven was living in New York and Smith was still residing in Chicago created huge barriers to communication. Early in March, Smith asked that the composer draw up a contract that would guide their working relationship, and, on March 21, he got his wish:

> This memorandum of Agreement made and entered into this twenty First day of March 1894 between Harry B. Smith of Chicago and Reginald de Koven of New York.
>
> Witnesseth that said Smith and de Koven hereby agree and bind themselves to collaborate in the writing and composing of a Comic Opera based on a scenario entitled Roy Rob—now in hands of said de Koven—said de Koven agreeing to write the music and said Smith the libretto.
>
> Said de Koven agrees to complete the music in time for a production in October or November next, and said Smith agrees to furnish the book completed in time to enable him to do so.

Said Smith agrees to make such alterations, changes and modifications in above named scenario as after discussion shall be deemed advisable and necessary to the satisfaction of said de Koven and also of Mr. F. C. Whitney.

> Said Smith also agrees to reside in New York or vicinity during period of collaboration required for completion of said opera and to devote all his time—when necessary—to such collaboration.
>
> All arrangements regarding the publication of book and music of said opera when completed to be the same as those at present existing between said Smith and de Koven for their operas The Fencing Master and the Knickerbockers.

By June, de Koven had completed the music for the first act and several of the songs in the second and third acts. The rest of the score was finished by the middle of August, and rehearsals began in New York for an October 1 opening in Detroit. The plot, turning on the efforts of Rob Roy MacGregor to restore Prince Charles Stuart (Bonnie Prince Charlie) to the English throne, is a kind of *Knickerbockers* in Scottish plaid, with Flora MacDonald cross-dressing as the Prince to save him from being captured by the English. To rescue her, Charles Stuart gets inside the prison and replaces her with an inebriated town crier. When Dugald MacWheeble, the Mayor of Perth, attempts to release "Flora" by disguising her as a "market woman," he, in fact, releases the town crier in a dress, and Flora's escape is made known. She is quickly recaptured and sentenced to the firing squad, and to prevent her being shot, the Prince turns himself in. Just as Bonnie Prince Charlie is about to be executed, however, Rob Roy and his wife, Janet MacWheeble, the Mayor's daughter, appear, leading a band of Highlanders who secure the escape of Flora and the Prince.

Rob Roy was played by William Pruette, the robust-voiced, Washington-based actor who had appeared in *The Tar and the Tartar;* Prince Charles Stuart was sung by tenor Barron Berthald, "one of the best tenors" on the light opera circuit; Mayor Dugald MacWheeble was acted by "first-class singing-comedian" Richard F. Carroll; Janet was played by Juliette Corden, whose voice was in "prime condition"; and Flora MacDonald was "magnificently" performed by Lizzie MacNichol. The opening night curtain in Detroit did not descend until after midnight because of the numerous encores called for by the audience, and, after the second act, the authors and producers were invited to give speeches.

Following the Detroit run, *Rob Roy* moved on to a week in Toronto, then straight to New York, where it opened at the Herald Square Theatre on October 29, 1894, and remained there for 168 performances. The New York critics echoed the endorsement of the reviews on the road and dubbed the work a success, emphasizing the merits of the book, as noted by the *Dramatic Mirror* (November 3, 1894):

> The libretto abounds in bright and at times exceedingly witty dialogue. The lyrics are charmingly sentimental, the war songs are spirited, and the verses allotted to the comedians abound in artistic comicality. Indeed, Harry Smith may be said to rank as one of our foremost librettists. *Robin Hood* revealed his talent; but *Rob Roy* has established his reputation on a permanent footing.

Once again, Harry B. Smith could look toward the new year with satisfaction. Not only did he have another hit on his hands legitimizing his work in the theatrical arena, he had also managed to stake a claim in a literary context as well with the publication of a book of verse, entitled *Lyrics and Sonnets*, by the Dial Press of Chicago. Dedicated to the memory of his recently deceased sister, Gertrude, the collection of eighty-two poems is divided into four sections, "Lyrics and Sonnets," "Egyptian Sonnets," "Rhymes in Many Moods," and "Bookish Ballads." Although the themes of the poems and the style of the writing are highly imitative of the classical models in Smith's personal library, many of the pieces provide a subtle insight into the author's private philosophies, independent of the witticisms and social commentary that marked his newspaper work and popular topical songs.

The new year brought the Smith family to Brooklyn, sharing a residence at 166 St. Mark's Avenue with Harry's mother, brother, and sisters, just as the two thousandth performance of *Robin Hood* was celebrated at the Broadway Theatre on January 10, 1895, with Reginald de Koven conducting The Bostonians' performance. Two months later, Sherwood Forest returned to Boston, where it broke the attendance record at the Tremont Theatre and drew $11,640 in a single week. *Rob Roy* followed on March 25, when the production moved to the Castle Square Theatre in Boston and met the same enthusiastic response that it had in New York. On April 2, the comic opera received a fair share of unintended publicity when tenor Barron Berthald left the role of the Prince to his understudy and was hurriedly transported to the Boston Theatre to sing the role of Lohengrin for Walter Damrosch's German Opera Company. The tenor scheduled to sing the role, Nicholaus Rothmuhl, had suddenly taken ill, and no one available in the Boston area was capable of singing the part, except for Berthald, who had sung the role in Europe. The curtain was delayed until the tenor could be fitted with a costume, and the opera began, Berthald going on without a rehearsal and giving "one of the finest performances of Lohengrin" seen in Boston. A month later, Damrosch signed the tenor to a contract with the opera company for the following season, to the dismay of Fred Whitney, who maintained the validity of *his* contract for future seasons. The fact that Whitney threatened to bring the matter to court added scandal to publicity, and ticket sales for the *Rob Roy* tour soared.

Smith notes that *Rob Roy* was produced fortuitously at a time when Scotch plaids were being advertised as the popular fashion and Scotch whiskey was becoming the preferred alternative to other kinds of alcohol. The bartender at the Herald Square Bar even created a drink called the Rob Roy, which became very popular. Fortunate timing, however, did not greet the next Smith–de Koven effort, scheduled to open in May 1895.

On November 28, 1894, a month into *Rob Roy*'s New York run, Smith registered for copyright a libretto called *Sylvia; or, The May Queen*, with music credited to de Koven on the title page. Like *The Dey*, this work was abandoned, this time in favor of a commission from Henry Abbey and Maurice Grau, managers of Lillian Russell, to produce a comic opera designed to highlight her abilities. Listening to Tchaikovsky's *1812 Overture*, Harry was struck with an idea for a libretto set in Russia during the French invasion of 1812. The plot involved Vera Ivanova, a gypsy fortune-teller, in love with Kasimir Androvitch, the heir to an estate. When Kasimir inherits a title, however, the class distinction between him and Vera makes it impossible for them to marry, so she goes to Moscow to become rich and famous, and succeeds because of her talents as a singer. Now courted by the elite, Vera encounters Kasimir at a masquerade ball, where he restates his love for her. Just as they are about to fall into one another's arms, it is announced that Napoleon has crossed into Russia and all the men in attendance are drafted into the Russian army (as luck would have it, to the tune of the *1812 Overture*). Following Kasimir to the front lines, Vera suddenly has a new career as a *vivandière*, Mata Hari–like, spying on the enemy. Kasimir acquits himself bravely in battle and, in the end, the lovers return to their simple Russian village, united in the firm belief that love conquers all. By the middle of April, the libretto was ready and registered for copyright as "*The Court Singer*, a Russian comic opera in three acts," and Harry had already contracted to compose another libretto for another star, Francis Wilson, the man who created the role of Cadeaux in *Erminie* on the American stage.

However, Lillian Russell was not in the mood to do a new show. Her recent divorce from Giovanni Perugini (Jack Chatterton) had strained her finances, and she was interested in nothing that was not already a proven success. She resisted having to rehearse the new opera at the same time she was appearing in a successful engagement of Offenbach's *La Périchole*, and she was upset by the fact that the run would have to be abridged because of Abbey's commitment to Smith and de Koven to produce their new opera by the middle of May. It is no surprise, then, that Lillian Russell did not like the role of Vera, nor was she especially good in it.

On May 17, Smith and de Koven's newest effort, now called *The Tzigane* (a name Smith claimed no one could pronounce), opened at Abbey's Theatre, closing on June 18 after a disappointing thirty-six performances. The reviews were harsh and unfriendly to both the star and librettist. She was judged to be unsuited "either by temperament or vocal training" for a satisfactory performance of de Koven's music, and Smith's dialogue was found to be "without merit of any sort." The *New York Clipper* (May 25, 1895) even chastised the author for writing in three acts:

> Mr. Smith should, by the way, write his books in two acts, for a third seems always to get beyond his control. . . . Mr. Smith has given us many an anticlimax in his third acts, not excepting that of "Robin Hood," but never has he succeeded in producing one so utterly stupid, so devoid of reasonable motive, and so palpably like the mouse that came out of the mountain, as is the puerile finish of this work.

Beginning September 9, *The Tzigane* opened in Boston to better notices, but by the second week of the run, it was sharing the bill with *La Périchole*. The Smith and de Koven work continued to play in tandem with Offenbach's comic opera throughout the national tour that followed, until it reached the Midwest when *The Tzigane* was dropped from the repertoire in favor of other proven works by Offenbach and Lecocq.

Lillian Russell

There are many reasons for the failure of the work. The production, though lavish, was underrehearsed, creating a lack of comfort with, and confidence in, the material. The Russian setting was of no particular interest to the audience at the time, so spectacular musical numbers such as the Cossack song, "We Ride, We Ride, We Ride from the Far Ukraine," a "Sleigh Bell Chorus," a "Dancing Bear Song," and a czardas, "Tell Me, Breezes," all attempting to evoke the Slavic culture, were unappreciated. Most importantly, the star was unhappy in her role, and, even though subordinate performers were praised for their efforts, Lillian Russell was the draw and audiences were disappointed. As Smith said repeatedly about *The Tzigane*, "the opera was one of the things that seem born to bad luck."

While the "Russian comic opera" was struggling at Abbey's, Harry was off to Chicago to attend the final rehearsals of his new "operatic burlesque" at the Schiller Theatre, called *Little Robinson Crusoe*. Produced by Thomas W. Pryor, back on track since the *Jupiter* debacle, the burlesque had music by Gustave Luders and W. H. Batchelor, who, as musical director for the theater, supervised the rehearsals along with the author. The opening, originally scheduled for Wednesday, June 12, was postponed until Saturday night to give the actors more time for rehearsal. Having just experienced the result of too little preparation with *The Tzigane*, Smith was determined to take all the time necessary to ensure that the actors were comfortable in their roles.

The plot begins at Ophelia Crusoe's (Marie Dressler) "anti-fat Summer Hotel," where Robinson Crusoe (Adele Farrington), a Marine captain, is enamored of Pollie Perkins (Sadie MacDonald), the sweetheart of Ben Bolt (Babette Rodney), the captain of a press-gang. A pawnbroker named Hockstein (George A. Beane), wanting revenge against Crusoe, whose marines have looted his pawnshop, talks Ben Bolt into "pressing him into service." Crusoe is summarily abducted, brought aboard ship, and headed out to sea when the vessel is shipwrecked and all aboard (virtually the entire *dramatis personae*) are cast upon a desert island where Dare Devil Willie (Edwin Foy), a canal boat captain, has built a saloon with the assistance of a "deaf-and-dumb salt water fairy." The survivors of the shipwreck start a theater and build a racetrack on the island for the amusement of the inhabitants, leading to a chorus number by women dressed as jockeys, and satirical presentations of David Belasco and Franklyn Fyles's *The Girl I Left behind Me*, Arthur Wing Pinero's *The*

Second Mrs. Tanqueray, and Paul M. Potter's dramatization of George Du Maurier's novel *Trilby*.

The Chicago critics called the piece a "great success," singling out the comic antics of the Canadian-born comedienne Marie Dressler and Edwin (Eddie) Foy, who entered in the middle of the first act on a canal boat, drawn by a donkey, singing "Let Me Off at Buffalo," one of the musical hits of the production (another was "Only One Girl in This World for Me," sung by a boy planted in the balcony, supposedly mesmerized from the stage).

While *Little Robinson Crusoe* made its way through the summer at the Schiller Theatre, *Ali Baba* was revived at the Chicago Opera House for an extended run. As Harry B. Smith returned to his family in Brooklyn, plans were already in the works for a national tour of his new burlesque beginning the last week of August, and *Rob Roy* was scheduled to open the next season at the Herald Square Theatre on September 2. More important, perhaps, was the announcement in the *Dramatic Mirror* (June 1, 1895): "In September two new operas will be produced, the librettos of which have been written by Mr. Smith, *The Mogul* [*The Caliph*], which Thomas Q. Seabrooke will present, and *The Wizard of the Nile*, in which Frank Daniels will begin a starring tour in opera. The music of the latter piece has been composed by Victor Herbert, and has greatly pleased all who have heard it."

Chapter 4

"Am I a Wiz?"

Like so many of Harry B. Smith's projects, *The Wizard of the Nile* began with a star. Comedian Frank Daniels had cut his teeth on the comic opera circuit in amateur productions and a brief stint with the McCaull Opera Company, but he became famous as an actor of farce comedies of the Charles H. Hoyt variety, in roles such as Old Sport, a drugstore clerk whose lifelong desire was to shake the hand of the man who shook the hand of John L. Sullivan, in *A Rag Baby*. In the mid-1890s, Daniels decided that he wanted to star in comic opera so, after a season with *The Princess Bonnie* Company, he elected to strike out on his own, under the management of Kirke LaShelle. Smith knew LaShelle when they both worked as newspapermen in Chicago. LaShelle had left the fourth estate for theatrical management and became the general manager for The Bostonians in 1892, where he remained until 1895, when he left to go into private management with his friend and associate, Arthur Clark, and organized the Frank Daniels Comic Opera Company.

As Smith remembers the story, he and his family were spending the summer at a resort on the New Jersey coast. He ran into LaShelle (who happened to be his neighbor there), and the conversation led to a lively discussion about their current projects. When LaShelle explained that he was looking for a vehicle for Frank Daniels, Smith took the opportunity to mention a story floating around his brain that he felt could be developed into a comic opera. The manager liked what he heard and contacted Daniels, who also approved. Harry agreed to shape the libretto for the star, giving him every opportunity to capitalize on his gifts as a comedian and his abilities as a singer. The only point of contention early on was the identity of the composer. Who would write the music for the piece?

Harry was in no hurry to suggest Reginald de Koven for the job. *The Wizard of the Nile* would not be his kind of opera, particularly because de Koven appeared inclined toward more serious work, devoid of the buffoonery and colloquial humor that appealed to audiences (if not the critics), and that seemed appropriate, if not absolutely necessary, to the project at hand. LaShelle suggested a composer he had known through The Bostonians, Victor Herbert, whose comic opera, *Prince Ananias*, had been produced by that company at the Broadway Theatre on November 20, 1894, while *Rob Roy* was on the boards at the Herald Square. Smith did not like the idea. He knew of Herbert's abilities as a cellist in the orchestra of the Metropolitan Opera House, but he had little confidence in Herbert's talent as a composer. *Prince Ananias* had not been a success, and Smith was disinclined to collaborate with another classically trained musician whose compositional skill and theatrical instincts were doubtful at best.

Although Arthur Clark seemed in agreement with Smith on this point, LaShelle insisted that Herbert at least be given an audition. Smith agreed to complete one act of the libretto and give it to Herbert to set to music. Two weeks after the composer received the material, he invited Smith, Daniels, Clark, and LaShelle to his home to hear the finished score to the first act. Although Smith, himself a pianist of some accomplishment, was deterred by Herbert's piano playing, he and the rest found the music delightful, and Herbert was engaged to compose the score.

Following the signing of the contract on January 16, 1895, with Victor Herbert, work on the project progressed quickly (almost as rapidly as the name of the opera changed from *The Wise Man of the Nile*, to *The Kibosh*, to *The Wizard*, and finally to *The Wizard of the Nile*), with most of the chorus hired by the middle of June and rehearsals set to begin at

Victor Herbert

the Casino Theatre on August 19. The work was premiered at the Grand Opera House in Wilkes-Barre, Pennsylvania, on September 26, followed by a monthlong pre-Broadway tour, including stops in Buffalo and Chicago, Smith's two hometowns. Everywhere along the way, audiences appeared to be charmed by the music and thoroughly amused by Smith's burlesque-like plot.

During a time of drought in ancient Alexandria, a magician named Kibosh (Frank Daniels) arrives with his apprentice, Abydos (Louise Royce), on Cleopatra's barge. Having "borrowed" the vehicle illegally,

Kibosh and associate are about to be decapitated when the magician claims to be able to cause the Nile to rise above its banks. Ptolemy, the King of Egypt (Walter Allen), promises Kibosh Cleopatra's hand in marriage if he can really accomplish such a miracle, and, serendipitously, the river manages to overflow just at the moment the magician waves his magic wand. Unfortunately, the Nile rises too high, flooding the entire country and forcing all the inhabitants to live on their rooftops, and Kibosh finds himself in trouble again. Cleopatra (Dorothy Morton), who has been flirting with her music teacher, Ptarmigan (Edwin Isham), also has an eye for the magician's apprentice, Abydos, who, in a weak moment, tells her that his master is a fraud. As a result, Kibosh is walled up alive in a pyramid, along with Ptolemy, who, taking the opportunity to gloat over his victim, remains too long inside the tomb. Abydos manages to redeem himself by rescuing his master by means of a secret passage, and the King of Egypt is rescued as well, after he pardons Kibosh and promises to give him a vast amount of money and the hand of Cleopatra. The magician takes the money but not the girl, who ends up waiting for the right man (her "Marc Antony") to come along.

The New York critics were highly enthusiastic about Smith's libretto, claiming that it had "life, originality, and humor." The *Dramatic Mirror* (November 16, 1895) noted that "In *The Wizard of the Nile* Mr. Smith is in his element, and has restored managerial confidence in his work, the commercial value of his librettos having been placed in serious jeopardy by the libretto he supplied for *La Tzigane*. His lyrics are dainty and rhythmical, and his comedy lines abound in telling humor." Several of Kibosh's songs were singled out for praise: "My Angeline," in which he laments his marriage to a "human fly" who "skipp'd at last with a gentleman friend who had starr'd as the 'bearded lady,'" and the topical patter, "That's One Thing a Wizard Can Do," with its lively, anachronistic lyrics:

When barbers grow talky my magic gets balky,
I change one into a dumb waiter straightway;
The sleeping car porter of money grows shorter,
I make him black boots and brush me without pay.
By magic I jolly the cable or trolley,
They stop for me gladly to get on or off;
The chronic soprano who bangs the piano
I quickly shut up with sprained wrist and a cough.

Also notable were the "Serenade" that opens the second act, with its chorus of Pages singing "Plunk plunk plunk plunk plinky plinky plunk plunk" like the strings of a mandolin (a device Smith used earlier in *Don Quixote*), and the finale of the same act with its self-conscious burlesque of the comic opera genre: "Stand back, stand back, and do not touch him yet,/ This is their last chance, this is their last chance for a duet."

In addition, one of the catchphrases of the opera—"Am I a wiz?"—became a colloquial expression in American slang. Frank Daniels tells the story that, during the performance of the opera, one of his pieces of business in the role of Kibosh was extracting eggs from the mouths of the other characters onstage. He would pat a character on the head and take an egg from the person's mouth, all the while exclaiming: "Am I a wiz?" Years later, he bought a farm in Rye, New York, and was given an English bulldog by producer Charles Dillingham. Soon he began to notice a decrease in the supply of eggs from his henhouse, and he spied his dog lurking guiltily around the area. He called to the dog and patted its head in a customary expression of affection when, as if on cue, out of its mouth came an egg. "Am I a wiz!" he gloated, neglecting to reprimand the dog.

After thirteen successful weeks in New York, *The Wizard of the Nile* went on tour, accumulating five hundred performances by the end of the 1896–97 season, and plans were under discussion for a production in Europe. Smith and Herbert began work on a new project, this time for The Bostonians who seemed relentless in their search for a successor to *Robin Hood*, still the most popular opera in their touring repertoire. A contract was signed by Smith, Herbert, Barnabee, and MacDonald on June 16, 1896, for a work called *The Serenade*, with a delivery date scheduled for October 1. Smith derived genuine enjoyment from his work with Victor Herbert, who seemed to possess a very different temperament from that of Reginald de Koven. The composer thought very little of much of de Koven's music, calling it "rubbish" on occasion, but he formed a collegial bond with Smith that extended through sixteen shows, nearly half of his total output.

Writing in 1931, Smith gave this description of Victor Herbert:

> Herbert was feverishly industrious and always seemed to work at high pressure, even when there was no necessity for it. When at work in his study, if he needed anything at the other side of the room, he had a curious habit of rushing after it as if he were highly excited about it. He was immensely popular with

his associates and extremely convivial. He was fond of good wine, beer and Irish whisky; but in thirty years' acquaintance with him I never knew him to be even slightly under the influence of these prohibited things. Table mates, one after another, would fade away, but he seemed to be above the weakness of an ordinary human drinker. His capacity—I say it in admiration—was Gargantuan. He used to visit me—we were near neighbors—and comment that mine was "a house full of books, and nothing to drink," though I fancied that we always offered a normal supply.

While Smith was engaged in creating the libretto for *The Serenade* and polishing a comic opera for Francis Wilson, composer Ludwig Englander, the one-time conductor for the Casino Theatre, was busy completing the score to one of Smith's unproduced librettos, *The Caliph*, scheduled to open on September 3, 1896, at the Broadway Theatre, with Jefferson de Angelis (well known as one of the leading comedians of Colonel McCaull's company) in his first starring role, replacing Thomas Q. Seabrooke, who had optioned the piece in spring 1895. Set in Bagdad [*sic*], the opera follows the adventures of Hardluck XIII (de Angelis), a Caliph with a desire to suppress crime who decides to shave off his hair and beard and go incognito among the criminal classes in order to study them. When the police come to arrest criminals, they carry away the Caliph as well because he is completely unrecognizable in his disguise and has no way of proving his true identity. His banished brother, Brikbrak (Alf. C. Whelan), who has become a pirate chief, whisks Hardluck out of jail only to force him to become a "bold, bad pirate" at sea. When the pirates attack a merchant vessel, Brikbrak discovers among the passengers his long-lost love, Djemma (Minnie Landes), the woman his brother had planned to marry. Hardluck manages to restore his throne and convince Brikbrak to give up his piratical ways by giving up the girl, sharing the throne, and making all of the pirate crew municipal officers.

The production, directed by Richard Barker, former company manager and stage director for Richard D'Oyly Carte in London, was commended for its spectacle, and de Angelis was praised as being "extremely diverting" and destined for popular success. However, the book was not judged to be among Smith's best. Even though the dialogue and the comic business were found to be amusing, critics complained about a lack of originality in the work, claiming that it was not really a comic opera at all but a burlesque or musical extravaganza. Dubbed a "quasi success," *The Caliph* held on for forty-eight performances at the Broadway Theatre and then moved out on tour.

Eleven days after *The Caliph* opened in New York, the comic opera Smith wrote for his old friend and fellow bibliophile, Francis Wilson, began a somewhat more successful run at the Knickerbocker Theatre. *Half a King*, based on *Le roi de carreau* by Eugène Leterrier and Albert Vanloo, tells the story of a traveling mountebank, Tireschappe (Francis Wilson), who, having adopted a young gypsy girl, Pierette (Lulu Glaser), features her in his company as a "ballad singer." Another mountebank, Mistigris (Peter Lang), has fallen in love with the girl, but she prefers the advances of the Duke de Chateau-Margaux's son, Honoré (Clinton Elder). Because the Duke (John Brand) is forcing his son to marry a girl of noble blood, the mountebanks help Pierette to impersonate the aristocratic girl, but when the ruse fails, the gypsy girl decides to give up her love and return to her itinerant lifestyle. When the troupe is eventually arrested in the "Court of Miracles" in Paris, Tireschappe reveals that when he discovered Pierette as a foundling, half of the king of diamonds was pinned to her baby clothes. The Duke De La Roche-Trumeau (J. C. Miron), possessing the other half of the playing card, recognizes the girl as his own daughter. He bequeaths her half his fortune, enabling her to marry her aristocratic boyfriend, and the mountebanks are set free.

Audiences and critics alike appeared to prefer *Half a King* to *The Caliph*. The music, also by Ludwig Englander, was found to be superior to that in the earlier show, although hardly inspired or original. Smith was criticized as usual for his use of American slang and topical humor in the piece, but he was also praised for providing "a consistent story, a *sine qua non* of comic opera that is not very strongly in evidence in *The Caliph*," and for producing a scenario that is both comic and romantic. Smith's lyrics were still the anachronistic social commentary audiences expected and enjoyed, as Tireschappe's number, "If I Were Really a King" indicates:

> If I were king, no titled snobs
> Should come across the waters
> To find themselves such easy jobs
> As marrying rich men's daughters.
> All barbers should be deaf and dumb,
> All tramps should keep their distance,

Cheap cigarettes and chewing gum
Should drop out of existence.
If I were really a king,
The girl, on her wheel, should more comfortable feel,
I'd declare knickerbockers the thing!
The poet who warbles of spring,
From a precipice high I would fling,
And the matinée hat should be perfectly flat,
If I were really a king!

The role of Tireschappe was judged to be most "congenial" to Francis Wilson, once again demonstrating Smith's ability to write for a star. Of the supporting cast, most of the bouquets went to Lulu Glaser, who had achieved celebrity four years earlier when she went on for the star, Marie Jansen, in the role of Angelina in the Francis Wilson production of *The Lion Tamer*. Critics noted a "delicious verve" that was "veritably Gallic" in her acting, and noticed a remarkable improvement in her singing. Like Smith and Wilson, Glaser was an avid book collector, and the trio enjoyed lively bibliophilic discussions during rehearsals, much to the surprise (and amazement) of other members of the cast.

Two weeks into the New York run of *Half a King*, on September 26, 1896, *The Wizard of the Nile* resurfaced as *Der Zauberer vom Nil* at the Carl Theater in Vienna, becoming the first American comic opera to be performed in any of the German-speaking countries. Franz von Jauner, the director of the theater, was highly enthusiastic about the work, calling it a success, although attendance was hardly what it had been in the United States. Still, Jauner promised to keep the opera in the repertoire and tour it the following season. If Smith and Herbert were disappointed with the royalties they received, they could console themselves in the knowledge that their work was receiving international exposure. Back in New York, sixty-four performances were enough for *Half a King* at the Knickerbocker Theatre before it followed *The Caliph*'s example and left on a national tour.

On November 2, a brief two months after Smith's collaborations with Englander opened in New York, *The Mandarin*, his latest effort with de Koven, appeared at the Herald Square Theatre. Another of the team's oriental operas, like *The Begum*, borrowing liberally in tone and style from *The Mikado*, as well as from the plot of *Jupiter*, *The Mandarin* had been

Lulu Glaser

commissioned by Charles Evans and W. D. Mann, the lessees of the theater, who were anxious to produce a new work by the team who wrote *Robin Hood.* The plot is set in the Chinese domain of Foo-Chow, under the rule of a Mandarin (George Honey) who covets the wife of Fan Tan (George C. Boniface Jr.), a carpenter. Because of a striking resemblance between the Mandarin and the carpenter, the potentate trades his magisterial robes for the garments of a laborer and goes into town, where he is dragged off to jail by the police. The carpenter, inebriated from a night on the town, is returned to the palace, where he sobers up to find himself decked out in silk and satin. Even though Fan Tan enjoys the attention of the Mandarin's twelve wives, he expresses loneliness for the company of his own wife, Jesso (Bertha Waltzinger), a statement that suggests his having taken a thirteenth wife, one more than the legal limit. Informed of the crime, the Emperor of China (Henry Norman) visits the Mandarin's palace, where he discovers Jesso and Fan Tan together in the midst of the twelve other wives. When the carpenter admits that Jesso is, in fact, his real wife, the Emperor sentences him to death, an execution that is prevented by the eleventh-hour appearance of the Mandarin, who explains everything to the Emperor's satisfaction.

In spite of a *dramatis personae* of silly burlesque-like characters resembling the names of teas (Pekoe, Oolong, Suchong), and excruciating puns (Sing Lo), critics were gratified that the libretto told "something akin to a consistent story" that kept "within the confines of opera *comique*" without an extended use of American slang and "current gags" in place of real comic dialogue. The music, though "unworthy of the composer of *Robin Hood*," was found to be pleasant enough, and, while *The Mandarin* would do little to enhance the reputation of its authors, the critic for the *Dramatic Mirror* (November 21, 1896) predicted that the opera "will presumably enjoy a fair amount of box-office prosperity for a season or two."

Although the reviews for the new opera were anything but raves, they were the least of the authors' worries. On November 14, the *Dramatic Mirror* published a report that the management of *The Mandarin* had infringed upon the copyrighted title of a comic opera, *The Mandarin Zune*, which had been produced in Providence, Rhode Island, the previous summer. The proprietors of *The Mandarin Zune* threatened a lawsuit to recover damages, but the case never went to court. It was certainly fortuitous that Smith and de Koven's "Chinese comic opera" closed after forty performances, before box-office success led to a legal battle.

As the year was drawing to a close, The Bostonians had begun to rehearse the new Harry B. Smith–Victor Herbert collaboration, retitled *The Serenaders.* They had done the preproduction design work in the fall but, due to the rigors of a touring schedule, rehearsals in earnest did not begin until the new year when the company was in residence in Washington, D.C., where Smith and Herbert were on hand to make changes and solve problems. The opening date was announced as January 14, 1897, in Buffalo but, when the company arrived in upstate New York, too much work still needed to be done. After several more postponements, *The Serenaders* finally premiered in Cleveland on February 17, on the last night of a three-day engagement, the first two performances devoted to *Robin Hood.* The first week of March, the opera was tested in Chicago, where it was welcomed enthusiastically as part of a Harry B. Smith festival. The *Dramatic Mirror* (March 6, 1897) reported:

> This is what might be termed "Harry B. Smith week" at the local theatres. The popular young Chicago librettist has been very much in evidence here lately with *Half a King* and *Robin Hood*, but tonight his words are being warbled and spoken at three local houses—in *The Wizard of the Nile* at the Grand, *The Serenaders* at the Columbia, and *The Mandarin* at the Great Northern.

Finally, on March 16, with the title changed back to *The Serenade*, Smith and Herbert's second collaboration opened in New York at the Knickerbocker Theatre. The story is centered on the serenade sung by Carlos Alvarado (W. H. MacDonald), an opera baritone, to win the affection of Dolores (Jessie Bartlett Davis), ward of the Duke of Santa Cruz (Henry Clay Barnabee), who wants the young lady for himself. While paying court to Dolores, Alvarado is also trying to escape the clutches of Yvonne (Alice Nielsen), who feels he has jilted her. The Duke sets out to kill the singer of the serenade, but he soon discovers that nearly everyone in town can sing the haunting melody. Robbed of quick and easy revenge, he is further harassed by Romero (Eugene Cowles), a schizophrenic brigand chief who is bloodthirsty one day and repentant the next, and his secretary, Lopez (William E. Philp), who take refuge at a monastery adjoining the convent where the Duke has sequestered Dolores. In the end, Yvonne discovers that she loves Lopez, the Duke collapses (to the music of the serenade), and Alvarado and Dolores are joined together.

Because he had employed the traditional operatic device of the recurring melody that had been heard at the Casino Theatre in 1892 with a production of Richard Genée's *Nanon*, Harry felt sure that he would be accused of plagiarism. He had always been one to cite his sources when a libretto was based directly on a known original, so, to give himself an alibi, Smith claimed to have based *The Serenade* on "an interlude from Goldoni." The Goldoni original, of course, did not exist, and most of the critics made no note of it, except perhaps chuckling to themselves at the perpetration of such a ruse. The one exception was the music critic, H. E. Krehbiel, of the *New York Tribune*, who, a half-dozen years before, had called *Robin Hood*, "a first litter of puppies fit to be drowned." Krehbiel took Smith seriously and suggested that the author was "probably indebted to a French version of Goldoni's work" because he did not believe that Smith could read Italian. Because the critic actually praised the show, noting the melodiousness of Herbert's music and Smith's fine plotting, the author never let Krehbiel know he had been duped.

The *Tribune* was not alone in its support for *The Serenade.* All the reviews were enthusiastic, hailing the show as "the best opera written since the days of *Robin Hood*," with Smith's libretto also cited as especially praiseworthy. The *Dramatic Mirror* (March 27, 1897) exclaimed:

> Mr. Smith's libretto is in every sense capital. The narrative, always well in hand, is carried along with admirable clearness and precision; the lyrics are daintily worded and delightfully characteristic; and the dialogue, subordinated more than is usual to the lyrical features, boasts an uncommon brightness and a commendable freedom from the reprehensible adjectival form of "gag" which has marred more than a few recent efforts in the way of libretto writing.

At the end of the second act, Harry B. Smith had the opportunity to accept the unanimous approbation of the crowd when he and Victor

Herbert were called on stage. The collaborators expressed their gratitude to the audience for appreciating their work so highly, and spoke of the respect and admiration they had for each other's work. Smith was then reminded of a theatrical aphorism that seemed particularly providential in his work with Herbert: when a comic opera is a hit, everyone attributes its success to the music; when it fails, everyone blames the libretto.

With *The Serenade*, Smith certainly had no axe to grind: everyone praised his contribution most highly, and even he felt that the libretto was his finest work. But his dealings with composers and critics had taught him not to expect adulation or even respect for what he did. He felt his job was simply to provide the soil from which beautiful music can blossom. As a result, he never seemed to be troubled by producers wishing to interpolate other material into his work. From his early experiences with the burlesque tradition, he knew that a show could change almost weekly, depending on popular fads, news reports, and the idiosyncrasies of the star. In an interview with the *New York Herald* (May 8, 1904), he explained:

> I have never had the slightest argument about interpolations. If my piece is artistic and complete, I find the manager does not want them, and if my piece is designedly for box office purposes only I am glad to welcome composers and their songs. In fact, then, to paraphrase a familiar saying:—"I care not who writes my country's songs if I may draw the royalties."

The Serenade continued at the Knickerbocker Theatre for seventy-nine performances, after which The Bostonians continued their national tour. Although the opera made a star of Alice Nielsen, she was not the original choice for the role. The Bostonians had selected Hilda Clark, a soprano who had seniority with the company, for the role of Yvonne, but when both women auditioned for the composer, Herbert chose Nielsen, a singer from Nashville, who had joined the company in San Francisco. Because Herbert threatened to withdraw the score if Nielsen did not play the role, a compromise was reached: Clark and Nielsen would alternate performances, with Nielsen opening in Boston, New York, and Chicago.

Barely a week later, Smith's latest collaboration with Ludwig Englander, *Gayest Manhattan; or, Around New York in Ninety Minutes*, opened on March 22 at Koster and Bial's Music Hall in New York City.

Alice Nielsen

Billed as "a vaudeville in three scenes," the show sought to capitalize on a new musical form, the revue, a kind of "topical extravaganza" satirizing life in the big city, popular fads, gossip, and theatrical performances—familiar turf for Harry B. Smith. Without a story as such, the evening followed the adventures of Auditorium Shortribs (R. A. Roberts) from Chicago and Anheuser Froth (Robert E. Graham) of St. Louis, who visit Central Park, the Stock Exchange, and Koster and Bial's, squandering all of their money along the way. An acting teacher, Delsarte Flam (Henry E. Dixey), and his students also provided an excuse for songs and take-offs of the latest Broadway hits. After eight performances, the vaudeville returned to the road and Smith returned to work, collaborating simultaneously with de Koven and Herbert on two separate projects, both scheduled to open in September 1897.

The first to appear was *The Paris Doll*, a musical comedy in three acts, with music by de Koven. It premiered on September 14 at Parson's Theatre in Hartford, Connecticut, a week after *The Wizard of the Nile* opened at the Shaftesbury Theatre in London. Although *The Wizard* was judged "tolerably coherent and intelligible," British critics did not appreciate Smith's libretto, finding it lacking in wit and too full of "Americanisms" to please an English audience. American critics were no more appreciative of *The Paris Doll*, a *Prince and the Pauper*–like tale in which an heiress, Cerise, is confused with a mountebank, Columbine (both performed by Vernona Jarbeau, whose costume changes were the hit of the evening). Although the advertisements promised a cast of forty, elaborate scenery, and a huge orchestra, popular and critical response was not good. Out of a sixteen-number score, only one song was singled out by the critics, "When Cupid Comes a-Tapping," and Smith's libretto, though integrated, was found to be below his standard, with too many "gaps between laughs." Neither Smith nor de Koven was in the mood to tinker with the show. Together they were working on another project scheduled to open at the end of the fall, and Smith was involved with two new operas with Victor Herbert, one of which was advertised to open the following week. Mercifully, *The Paris Doll* was allowed to expire before it reached New York.

Rand's Opera House in Troy, New York, was the site for the premiere, on September 20, of Smith's next collaboration with Victor Herbert, *The Idol's Eye*. Designed as another vehicle for Frank Daniels, who had just recently completed the national tour of *The Wizard of the*

Nile, the comic opera was inspired by an old Chinese law that requires anyone rescuing a would-be suicide to assume complete responsibility for that person's actions. The plot centers around Abel Conn (Daniels), an aeronaut seeking adventure in India, who saves the life of Jamie McSnuffy, a Scottish kleptomaniac, who has stolen a ruby (the "Eye of Love") from the Rajah. To escape being captured by the Brahmins who are searching for the ruby, McSnuffy conceals the gem in Conn's coat, and because of the magic power of the ruby, all the women suddenly fall in love with Conn, including Damayanti (Norma Kopp), the Rajah's favorite Nauch girl. When she reveals that there is a similar ruby (the "Eye of Hate") in the eye of an idol hidden in the jungle, Conn, unaware that he possesses the original gem, decides to lead an expedition to find it so that the Brahmins can take a ruby back to the Rajah. Maraquita (Helen Redmond), the beautiful daughter of a Cuban planter named Señor Pablo Tobasco (Will Danforth), and her boyfriend, Ned Winner (Maurice Darcey), an American novelist who must raise $100,000 before her father will allow him to marry her, are also interested in discovering the ruby, because its value is precisely the sum required for them to wed. At the temple, McSnuffy steals the idol, forcing Conn to take its place and pretend to "come alive," fulfilling a native prophecy. His deception is soon discovered, but Conn escapes being tortured by the propitious arrival of English soldiers, who bring news that McSnuffy has inherited a fortune. Because the Scotchman was a would-be suicide, he ceased to exist in the eyes of the law, and his fortune is turned over to Abel Conn. Maraquita and Ned are given the Eye of Love so that they can get married, and the Eye of Hate is returned to the Rajah.

A week before *The Idol's Eye* reached New York City, the second of Smith and Herbert's collaborations, *Peg Woffington*, opened at the Lyceum Theatre in Scranton, Pennsylvania. It was written and composed especially for Camille D'Arville, the original Katrina in *The Knickerbockers;* D'Arville commenced her touring season by premiering the new work on October 18 to a large and appreciative audience. Based loosely on the historical novel *Peg Woffington*, by Charles Reade, the opera tells the story of the eponymous actress (D'Arville), who has taken residence in the country to recapture her youth. In the guise of a milkmaid, she joins a touring theatrical troupe managed by Joe Wattles (Albert Hart), a low comedian. While in the company, she discovers that her lover, Captain Adair (Hugh Chilvers), has fallen in love with an heiress. To avenge herself, she re-creates one of her most famous roles,

Harry Wildair from George Farquhar's *The Constant Couple*, and, dressed like a soldier, attempts to seduce the heiress away from her lover, provoking three duels in the process. Although her adventures lead her in and out of danger and often on the wrong side of the law, Peg recaptures her captain and gives up country life.

After Scranton, where Smith's libretto was criticized for an excessive amount of "gags and topical allusions," the Camille D'Arville Opera Company moved to the Lafayette Square Opera House in Washington, D.C., where another large and enthusiastic crowd greeted the new opera. The *Washington Post* (October 26, 1897) suggested that the libretto was a hurried effort, full of "excellent material" that was "not well knitted together." The score was considered "sprightly" and "much more creditable than the book," full of lively dances, a "dashing waltz song," and a bagpipe song, "a delicious bit of musical drollery," with lyrics "slightly reminiscent of Gilbert." The critic found merit in the performances and in the physical production, and concluded that "if the first act can be put on par with the second, the piece is a success." Because *Peg Woffington* opened in Washington, D.C., on the same day that *The Idol's Eye* opened in New York, neither Smith nor Herbert was available to tinker with the show. It was rumored that J. Cheever Goodwin had been engaged to "repair" the opera during the Washington run, but if he did indeed rewrite the piece, he did not improve it sufficiently for the Camille D'Arville Opera Company to chance a run in New York City.

On October 25, Frank Daniels returned to New York City when *The Idol's Eye* opened at the Broadway Theatre. The audience was filled with the star's supporters, calling for encores throughout the performance and, although the reviews were mixed, clearly the audience was thoroughly entertained. The *Dramatic Mirror* (October 30, 1897) typified the critical reaction to Smith's book, noting that the author "has not supplied a libretto that abounds in humor of the highest order, but the plot at least is less conventional than that of the average comic opera of English or American make. The dialogue is often clever, and seldom sinks to actual dullness, and the lyrics are bright and dainty." The *Washington Post* (October 27, 1897) agreed, emphasizing that "the librettist has illustrated his plot with many witty points, quick and epigrammatic dialogue, grotesque characters, and funny lyrics." Critics found Herbert's music "tuneful and spirited" if not particularly inspired or original, and popularity was predicted for much of the score. Daniels "was as comic and grotesque as ever," and the rest of the cast "contributed to the high standard of the production," directed by Julian Mitchell, nephew of the star actress, Maggie Mitchell.

After fifty-six performances in New York, Daniels and company went back on the road, now with two Smith-Herbert comic operas in the repertoire. Meanwhile, Harry B. Smith joined Reginald de Koven in the audience at the Broadway Theatre for the opening of their next comic opera, *The Highwayman.* Set at the end of the eighteenth century, the opera tells the story of an Irish soldier of fortune, Dick Fitzgerald (Joseph O'Mara), who has been ruined by a gambling government attaché, Sir John Hawkhurst (Edwin White). In an attempt to retrieve his fortune, Dick takes to the road as a highwayman, "Captain Scarlet," winning notoriety as well as a price on his head. Lady Constance Sinclair (Hilda Clark), a court lady who loves Fitzgerald, dresses as Captain Scarlet to hold up a stagecoach carrying Hawkhurst, who has appropriated the pardon Lady Sinclair obtained for her lover from the King. Captain Rodney (Van Rensselaer Wheeler), one of Horatio Nelson's officers, also masquerades as the highwayman to elope with his sweetheart, Pamela (Maud Williams), daughter of Sir Godfrey Beverley (George O'Donnell), a Baronet who wants his daughter to marry an Irish nobleman, Lord Kilkenny (William S. Corliss). Toby Winkle (Harry MacDonough), hostler at an inn called The Cat and the Fiddle, also dresses as Captain Scarlet to impress his sweetheart, the barmaid, Doll Primrose (Nellie Braggins), who will only marry him if he proves himself to be a "hero."

In pursuit of the real Captain Scarlet (and a thousand-pound reward) are Constable "Foxy" Quiller (Jerome Sykes) and Lieutenant Lovelace (Reginald Roberts), of the militia. They arrest the three bogus highwaymen, allowing Fitzgerald to escape as a lame peddlar and reappear as Lord Kilkenny, the man supposed to marry Lady Pamela, in an attempt to free the others. The ruse is discovered when the real Lord Kilkenny arrives, but Constance, once jealous of Dick's attentions to Pamela, is now convinced of his affections and produces the pardon she stole from Hawkhurst in time to save the day.

After a short pre-Broadway tour, *The Highwayman* opened on December 13, 1897, and Smith and de Koven had another hit on their hands, a romantic comic opera that pleased audiences and critics alike. Reviewers praised the absence of anachronism, slang, and horseplay in

Smith's book, the *Dramatic Mirror* (December 18, 1897) being characteristically eloquent:

> Mr. Smith revels once more in the picturesque period of his successful *Robin Hood*, and his libretto and lyrics are a continual delight, brilliant with quaint conceits of humor and containing more than a few highly meritorious versifications. The pretty love story is charmingly handled, and the comic elements are construed with a delicacy with which, unhappily, recent so-called comic operas have had nothing to do.

De Koven's score was judged to be one of his "most melodious" if not original, and the cast and physical production were unanimously praised, with special laurels given to Joseph O'Mara, Hilda Clark, Harry MacDonough, and Jerome Sykes.

The Highwayman remained at the Broadway Theatre through spring 1898. The program for April 4 announced the 175th performance of the work scheduled to close on April 16 in order to commence a national tour. Not only was the opera a great success for the librettist, it also marked the last time in America Smith would make a curtain speech on the opening night of any of his shows. In his autobiography, he explains why:

> Up to that time I had always responded to any call for the author, however threatening. "The Highwayman" had played in Philadelphia before coming to New York. In my ill-chosen remarks I alluded to this and said that actors felt that there was "only one real *first* night—that in New York." Some of the Philadelphia reviewers resented this and intimated that when I next asked the patronage of Philadelphia for a new opera I would find Nemesis on the job. My next piece in Philadelphia was "The Fortune Teller," and if that Victor Herbert opera had not been a sturdy infant the criticisms would have killed it. This experience cured me of taking curtain calls. For the next play, I wrote a speech for the comedian to deliver before the curtain; but one of the newspapers said "Mr. Sykes' speech was so clever that it is a pity he did not write the libretto." After that I left the entr'acte oratory to others.

The new year continued Smith's phenomenal record of touring shows with *The Idol's Eye* in Boston, and *The Fencing Master* and *Gayest*

Manhattan back for weeklong runs in New York. On January 27, Smith and de Koven possibly received the greatest of all compliments when *The Highwayman*, still playing at the Broadway Theatre, was burlesqued as *The Wayhighman* at Weber and Fields's Broadway Music Hall. Smith judged the satire, written by Edgar Smith and Louis De Lange, with music by John Stromberg, "much better entertainment than the opera," with an exceptionally strong cast of merrymakers who performed the piece as Smith might have written it in his old burlesque days. In one scene, Foxy Quiller (Peter Dailey) appeared disguised as a billiard table; in another, Captain Rodney (Sam Bernard) carried his ship and the ocean on which it sailed around with him. Reviewers found the holding up of the stagecoach to be especially amusing. The *Dramatic Mirror* (January 29, 1898) explained: "When the stage rolled on, after a great noise, it turned out to be one of the 'Owl' lunch wagons which stand at the side of the streets in New York. It was drawn by four supers made up as horses, and at the command of the Highwayman they threw up their front legs."

Following the satire of *The Highwayman*, Weber and Fields invited Harry B. Smith to collaborate in the creation of their burlesques at the Music Hall. Although he felt that Edgar Smith needed no help in terms of satirical imagination, Smith agreed to join the team and signed a contract with Weber and Fields to be their lyric writer and co-author of the burlesques. Characteristically, Smith found himself spending the spring and summer working on a variety of projects: a new opera for Alice Nielsen with music by Victor Herbert, another vehicle for Francis Wilson with music by Ludwig Englander, and a satirical series for Weber and Fields. Even though the next new Smith libretto would not be seen in New York until the fall, his earlier work was hardly forgotten. The Bostonians returned to Wallack's Theatre in the spring with *Robin Hood* and *The Serenade*, Daniels was back in *The Wizard of the Nile* at the Broadway Theatre, and *The Highwayman* was doing excellent business at Hammerstein's Harlem Opera House.

Smith recalled that when Oscar Hammerstein first became an impresario, he commissioned Smith and de Koven to produce a musical version of *Trilby*, based on Paul M. Potter's dramatization of George Du Maurier's novel. After the first act had been completed, however, it was discovered that too many people claimed to own the rights to the novel and the play to make the project financially profitable for the authors and producer. Neither the creative team nor Hammerstein were interested in pursuing a production of a property they knew from the outset would not make money, and the project was speedily discarded.

Obeying his doctor's orders, Harry spent the summer resting in London, returning just as the fall of 1898 exploded with the flurry of his new shows. *Hurly Burly* was first to open, on September 8, at Weber and Fields's Broadway Music Hall, where every seat, box, and inch of standing room was filled with "fun-loving New Yorkers" anxious to laugh at the follies of the day. What they saw was Harry B. and Edgar Smith's more-or-less integrated story beginning at a villa on the Thames River where a chorus of "athletic girls" brag about feminine prowess in boxing, riding, and eating. They are interrupted by the entrance of Tottie Cambridge (Nelly Beaumont) and Sissy Oxford (Josephine Allen), former actresses, now wives of British Peers, who, explaining how athletics relieves the boredom of marriage, engage in a burlesque-style boat race. A shot is heard offstage, followed by the entrance of Michael McCann (John T. Kelly) just returned from shooting buckwheat cakes for breakfast. The conversation turns to Abel Stringer (Peter F. Dailey), McCann's son-in-law, who has been in England less than a year and has succeeded in managing all of the theaters in London. Although Tottie and Sissy think highly of him (he found them their Peers), McCann complains that Stringer became successful by bleeding him of money, just like Lord Chumpley (Charles J. Ross), who left him a huge hotel bill to pay before disappearing in the Klondike. McCann is so in need of money now, he decides to raffle off his estate to pay his debts.

Both Chumpley and Stringer appear, arguing over a woman whom Chumpley swears Stringer stole from him. Having made a fortune in the Klondike, Chumpley decides to open a vaudeville house in London to complete with Stringer's theatrical ventures. Enter Herr Weinschoppen (Joseph Weber) and Herr Bierheister (Lew Fields), two inebriated Dutch comics whose experiment with hypnosis (in a long comical routine) is interrupted by the appearance of Suzzannah (Rose Beaumont), a young theatrical advance agent, who winks seductively at men to get them to buy tickets to her next play. Weinschoppen and Bierheister fight over which one of them was the recipient of the girl's wink, but when the men discover her real intentions, they quickly button their pockets and turn their attention to a huge box on the stage. Another Dutch comedian, Solomon Yankle (David Warfield), enters, claiming to be one of Roosevelt's Rough Riders. He examines the box and tells the sots that there is a "Gipsish mummy" inside, showing them how to open the container. They push on the box and out comes Cleopatra (Fay Templeton), who is confused by her surroundings. Stringer reappears, and immediately falling in love with Cleopatra, who thinks that he is Marc Antony, he runs off with her. Weinschoppen and Bierheister plot to blow up Stringer's house when the clock strikes nine, in revenge for his stealing their mummy. Solomon runs off to plant the bomb as McCann enters to draw the winning entry from the raffle. Bierheister is discovered to be the winner as an explosion brings down the curtain on act one.

The second act takes place in the bar of a London musical hall, where Weinschoppen and Bierheister lose all their money gambling while patrons and barmaids criticize the play, and the third act takes place on the roof of the "Cleopatra flats, in Egypt," with a burlesque of Victorien Sardou's play *Cleopatra*, which had been performed by Fanny Davenport and her company at the Fifth Avenue Theatre in January 1898. Although the audience "howled themselves hoarse" during the performance and filled the stage with flowers for over ten minutes after the final curtain, the Cleopatra satire did not turn out to be popular. Within a few short weeks, the Egyptian element was dropped and another burlesque added, this time of a more recent production, *The Turtle*, Joseph W. Herbert's adaptation of Leon Gandillot's farce, *La Tortue*, produced by Florenz Ziegfeld Jr. on September 3, 1898.

Harry B. Smith had little time to tinker with the Weber and Fields show, however, because as soon as it was open, he was off to Toronto where his latest collaboration with Victor Herbert was scheduled to open on September 14 at the Grand Opera House. *The Fortune Teller* was written for Alice Nielsen, who had left The Bostonians in April following a salary dispute and formed her own opera company. For the story, Smith borrowed from *The Paris Doll*, his collaboration with de Koven that involved two women who looked alike. In *The Fortune Teller*, Irma (Nielsen) is an heiress in love with Captain Ladislas of the Hungarian Hussars (Frank Rushworth). Her ballet teacher, Fresco (Richard Golden), assists in promoting the attentions of Count Berezowski (Joseph Herbert), but Irma will have nothing to do with the Count. She disguises herself as her brother, Fedor, and escapes from the ballet academy, leaving a suicide note to be discovered by her teacher.

Fresco's bereavement at the loss of his star pupil is interrupted by the arrival of a gypsy fortune-teller named Musette (Nielsen), who bears a striking resemblance to Irma. Fresco plans to pass her off to the Count as Irma, but Sandor (Eugene Cowles), Musette's gypsy sweetheart, helps her to escape from the Count's chateau just as the marriage preparations are under way. Irma, disguised as Fedor, arrives just in time to step in as the Count's fiancée, when she learns that the real Fedor has been reported as a deserter and is being hunted by the military police. Because of her disguise, Irma is mistaken for her brother and threatened with arrest by the Hussars, until Captain Ladislas reveals that Fedor is really his sweetheart, Irma, and all is forgiven.

Following a successful opening in Toronto, Smith was back in New York for the premiere of his latest show for Francis Wilson, *The Little Corporal.* Inspired by the pronounced resemblance between Wilson and Napoleon Bonaparte in the Emperor's "leaner" days, he developed a story around Napoleon's campaign a hundred years earlier in Egypt.The action begins in a fishing village in Brittany where the Marquis de St. Andre (Denis O'Sullivan) and his valet, Pierre Petitpas (Francis Wilson), in an attempt to show loyalty to Napoleon, join his expedition to Egypt masquerading as scientists. Adele de Tourville (Maud Lillian Berri), the Marquis's sweetheart, and her sassy stepsister, Jacqueline (Lulu Glaser), enlist as canteen girls to be with the men. In Egypt, the staunchly royalist Marquis finds himself in trouble, having written a satire against Napoleon. His valet, bearing a striking resemblance to Bonaparte, manages to impersonate the general long enough to secure his master's release. However, before he can rid himself of the disguise, the camp is attacked by Arabs who carry off Petitpas, believing him to be the real Napoleon, and the rest of the French battalion. When the captors attempt to ransom their prisoners, they discover the hoax and condemn their captives to death. In a device somewhat reminiscent of the idol coming to life in *The Idol's Eye*, Petitpas takes advantage of superstitions attached to a statue of Memnon and manages to save the day and win the affections of Jacqueline.

The Little Corporal opened on September 19 at the Broadway Theatre to highly enthusiastic reviews. Smith's book was judged his best since *Robin Hood*, "refreshingly free from irrelevant burlesque and horseplay." Ludwig Englander's score was praised for its "fluent melody," and the role of Petitpas was considered "by all odds the best work" produced by Francis Wilson, rare praise indeed. Recalling his earlier triumph in *Erminie*, the *Dramatic Mirror* (September 24, 1898) added, "His Petitpas is as unique a comic creation as his Cadeaux. It proves that Mr. Wilson only needs an original conception like this to take rank as the most legitimate comedian on the operatic stage. The composer and librettist of the new opera shared equally in Mr. Wilson's success."

Smith recalled that everyone liked the book to *The Little Corporal*, even the English director, Richard Barker, who typically denigrated everything American, except the money. As the librettist told the story:

> At a rehearsal of "The Little Corporal," when some one remarked that a certain situation was very effective, Mr. Barker proclaimed before the whole company that it was good; but added, "Smith couldn't have written it. It must have been written by some great Frenchman." I was in a rear seat of the darkened auditorium and overheard this curious combination of compliment and insult. Thinking that the best reprisal was to get some fun out of it, I asked Howe and Hummell, the criminal lawyers, to write Mr. Barker a letter, saying that his statement before the company was libelous and that I intended to bring suit for heavy damages. It was thought likely that Mr. Barker would be afraid of some barbarous law that we might have in our outlandish country. When he received the attorney's letter, he sent me a deferential apology, excusing himself on the ground that his gout was very bad. After this episode he treated me as a protégé who under his tutelage might amount to something. He was a great old boy and used to direct rehearsals with a megaphone and a police whistle. When anything went wrong, he had all the calmness and dignity of a cat in a fit.

After sixty-eight well-attended performances at the Broadway Theatre, *The Little Corporal* merrily headed out on the touring circuit.

On September 26, merely a week after *The Little Corporal* opened in New York, *The Fortune Teller* began a forty-performance run at Wallack's Theatre, marking Alice Nielsen's debut in New York as the star of her own company. The first night's audience was filled with her admirers and encores were numerous, but the warm reception of the crowd was not entirely indicative of the reviews. Although critics admired Smith's lyrics, the librettist was again roundly criticized for his use of slang in a book that was "singularly incoherent" and "weak, both in invention and romantic interest." Reviewers liked Nielsen's "sweet voice" but found her to be less than a "finished comedienne" or a star of the "first magnitude," blaming much of her deficiency on the overcomplicated plot that was more "exasperating" than amusing. While the supporting cast was found only to be more-or-less acceptable, Herbert's music was praised as "tuneful," and the production was judged to be "sumptuously mounted."

On opening night, when the audience called for the authors to make speeches, Herbert readily complied, but the usually garrulous Harry B. Smith was nowhere to be found. His experience with the Philadelphia critics, who roasted *The Fortune Teller* during its pre-Broadway run because of Smith's ill-advised remarks at the opening of *The Highwayman*, had turned him against making curtain speeches. In his place, Nielsen was called upon to speak a few words, but she, realizing her minimal improvisational skills, demurred. An anonymous voice from the auditorium called for Herbert to strike up a march, so the rotund composer happily climbed into the orchestra pit to conduct the orchestra, and the librettist was off the hook.

At the beginning of November, after five weeks in New York, *The Fortune Teller* was off on a two-year national tour, and Smith's latest contribution to Weber and Fields, *Cyranose de Bricabrac*, opened on November 3 at the Music Hall to another packed house. *Hurly Burly* continued as a one-act prelude to Edgar and Harry B. Smith's travesty of Richard Mansfield's recent (October 3) production of Edmund Rostand's *Cyrano de Bergerac*, with Cyranose (Lew Fields), a "champion middleweight duelist, poet meddler, rubber neck and nose specialist," Ragamuffin (Joseph Weber), "author of half-baked verses; the only poet who ever has any 'dough,'" Christmas de Newcadet (Charles J. Ross), "long on looks, short on brains," and his sweetheart, Roxy (Fay Templeton). The *dramatis personae* also includes a number of punningly contrived French names that exhibit the work's brand of humor: Count Absinthe-Frappé, Count Patsy de Clam, Count Vive l'Armée, Count Crackerjack de Hackensack, Count Bordeaux de Marseillaise, Duchesse de Crême de Menthe, Baron Nicnac de Kodac, among a long list of others.

In the first scene of the burlesque, a play-within-a-play was presented, a parody of Hall Caine's sentimental play, *The Christian*, called *The Heathen*, portraying the trials of one John Sloppyweather (Charles J. Ross), a theatrical shoemaker and "sole-saver." Because most of his lines were puns on the words "sole" and "soul," the audience seemed to find the character most unfunny. However, once the *Cyrano* plot got under way, the laughs began and did not stop until midnight.

Criticizing only the length of the production, the reviewers were complimentary about the performances, the dialogue, and the songs, singling out "Moonlight Serenade" and "Keep Away from Emmeline" for special praise. Imported from the original *Hurly Burly*, and sung by Templeton, "Keep Away from Emmeline" was one of John Stromberg's syncopated proto-ragtime coon songs; it displayed Smith's facility in writing in a kind of "minstrel-show" idiom:

I want ah wahn yo' all agains' a lady,
I got to show her up although I hate ter,
She swahs she loves a moke till she finds 'at he is broke,
Den she drops him like a smokin' hot pertater,
Her maiden name is Emmelina Winger,
Her colah am de pales' choc'lut cream,
When I tink about de dough dat I wasted on her so,
I skusly can believe it aint a dream.

After ten sidesplitting weeks, *Cyranose* was replaced on January 19 by *Catherine*, a parody of Henri Lavedan's "doleful, tear-stained" French play of the same title, which had received its American premiere in October 1898, with British-born actress Annie Russell in the title role. In the burlesque, Catherine Villun (Fay Templeton), a "poor, but proud girl," supports herself, a father (David Warfield), two brothers, Paul (Joseph Weber) and Frederick (Lew Fields), and a sister (Rose Beaumont) by giving sewing machine lessons. They live in a poor apartment in Paris where she is visited by the penniless Duke de Coocoo (Charles J. Ross), who wants to marry her. She prefers the attentions of George Mantlepiece (John T. Kelly), but consents to marry the Duke because he is much worse off financially than the man she really loves. The Duke is happy to let Catherine provide for him and his mistress, Helene de Gristle (Mabel Fenton), and the entire family move into the run-down chateau with the newlyweds.

In the satire, Weber and Fields (without using their characteristic Dutch dialect) play two nasty young boys dressed in Lord Fauntleroy suits, who blow spitballs at their sister's suitors, and a number of drolly named characters again crowd the *dramatis personae:* Countess de Brie, Baroness de Roquefort, Count de Spoons, and Count de Monnae (well in anticipation of Mel Brooks's use of the character in *History of the World, Part One*). The critics called the burlesque "a tremendous hit," praising the funny lines and amusing situations, the fine performances of the actors, Julian Mitchell's staging, and the songs. Templeton evidently scored the hit of the production with the Smith-Stromberg companion piece to "Emmeline" called "What! Marry Dat Gal?" another syncopated coon song, with a colorfully colloquial, if ethnically stereotypical lyric.

Harry B. Smith found director Julian Mitchell, who had recently staged Charles H. Hoyt's *A Trip to Chinatown*, to be a master of his craft, if somewhat irritable and almost totally deaf (he staged musical numbers by the vibrations he felt on the piano). Smith recalled that:

> When anything went wrong at rehearsal, frantic with wrath, he would throw his hat on the stage, frequently to the complete ruin of the headgear. At the first rehearsal of a new burlesque, just as Mitchell was about to begin, he was informed that there was a hamper for him at the stage door. It was opened, and found to be filled with an assortment of old hats.

In addition to those songs already mentioned, Smith composed a number of catchy lyrics for the various permutations of *Hurly Burly* that functioned as the first act of the entertainment at Weber and Fields's Music Hall, all with music by John Stromberg, the musical director of the establishment. His "Little Old New York Is Good Enough for Me" anticipated Bock and Harnick's "Little Old New York Is Plenty Good Enough for Me" in their musical *Tenderloin*, as "Lydy Wot Is Studin' for the Stige," a lyric borrowed from *The Paris Doll*, looked forward to a catalog of performance satire numbers like Noel Coward's "Don't Put Your Daughter on the Stage, Mrs. Worthington." Also popular were "A Large Cold Bottle and a Small Hot Bird," introduced by Templeton, and "Maud," introduced by John T. Kelly, the Irish comedian in the company.

Catherine was barely a week old at the Music Hall when Smith traveled to Toronto to be present at the opening of *The Three Dragoons*, his most recent collaboration with de Koven. The usual "large and enthusiastic" crowd filled Her Majesty's Theatre on September 23 to catch the first glimpse of Smith's adaptation of Étienne Tréfeu's *Les trois cadets de Gascoyne*, and from all reports, the opera scored an "emphatic success," with every major musical number being encored. The story told of three officers in the British army, Jack Sheridan (Joseph O'Mara), Bob Leslie (William H. Clarke), and Archie Cameron (Robert S. Pigott), who find themselves in Portugal during the Peninsular War. They discover that they have been left an inheritance by an old merchant whose life they had saved during the war, but a clause in the will stipulates that Donna Inez de Lara (Marguerite Lemon), the merchant's niece, must marry one of the soldiers by midnight, February 28, and the officers are led to believe that the husband will get the entire fortune. Inez's plan to announce her decision at a masquerade ball is not entirely welcomed by the men, each of whom already has a girlfriend. However, Jack's *inamorata*, Columbine, a girl he met at a carnival in Paris, is none other than Inez, who hides that fact from him until the eleventh hour. When she selects Jack as her husband, Inez also reveals another clause in the will that allows the two other men to share in the fortune, and the opera ends with three pairs of lovers, happy and rich.

The critics in Toronto found the libretto "fairly lucid" with "particularly bright and clever" dialogue and many "original" scenes. Smith's continuing debt to W. S. Gilbert was strongly in evidence in the lyrics, especially with the opening number, "Then with Cachucha, Fandango, Bolero," borrowing directly from *The Gondoliers*. He also stole from himself, appropriating the duet "When Cupid Comes a-Tapping" from *The Paris Doll*. De Koven's music, though below his usual standard, was judged "pretty" with an "unmistakable swing," and the physical production was praised as "splendid." Both the librettist and composer were called upon to give speeches, and W. A. Tremayne reported in the *Dramatic Mirror* (February 4, 1899) that Smith actually did say a few words to the crowd, availing himself of the luxury of being in Canada.

The Three Dragoons opened at the Broadway Theatre in New York City on January 30, 1899, to another large audience that greeted the opera with hearty applause and repeated calls for encores. The reviewers, however, finding it necessary to compare the new work with *Robin Hood*, found it "artistically far inferior" to the earlier show, even though they predicted it would be a commercial success. Comparisons with Gilbert and Sullivan still hounded Smith and de Koven, with the *Dramatic Mirror* (February 4, 1899) noting:

> Messrs. Smith and De Koven, like Gilbert and Sullivan, work well in comic opera harness, but the work of these two teams differs very essentially. Mr. Gilbert possesses art of the highest order, and Mr. Sullivan is generally acknowledged to be a thorough master of harmony. Mr. Smith's librettos have flashes of wit, to be sure, but a very large proportion of his would-be humorous dialogue simply abounds in American slang and bombastic phraseology. Mr. De Koven, like his co-worker, is

> clever in his own line, but he seems to have exhausted whatever musical originality he possessed in *Robin Hood.*

Nonetheless, the music was judged "pleasing though reminiscent," the dialogue was found "diverting though slangy," Julian Mitchell was applauded for his "efficiency" as a stage director, and the visual production was praised as "sumptuous." Neither a hit nor a failure, *The Three Dragoons* left the Broadway Theatre after forty-eight performances to join its fellows on the touring circuit, and rehearsals began for Smith's latest exercise in lunacy for Weber and Fields.

Helter Skelter opened at Weber and Fields's Broadway Music Hall on April 6, 1899, splitting the bill with the popular parody of *Catherine.* The new entertainment was a series of travesties on the hit plays of the current season: Raleigh and Hamilton's *The Great Ruby* playing at Daly's Theatre, Carton's *Lord and Lady Algy* at the Empire Theatre, Pinero's *Trelawny of the Wells* at the Lyceum, Grundy's *The Musketeers* at the Broadway Theatre, and Belasco's adaptation of *Zaza* at the Garrick Theatre. The last play, based on a French original by Pierre Berton and Charles Simon, starred Mrs. Leslie Carter, the "American Sarah Bernhardt" as "the other woman" who goes to her lover's wife to talk her into giving him up, but who is ultimately deterred by the lover's young daughter.

In the burlesque, Mabel Fenton played Zaza, satirically re-creating the mannerisms and speech patterns of Mrs. Carter's performance, and the young child was replaced by a French poodle named Toto (Richard Garnella), whose wise remarks persuaded Zaza to give up her lover. While Fay Templeton imitated actress Ada Rehan in the "Sleepwalking Scene" from *The Great Ruby,* where Weber and Fields appeared as a pair of diamond thieves, and Charles J. Ross burlesqued actor William Faversham in the "Drunken Scene" from *Lord and Lady Algy,* it was the beautiful chorus girls in several changes of costume, the elaborate scenery, and clever songs by Smith and John Stromberg that drew the attention of the spectators and critics. "My Josephine," a new "instantaneous hit" of the coon song genre, was introduced by Peter F. Dailey to much applause, but it was John T. Kelly's multi-encored rendition of the aptly named ditty "Popularity" that marked the evening's biggest musical success.

After *Helter Skelter* closed at the end of May, Smith copyrighted a comedy called *A Busy Woman,* and a musical, *Wild Oats,* both written during his free time in the spring while he was adapting *Les Fêtards* by

Maurice Hennequin, Antony Mars, and Victor Roger for George Lederer, the manager of the Casino Theatre in New York City. Lederer's house librettist, Charles McLellan, had left the Casino to supervise the production of his musical *The Belle of New York*, in London, where it became a long-running hit and the first American musical to run over a year in that city. In McLellan's absence, Harry was hired to provide lightweight summer fare for audiences looking for beautiful girls, hummable tunes, eccentric dancing, and a suggestively naughty plot, all wrapped up in gorgeous costumes and elaborate scenery.

The first of Smith's Casino shows was *The Rounders*, his loose adaptation of *Les Fêtards*, which opened in the midst of a thunderstorm on Wednesday, July 12, 1899. In spite of the miserable weather, the Casino was crowded to the rafters and, according to the *New York Times* (July 13, 1899), there was never a livelier opening night at that theater, nor had any show been as well received in the past two years. The slightly naughty plot involved the Marquis De Baccarat (Harry Davenport), who is married to an American Quaker wife, Priscilla (Mabel Gillman). Because she carries her modesty to the extreme, the Marquis goes to Thea (Phyllis Rankin), a prima ballerina, to find more "ardent" affection. At Biarritz, Priscilla discovers the nature of the business that takes her husband to Paris so frequently, and she decides to follow him on his adventures. Having overheard a conversation between the Marquis and the dancer, the wife decides to win back her husband by beating him at his game. She borrows one of Thea's sexiest costumes and flirts with Maginnis Pasha (Thomas Q. Seabrooke), an Irishman in the court of the Sultan of Turkey and the Marquis's rival for Thea's affections, making him believe that she is really the dancer. So successfully does she carry off the flirtation that her husband finds it difficult to believe that she remained faithful to him. Priscilla, however, manages to convince her husband of her fidelity and of her newfound passion, and the Marquis vows never to cheat on his wife again.

The reviews made great mention of the morality (or lack thereof) in the piece, creating just enough scandal to keep the entertainment running into the fall. Smith was praised for expurgating "much of the nastiness of the original," even though many "unnecessary and undesirable" vulgar lines and profanities remained. The dialogue had some "fifty lines that call forth roars of laughter" and was full of "good jokes, both old and new." Smith's lyrics were found to be "all excellently made," and Ludwig Englander's music was considered his best work to date. The reviewers predicted a successful run for *The Rounders*, with the *New York Times* (July 13, 1899) concluding that "in the matter of fun and tunefulness it excels all its recent predecessors."

It was in this production that Smith first encountered a young singer-actress by the name of Irene Bentley, who had joined the Casino chorus two years earlier. Smith recalls that the young lady was a plucky little chorine who managed to spark his attention, as well as that of comedian Dan Daly, who, as the Duke De Paty Du Clam, had two satirical songs, "What's the Use of Anything?" and "Same Old Story," both of which allowed him to exhibit his characteristically down-in-the-dumps demeanor. In his autobiography, Smith tells of a grueling rehearsal:

> At another session that lasted nearly all night, Daly was rehearsing one of his songs when he noticed Irene Bentley trying to repress a yawn. He stopped singing and growled, "I'm a so-and-so if you're going to yawn when *I'm* singing," and added a string of expletives.
>
> "I'm a so-and-so if I don't yawn when I please," replied the usually demure Miss Bentley, and gave a ludicrous imitation of his language and manner. Daly was too amazed to answer; no one had ever defied him before; but a little later he appeared with a bottle of his favorite Piper Heidsieck and said to the stage director, "Give this to Miss Bentley. The poor little thing looks tired out."

Irene became a favorite of George Lederer, who sought to advance her from the chorus to leading roles, often requesting his resident playwrights to beef up her parts, something Smith was always delighted to do.

While *The Rounders* was enjoying a lucrative run at the Casino Theatre, Smith was busy working with Victor Herbert on three new comic operas, *Cyrano de Bergerac*, *The Singing Girl*, and *The Viceroy*. In addition, he was producing the lyrics for the next installment at Weber and Fields's Music Hall. The theater was completely refurbished during the summer months with rose-colored decorations in the auditorium and a newly painted drop curtain. With the new trimmings came a change in personnel. The two leading ladies, Mabel Fenton and Fay Templeton, were no longer with the company, and Weber and Fields were in the market for a new star. Lew Fields suggested Lillian Russell, the "Queen of Comic Opera," and the highest-paid actress on the American stage. After going through a litany of reasons why the woman would not be the least

Irene Bentley

bit interested in doing burlesque comedy, and how they didn't have the money to pay her, Weber and Fields decided to throw caution to the wind and make Russell an offer.

The lady was often seen at the Sheepshead Bay racetrack, so Fields was off to the races to negotiate. He found her in the company of Jesse Lewisohn, the copper millionaire, who volunteered an introduction. The story goes that when Fields met her, Lillian Russell was in the process of choosing a horse for the next race: She took out a hairpin and stuck it through the racetrack program. Wherever the pin stabbed through the name of a horse, that was her choice for the race. After explaining the system to Fields, he suggested that if she used a fork instead of a hairpin, she could pick "winner, place, and show" all at once. The lady smiled at the thought, so Fields wasted no time in asking if she might consider joining his company. The question brought an even larger smile from the star. Fields persisted, asking how much she would ask to appear at the Music Hall; Russell replied: $1,250 per week, a guarantee of thirty-five weeks, and the managers pay for all of her costumes. Without missing a beat, Fields accepted the terms and announced, "Rehearsals begin in August."

August was a busy month for Harry B. Smith. While continuing work on the seemingly bottomless stack of ongoing projects, he was in rehearsal simultaneously with three of his favorite stars: Francis Wilson, scheduled to open in *Cyrano de Bergerac* at the Academy of Music in Montreal on September 11; Lillian Russell, waiting to make her burlesque debut in *Whirl-i-Gig* on the 21st; and Alice Nielsen, working toward a late-September early-October premiere of *The Singing Girl.* Even with a score by Victor Herbert, *Cyrano de Bergerac* seemed doomed from the outset. The star appeared uncomfortable in the title role, failing miserably in the attempt to be both a romantic lover and low comedian simultaneously. Lulu Glaser, the Roxane, could act the role with assurance but she was unable to sing the music, a significant deficiency as the leading lady in a comic opera.

When the show opened on September 18, 1899, at the Knickerbocker Theatre in New York, the book credited to Stuart Reed (one of Smith's pseudonyms) was criticized for its colloquialisms and topical humor, the stars were found to be out of their element, and the large chorus was taken to task for singing badly. Smith's lyrics were found to be pretty and amusing, but the comedy was deemed inappropriate. Herbert's music, though poorly sung, was applauded, as were the supporting actors, the costumes, and the scenery. An attempt to rework the show during the beginning of the run led to a "revised" opening on October 9. Neither the public nor the critics altered their original opinions of the opera, and *Cyrano de Bergerac* left the Knickerbocker Theatre after a mere twenty-eight performances.

More successful was *Whirl-i-Gig*, "a dramatic conundrum in two guesses," at Weber and Fields's Music Hall. A week before the September

21 opening, tickets for the first night were auctioned, with Jesse Lewisohn buying two boxes for $1,000 and the likes of Diamond Jim Brady, Abe Hummell, Stanford White, and William Randolph Hearst bidding up to $750 for the remaining boxes and $100 for the orchestra seats. The latest bit of nonsense began just outside the gates to the Paris Exposition of 1900 at the Stars and Stripes Hotel, operated by Josh Boniface (Peter F. Dailey). Sigmund Cohenski (David Warfield), the wealthy president of the "Matzo Trust," is vacationing at the hotel with his daughter, Uneeda (Irene Perry), who, much to her father's chagrin, falls in love with Captain Kingsbridge (Charles J. Ross), a naval officer. Among the other guests are Harold Gilhooly (John T. Kelly), an Irish-Italian with a trained bear, Bruno (George Ali), and Fifi Coocoo (Lillian Russell), an adventuress who hopes to bilk Cohenski of his money.

The second half of the bill was *The Girl from Martin's*, a spoof of Georges Feydeau's French farce, *The Girl from Maxim's*, then playing at the Criterion Theatre, transferring the locale from Paris to a popular nightspot near Times Square. During the proceedings, Russell introduced two Harry B. Smith–John Stromberg songs: the "catchy" and much encored "The Queen of Bohemia," and the "The Brunette Soubrette"; Dailey sang the latest of the songwriters' coon songs, "Say You Love Me, Sue," encored a half-dozen times.

While the merriment continued to draw standing-room-only audiences to the Music Hall, Smith was off to Montreal for the October 2 opening of *The Singing Girl* at Her Majesty's Theatre. The next in his series of collaborations with Victor Herbert, *The Singing Girl* had a book by Stanislaus Stange, an English-born actor-turned-playwright. Even though Smith was responsible only for the lyrics of the comic opera, the plot is what an audience would expect from one of his librettos. In Linz, Austria, in 1820, Duke Rudolph (Eugene Cowles) passed a law stating that a courtship license must be procured before a couple of the opposite sex may converse in public; and should they kiss, they must get married immediately, or face life imprisonment. Count Otto (Richie Ling) comes to Linz and finds love with Greta (Alice Nielsen), a girl who sings for money, but they do not dare to meet because Duke Rudolph bears a grudge against Otto and would imprison him for life if he were seen kissing a girl, even if he wanted to marry her. The Minister of Police, Aufpassen (Joseph Cawthorn), is also in love with Greta, and to avoid his attentions, she exchanges clothes with her brother, Stephan (John C. Slavin). Dressed as her brother, she is caught kissing the Duke's sister,

Marie (Lucille Saunders), and both are imprisoned for refusing to get married, while Stephan, dressed as his sister, attempts to discourage the advances of both the Minister of Police and an old Casanova named Prince Pumpernickel (Joseph W. Herbert). When Greta escapes from jail (with the assistance of Count Otto), she discovers that she either has to marry Prince Pumpernickel or go back to prison. Aware that her brother punched the old roué, she consents to the wedding; as expected, the Prince prefers life imprisonment to marrying a lightweight boxer, and Greta is free, just as Count Otto is incarcerated on a trumped-up charge. In the end, Duke Rudolph finds a woman he can trust and, in his excitement, he repeals the courtship laws, freeing everyone from prison, and Otto and Greta get married.

After successful stops in Toronto and Buffalo, *The Singing Girl*, marking Alice Nielsen's return to New York City as a star, opened at the Casino Theatre on October 23, 1899, to unanimous popular acclaim and generally positive reviews. Stange's book was considered "plausible" and "humorous," even though the jokes were old (a criticism typically leveled at Harry B. Smith), and reviewers applauded Smith's "skill as a rhymester." Most of the critics considered the score "excellent in construction," an "inexhaustible fund of pretty melody," and some of Herbert's very best work. Alice Nielsen was judged charming and winsome, "fresh, vivacious and unaffected" in a role that fit her "like a tailor-made gown." At the height of its popularity, *The Singing Girl* left the Casino Theatre after eighty performances to begin a national tour in repertoire with *The Fortune Teller*.

On October 26, 1899, three days after *The Singing Girl* opened in New York, the second part of *Whirl-i-Gig*, *The Girl from Martin's*, was replaced by another satire, *The Other Way*, a parody of *The Only Way*, Freeman Wills's dramatization of Charles Dickens's novel *A Tale of Two Cities*, then performing at the Herald Square Theatre. The traditional characters, Sydney Carton, Charles Darnay, Doctor and Lucie Manette, become Kidney Tartun (Peter F. Dailey), Charles Darnation (David Warfield), Doctor Manicure (John T. Kelly), and Lucie (Irene Perry) in the burlesque, with Lillian Russell appearing as "The Vengeance," dressed in a French peasant costume. Weber and Fields played dual roles, first appearing as the President of the Tribunal and the Public Prosecutor. At the end of the spoof, they reappear as Marquis de Balloon and Marquis de Fidget, playing a card game that recalled the gambling sequence in *Hurly Burly*.

Although the satire and the company were enthusiastically received by the audience, who laughed merrily throughout, and the critics, who called the show "another solid success," it was Lillian Russell and another Smith-Stromberg song that received most of the attention. The *Dramatic Mirror* (November 4, 1899) reported that Russell "showed marked improvement in her acting. She has taken a new lease of life since she joined this company, and it is interesting to watch the way in which she has fallen into the jolly humor which pervades the entire organization. She sang a coon-song called 'When Chloe Sings,' which has a catchy melody entirely different from the average rag-time ditty, and made a decided hit with it." If Russell bore Smith any residual ill will after *The Tzigane*, it was quickly eradicated as he and John Stromberg created hit after hit for her to sing at the Music Hall.

Harry certainly knew how to write for the divas of the musical theater, from Fay Templeton, to Marion Manola, Jessie Bartlett Davis, Marie Tempest, Camille D'Arville, Alice Nielsen, Mabel Fenton, and Lillian Russell. Many other women crossed his path as his career moved into the twentieth century: Lulu Glaser, Eva Tanguay, Grace Van Studdiford, Nora Bayes, and Irene Bentley. But few left so indelible a stamp on the American public as "The Maiden with the Dreamy Eyes," Anna Held.

Chapter 5

"I'd Like to Have a Photograph of That"

Dark and diminutive, with a voice unequal to her charms, Anna Held was a Polish-Parisian import of the young impressario Florenz Ziegfeld Jr. Together, they burst into the New York theater scene with Ziegfeld's 1896 revival of Charles H. Hoyt's farce, *A Parlor Match*, in which Held made a brief appearance singing, "Won't You Come and Play with Me." She was naughty enough to be beloved by the public and beautiful enough to be accepted by the critics, who nevertheless seriously questioned her acting and singing abilities. After Ziegfeld designed an elaborate publicity campaign that included reports about her bathing in milk and saving an elderly judge from death when his coach went out of control, and stunts like kissing contests and three hundred men pulling Anna's hansom cab up Broadway, Anna Held became a household name with hordes of manufacturers seeking her endorsement on their products. Anna had arrived in every way but artistically. She was paid extravagant sums to showcase her talents in musicals (*La Poupée*) and farces (*A Gay Deceiver*, *The French Maid*), but the results were always the same: bad reviews for everything but her appearance. Her (common-law) husband, Ziegfeld, finally went to his old acquaintance Harry B. Smith for a solution to the problem. If he wanted a musical designed to make the most of Held's strengths, who better than Smith, whose career was spent writing for stars and their particular talents.

It was Held who suggested *La femme à papa*, a French vaudeville by Alfred Hennequin and Albert Millaud with music by Hervé, for adaptation. It had been a success for French megastar Anna Judic in Paris and in New York, and Anna believed that it would be a good vehicle for her as well. Smith found the plot rather thin, so he added material from another of Hervé's popular comédie-vaudevilles, *Mam'zelle Nitouche* (libretto by Millaud, Henri Meilhac, and Ernest Blum), and came up with *Papa's Wife*. Since Florenz Ziegfeld Jr. wanted an air of highbrow legitimacy for the show, Reginald de Koven was engaged to compose new music for Smith's adaptation.

Harry had completed the libretto well in advance of rehearsals beginning in September so that Anna could spend the summer learning her lines and studying English pronunciation. Her language deficiencies had caused her great embarrassment in the past, and she was not about to supply her critics with any more ammunition if she could help it. Even after months of intensive study, however, Anna was far from perfect. Having attended a dress rehearsal of the show in New York City, producer-playwright David Belasco quipped that he could not understand a single word she said. Ready or not, Held opened in *Papa's Wife* at the Boston Theatre on October 30, 1899, the first leg of the pre-Broadway tour. She portrayed Anna, a naive convent girl who is married to the Baron Florestan de la Boucaniere (Henry Bergman), an old roué who is more of a ladies' man than his son, Aristide (Henry Woodruff), who, in turn, hopes that this somewhat unorthodox union will straighten out his father. Unfortunately, the old rake is still smitten by the charms of his old flame, a burlesque queen, Coralie (Eva Davenport), so Aristide tries to assist Major Bombardas (George Marion), his father's rival in Coralie's affections, in his pursuit. However, since Anna has discovered during their honeymoon that her husband is more interested in dancing girls than convent types, she begins to behave like them. Soon she is mistaken for Coralie by her former music teacher, Celestin (Charles A. Bigelow), her stepson, her husband, and Major Bombardas, who takes her to lunch and gets her drunk. The mistaken identity is unraveled at the

Anna Held

end and, reading her wedding license, Anna discovers that she is married not to the Baron but to his son, and all ends happily.

The Boston notices were highly supportive and, surprisingly, made little issue of the naughtiness of the plot. In Philadelphia, the response was equally positive and as many as ten curtain calls were demanded of the star. The "Automobile" number that ended the first act featured Anna Held's own Dion-Bouton as part of the choreography, an innovation certainly, because automobiles were still relatively new to the streets. Although the vehicle was troublesome in Philadelphia—at one performance Ziegfeld had to drive it himself so that the musical number could finish—it was in perfect working order when *Papa's Wife* opened at the Manhattan Theatre in New York on November 13. The New York critics, though lavish in their praise for Held, were (typically) mixed in their appraisal of Smith's book, some calling it "thin" and "suggestive," others "amusing," "smart," and "up to date." In characteristic fashion, Smith capitalized on the latest novelties of the day, including the Automobile number. Photography was becoming the rage, so Aristide got to comment on the trend with "I'd Like to Have a Photograph of That." And the popular coon song idiom found its way into the proceedings via Papa's valet, Tobias (Dan Collyer), who followed the opening chorus girls' number with "I'm 'Fraid Dis Snap Is Mos' Too Good to Last."

Critics continued to complain about Smith's use of topical songs and idioms in his shows, even though they provided much of the humor and good-natured fun in the entertainment. Critic Edward A. Dithmar, however, did seem to appreciate their function. Calling Smith "that distinguished American jester," in the *New York Times* (November 19, 1899), he wrote: "a French subject treated from the point of view of American humor, has not been excelled in the desirable elements of fun and vitality this season. Nothing else now in town is quite so funny as Papa's Wife, and I do not recall a recent production of this kind of musical piece nearly so pleasing to the eye." It was with this production, incidentally, that Ziegfeld began his reputation as a "connoisseur of pulchritude," with sixteen "dazzlingly attractive" girls in the chorus, and his leading lady in a variety of expensively tailor-made costumes.

Papa's Wife also marked the beginning of a number of projects for Smith where the score was produced by a committee of composers. Even though de Koven sought to create musically integrated scores and resisted interpolations in his comic operas, his music for this entertainment was less important than the star. Held had elected to sing "The Song of the Colonel" from Hervé's original score, so it was imported, no questions asked, and by the time the show had reached New York, de Koven was joined by A. Baldwin Sloane, writer of "Heaven Will Protect the Working Girl" and other popular hits, as composer of record.

Papa's Wife remained at the Manhattan Theatre for 147 performances, closing there on March 31, 1900, to begin a five-week tour. About a month after Held opened in New York, Smith was responsible for the lyrics of another burlesque added to *Whirl-i-Gig* at Weber and Fields's Music Hall. *Barbara Fidgety*, a spoof of Clyde Fitch's play *Barbara Frietchie*, then in performance at the Criterion Theatre with Julia Marlowe in the leading role, replaced *The Other Way* on December 7. The Civil War of the original play was rewritten as a mayoral election in the town of Frederick, Maryland, where Barbara (Mabel Fenton) finds herself in love with one of the candidates, Captain Grumbler (Charles J. Ross). Colonel Jagley (Peter F. Dailey), the Fidgetys' next-door neighbor, sang the hit song of the performance, "The Colonel," another of Smith's collaborations with John Stromberg that earned multiple encores on opening night.

While *Barbara Fidgety* was doing excellent business at the Music Hall and *Papa's Wife* was enjoying a spirited run at the Manhattan, Harry completed a sequel to *Robin Hood*, a three-act comic opera called *The Sheriff of Nottingham*, and was polishing up his next opus for George Lederer at the Casino Theatre, scheduled to go into rehearsal in February. On February 12, 1900, *The Viceroy*, the last of the shows Smith had been working on with Victor Herbert the previous spring, was produced by The Bostonians during the West Coast leg of their national tour at the Columbia Theatre in San Francisco. Borrowed from Lecocq's *Le Pompon*, the plot, set in sixteenth-century Sicily, involved the conflict between a usurping Viceroy (Henry Clay Barnabee) and Tivolini (Helen Bertram), the heir apparent, a pirate chief and his rival for the affections of Beatrice (Grace Cameron). Tivolini, who was arrested while courting Beatrice, manages to escape and convince the usurper to relinquish his claims to the throne and the girl. However, the critics were at odds in their assessment of the work, and The Bostonians, hoping for crowded houses, returned to *The Serenade* and *Robin Hood* to end their three-week engagement.

On March 8, Smith was back at the Music Hall with lyrics for *Sapolio*, "a clean travesty on *Sapho*," Clyde Fitch's dramatization of Alphonse Daudet's novel at Wallack's Theatre that had been closed by

Marcia Van Dresser as Fioretta, the Viceroy's daughter,
and Henry Clay Barnabee in *The Viceroy*

the police on March 5. As temptress Fannie Legrand in *Sapho*, British actress Olga Nethersole had won great acclaim and notoriety, especially when obscenity charges were leveled against her for performing the role. Satirizing her performance in the burlesque was Australian-born actress May Robson, engaged on a moral crusade to make Paris "nice and clean." The hits of the evening were two more Smith-Stromberg coon songs, "He's My Steady," performed "in short skirts" by Irene Perry, and "De Cake Walk Queen," a featured dance by "the wonderful Bessie Clayton."

Barely two weeks later, *The Casino Girl* opened at the Casino Theatre with a libretto by Smith and music by Will Marion Cook, Harry T. MacConnell, Ludwig Englander, Arthur Nevin, and John H. Moore. Designed as an American version of the London Gaiety Theatre musicals, the bare thread of a plot involves Laura Lee (Mabelle Gilman), a former chorus girl at the Casino Theatre, who goes to Egypt to escape the attentions of "stage-door-Johnnies" and become "Mam'zelle Estelle," the proprietress of a millinery shop. There, she falls in love with Percy Harold Ethelbert Frederick Cholmondeley (Virginia Earle), a doctor. Their romance is thwarted by the Khedive of Egypt (Sam Bernard), who desires Laura for his harem, and Fromage (Albert Hart) and Potage (Louis Wesley), two crooks posing as policemen, who convince the authorities that Percy is really a famous thief. Once the doctor is arrested, Laura Lee must rely on the help of a Chicago society matron, Mrs. H. Malaprop Rocks (Carrie E. Perkins), and her daughters, Roxy Rocks (Ella Snyder), Carrie Rocks (Mayme Gehrue), and Lotta Rocks (Irene Bentley), to effect Percy's release. After a series of disguises and mistaken identities, Laura Lee and Percy are finally off to the altar. If the plot recalls earlier Smithian dramatic situations, the lyrics did as well. In fact, Smith borrowed "The Naughty Little Clock," a song about "how quickly time flies," from *The Three Dragoons*. The reuse of material was not unique to this instance. The song "When Cupid Comes a-Tapping," used in *The Three Dragoons* (1899), was previously heard in *The Paris Doll* (1897), and the lyric to "The Lydy Wot Is Studin' for the Stige," originally written for that show, was subsequently recomposed by John Stromberg and used in the Weber and Fields's entertainments.

The *Dramatic Mirror* (March 24, 1900) found Smith's libretto "not a scintillating corollary of brilliants. Some of the lines are amusing, some of the lyrics are neat, but more suggesting the need of the fixing up that always comes to the aid of Casino productions, and usually eventuates gloriously." The *New York Times* (March 20, 1900) emphasized the paper-thin plotting, but offered a possible explanation as well: "There is no story to speak of in 'The Casino Girl.' But then Casino audiences do not go to hear stories. They want to see pretty and shapely girls, brilliant lights, and flashing eyes. They want handsome costumes and handsome scenery, and Mr. Lederer has given them this and more."

Smith was not concerned with critical reviews. The April 1 edition of the *New York Evening World* announced that he was earning $100,000 yearly from his royalties. In spite of what critics thought, his work was extremely popular with audiences. On April 2, *The Casino Girl*, originally in three acts, was abbreviated to two, and it continued to play to enthusiastic audiences for a total of ninety-one performances. A week later on April 9, The Bostonians appeared with *The Viceroy* at the Knickerbocker Theatre to generally poor reviews. Even though critics found much that was good to say about Victor Herbert's music, Smith's book was judged to be nothing but a pale remake of *Robin Hood* designed to feature The Bostonians, who "could not be induced to change their time-honored manners and customs." The Viceroy was the Sheriff of Nottingham, speaking again in platitudinous puns; his lieutenant, Corleone (William H. Macdonald), was Will Scarlet; Tivolini (Helen Bertram) was the obligatory trouser-role of Allan-a-Dale. After twenty-eight performances, *The Viceroy* gave way to a week of *Robin Hood*, beginning May 7, followed by a week of *The Serenade*. On June 25, *The Rounders* returned to the Casino Theatre for another thirty-five performances and, just as that show developed a stride, on July 11, *The Casino Girl* opened at the Shaftesbury Theatre in London and became the most successful American musical comedy export after *The Belle of New York*.

However, Harry did not enjoy his London experience with Henry Lowenfeld, then the manager of the Shaftesbury Theatre. Lowenfeld assumed both the right and necessity to tinker with the show, making changes in the cast after opening night and altering the text as he saw fit. Smith found himself disagreeing with many of Lowenfeld's choices, so he offered to sell him the play outright instead of accepting the usual royalty per performance. After some discussion, the sum agreed upon was £1,000. The manager wrote the librettist a check, which he cashed the very same day, worried that Lowenfeld would realize he had been duped and change his mind. Smith did not realize it at the time, but in spite of the alterations, *The Casino Girl* played to the end of the year and made Lowenfeld a very rich and happy man.

The British critics generally found Smith's libretto clever, full of "pleasant jokes and business," and his lyrics were considered "for the most part really humorous in idea and execution," though none of the reviewers felt that he was up to par with W. S. Gilbert. The English vocal score of *The Casino Girl* indicates a change in the *dramatis personae* from the original Broadway characters and the interpolation of several of Smith's lyrics from other shows, including "The Tattooed Man" from *The Idol's Eye*, which was recomposed by Arthur Weld, and "American Heiresses" from *The Rounders*.

Smith's battles with producers continued throughout July. When he returned to New York after the opening week of *The Casino Girl*, he discovered that his newest project, *The Cadet Girl*, scheduled to open at the Casino Theatre following *The Rounders*, had been blocked by George Lederer because of a dispute with A. H. Chamberlyn, the Boston-based producer of the new show. In response, Chamberlyn looked for another theater, finally securing the Herald Square Theatre with an opening scheduled for July 23. Lederer retorted by ordering Virginia Earle, the leading actress in the company, whom he had loaned to *The Cadet Girl* company, to leave that production and report back to the Casino Theatre for rehearsals of *The Belle of Bohemia*, advertised to open in September. Lulu Glaser was hired as a replacement, but the weekend before the show was to open, she announced that she could not appear. Christie MacDonald was subsequently engaged in her place, and the opening night was postponed so that the new leading lady could actually learn her lines.

On July 25, *The Cadet Girl*, Smith's adaptation of *Les demoiselles de Saint-Cyriens*, by Paul Gavault and Victor de Cottens, with music by Louis Varney, finally appeared at the Herald Square Theatre. New music was supplied by Smith's frequent collaborator Ludwig Englander, and additional lyrics were provided by J. Cheever Goodwin. The fairly complicated plot involved the execution of a will made 150 years earlier by an eccentric marquis in which a fortune, having been held in trust for a century and a half, would be bequeathed to whichever of his female descendants has the best figure. The contestants are required to pose in the nude, and the first foreigner to enter the room after the will is read is to be chosen as the judge. One of the descendants is Marguerite (Adele Ritchie), a pupil in a seminary, while the other is a café keeper's wife Antoinette (Christie MacDonald), who likes to dress in military attire (another trouser-role). The Baron Chartreuse (Dan Daly) is a kleptomaniac who steals art treasures to put into his museum. If the female claimants fail to comply with the provisions of the will, the fortune goes to his museum, so the Baron does his utmost to prevent the women from satisfying the requirements. His efforts are of no avail, however, because Antoinette has no qualm in taking off her clothes, and Marguerite refuses to compete. Antoinette is judged the winner, and being as generous as she is pulchritudinous, she divides the inheritance with her cousin.

The critics showed little tolerance for the production, except for Christie MacDonald and Dan Daly, whose work was roundly praised. Smith's contribution was described as "weeding out certain risqué passages and . . . planting a choice collection of Smithian 'gags,' couched in Broadway slang." The dialogue was judged "unfunny," and the music below expectations, with Varney's original score found superior to Englander's additions. None of Smith's songs were considered hits, nor were Goodwin's additional songs, "Gottet Got" and "I Annex It," noticed for special mention. *The Cadet Girl* limped along for forty-eight performances and quietly faded away on the touring circuit.

On August 6, two weeks after *The Cadet Girl* opened, the Casino Theatre mounted a production of *The Casino Boy*, a travesty of *The Casino Girl*, composed by Harry T. MacConnell and written by Robert B. Smith, Harry's twenty-five-year-old brother. Robert had grown up in Brooklyn, after the family moved back east in the early 1880s. Like Harry, Robert was a newspaper man, having served for some time as a reporter for the *Brooklyn Eagle*, and like his older brother, he was quickly drawn to performing in amateur theatricals. Acting led to writing, and by the time he was twenty, Robert had composed the libretto of a comic opera that was produced at the Brooklyn Academy of Music. The response to his work was sufficiently encouraging for him to leave his newspaper job and begin a career as a theatrical press agent and author of burlesques and vaudeville routines. The burlesque of *The Casino Girl* marked the first of many times Robert would be associated with his brother on a Broadway show. Nearly three weeks into the run of Robert's show, Harry registered three musical comedy librettos for copyright—*The Belle of the Beach*, *The Belle of the Halls*, and *Belles and Beaux*—and, as if the pattern of capitalizing on female pulchritude in the titles of musical shows were not obvious enough, he was in rehearsal for his next show at the Casino Theatre, *The Belle of Bohemia*.

Scheduled to open at the Hyperion Theatre in New Haven, Connecticut, on September 22, *The Belle of Bohemia* was a variation on Plautus's *Menaechmi*, the mistaken-identity plot Harry had been using since *Jupiter*. In this incarnation, Adolph Klotz (Sam Bernard), a Coney Island photographer, married to Katie (Virginia Earle), a singer, bears an amazing resemblance to the also-married Rudolph Dinkelhauser (Dick

Bernard), a well-to-do brewer. As a result, Dinkelhauser gets thrown into jail for indiscretions committed by Klotz while under the influence, and Klotz manages to set himself up in the brewer's mansion in Newport. As in *Jupiter*, the men attempt to play the husband with the wrong wife, again with calamitous results. Adding to the confusion, a local politician, Phelim McDuffy (D. L. Don), and his "matinee girl" daughter, Geraldine (Irene Bentley), try to swindle Dinkelhauser out of a Swiss chateau he inherited from a distant uncle. This requires the entire cast to travel to Switzerland, where in front of a beautiful Alpine panorama, the identities are set right and the inheritance is secured.

On Friday, September 21, the day before *The Belle of Bohemia* premiered in New Haven, its producer, George Lederer, sued A. H. Chamberlyn, producer of *The Cadet Girl*, for $20,000, alleged back royalties for Casino plays produced at Chamberlyn's theaters in Boston. On the following day, Chamberlyn countered the suit by attaching all the scenery, costumes, and box-office receipts from Lederer's production, claiming that he was owed $9,000 by the New York producer because of an unpaid debt, and a marshal and four police officers were sent to stand guard to ensure that *The Belle of Bohemia* would not leave New Haven. After much clever legal maneuvering by Herman Oppenheimer, Lederer's business manager, the production managed to pack up and return to New York City, just in time for its Monday night opening at the Casino Theatre.

Given the critics' complaints that the "costumes were distinctly not up to the Casino average" and the road signs used in the scenery were misspelled, the show might have been better off had it remained locked up in New Haven. Nonetheless, Smith's book was praised as "full of easily appreciated fun," providing a "coherent farce, with a serviceable story and characters whose comings and goings, if often astonishing, are at least understandable." The indefatigable Ludwig Englander's music was found to be a pleasant grab bag of coon songs, love songs, and topical songs, with an especially effective (and comically melodramatic) first-act finale that consciously travestied grand opera.

The topical songs that Smith composed for the production all came from his traditional stock: "The Matinee Girl," noting the practice of autograph-seeking beauties, hounding their favorite stars; "The Girl Who Is Up to Date," about the "new" woman's ability to handle men, cleverly, aesthetically, and athletically; "Amateur Entertainer," burlesquing a variety of popular singing styles; and "He Was a Married Man," detailing all the hardships married men are willing to encounter just to get away from their wives. Still, the songs were wittily phrased and polished, and the critics had little complaint with the material.

Although Smith recalled that, on opening night, the comedy hit of the evening was the (unintentional) moon effect that upstaged the action onstage because of its strange and unpredictable shapes, the technical glitches were quickly repaired and *The Belle of Bohemia* settled into a lucrative run before setting off on tour in November. No sooner had the Casino show opened when Smith found himself in rehearsal with *Foxy Quiller*, a kind of sequel to *The Highwayman*, starring Jerome Sykes in the role he had created. Sykes had been so successful in New York and on the road as Constable Quiller that the Theatrical Syndicate producers, Marc Klaw and Abraham Erlanger, commissioned Smith and de Koven to compose a new comic opera for him, focused on that character.

The plot began in Portsmouth, England, where the captain of a ship, Ned Royster (W. G. Stewart), is robbed of all his money by a dwarf, Kimono (Adolph Zink), traveling with Walsingham Binks (Harry MacDonough), an itinerant actor (and "neglected genius"). Ned's girlfriend, Daphne (Grace Cameron), has a father, Abel Gudgeon (Louis Casavant), a rich shipbuilder who will not permit the couple to marry unless Ned recovers his money. Foxy Quiller (Jerome Sykes) is subsequently called in to find the thief. His "deductive, inductive and seductive" reasoning leads him to believe that the thief is hiding in Corsica, so nearly the entire *dramatis personae* sets sail for that island in Ned's ship. There, Quiller discovers the money in his own valise (having been placed there by the dwarf), and he finds it necessary to arrest and send himself to jail. Before he can be executed for the crime he did not commit, the real culprit confesses, and all ends happily.

Following a three-week tryout tour, *Foxy Quiller* opened at the Broadway Theatre on November 5, 1900, to poor notices and lukewarm patronage. Even though Sykes was applauded for his comic abilities, his talent was insufficient to make the opera a success. De Koven's music was found lacking in "novelty or brilliancy," and Smith's libretto was roundly criticized for its thin plot and irrelevant attempts at humor. The *Dramatic Mirror* (November 17, 1900) complained, "The attempts at humor are forced and thin, and Quiller's peculiar phrases, spoken in the third person, become as wearisome to hear as they must have been to Mr. Smith to manufacture. It is the old story of overworking a good thing, and

Jerome Sykes as Foxy Quiller

another demonstration of the futility of endeavoring to sequelize stage characters with success."

Although the critics found little to applaud about the show, Smith did provide Sykes with a show-stopping entrance number, "Quiller Has the Brain," a "list" song about Quiller's obvious superiority to the great men in history:

You talk about your Plato,
And your Socrates and Cato,
But I must say without intending rudeness,
Their talk was merely driveling;
Their wisdom only frivoling,
Compared to my extraordinary shrewdness.
Napoleon and Nero,
Were a cipher and a zero,
And Bacon wasn't wiser than a miller.
All other names diminish
To a microscopic finish
When brought into proximity with Quiller.
For Quiller has the brain and Quiller has the arm,
A frown that is a terror, but a smile that has a charm,
To turn the coyest damsel to a cooer and a biller.
Don Juan was an amateur compared to Foxy Quiller.
The rest of the detectives
When they gaze on him grow iller;
A lot of children they, not men,
They're just a Kindergarten
When compared to Foxy Quiller.

Following an opening week of discouraging business, Smith contacted Erlanger and offered to dispense with his royalty because the production was not a success. As Smith tells the story, "I did not hear from him for a week and then he wrote that he had not yet recovered from the shock; that such a proposal had never been made to him before. He added that, if the piece had been a tremendous success, he would not have felt called upon to increase the rate of royalty; so, to be consistent, he declined the proposition."

After fifty performances, *Foxy Quiller* had worn out its welcome in New York and left for the road, where the inexhaustible *Robin Hood*, *The Serenade*, *The Singing Girl*, *Papa's Wife*, and *The Belle of Bohemia* were still going strong through the holidays. Although Smith had not had a production in 1900 that significantly added to his reputation, he was able to point to something that had never been done before. In that year, R. H. Russell, a New York publisher, issued a collection of Smith's *Stage Lyrics*, marking the first time an American lyricist would be legitimized in a poetic anthology of his work.

The new year brought Harry again to London when *The Belle of Bohemia* began a ten-and-a-half week run at the Apollo Theatre on February 22, 1901. While in England, Smith completed the libretto of another three-act musical comedy, *The Roll of the Drum*, and polished up the dialogue of a comic opera, *The Prima Donna*, scheduled to go into rehearsal in March. He had to miss the cordial reception afforded the revival of *The Casino Girl* at the Knickerbocker Theatre on April 8 because he was due back in London the next day for the opening of *The Fortune Teller* at the Shaftesbury Theatre with Alice Nielsen's company. For the London production, Smith and Herbert had written a new song for Sandor (Eugene Cowles) to sing in the third act, "O Sing the Praise of the Sword," but at the last minute, "Cupid and I" from *The Serenade* was added as well. Smith was glad that Herbert's commitments to the Pittsburgh Symphony had kept him in the United States, because he was sure that the composer would not have permitted the interpolation. The British response to the production was unsurprisingly mixed. Audiences and critics alike appeared to enjoy the music and the performers, but few seemed to appreciate the lack of originality in the libretto. Even though one critic called the show "a triumph," *The Fortune Teller* only managed eighty-eight performances and closed on July 11 when Alice Nielsen was ordered by her physician to take a long rest.

Immediately following the London opening, Harry headed back to New York for the premiere of *The Prima Donna* at the Herald Square Theatre on April 17. Advertised as a "musical farce," with a score by Aimé Lachaume, *The Prima Donna* was based on a French farce, *Le Siège de Grenade*, by Henri Chivot and Alfred Duru. It told the story of Angela Chumpley (Lulu Glaser), the "prima donna" of the Frivolity Theatre in London, who marries a composer, Meyerbeer Supnoodle (Herbert Cawthorne). The marriage causes Supnoodle's father to disinherit him, so the couple move to Paris where an Egyptian Pasha (Gilbert Clayton) falls in love with Angela, providing an excuse to move the action to Cairo, where a series of Smithian mistaken identities and misunderstandings are sorted out amid a "merry, merry" chorus of diaphanously dressed beauties.

The piece had been scheduled to open at an earlier date with Mabelle Gilman in the leading role, but a providential illness prevented the actress from appearing and Lulu Glaser was engaged on short notice as her replacement. Although producer Chamberlyn postponed the opening several times so that Miss Glaser could have more rehearsals, the critics argued that the public would have gained "had the postponements been continued *ad infinitum.*" The book—originating in the "Harry B. Smith Libretto Foundry"—was dismissed as "halting and muddled," "dull and inane," and "far less humorous than the average burlesque." The music was said to lack hummable melodies, "color, variety and spirit," and the producer was brought to task for considering the work stageworthy. The *New York Times* (April 18, 1901) was particularly articulate in its blame:

> Just why theatrical managers believe that the public loses its senses in the Spring no one has been able to find out, but it is a familiar fact that about this time every year, what is called "the silly season" begins. This delectable period was begun in proper form last night at the Herald Square Theatre, with the production of . . . "The Prima Donna." The dramatic conception of this unique work is credited to the prolific Harry B. Smith, while the music was composed—or at any rate, written down—by Aimé Lachaume. The combined efforts of these two gentlemen have produced something which cannot be described. That it has a plot was suspected, and, indeed, argued by the exclamatory utterance of certain lines designed to make the audience believe that some one had married some one, or was trying to marry some one, or was willing to do so for a consideration. But this plot was able to get its head above water only once in a while.
>
> For the rest of the time it was submerged beneath a sea of hopelessly silly dialogue, and frequent, cheap, and foolish music. There is nothing more enjoyable in a theatre than a piece of good fooling, but—there are fooling and fooling, and it is not wise to try to fool the public when the public expects you to fool for it. Witless chatter and pointless songs, meaningless actions and insignificant comings and goings can hardly be carried to popularity by pretty figures, high kicking, and low dressing. . . . "The Prima Donna" is tenuous; it is diaphanous; it is almost invisible.

As Smith's latest critical disaster wound down to its thirty-six-performance limit at the Herald Square, Anna Held returned to New York with *Papa's Wife*, celebrating its five hundredth performance on May 7. The Ziegfeld production completed a commercially successful two-week engagement at the Grand Opera House on May 17, and Anna was ready to take the summer off to prepare for her next Harry B. Smith adaptation, *The Little Duchess*, scheduled to go into production in the fall. As she began to memorize her lines for the new show, the author was busy polishing the dialogue for *The Strollers*, his adaptation of a recent megapopular Viennese musical, *Die Landstreicher*, by Leopold Krenn and Carl Lindau with music by Carl Michael Ziehrer.

In Smith's version, *The Strollers* traces the adventures of a pair of tramps, August Lump (Francis Wilson) and his wife, Bertha (Irene Bentley), who are arrested as "suspicious persons" in a small Austrian village. They manage to escape from jail in the clothing of Prince de Boomsky (Harry Gilfoil), an old roué, and Mimi (Marie George), his little ballet girl, who have come to the police station to report the theft of some jewels. The Lumps, who are subsequently mistaken for the Prince and his girlfriend, have discovered the gems and happily return them to Mimi to collect the $5,000 reward. The Prince, however, wanted his girlfriend to have paste, not the real thing, so the Lumps have to reappropriate the jewels at an elaborate garden party and replace them with fakes, only to discover that both sets of gems are paste.

George Lederer's production of *The Strollers* opened on June 24 at the Knickerbocker Theatre in New York, the music provided by Ludwig Englander with additional help from Gus Edwards, Jean Schwartz, and Evans Lloyd. Smith's book was embellished as well with additional lyrics by Jeff T. Branen, Will D. Cobb, and William Jerome. To some critics, the added material did not help the libretto, which was dubbed "a stupid book; an exhaustive book; a book full of jokes decrepit and inane; a book that hasn't a bowing acquaintance with real wit." The *Dramatic Mirror* (July 6, 1901) denigrated the show as representative of the new style of "American musical comedy" with "an abundance of chorus girls; a reminiscent score, seasoned with rag time; a libretto stocked with stale and vulgar jokes and horseplay *ad lib.* for the comedians." Such things, however, were the stock in trade of summer entertainment and, for some critics, the very qualities that would guarantee *The Strollers* its measure of success. The *New York Times* (June 25, 1901), for example, calling Smith "the librettist-in-ordinary to the United States," argued that *The Strollers* was "as good as anything of its kind lately presented in New York, and in many respects much better."

However, Smith was far too busy to concern himself with reviews. As soon as one show opened, he was hard at work on his next half-dozen assignments, clearly unaffected by a string of bad notices. It was obvious he knew how to write for audiences, producers, and stars—the people paying his royalties. What was less apparent, however, was the fact that he generally agreed with his critics. In an interview with the *New York Herald* (May 8, 1904), Smith articulated the difficulties of being a expert librettist in terms that echo his severest critics:

> [T]he secret of writing for the stage is a knowledge of construction, and the most difficult kind of stage construction is the writing of librettos. Writing a good play is comparatively child's play. . . . A playwright, given a story and characters, has merely to arrange his story, develop it logically and naturally, and establish certain climaxes which shall terminate his acts. A librettist must do this and much more. After constructing his play, he must take it all to pieces, find places for his songs, and then write his songs. He must also—in a real comic opera—carry on the action of his play to music and verse. He must plan the play musically as well as dramatically. He must bear in mind always the limitations of the musical piece, one of the chief of which is that his play will be acted by people who are singers primarily and actors secondarily. . . . Mind you, I am speaking of really meritorious librettos. The average musical play written in America nowadays is beneath critical consideration. It is ridiculous to speak of "construction" in connection with them. There is no construction. I saw a musical piece this week which bore all the appearance of having been written in a lunatic asylum. There had been a plot, but it had been forced into the background to such an extent that when an allusion was made to the story the matter became all the more incoherent. Otherwise it was a succession of songs, some of them pretty and lively. . . .
>
> A great many pieces put together in this way have considerable success. I have been guilty of aiding and abetting some of these conspiracies. I think the cause of the existence of this kind of musical piece is the managerial fear that the "show" will be slow. Whenever the plot of a piece appears the tempo is necessarily slower than that of mere comic incident. Then, the average manager fears the play will drag, and the edict is, "Cut out the plot and put in a coon song."

As *The Strollers* had begun to settle into a comfortable canter at the Knickerbocker, Smith was off to Buffalo where he "aided and abetted" another plotless musical, composing the lyrics for *The Rogers Brothers in Washington*, opening at the Star Theatre on August 19, 1901. Conceived by John J. McNally as a vehicle for the popular Dutch comedians, the loose and farcical plot begins at the Democratic Club in New York City, where Carlos Chauffs (Gus Rogers) and Louis Lauffs (Max Rogers) are dummy candidates for a congressional seat. This provides the excuse for moving the action to the "Botanical Gardens" (with a view of the Capitol) in Washington, D.C., and then up to the "Court of Fountains" at the Pan-American Exposition in Buffalo, New York, where the bogus politicians chase the wrong women and mingle with the wrong people.

Smith penned a number of up-to-date lyrics for the farce: an opening number, "The Girl of Greater New York"; a political satire, "Get Next to the Man with a Pull"; a "new-woman" song, "In the Swim"; and a specialty number, "An Englishman's Ideas of Rag-Time." The runaway hit of the production, however, was "The Wedding of the Reuben and the Maid," a spoof of Leslie Stuart's "Tell Me, Pretty Maiden," from *Florodora*, the popular British import in the midst of a long engagement at the Casino Theatre. Advertised as a "cyclonic success," the patter song relates the adventures of country bumpkins coming to the big city on their honeymoon:

> As he had been to town before, he thought he knew his biz,
> One always likes to think he knows his biz,
> The cabman hollered "hansom" Reuben said, "You bet she is"
> One always likes of course to think she is,
> One cabman hustled Reub into a rattle trap coupé,
> You know one doesn't always like to pay,
> Another cabman grabbed the maid and drove the other way,
> One doesn't like a wedding trip that way.

Calling the lyrics "clever" and Maurice Levi's music "fetching," critics predicted immediate popularity for the number, which was judged a fitting sequel to Levi's previous hit "When Reuben Comes to Town," from *The Rogers Brothers in Central Park* (1900).

After an extraordinary run in Buffalo to record-setting business, on September 2 the production moved to the Knickerbocker Theatre in New York City, recently vacated by *The Strollers* after seventy performances. There, *The Rogers Brothers* played to audiences more accustomed to vaudeville houses and cabarets for forty-nine showings before going out on tour. Not surprisingly, the New York critics applauded the scenery and

"The Wedding of the Reuben and the Maid" from *The Rogers Brothers in Washington*

the chorus girls, but found little of value in the production except for the "few admirable musical numbers" by Smith and Levi that were "the only truly bright spots in the programme."

Harry B. Smith had little time to spend with *The Rogers Brothers* for, a week after their New York opening, he was in Philadelphia, where his next three-act musical farce, *The Liberty Belles*, was scheduled to premiere at the Chestnut Street Theatre on September 9. This project was something of a departure for Smith in that he was not only the librettist and lyricist, he was also the co-producer with Marc Klaw and Abraham Erlanger, whose Theatrical Syndicate also managed *The Rogers Brothers* and *Foxy Quiller*. As Smith described the sequence of events, he suddenly became possessed by "delusions of grandeur" at the beginning of the 1901–02 theater season and thought it would be "fun" to produce a show and pay himself a royalty. He set out to write a surefire hit, guaranteed not to lose money, and approached Klaw and Erlanger with his scenario, and the request "to be their partner with a one-third interest." The syndicate bosses were shocked that any writer would be foolish enough to risk his own money on one of his own plays, but, recalling that they declined Smith's earlier offer to defer royalties for *Foxy Quiller*, they decided to accept his current proposition. Smith then proceeded to draft his sure thing:

> With a crafty economy which I had never considered before I evolved a piece for which the costumes in the first act should cost nothing and those in the second act very little. The scene of the first act was to be the dormitory of a girls' school, the pupils getting together for a supper party after the authorities had retired for the night. The girls were to wear nightgowns, pajamas and negligees, and the economical theory was that each would prefer to buy her own in order to look as pretty as nature would allow. The scene of the second act was to be a cooking school and the girls were to wear dainty but inexpensive frocks. The only outlay for costuming was to be for summer gowns in the last act.
>
> I wrote the piece, lyrics and all, in three weeks. This important fact was afterward paragraphed and one friendly reviewer in Chicago said that he thought it quite remarkable till he saw the play and then he wondered what I had been doing all that time.

For the first time in his career, Harry took an active participation in the casting of a show, interviewing chorus girls in depth, with the kind of rigor normally spent on principal roles. Though he was perceived as a dilettante, a source of amusement in the managerial offices, Smith's methods did pay off: *The Liberty Belles* boasted a bevy of beauties who could sing, dance, *and* act, something of a rarity on Broadway.

The Philadelphia critics were agog about the first scene in the show, featuring girls in nightgowns discovered in their dormitory room. One even exclaimed, varying Smith's lyric from *Papa's Wife*, "You'd like to have a photograph of that." After so "shocking" an opening, the rest of the plot seemed predictably tame. Margery Lee (Etta Butler) is engaged to Phil Fullerton (John Slavin), a "Columbia boy," and Dorothy Grey (Sandol Milliken) is secretly married to Jack Everleigh (Harry Davenport), who goes to Annapolis. The boys disguise themselves as burglars to break into the girls' dormitory and visit their sweethearts, but their prank causes Dorothy's marriage to be revealed and both girls to be threatened with expulsion.

Faced with the abrupt termination of their scholastic careers, Dorothy and Margery decide to run away and open a cooking school, accompanied, of course, by their husband and fiancé. They soon find themselves short of funds, and although Jack and Dorothy both have wealthy uncles (Harry Gilfoil, J. C. Marlowe), each has placed conditions on an inheritance: Jack's uncle will only leave his fortune to his nephew's heir, and Dorothy's uncle will only give her money if she remains single. To deceive Jack's relative, the couple borrows a baby, and to deceive Dorothy's uncle, Margery pretends to be Jack's wife. Such a ruse could not remain undetected for long, and the uncles visiting the couple threaten to disinherit the pair. In the end, at a Florida hotel, Phil Fullerton manages to save the day by cross-dressing as a Cuban widow (recalling Brandon Thomas's popular farce, *Charley's Aunt*) and seducing the uncles into forgiving Jack and Dorothy.

On September 30, *The Liberty Belles* opened at the Madison Square Theatre in New York, and it remained there for a respectable run of 104 performances. Like the Philadelphia critics, the New York reviewers were drawn to the "gross exploitation of feminine underwear" in the opening scene, some even considering such things out of place in a "first-class" theatre. The music, composed by a committee that included Aimé Lachaume, Ludwig Englander, Clifton Crawford, L. G. Gottschalk, A. Baldwin Sloane, Harry T. MacConnell, Alfred E. Aarons, William Accooe, and Herbert Gresham, was thought to be tuneful, even if only of "ephemeral value," and Smith's book, though "thin," kept the stage "alive with light and life and color." The *New York Times* (October 1, 1901) concluded, "The success of 'The Liberty Belles' lies in the liveliness, the tunefulness, and snap of the entire company. In the comedy is the thoughtlessness of a farce, the swiftly shooting colors of the pantomime, and care free good humor." If nothing else, Smith knew how to keep an audience entertained.

Because he was involved as producer of *The Liberty Belles*, Smith had little involvement in the out-of-town tryouts of Anna Held's next vehicle, *The Little Duchess*, his adaptation, with music by Reginald de Koven, of the French vaudeville *Niniche*, by Alfred Hennequin, Albert Millaud, and Émile de Najac (music by Marius Boullard). Reports from Baltimore and Washington were excellent, and the show, scheduled to open at the Casino Theatre on October 14, promised to be a suitable successor to Leslie Stuart's *Florodora*, which had just closed there after 553 performances, the most successful British import to date.

Claire de Brion (Held), a Parisian actress, assumes the title of the "Little Duchess" at Ostend in order to avoid the creditors hounding her uncle, the dissipated Count Cassibianca (George Marion), who expect her to pay the bills he accrues in Paris. While at the shore, she becomes a much sought-after "belle in a bathing suit," though her affections are directed to Captain Ralph Egerton (Sydney Barraclough), an English officer. At the end of the first act, Claire discovers that her uncle's creditors have seized her apartment in Paris and intend to auction off all of her belongings. So everyone goes to Paris to straighten out Claire's financial matters, and after two acts of disguisings and elaborate costume changes, the "Little Duchess" solves her problems and finds love.

The audiences loved it. By the end of the first week, the show had set a box-office record for the theater (even surpassing *Florodora*). Producer Florenz Ziegfeld Jr. knew he had another hit on his hands, even though the critics were not entirely amused, some calling Smith's book "inane" and "vacuous" and Reginald de Koven's music "tantalizingly familiar." Offering a rare positive vote, the *Dramatic Mirror* (October 19, 1901), usually opposed to this kind of show, called the book "a serviceable peg on which to hang a plentiful portion of musical numbers," just what Smith intended, and applauded the author for supplying "a cluster of lyrics that rank among his best," and furnishing "the numerous comedians of the company with liberal chances for laugh-making." All the critics, however, agreed on one thing: spectacle was the strong point of the production, and the costumes, scenery, and properties were "the limit in luxury." Again, Harry had done his job well, and having provided excuses for costume changes and spectacular devices in his script, he did not bog down the evening with plot. In fact, when the production left for a long national tour, he added a tongue-in-cheek announcement on the program: "Owing to the length of the performance the plot has been eliminated."

On January 17, 1902, *The Little Duchess* celebrated its one hundredth performance at the Casino Theatre. Ten days later, Smith and de Koven were back at the Garden Theatre when The Bostonians introduced New York City to *Maid Marian*, the long-awaited sequel to *Robin Hood*. The story begins just as Robin (Frank Rushworth) and Marian (Grace Van Studdiford) are about to get married. Their nuptial plans are interrupted by the King's edict, sending Robin to the Crusades, much to the delight of the Sheriff of Nottingham (Henry Clay Barnabee), who, still eager to appropriate Marian's land, takes the opportunity of Robin Hood's absence to unite the girl to Guy of Gisbourne (W. H. Fitzgerald). Little John (W. H. MacDonald), Will Scarlet (Allen C. Hunckley), Friar Tuck (George B. Frothingham), and Allan-a-Dale (Adele Rafter) come together to help Marian frustrate the Sheriff's plans, and they all go to the Holy Land in search of Robin Hood.

Once in Palestine, Marian is captured by Saracens, only to be speedily rescued by Robin Hood. Their happiness is short-lived, however, because the Sheriff (who has followed Marian) connives to have Robin recaptured (along with Marian and the rest of his merry men) so that he can take possession of his property. Needless to say, Hood and company escape from the Holy Land and return to Robin's castle, where they find the Sheriff and Gisbourne celebrating their victory. The festivities are interrupted by an order from the King banishing the Sheriff and his minion, and Robin and Marian finally enjoy the luxury of getting married.

Critics were generally universal in their praise, some even suggesting that *Maid Marian* was the finest Smith–de Koven collaboration since *Robin Hood*. Reactions to de Koven's music were mixed, some calling it the best thing he had done since the earlier show, and others, "a very satisfactory average of melody and harmony." Smith's book was roundly praised for presenting a "plausible and entertaining" plot "in a very lucid and effective fashion," and applauded for not weighing it down with "up-to-date" jokes. Irrespective of good reviews, audiences still preferred the original to the sequel, and *Maid Marian* remained at the Garden Theatre for only sixty-four performances before joining *Robin Hood* and *The Serenade* in the active touring repertoire of The Bostonians.

As *Maid Marian* began its run, Harry's attention was drawn to his next project. It had been suggested to him that he and two of his newspaper colleagues from Chicago, George Ade and Peter Dunne, should form a company "for the wholesale manufacture of comedies and musical plays." George Ade, who had joined the *Daily News* during Smith's last days with the paper, had just struck gold with the libretto for *The Sultan of Sulu* in Chicago, and Dunne had found fame as the creator of the fictional Chicago bartender "Mister Dooley." The three friends met regularly to discuss the possibilities of establishing such a manufacturing company, but typically, the conversation involved more reminiscing than forward thinking. At one point, Dunne glibly suggested that the formation of such a corporation would probably be in violation of the Inter-State Commerce Law. Whether or not he was serious, the project never materialized.

The end of April brought Smith again to the Garrick Theatre in Philadelphia, for the opening of *The Wild Rose*, another musical comedy produced by George Lederer, with music by Ludwig Englander. The typical Smithian plot involves Rose Romany (Irene Bentley), the daughter of Count von Lahn (William Black), who was raised as the daughter of Mirabel (Carrie E. Perkins), one of the gypsies, and is now being forced to marry Mahomet (Albert Hart), the chief of the gypsy band, who knows her true identity. Because Rose loves Rudolph von Walden (David Lythgoe), a young military officer, Mirabel, who also loves Mahomet, drugs the gypsies' food with a sleeping potion so that Rose and her sweetheart can escape. Victor Hugo de Brie (Junie McCree), a newly wed playwright and aeronaut, and his wife, Vera von Lahn (Marie Cahill), the supposed daughter of the Count, land in a balloon just as Paracelsus Noodles (Edwin "Eddie" Foy), an itinerant hypnotist's assistant, accidentally wanders into the gypsy camp and is taken prisoner by the inhabitants, who think him a police spy. To prove he is not a spy, he claims to be a professional mesmerist who can put the entire camp under a trance, and he succeeds with the assistance of drugged food in putting everyone to sleep. Paracelsus, Rose, and Rudolph escape from the gypsy camp in de Brie's balloon, and they fly to a nearby German Rathskeller frequented by French and German soldiers. The trio disguise themselves as waiters to elude the gypsies on their trail, and they discover the secret of Rose's birth, and the fact that her father, Count von Lahn, is present at the inn. Von Lahn and his real daughter are united, and Rose, no longer a gypsy, can marry the soldier she loves. Everyone is happy except for Vera, who turns out to be a real gypsy, and de Brie, who suddenly realizes that his wife cannot support him.

Smith had completed a draft of the libretto in 1901, calling it *The Mesmerist*. As he began to rework the piece, he engaged the help of playwright George V. Hobart, who basically assisted with the lyrics, although he received co-librettist credit in the reviews. The opening in Philadelphia was not encouraging, and a number of composers and lyricists, including Clifton Crawford, Will Marion Cook, and Cecil Mack, were engaged to strengthen the score. When *The Wild Rose* opened at the Knickerbocker Theatre on May 5, 1902, the New York reviews were positive, thanking Smith for creating an amusing and "coherent, consistent plot in these days of tommyrotical libretti," with only a "comparatively slight amount of horseplay." Unfortunately for Ludwig Englander, the two biggest musical hits of the evening were interpolations: "The Little Gypsy Maid," composed by Will Marion Cook with lyrics by Smith and Mack, and sung by Irene Bentley; and "Nancy Brown," a song about a young man who came to town "in search of a girl whose father owned half of New York," written by Clifton Crawford and sung by Marie Cahill, earning her six encores.

During the musical comedy's 136-performance run, the Cornelius Vanderbilts paid the company $5,000 to perform the show at their mansion in Newport, Rhode Island. While the cast was rubbing elbows with the upper crust, Harry began working on *Nancy Brown*, a musical designed to capitalize on the success of the interpolated song, registering the libretto for copyright on November 4, 1902. His hopes for interesting a producer in the project were discouraged with the discovery that Clifton Crawford, the composer of the song, had written his own musical on the same subject, and Frederic Ranken, a popular play-doctor and librettist, was laboring on yet another version called *Nancy Brown; or, The Bey of Bally-hoo*. Ranken's version was the only one to be produced, opening in February 1903 with Marie Cahill reprising her rendition of the popular song.

As always, Harry B. Smith had no time to lament lost opportunities. *The Billionaire*, Smith's first collaboration with German composer Gustave Kerker, who had composed the music for the remarkably successful *The Belle of New York*, was scheduled to open at Daly's Theatre in New York just after Christmas, on December 29, 1902. Smith had written the musical for Jerome Sykes and Klaw and Erlanger in the hopes of repaying them for the failure of *Foxy Quiller*. The plot revolves around John Doe (Sykes), a man so wealthy that he has a "controlling interest in the earth." He goes to Nice, where he meets Pansy Good (Nellie Follis), a girl from Iowa who traveled to France to learn how to succeed in show

"The Little Gypsy Maid" from *The Wild Rose*

business. Doe is so impressed with the girl that he offers to buy her a theater in New York and make her a star. Pansy accepts his offer, and John takes the entire population of Nice with them back to New York so that he can count on a supportive audience for Pansy's debut.

The second act opens in Doe's theater, showing a curtain, stage, footlights, orchestra seats, and proscenium boxes, with patrons being led to their places by "two very fresh ushers." Lackluster vaudeville entertainment follows for the amusement of Doe's ready-made audience, and the attempt to make Pansy a star has the look of failure. Abruptly the scene changes to a racetrack in Longchamps, France, where Doe is hoping to win the race to make up the money lost in his theatrical venture. Too overweight to fit in his jockey suit, Doe is convinced of the futility of trying to ride the horse himself, and he allows Pansy to ride on his behalf. She wins the race, and John Doe is once again a wealthy man.

The *New York Clipper* (January 3, 1903) found the music pleasing and the book "full of bright lines and witty dialogue," but not all of the critics were amused by the musical farce. Most called it deficient in both respects, with only one catchy song and a book "as cut and dried as a piece of salted codfish." The *Dramatic Mirror* (January 10, 1903) quoted the two best jokes in the piece: "You are so refined—I ought to be; my father used to own a refinery," and "I will now sing a song, written expressly for me, by an express man." Such witticisms were greeted enthusiastically on opening night by an enormous crowd, though some audience members, like Reginald de Koven, managed to sleep soundly through the first two acts, completely missing the musical staging by Ned Wayburn, making his move from performer to choreographer. Fortunately, Jerome Sykes was "legitimately funny" enough of the time to keep most of the audience awake, and *The Billionaire* ran a respectable 104 performances to good business before going on tour.

The new year saw another Smith musical comedy open in Boston, this time with a libretto in collaboration with Frederic Ranken. *The Jewel of Asia* premiered at the Park Theatre on January 26, 1903, produced by George Lederer, with music by Ludwig Englander, and starring James T. Powers, another favorite comedian on the musical theater stage, in the role of Pierre Lerouge. Pierre is a French art student (and part-time waiter) painting a picture called the "Jewel of Asia." A Turkish Pasha (George O'Donnell) comes to France with his dozen wives, the favorite of whom, Zaidee (Eloise Morgan), is known as the "Jewel of Asia" as well. Yussuf Potiphar (Clifton Crawford), a Turkish prince and heir to the late Badeg Pasha, is in love with this "Jewel" and follows her to Paris, where he hopes to meet with her secretly. To accomplish this, Yussuf disguises himself as a waiter, borrowing Pierre's uniform, leaving the artist-waiter his Turkish suit and vest. Once Pierre puts on the prince's clothes, he is whisked away to Turkey, mistaken for the real prince, followed by his sweetheart, Mimi (Rachel Booth), and Madame Hersillie (Carrie

Perkins), the owner of the restaurant where he works. Hersillie is after the painting, and Sergeant Lafitte (Henry Short), Mimi's father, is after his daughter and the restaurant owner, whom he loves. In Turkey, the mistaken identity is discovered, Yussuf Potiphar takes possession of his inheritance, including the "Jewel" he loves, and Pierre marries Mimi.

The Boston opening had been postponed a number of times to allow for more rehearsal. When an audience was finally allowed to see the work, the critics were enthusiastic about the performances, the book, and Englander's score, even though one of the songs especially applauded, "Everybody Wants to See the Baby," was an interpolation composed by Bob Cole and James Weldon Johnson. Two weeks later, on February 16, the show appeared in New York at the Criterion Theatre, where the opening proved to be a comedy of errors. Blanche Ring had replaced Eloise Morgan in the title role, new dialogue and business had been added to the show, and the cast was underrehearsed. Neither Ring nor Powers was letter-perfect in their roles, and Clifton Crawford forgot so many of his lines that he had to walk to the wings to hear the prompter shout them out. Even the props did not work: the curtain in Hersillie's restaurant fell down as she attempted to close it, and an electric light globe exploded in front of the audience. The crowning glory, however, came when the conductor nearly fell asleep at the podium and the prompter had to stick his head from behind the curtain to cue the music.

Needless to say, the reviews of that performance were mixed. Special attention was drawn to Ring's "good and consistent" impersonation of a "mechanical doll," even though the device was thought to be old-fashioned and far-fetched. Evidently the device was popular enough with audiences for Smith to build an entire musical around it, *A China Doll*, in 1904. The libretto was criticized for having an overabundance of venerable "turkey" jokes—"turkey wings," "gobbler's feathers," "light and dark meat"—but praised for keeping the humor "refined and clean," and generally "above the ordinary."

After sixty-four performances in New York, *The Jewel of Asia* left in the spring to join the touring circuit, and Smith was back at work with Gustave Kerker on a new summer musical for George Lederer, *The Blonde in Black*, advertised to open on June 8, 1903, at the Knickerbocker Theatre. The show had originally been called *The Gibson Girl*, but when American illustrator Charles Dana Gibson threatened legal action over the appropriation of his trademark, the title was quickly altered. Smith and Lederer designed the show as a starring vehicle for Blanche Ring, who played Flossie Featherly, an American in Paris, who is employed teaching the cakewalk, but secretly yearning to play "Camille." The action opens at a ladies' clothing establishment operated by Gaston Roulette (Harry Conor), which also serves as the headquarters for his "Domestic Fidelity Trust Company." Gaston not only sells dresses, he peddles matrimonial insurance, guaranteeing a wife's fidelity or the husband gets his money back. Into the shop comes Flossie to pick up her dresses when she suddenly finds herself in the middle of a series of domestic squabbles that seem to center around a painter, Van Dyke Beard (Charles H. Bowers), and his desire to use a Wagner diva, Elsa Beckmesser-Carrousel (Violet Halls), and Bettine (Rose Beaumont), Roulette's own wife, among other "insured" women as his models. Because Elsa's husband, M. Carrousel-Ladjos (Max Freeman), a Hungarian ballet-master, is both fiery and jealous, Roulette attempts to direct the artist's attentions toward Flossie to avoid having to pay on the insurance policy, and to save his skin. The American manages to straighten out the domestic difficulties through a clever misdirection of letters and a number of fast-paced ragtime numbers.

The musical was clearly designed as a summer entertainment: peppy music, an easily digestible plot, and pretty "hat-bobbing" showgirls wearing handsome gowns in exotic settings. Many of Smith and Kerker's songs were singled out for praise: "Mademoiselle Kek-Wak," a ragtime dance that ends act one; "Banjo Serenade," in which the chorus vocally mimics the plucking of the banjo; an inebriated "Champagne Song" for Bettine; and "Angels without Wings," a trio that enumerates the virtues of women. The *Dramatic Mirror* (June 20, 1903) thought the show was superior to the usual summer fare, with well-drawn characters and a real plot that "appears frequently enough to hold the play together." None of the other critics were convinced, however, with the *New York Herald* (June 9, 1903) complaining that, even though the cast was well rehearsed in the material, the "stupid" book "wasn't worthy of Harry B. Smith." In spite of critically acclaimed performances by Blanche Ring and much of the rest of the cast, the audience did not take to *The Blonde in Black*, and the show retired gracefully from the Knickerbocker Theatre after five weeks.

Smith spent the rest of the summer polishing the musicals scheduled to open in the fall and working out the production details for *A Girl from Dixie* (often refered to as *The Girl from Dixie*), a show he had been inspired to write in the autumn of 1902 because of the typically enthusiastic response "Dixie" receives when played in a restaurant. Because northerners seemed to welcome the song in a casual setting, Smith felt that it would be a sensation performed on stage in an appropriate situation. Smith had enjoyed his experience as co-producer for *The Liberty Belles* and was determined to produce *A Girl from Dixie* himself, taking Nixon and Zimmerman, members of the Theatrical Syndicate, as his partners. During the summer, in a rare collaboration with the syndicate, Sam S. Shubert joined the project, replacing Smith as titular producer of the show.

The musical comedy gave its world premiere on September 7, 1903, at Young's Pier Music Hall in Atlantic City, New Jersey, and by the time it reached the Madison Square Theatre in New York City on December 14, no less than thirteen composers were credited with the score. "Dixie" had been interpolated into the second-act finale, but the response to the

MESSRS. SAM S. SHUBERT AND NIXON & ZIMMERMAN

PRESENT

A GIRL FROM DIXIE

A Musical Comedy, in Two Acts, by H. B. SMITH.

CAST OF CHARACTERS.

LORD DUNSMORE, "object, matrimony" .... FERDINAND GOTTSCHALK
LUDWIG REGENBORGEN, village music teacher .... D. L. DON
JACK RANDOLPH, professor of everything, at the Grammar School, Tamarack, Maryland .... ALBERT HART
SQUIRE MINK, of the Tamarack bar, legal and otherwise .. GEORGE A. SCHILLER
EDWARD BRANDON, a lawyer's clerk .... CHARLES H. BOWERS
NICK CALVERT, a school boy .... WILMER H. BENTLEY
NAPOLEON LEE, who "worked for de Calverts when dey all was rich," CHARLES K. FRENCH
MARIA LOUISA, his wife .... CHARLES H. SHEFFER
JEFFERSON PAYNE (school boys) .... ALBERT J. MARSHALL
BOB MARSHALL (school boys) .... VERNON H LEE
BILL DOUGLAS .... D. M. LUMSDEN
JIM SMALL .... W. L. HOBART
KITTY CALVERT, "best old family in Maryland, and the worst old clothes," IRENE BENTLEY
BESS JACKSON .... EVELYN NESBIT
MAUD MABEL EARL, whose papa owns the cigar factory .... DOROTHY DONNER
IMOGENIA .... ROSE HART
SALLY SUMPTER (school girls) .... ESTHER LYONS
MALVINA CARROLL (school girls) .... BELLE DESMOND
DORA (college girls) .... MABEL VERNE
ALIC (college girls) .... ADA VERNE
EDITH (college girls) .... OLGA MAY
HELEN (college girls) .... LORRAINE OSBORNE

MEMBERS OF THE HORSE SHOE HUNT CLUB—Misses May, Smyth, Grant, Muller, Holmes, Verne and Osborne. Messrs. Marshall, Lee, Booley, O'Brien, Hobart and Bentley.

USHERS AT KITTY'S WEDDING REHEARSAL—Messrs. Roberts, Bohannon, Pooley, Brengle, Lumsden, McArthur, Hall, O'Brien, Hobart, Lee and Marshall.

BRIDESMAIDS—Misses Grant, May, Osborne, A. Verne, M. Verne, Holmes, Smyth and Muller.

Playbill for *A Girl from Dixie*

tune in a theater was precisely the opposite to that in a restaurant, and the song was cut after a week. The plot of the musical, set in the South just after the Civil War, involves Kitty Calvert (Irene Bentley), a descendant of a poor though aristocratic Maryland family who suddenly inherits a fortune. The money really belongs to Nick Calvert (Wilmer H. Bentley), Kitty's cousin, but he generously lies about his parentage so that Kitty may keep the cash. As soon as Kitty, his stepdaughter, begins to behave like an heiress—going to a fashionable college and keeping a luxurious home in New York City—Angelo Catalani (Arnold Daly), a disreputable Italian musician, arranges a marriage between her and Lord Dunsmore (Ferdinand Gottschalk), an opportunistic member of the British nobility. When the time for the dowry settlement arrives, however, it comes out that Nick, not Kitty, is the rightful heir, and Lord Dunsmore immediately loses interest in the girl. Free of her responsibility to marry into the aristocracy, Kitty finds happiness with Edward Brandon (Charles H. Bowers), a young lawyer, and Nick, who ultimately divides the fortune with his cousin, marries his sweetheart, Bess Jackson (Evelyn Nesbit).

A Girl from Dixie was the second show that Smith wrote as a vehicle for Irene Bentley, the chorus girl George Lederer wanted to turn into a star. Critics were not effusive about Bentley's first starring role in *The Wild Rose*, suggesting that her acting was unexceptional, her voice sweet but thin, and her personality far from magnetic. To make the actress as comfortable as possible, Smith had fashioned the character of Rose after Bentley's role in *The Strollers*, even to the point of interpolating one of her songs from that show. The best the critics could say about her performance, however, was that she was vivacious and comely in the role. In *A Girl from Dixie*, the notices were not much better. The *New York Clipper* (December 19, 1903) praised her for looking good in a variety of costumes and being expressive in her songs, but noted that "her vocal powers are not well developed, for she does not attempt any sustained effort in singing or reaching high notes." The *Dramatic Mirror* (December 26, 1903) complimented her on a vivacious and lively performance that pleased the audience, but complained that she made "no attempt at characterization, and varied her dialect between Southern, lower East Side, and Tenderloin with the utmost unconcern." It did not seem to matter to the author (and producer) that his leading lady was not in the same league as Marie Cahill, Blanche Ring, or Lulu Glaser, as far as the critics were concerned. To him, she was bright and beautiful and extraordinarily clever, and Harry was in love with Irene Bentley. Smith and his wife,

Lena, had been leading separate lives since the turn of the century. Much of his royalty income was spent in an attempt to win a reasonable financial settlement with his soon-to-be former wife, though, even after the divorce was granted, hundreds of letters passed between them regarding Lena's ever-increasing monetary demands.

Smith's romantic attentions to his star did not cloud his managerial responsibilities. Like *The Liberty Belles*, *A Girl from Dixie* was designed as cheaply as possible, with a relatively small cast, no extravagant settings, and the few opportunities for elaborate costumes reserved for the star. A number of composers were hired to provide a popular-sounding *potpourri* score aimed at producing hits, and hits there were. "The Sunflower and the Sun" by Will Marion Cook, and "The Lover's A.B.C." and "Bubbles," both by Max Witt, were singled out as the most attractive musical numbers. "Bubbles" even allowed for an inexpensive, though impressive, stage effect that involved everyone on stage blowing soap bubbles that glistened "like opals" under red and green lights. Critics complained that the production looked "economical" on every level, and the audience, for once, was in agreement. The show only managed twenty-six performances in New York, and never to a full house.

On September 14, 1903, the week after *A Girl from Dixie* opened in Atlantic City, the Frank Daniels Opera Company, under the management of Charles Dillingham, presented *The Office Boy* for the first time at the Star Theatre in Buffalo, New York. The show had been originally announced in the *New York Clipper* (June 20, 1903) as a vehicle for Frank Daniels, with Clifton Crawford advertised as composer, but by the time Smith's adaptation of *Le jockey malgré lui*, by Paul Gavault and Maurice Ordonneau (music by Victor Roger), went into rehearsal, Ludwig Englander was the composer of record. While the star and writers were highly experienced in creating and touring a musical, the thirty-five-year-old manager was not. Charles Dillingham had been the drama critic for the *New York Evening Sun*, and a press agent and production assistant for producer Charles Frohman, but he had never before produced a show on his own. On November 2, when *The Office Boy* opened at the Victoria Theatre in New York City, it was the beginning of a long and successful career for the producer, and an association with Smith that would last the rest of their lives.

Smith enjoyed Dillingham. He was a fine gentleman with taste and enthusiasm and an irrepressible predilection for practical jokes. Early on in their association, the producer convinced a young actress that William

Shakespeare was an old friend of his father and that he was in possession of some of their correspondence. To carry off the ruse, he even went so far as to create an antique-looking letter addressed to "My beloved friend Dillingham," and signed, "Thine sincerely, William Shakespeare." The actress made a fool of herself convincing her friends that the document was genuine, until she discovered that Shakespeare had, in fact, died in 1616 and could not have known the producer's father. Though the woman was less than amused at being deceived so easily, Smith took an immediate liking to the deceiver.

The Office Boy begins in a law office where the secretaries and office boys all want to be opera singers. They threaten to go on strike to collect their back pay, but since their salaries are locked up in the safe, they have to wait until two burglars sneak into the office and blow the safe open. From the rubble emerges Noah Little (Frank Daniels), an office boy who had fallen asleep inside the apparatus. He explains that he is in love with Euphemia (Louise Gunning), an aristocratic girl, whom he has led to believe that he is a member of the firm. Euphemia's father, Tobias Van Twiller (Sydney Toler), owns a private racetrack behind his mansion. When Noah goes to the house to deliver a message for the firm, he is mistaken for a famous jockey, Rider Little (Alfred Hickman), and forced to put on a jockey's uniform and ride a feisty colt. When he returns battered from the ordeal, he tells Euphemia that he is only an office boy, but in typical musical comedy fashion, she loves him anyway.

Although the plot was flimsy, the critics did not appear to care. There was just enough fun and music to allow the star's personality to shine through, and that, by itself, could propel the evening. The *Dramatic Mirror* (November 14, 1903) described Daniels's role as one that gives free reign to the exploitation of his comic abilities:

> He is a born comedian, and is gifted by nature with a very mobile countenance. Every muscle of his face is as well trained as the biceps and triceps of Sandow, and he makes each do its full duty for the amusement of the public. Each new contortion of the eyebrows, chin, forehead and cheeks was good for a laugh, and as one or all of the muscles were kept in constant motion the audience was very happy while the star was on the stage.

After the first act, Daniels interpolated a burlesque comedy monologue that made such a hit with the audience on opening night that it was permanently added to the show.

Typical of star vehicles, not all of the musical hits of the performance had lyrics by Smith or music by Englander. Daniels was particularly successful with a much encored interpolation, "I'm on the Water Wagon Now," by Paul West and John W. Bratton, and his opening number, "I Thought Wrong," was by R. G. Knowles and Richard Morton. Eva Tanguay, however, in the role of Claire de Lune, scored hits with two of Smith and Englander's tunes, "Summer Proposals," a character patter song, and "Plain Mamie O'Hooley," a Bowery-style waltz, in which she was joined by Daniels and two boys from the chorus, impersonating Bowery hoodlums. As Euphemia, Louise Gunning had romantic waltzes, coloratura marches, and *schottische* ditties, all designed to show off her celebrated top notes. The sweetness of her voice was hampered, however, by poor articulation, a deficiency that extended to the dialogue as well. Among the supporting actors whose work was noticed by the critics, Sydney Toler, who would become famous as Charlie Chan on film, was judged "amusingly dignified" as Euphemia's father.

Everything about the production was expressive of Dillingham's style of producing: the chorus was large and good-looking, the book and musical numbers were tight and attractively staged, and the costumes and scenery were lavish, but all in good taste. Frank Daniels kept the machine running for sixty-six performances in New York before the company headed out for a long and lucrative tour, while Smith and Dillingham had already moved on to other projects. A week after *The Office Boy* opened at the Victoria Theatre, producer and librettist were in Washington, D.C., about to unveil Metropolitan Opera diva Fritzi Scheff in her comic opera debut.

Chapter 6

"If I Only Had a Theatre on Broadway"

Viennese lyric soprano Fritzi Scheff had come to America in 1901 under contract with impressario Maurice Grau to sing at the Metropolitan Opera House. While she performed important principal roles—Papagena in Mozart's *Die Zauberflöte*, Musetta in Puccini's *La bohème*, Cherubino in Mozart's *Le nozze di Figaro*, Nedda in Leoncavallo's *I pagliacci*—Scheff was dissatisfied. She had come to America to be a headliner, and she soon realized that the Metropolitan Opera House was not the place for her. She began to explore the possibilities of appearing in operettas where her lyrical voice could be put to more lucrative (if not better) use, and in March 1902, the *Dramatic Mirror* announced that, under the management of the Shubert Brothers, Scheff would star in a new Smith–de Koven comic opera in the coming season. However, the singer did not like de Koven's music, so nothing came of that project, but Fritzi was still determined to appear in light opera. Almost a year passed before the *Dramatic Mirror* (February 21, 1903) revealed that the singer was to be under the management of a relatively unknown producer, Charles

Dillingham, and that her operetta debut would be an adaptation from the French, later revealed to be Ivan Caryll's *The Duchess of Dantzig* (based on *Madame Sans-Gêne*, by Victorien Sardou and Emile Moreau). Even though Ziegfeld had been courting the singer to appear in his production of *The Red Feather*, Scheff decided to go with the lesser-known producer. A composer she did not like, de Koven, was writing the music for Ziegfeld's show, and Dillingham had promised her $1,000 a week, substantially more than she was earning in grand opera, and sumptuously mounted vehicles that would showcase her talents.

Early in the summer, the diva changed her mind about the project, and Dillingham commissioned Smith and Victor Herbert to provide a vehicle for his temperamental, albeit charming, Viennese songbird. Smith produced another period libretto, *Babette*, set in seventeenth-century Europe during the Spanish occupation of the Netherlands. The title character, a professional Dutch letter writer (Scheff), tries to intercept a message from the King of Spain to the King of France (Erroll Dunbar). Helped by her father, Mondragon (Eugene Cowles), a soldier of fortune, and her sweetheart (Richie Ling), a painter named Marcel—all pretending to be itinerant performers—she convinces the stagestruck Spanish messenger, Baltazar (Edward J. Connelly), and his daughter, Vinette (Ida Hawley), to travel disguised as strolling players while she and her companions masquerade as Spanish emissaries. The ruse is discovered and Babette and company are imprisoned, but she manages to gain the pardon of the French King by charming him with her singing voice. Having forestalled Spain's negotiations with France, Babette and Marcel get married.

The plot is historically inaccurate since the Spanish occupied the Netherlands in the sixteenth century, but the spectacle afforded by setting the third act at Versailles was of far more importance, and neither Victor Herbert nor Fritzi Scheff were concerned with the historical truth. Herbert enjoyed the opportunity of writing for a singer of Scheff's caliber, and the diva, enraptured by Herbert's music, was thrilled with a role that would allow her to play a peasant girl, a strolling player, a Spanish cavalier, and a French court lady.

Babette, a "romantic comic opera," opened at the New National Theatre in Washington, D.C., on November 9, 1903, to a large and sophisticated audience made up of Capitol Hill dignitaries, including President Theodore Roosevelt and his family. The crowd and the critics greeted the work, the star, and the spectacle with great enthusiasm. The book was thought to be "thoroughly interesting," the music was in

Herbert's "happiest vein," and the star judged to have "unique ability" and a "magnetic personality." The company of thirty-two speaking roles and a chorus of sixty were found to be "talented" and "effectively strong and tuneful," and the production was lauded for its "splendid scale."

A week later, *Babette* was welcomed by an appreciative New York audience at the Broadway Theatre. The critics were unanimous in their praise of the star, the music, and the production, but mixed in their view of Smith's text. The *New York Clipper* (November 21, 1903) called Smith's lyrics "well turned and clever," and the book "a very convenient peg on which to hang the many bright features of the performance." The *Dramatic Mirror* (November 28, 1903) was less tolerant, saying that the plot is "far from strong, and its mechanism is generally annoyingly crude." The *New York Times* (November 17, 1903) was even harsher:

> Mr. Smith is known as one of the largest manufacturers in this country of comic opera librettos, which of late years have been remarkably free from comic spirit in their conception and of wit in their dialogue, and the book of *Babette* has little that will tend to injure the reputation.

As *Babette* was beginning its Broadway career, the *Dramatic Mirror* (November 28, 1903) announced that it would close on January 4, 1904, to accommodate another production scheduled to open at the theater. A week later, Fritzi Scheff and company were at the Colonial Theatre in Boston, starting a tour that would take *Babette* throughout the East and Midwest for the rest of the season.

Harry continued to pump out librettos, both on commission and on speculation. He completed two musical comedies trading on orientalism in March, one named for a Japanese camellia, *Japonica*, and the other, titled *A China Doll*, capitalizing on the mechanical doll routine in *The Jewel of Asia*. On May 10, 1904, he registered for copyright a unique mixed-racial script called *The Southerners*, produced on May 19 by George Lederer at the Hyperion Theatre in New Haven, where it scored a great success. On May 23, the show opened on Broadway at the New York Theatre, advertised as "A Musical Study in Black and White," and attributing its book and lyrics to Will Mercer, a pseudonym for Will Marion Cook, who also composed the music, and Richard Grant, a pseudonym for Harry B. Smith. The plot begins in the present as Uncle Daniel (Eddie Leonard in blackface), a former slave, dreams of the old days on his master's plantation in 1830. Leroy Preston (William Gould) is a benevolent slaveholder whose inclination to free his slaves is blocked by his need to remain socially acceptable to his neighbors. After an argument with his sweetheart, Polly Drayton (Elfie Fay), he goes off the join the navy, leaving instructions that his slaves may only be transferred to plantation owners who are inclined to treat them kindheartedly. Once he is gone, Brannigan Bey (Junie McCree), a villainous and oppressive "Irish Turk," attempts to take possession of the slaves so that he can own Parthenia (Vinie Daly), a light-skinned slave girl, the longtime object of his lust. Polly disguises herself as a sailor so that she can follow Preston to sea and inform him firsthand about what is happening at his plantation. The couple resolves their differences, and Leroy returns home in time to prevent his slaves from being sold to Bey.

The Southerners was among the earliest attempts to present an integrated cast on the Broadway stage. White actors played all the speaking roles while African American performers appeared in specialty acts, such as a sextette of children in "squirrelesque garb" performing "The Chipmunk and the Squirrel," and a singing and dancing chorus, with Ida Forsyne featured as a solo dancer and Abbie Mitchell, Will Marion Cook's wife, a vocal soloist. The reviews were quick to note the tension in the audience on opening night when a racially integrated cast appeared onstage. The *New York Times* (May 24, 1904) noted that patrons "trembled in their seats" when a real African American chorus appeared to dance the cakewalk. Once it appeared that "the spirit of harmony" would overcome racial boundaries onstage and off, the *Times* concluded: "There is a large public for this sort of thing, and beyond question it will carry the show well into the summer months. For those who like black and white, this black and white is all right." The *New York Clipper* (May 28, 1904) found that the "bright" lyrics and racial issues more than made up for the absence of plot and witty dialogue, and the *Herald* (May 24, 1904) predicted that the show "will catch Broadway surely." Smith and Cook produced a ragtime score ranging from haunting ballads, "As the Sunflower Turns to the Sun," to spirited marches, "It's Allus de Same in Dixie," with "Dandy Dan" and "Mandy Lou" (lyrics by R. C. McPherson) singled out as the musical hits of the evening.

The critics were too hopeful in their expectations of the musical's drawing power, because after thirty-six performances, *The Southerners* was withdrawn. Harry B. Smith continued to produce, however, and on August 8, three more scripts were registered for copyright, two comedies, *Our Friend the Baron* and *The Second Fiddle*, and a musical comedy adapted from *The Blonde in Black*, called *The Sambo Girl.* The ink

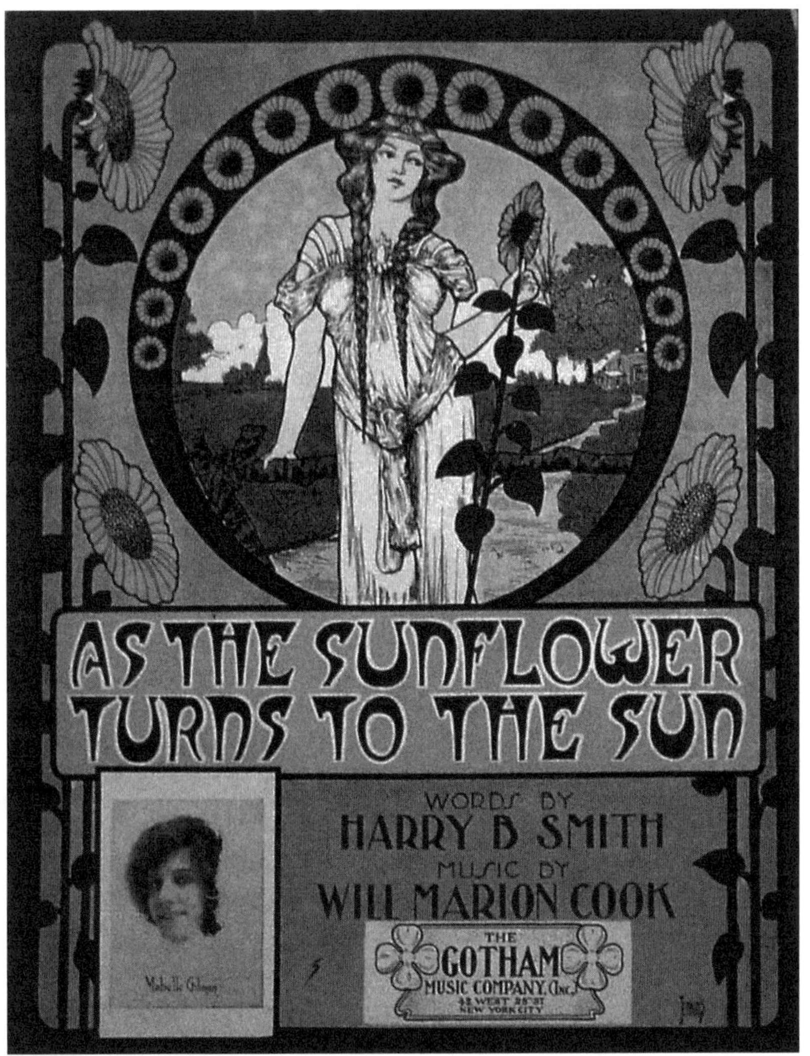

"As the Sunflower Turns to the Sun" from *The Southerners*

was hardly dry on the copyright forms when Smith was back in rehearsal with two shows: his next collaboration with Ludwig Englander, *A Madcap Princess*, advertised to open at the Knickerbocker Theatre on September 5; and *The Sambo Girl*, composed by Gustave Kerker and scheduled to premiere on the same day at the Nesbitt Theatre in Wilkes-Barre, Pennsylvania.

Smith based the libretto for *A Madcap Princess* on Charles Major's novel *When Knighthood Was in Flower*, and wrote it as a vehicle for Lulu

Glaser, once the leading lady of the Francis Wilson Company. The plot follows Mary Tudor (Glaser) as she defies her brother, Henry VIII (William Pruette), and his order that she marry the decrepit King of France. She escapes from court cross-dressed as a young man and, in the last act, manages to be united with her true love, Charles Brandon (Bertram Wallis), at the Bow and String Tavern in Bristol.

This new Charles Dillingham production was "sanely enjoyed" by a large audience on opening night, and the critics applauded it as an entertainment that merely entertained, free from "pestilential 'song hits'" or topical "advertising matter" in the libretto. The *Dramatic Mirror* (September 17, 1904) offered an unusually detailed assessment of the authors' work:

> *A Madcap Princess* is real comic opera, and as such it is welcome to the local stage. Faults it has in plenty, but the form is there, and is much to be admired. The plot is legitimately worked out, and the score, while not brilliant, is a complete musical structure. Particularly pleasing was it to hear real finales in place of the now customary medleys. The main fault with the piece is that it is entirely too plainly a vehicle for a star. However important and interesting a person the late Mary Tudor, Princess of England, may have been she was not the sole representative of the human race in her day and generation. But she is made to appear almost so in the opera, and the result is that the spectator yearns now and again to turn his gaze from the central figure to the other personages in the picture. . . . Another fault—possibly, to an extent, a necessary fault—is the employment by Mr. Smith of modern terms, allusions and slang in the dialogue. Princess Mary Tudor spoke in the language that is best employed by Sixth Avenue sales ladies and cashiers during their exuberant hours at Coney Island. Surely an English Princess should speak the King's English. The lyrics were neither above nor below Mr. Smith's standard.

After forty-eight performances, *A Madcap Princess* headed out on tour, where it regularly crossed paths with *The Sambo Girl*, designed as a starring vehicle for Eva Tanguay, now advertised as "The Queen of Vivacity." Produced by F. M. Norcross, the show is simply a remake of *The Blonde in Black*, with new *dramatis personae* and all blonde and black allusions removed. The musical hits of the earlier show composed by

Gustave Kerker are retained, and amplified with four interpolated songs composed by Harry O. Sutton with lyrics by Jean Lenox: "In the Studio," "My Little Firefly," "Ragtime," and "I Don't Care," soon to become Eva Tanguay's signature tune. Smith added material as well, most notably, "Morality's a Matter of Geography," borrowed from *The Billionaire*, and "If I Only Had a Theatre on Broadway," a topical song borrowed from the libretto of *A China Doll*, spoofing popular celebrities such as Sarah Bernhardt, Henry Irving, and Ellen Terry, as well as current theatrical practices:

I'll introduce a feature that I'm very sure attracts
Preventing thirsty men from going out between the acts
A pipeline from the nearest bar will run to ev'ry guest
You only press the button and the bar-keep' does the rest.
So you can get most anything from Burgundy to Bass
By just pretending to look through my patent opera glass.
All stingy men will like this for they will not have to treat
It will save a lot of trouble, also save the ladies' feet.

The Sambo Girl, advertised as *The Musical Spark*, did well in Pennsylvania. Critics in Wilkes-Barre found Kerker's music "original and tuneful" and Smith's book funny, with "a laugh in nearly every line." When *The Sambo Girl* moved to the Columbia Theatre in Washington, D.C., on September 26, however, the reaction was wildly different. The *Washington Post* (September 27, 1904) announced apologetically that Eva Tanguay chose the wrong vehicle to display her stellar qualities. Pleased to note the presence of a beautiful chorus, handsome staging, and the occasional catchy melody, the reviewer felt that the book was lacking in coherence, the characters were uninteresting, and the comedy was forced "from beginning to end." Even the star's entrance, when Tanguay is literally "thrown through the window" by a series of loud explosions, seemed to miss its mark. Designed to unveil the actress in a breathless flurry of excitement, Smith followed the spectacular stage business with a long explanatory monologue, filled with antique puns, perhaps better suited for vaudeville than musical comedy:

You see I started out from the Hotel de Veal, that's where they give you cutlets for dinner every day. Yes; started out in my little pink auto. Oh, you should have seen us as well scooted down the Boy de Boloney. That's where the sausage factory

Eva Tanguay in *The Sambo Girl*

> is. . . . We knocked a chip of Toolerees and broke a piece out of the Loover. Twenty Johnny Dams followed us yelling blue murder. . . . All of a sudden—bif-bang! we ran into the Art dee Triumphy.

It is not surprising that the Washington reviewer concluded that *The Sambo Girl* resembled an elaborate variety show.

The day Eva Tanguay opened in Washington, Harry registered a one-act comedy for copyright, an up-to-date farce called *Seeing New York*, and started polishing his old adaptations of *Fatinitza* and *Boccaccio* for Fritzi Scheff and Charles Dillingham. While waiting for his next scheduled opening in New York, he also started an adaptation of *Giroflé-Girofla*, by Albert Vanloo and Eugène Leterrier (music by Charles Lecocq), and another musical comedy libretto for Victor Herbert.

On November 19, 1904, *A China Doll* opened at the Majestic Theatre in New York after several months on the road. Produced by Fred C. Whitney—the Detroit producer who had so much success with the Smith–de Koven opera *Rob Roy*—scored by Alfred E. Aarons, a popular ragtime composer, and written by Smith in collaboration with his brother, Robert, the musical told the story of a Mandarin's daughter, Pee Chee San (Helen Royton), whose mechanical doll has been stolen. She refuses to marry Hi See (Corinne), the son of the local police chief, Sing Lo (Arthur Cunningham), until the toy is recovered. In Hong Kong, where the action takes place, it is customary to pay a reward to the thieves, so Hanki (George C. Boniface Jr.), a juggler, and Hoochee (Albert Hart), a "cannon-ball tosser," persuade Cerise (Adele Rafter), a Paris milliner, imported as a governess to the Mandarin's daughters, to impersonate the doll so that they can claim the reward. In the second act, the bogus thieves discover that, in Hong Kong, it is also customary to execute the thieves after they have received the reward, so that the owner can recover both his property and the reward money. Matters become even more complicated when a local fisherman appears with the original mechanical doll, and Pee Chee, who was content with the bogus doll, now refuses to marry Hi See until the matter of the two dolls is resolved. Hanki and Hoochee disguise themselves as agents of the gods and convince the chief of police to release his prisoners, while Cerise changes back to the French milliner. With only a single doll left, Pee Chee embraces it as her own and marries Hi See.

The *New York Times* (November 20, 1904) noted that the book was "capable," and provided the possibilities for a "lively variety of effects," but had only a few "of the simon pure Smith scintillations of wit." A possible reason for this is the fact that the show that opened in New York was not the show Harry and Robert Smith wrote for the road. An earlier text shows half the characters with different names and identities, the most notable difference appearing in the role of Cerise, which does not exist in the original version. In the earlier text, Bonnie Brierly, an American vaudeville singer, impersonates the mechanical doll and, in the last scenes of the musical, disguises herself as a Parisian chanteuse to seduce the chief of police into letting her friends off the hook. When the show was "hurriedly polished and rubbed up" for New York, Bonnie's climactic French impersonation became the entire character. In addition, the original *dramatis personae* allowed foreigners to be the bogus thieves and criminal investigators. Instead of Hoochee and Hanki, the group consisted of Walker Foote, the manager of the Trans-Pacific All-Star Vaudeville Company, Sampson Muckles, a strong man, Daniel Gaggs, a clown, Barker, a glass eater, and La Belle Daisy, a tightrope artist and juggler.

The existence of American performers in Hong Kong allowed for cross-cultural humor that is out of place in the New York script. Early in act one, Barker is tossed out of a shop by two Chinamen who denounce him in Chinese. He complains about not being able to eat breakfast because the vase he began to chew contained the ashes of one of the grandparents of the shopkeepers. His companions attempt to console him:

> MUCKLES: It is pretty tough on you to live in a country where they don't use glass windows.
>
> GAGGS: Cheer up, Barker, as long as you're in China you'll never have a pane in your stomach.
>
> BARKER: I'm sick of China.
>
> WALKER: Well, don't eat so much of it. What can you expect? Last time the doctor prescribed for you, you threw away the medicine and ate the bottle.
>
> MUCKLES: It's those looking-glass sandwiches you're always eating between meals.
>
> WALKER: I told you to stop eating thermometers. It's the Fahrenheit of impudence. They're bound to affect you by degrees.

Although the puns are of the groan-eliciting variety, coming from American vaudevillians who trade on such things, they are hardly inappropriate. To put lines such as these into the mouths of Oriental characters creates a very different impression. It is no wonder that the large opening night audience greeted the show less than enthusiastically, even though the production had been elaborately mounted, using real silk and

Oriental colors, and several of the Smith-Aarons songs ("How to Be Happy Though Married," "The Dew on the Heather," and "Mistakes Are Apt to Be Made") were warmly received. *A China Doll* ultimately failed to find an audience and closed after eighteen performances, nearly two weeks short of its advertised four-week engagement.

On November 21, two days after Smith's oriental musical appeared at the Majestic, his play *The Second Fiddle* was hurriedly unveiled at the Criterion Theatre by Charles Dillingham, in an attempt to take advantage of the theater's sudden availability. R. C. Carton's *The Rich Mrs. Repton* had closed there abruptly after five performances, and Dillingham saw an opportunity for bringing Smith's play, then in the midst of a western tour, straight to Broadway. Produced as a vehicle for Dutch comedian Louis Mann, *The Second Fiddle* gave its world premiere on September 12, 1904, at the Star Theatre in Buffalo, New York. Based on a story Smith had written for the literary magazine *The Current*, the plot involves Leopold Baron von Walden (Mann), a composer with an opera no one wants to produce. He leaves Vienna, where he played second fiddle in an orchestra, and travels to Paris, where his stepsister, Paula (Georgia Welles), has a job singing in an opera chorus. She has been guaranteed the leading role in a new opera by Count Alfred de Cardinet (Percy Lyndal), provided she will marry him. When she learns of Leopold's unfortunate circumstances, she accepts the Count's conditions to benefit her brother, and Leopold, realizing that the Count has stolen the opera from him, refrains from revealing the theft so that his sister can have her big break.

Paula, it seems, was chosen as the replacement for the original leading lady, Fanchonette (Dorothy Revell), who took ill during rehearsals. When the diva discovers that a rich Russian baron (William Hassan) plans to attend the performance, however, she miraculously recovers from her illness. To safeguard his sister's opportunity, Leopold masquerades as the Russian baron and convinces Fanchonette to elope with him before the opera begins. Paula's operatic debut is a triumph, and the date for her wedding to Cardinet is set. Just as the ceremony is about to take place, Leopold's original manuscript is discovered in the possession of the Count, who is unmasked as a thief. Paula is spared a marriage to a man whom she does not love, and Leopold is feted as a brilliant new opera composer.

In an attempt to avoid the critics calling the play "typically Smithian," Harry presented it under the pseudonym Gordon Blake, and to some extent, the stratagem worked to his advantage. The *Dramatic Mirror* (December 3, 1904) predicted that the play "is sure to be a box-office success, for it all goes with a whoop and rush that allow no time for reflection, and the world will laugh with it." And even though critics found little "art" in the writing or production, they admitted that *The Second Fiddle* was a distinctly funny play, "for those who want to forget and roar." The greatest complaint, oddly enough, was leveled not at the author, but the star, whose Dutch dialect comedy and eccentric mannerisms tended to remove any semblance of reality from the character. One critic even expressed interest in seeing the role played "straight," just as it was written, "by a good comedian who had distinction of manner and real pathos." Rare certainly were notices claiming that Smith's writing was superior to his performers.

In his autobiography, Smith reported having trouble with Louis Mann during rehearsals for *The Second Fiddle*. Evidently, the author objected to the changes Mann intended on making to the script, and a mildly heated argument ensued. Exasperated by Smith's insistance on preserving the original text, Mann attempted to reason with him, and playing upon the author's well-known appreciation of Elizabethan theater, he said, "Why, you shouldn't mind my making suggestions. Shakespeare got some of his best results working with Garrick." Smith was no stranger to "improvements" made to his shows by star comedians, even though, as often as not, the substitution of slang and horseplay for the author's original attempt at humor weakened the text. If the interpolations succeed, the critics generally praise the actors. If they fail, the blame rests solely with the author for filling the script full of gags. In the *New York Herald* (May 8, 1904), when asked if a writer could protect his work against unwanted "improvements," Smith replied:

> An author, if he is moderately amiable, does not wish to add to the annoyances of manager and company by saying: "Produce my piece as it is written or I take my toys and won't play in your yard." A manager may object to a comedian's introduction of objectionable features, but if he protests Mr. Comedian may say, "I'll do it your way, but it will be a failure." Then the manager gets frightened and says, in effect, "Go ahead; make it funny any way, no matter how you do it.". . . A comedian told me once that he had put a hundred and sixteen laughs into the American version of a successful English piece. Next time I

> saw him he assured me that he had put nearly two hundred laughs in the piece. All the same, the play was a failure in America, although a great success in England. I suppose the American comedian had made it so funny that audiences couldn't stand it.

The Second Fiddle remained at the Criterion Theatre for a month, long enough to pay its bills and return to the road. Just as it was closing, the day after Christmas, Fritzi Scheff was opening in Franz von Suppé's *Fatinitza* at the Broadway Theatre in a new up-to-date adaptation by Harry B. Smith. A month later, she appeared in Smith's version of Charles Lecocq's *Giroflé-Girofla*, and completed her three-month engagement in March with Smith's revised adaptation of *Boccaccio*. The critics applauded Scheff in every role, but found Smith's topical allusions and modernization of text only successful in *Fatinitza*, where the original comic situations were substantial enough to support the changes.

In spring 1905, Harry completed three new musical comedies, *American Girl*, *Papa's Bride*, and *The Parisian Model*, the last designed as a vehicle for Anna Held, who had not had a Broadway success since *The Little Duchess*. Waiting for *Miss Dolly Dollars*, his next musical comedy with Victor Herbert, to go into rehearsal at the end of the summer, Smith produced another full libretto, *The Belle of Hong Kong*, registered for copyright on August 9, 1905, and a synopsis for *Omar*, a musical treatment of the Persian poet Omar Khayyam, advertised in September 1905 as having been purchased by Dillingham for a production in January 1906.

On August 30, 1905, *Miss Dolly Dollars*, a vehicle for Lulu Glaser, received its world premiere at the Lyceum Theatre in Rochester, New York. An American girl, Dolly Dollars (Glaser), is the daughter of Samuel Gay (Charles Bradshaw), a "condensed soup magnate," who wants his daughter to marry into European nobility. The Gays rent the English estate of the bankrupt Lord Burlingham (Melville Stewart), with whom Dolly fell in love at first sight while crossing the English Channel. At the estate, Burlingham's secretary, a bookworm named Finney Doolittle (R. C. Herz), falls in love with Bertha Billings (Olive Murray), Dolly's maid, and passes himself off as the lord of the manor. The real Lord Burlingham, consequently, plays the role of Dolly's chauffeur, much to her delight because she had vowed never to fall in love with a title. Her father discourages the relationship, preferring his daughter to pay her attentions to the many titled young men who seek to marry her, but his objections to the love-match are quickly withdrawn when it is revealed that the man she loves is a Lord.

After a triumphant opening in Rochester, *Miss Dolly Dollars* moved to the Knickerbocker Theatre in New York on September 4, where critics predicted it would "entertain New York audiences for a good many months to come." Though neither the score nor the book was considered the best work of the collaborators, the show was found to be "the best vehicle" to date to display Glaser's talents. Two songs were singled out by the notices for popularity: "An Educated Fool," a patter song in which Doolittle wonders why he knows nothing about money; and Lord Burlingham's chauvinistic waltz, "A Woman Is Only a Woman (But a Good Cigar Is a Smoke)," a sentiment borrowed from Rudyard Kipling. Although there was a lot right with *Miss Dolly Dollars*, the less-than-enthusiastic reviews destined the show for a short run. Even with transferring the production to the New Amsterdam Theatre on October 16, producer Dillingham only managed to log fifty-six performances in Manhattan before dwindling receipts sent *Miss Dolly Dollars* out on tour.

Shortly after the Smith-Herbert musical premiered in Rochester, another Smith musical opened on the road, with music by Bohemia-born composer Karl L. Hoschna, who was making his musical comedy debut. Produced by B. F. Forrester, Smith's "musical comedy with melodramatic trimmings," *The Belle of the West,* gave its first performance at the Weller Theatre in Zanesville, Ohio, on September 1, 1905. The story involved Virginia Lee (Florence Bindley), a Washington girl who accepts a position as schoolteacher in a western mining town. All of her students are full-grown, rough-and-ready men, with the exception of Bob Randolph (Jack Randolph), a young lad from New York, who is the teacher's pet. Jealous because Randolph has won Virginia's affections, the other men accuse him of robbing a stagecoach. Just as the New Yorker is about to be strung up for a crime he did not commit, Virginia manages to uncover the real culprits, and saves her sweetheart's life.

The Belle of the West took a long pre-Broadway tour, including a major stop at the Great Northern Theatre in Chicago, before opening in New York at the Grand Opera House on November 13. Though the critics were much impressed with Florence Bindley, whose popularity was so great that she could "carry a worse play than her present vehicle," neither the book, which seemed more like a collection of vaudeville turns than a musical comedy, nor the music received better than lukewarm notices. A few songs were singled out as having been encored on opening night: "Holding Hands," "My Little Lassoo," and "The Frog and the Owl." But even though the last named was performed by the star in her famous diamond dress, "always sure to create a sensation," it was not sensational enough to sustain the show for more than a week in New York.

Smith, however, appeared unconcerned with the recent string of lackluster runs, and continued manufacturing scripts at an incredible rate. He had recently completed the text of a comic opera for John Philip Sousa, scheduled for production in the spring, a "musical fantasie" called *Bric-a-Brac* was registered for copyright on October 9, 1905, and *The White Cat*, adapted from the Drury Lane pantomime by J. Hickory Wood and Arthur Collins, was already in rehearsal for a November 2 opening at the New Amsterdam Theatre, which had just been vacated by *Miss Dolly Dollars*.

In 1901, Theatrical Syndicate producers Klaw and Erlanger began to import pantomimes from Drury Lane in London in an attempt to reproduce the spectacular extravaganzas produced by David Henderson at the Chicago Opera House. Their initial experiment, *The Sleeping Beauty and the Beast*, ran a lucrative 241 performances, and the producers did not hesitate to capitalize on their success. *The White Cat* was their most recent British import, and Smith was hired to Americanize the text and provide lyrics to Ludwig Englander's music, with Jean Schwartz (music) and William Jerome (lyrics), Klaw and Erlanger's house songwriting team, contributing a number of songs as well.

The fantastic story (based on Madame d'Aulnoy's fairy tale, *La chatte blanche*) takes place in the Kingdom of Malaria, where King Jonah the Thirteenth (William T. Hodge) sends his three sons out to find the "magic golden net," promising that the winner will receive his crown. Prince Paragon (Edgar Atchison-Ely), Prince Plump (Herbert Corthell), and Prince Peerless (Maud Lambert) set out in search of the golden net, Peerless engaging the help of Princess Chiffon (Edith St. Clair), who has been transformed into a huge white cat by Hecate (Harriet Worthington), a bad fairy. Together, they manage to find the treasure and fall in love, and when the prince introduces the cat at court as his intended bride, the huge white feline transforms into a beautiful princess. In addition, the *dramatis personae* included a dancing ape (Hugh J. Ward), a burlesque comic in the guise of a superannuated fairy (William Macart), and Castilian dancers and troubadours imported from the Royal Theatre of Madrid.

The critics found the spectacle to be beyond anything previously produced by Klaw and Erlanger on the New York stage. The ballets, supervised by Ernest D'Auban, ballet-master, and Herbert Gresham and Ned Wayburn, stage directors, were judged "elaborately beautiful beyond the power of words to adequately describe." The music and lyrics were found attractive for the most part, but Smith's pun-filled book was considered "sadly lacking in humor" and surpassing the City Directory in dullness. The *Dramatic Mirror* (November 11, 1905) spoke for the rest of the critics when it suggested, "Heard by a deaf man or witnessed by a child, the piece would probably be very entertaining."

Totaling forty-six performances, *The White Cat* left the New Amsterdam Theatre before Christmas, leaving Klaw and Erlanger to wonder if perhaps the vogue for such entertainments had passed. Despite yet another failure, Smith pressed on. He registered three new scripts for copyright in February 1906: a musical comedy, *Masquerading Girl*, the libretto for Charles Dillingham, *Omar, Jr.*, and *King for a Day*, the comic opera he had been working on with John Philip Sousa about to go into rehearsal. On March 26, Smith joined Klaw and Erlanger, George M. Cohan, Sam Harris, and his one-time collaborator John J. McNally at the Court Square Theatre in Springfield, Massachusetts, for the world premiere of the new Sousa opera, under a new title, *The Free Lance.*

The story involves the bankrupt kingdoms of Braggadocia and Graftiana, each believing the other is wealthy. The Emperor of Braggadocia (Felix Haney) hopes to marry his daughter, Princess Yolanda (Nella Bergen), to Prince Florian (George Tallman), son of the Duke of Graftiana (Albert Hart). Although the parents are in agreement concerning this union, the Prince and Princess, who have never met, resent being merchandized and run away. The Emperor forces Griselda (Jeanette Lowrie), a goose girl, to masquerade as the Princess, and the Duke convinces Sigmund Lump (Joseph Cawthorn), a goatherd and one-time bandit chief, to take the Prince's place at the marriage ceremony. Because Griselda and Sigmund are already man and wife, it is no concern of theirs to be joined together a second time. Meanwhile, Prince Florian and Princess Yolanda, both disguised as peasants, have met one another and fallen in love.

After the wedding, each country discovers that the other has no money, and war is declared. Griselda, still thought to be the Princess, is made captain of Braggadocia's all-woman army, and Lump, as the Prince, leads the manly troops of Graftiana until his disguise is penetrated. Just as he is about to be executed, Mopsa (Fanny Migley), a sorceress, appears and restores Sigmund's former powers (he used to be a bandit chief with great strength in his hair until Mopsa cut it off). Once again incredibly strong and fearless, Lump hires himself out as a "free lance," a soldier on both sides of the conflict, and cleverly manipulates the war so that neither side can actually win. When a truce is called and his demands for ransom cannot be met on either side, he declares himself Sigmund I, ruler of both countries, with the blessing of the Prince and Princess, too much in love to care about who runs the government.

The Springfield critics were delighted with the production, dubbing it an immediate "hit," with lively music, an amusing book, and lyrics that had popular appeal. The first night audience called for so many encores that the performance lasted nearly four hours. Smith was happy in his collaboration with Sousa, finding no fault whatsoever with the composer, except for his piano playing:

> When Sousa played on the piano his march finale for the second act of our opera, it did not seem like a Sousa march. It sounded more like "The Maiden's Prayer" played by the little girl next door. The composer assured me that he thought it one

Jeanette Lowrie, Joseph Cawthorn, and Nella Bergen in *The Free Lance*

of his best. "Play 'The Stars and Stripes Forever,'" I suggested. He did so, and on the piano it did not sound any better than the new march, so I concluded that the latter might be good. And so it was, though it was not really heard at its best in the opera until one night when the composer was observed in the audience and called upon to conduct. The effect of the march with Sousa wielding the baton was electrifying and the audience cheered.

Sousa conducted a performance of *The Free Lance* on April 12 in Philadelphia, and the *Philadelphia Press* (April 13, 1906) noted that the performers onstage and musicians in the pit were so invigorated by the pulse of the music and cheers of the crowd that they began to march through the audience.

A week after the successful opening of his comic opera, Smith was in Chicago for the premiere of *The Three Graces*, his new three-act musical play, produced by the Chicago Opera House and scored by Stafford Waters, composer of the popular Blanche Ring standard, "The Belle of Avenue A." A large crowd gathered on April 2, 1906, to welcome the latest effort from the hometown celebrity, but what they witnessed was the plot of *Erminie*, in which the vagabond thieves of the earlier show, Cadeaux and Ravennes, have been rechristened Owen Muchmore (John Slavin) and Grimaldi Grimes (Frank Farrington). Muchmore and Grimes rob an Irish Earl (Sydney De Grey) and his son, Viscount Kilkenny (Bert Weston), of their clothes and luggage, and register at a hotel in the Catskill Mountains under the identity of the two noblemen. They discover a will among the stolen possessions, revealing that the Earl and his son are looking for the heiress to an Irish estate, and the only means of identifying her is through a particular ring, a familial heirloom, in her possession.

At the same hotel are boarded three young ladies, each with the designated ring and the name of Grace: Grace Carryl (Trixie Friganza), Grace Lyndon (Mabel Harrison), and Gracia Lindonia (Amy Ricard). One of the stipulations in the will is that the girl is supposed to marry the Viscount, so as Owen interviews each young lady, he flirts with her as well. But the thieves are not satisfied with their latest haul, so when everyone is off to bed, they set out to rob the hotel, only to be arrested in the attempt. Meanwhile, the real Earl and Viscount have been living in a cave, dressed in the clothing of the thieves. The following afternoon, the hotel guests picnic on the grounds (in a scene highly reminiscent of *Amaryllis*, one of Smith's earliest pieces) and the Earl and Viscount sneak among them, stealing food from deserted lunch baskets. Muchmore and Grimes, released for lack of evidence, reappear in a variety of disguises until they encounter their victims wearing their old clothes. They try to pass off the Earl and Viscount as the real thieves, but the tables are turned and the noblemen regain their possessions and find the Irish heiress.

The critics were unable to see beyond the obvious similarities to *Erminie*, the *Chicago Tribune* (April 3, 1906) calling *The Three Graces* "one of Mr. Smith's 'off books,'" completely lacking in originality. Even though the reviewers admitted that there were "occasional flashes" of Smithian humor and that the lyrics were "fairly" successful, the show was dubbed a flop. Even after the notices, Chicago audiences supported the show valiantly for ten weeks, often stretching the performance time to midnight with repeated demands for encores of nearly every number and long ovations after every act. At the beginning of May, Smith returned to revise the libretto, and, as of May 21, the musical was cut to two acts and comedienne Edna Wallace Hopper and prima donna Helena Frederick were added to the cast. Although the Chicago engagement was highly popular and extremely lucrative, the lack of critical support discouraged the Opera House from attempting a New York run.

Two weeks after *The Three Graces* appeared in Chicago, *The Free Lance* was in New York, at the New Amsterdam Theatre, earning the same popular and critical response it had received previously in Springfield and Philadelphia. The *Dramatic Mirror* (April 28, 1906) praised the work as "a genuine comic opera . . . not a musical comedy," with bright dialogue and lyrics "written in a capital vein of humor." Even Smith's characteristic puns and groan-eliciting jokes were considered "pardonable because of their wit and originality." The *New York Clipper* (April 21, 1906) agreed, reiterating that Smith contributed a "briskly moving, interesting book, some bright lyrics and some funny lines." The critics were unanimous in their praise of the music and the performances, and the opening night audience was as enthusiastic as any that greeted a Harry B. Smith production. But the show was too much a comic opera to appeal to popular tastes, and after thirty-five performances, *The Free Lance* left on a six-month tour across the United States.

During the summer, while *Miss Dolly Dollars* and *The Free Lance* were touring, Smith registered the *Paris Model* (an early draft of *The Parisian Model*) for copyright, renewed his working relationship with Victor Herbert, who had been engaged as composer for *Omar, Jr.*, and put the finishing touches on *The Rich Mr. Hoggenheimer*, another collaboration with Ludwig Englander, scheduled to appear in New York in October 1906. Producer Charles Frohman had commissioned Smith to create a vehicle for Sam Bernard, centered on the character of Piggy Hoggenheimer, the role played by Bernard with great success in *The Girl from Kay's*, a British musical by Ivan Caryll and Owen Hall, the pseudomym of journalist James Davis, imported on November 2, 1903, the same day Smith's *The Office Boy* opened in New York.

On October 3, Smith's latest vehicle for Anna Held, *The Parisian Model*, appeared at the Chestnut Street Opera House in Philadelphia. This time around, Anna played "Anna," a model in a Parisian fashion salon who becomes an heiress to one million francs. She is in love with a young artist, Julien de Marsay (Henry Leoni), who has been painting her picture and who does not believe that Anna came by the money honestly. Instead of using any of Anna's money, he hopes to sell his painting in order to become rich enough to marry her, but Violette (Truly Shattuck), jealous of his affection for Anna, steals the portrait. To enable Julien to show the picture to prospective buyers, Anna steps behind the frame and pretends to be the painting. Before the couple finally tie the knot at the final curtain, however, we are treated to the antics of Silas Goldfinch (Charles Bigelow), an American millionaire chased by his wife (Mabella Baker); during the course of the play, Goldfinch disguises himself as a Mexican, Paderewski (a Polish pianist), and an old woman. The plot is also embellished with the spectacle of six chorus girls whose apparent nakedness is hidden by canvases on easels in the "I'd Like to See a Little More of You" number, sixteen chorus girls with bells on their legs and feet, laying on the floor and wiggling out a tune in the "Bells" routine, and a roller-skating finale with Anna and the entire female chorus skating around the stage. After having produced a number of clean libretti, Smith was back to work for Ziegfeld, who encouraged him to be naughty.

Cries of indecency began to hound the production on tour. In addition to the display of "nude" girls as artists' models, Held changed costume eight times during "A Gown for Each Hour of the Day," onstage in

The roller-skating chorus in *The Parisian Model*

view of the audience, with only the chorus girls providing any kind of screen. Even worse, Anna's friend, Gertrude Hoffman, cross-dressed as a man, danced a suggestive *pas de deux* with her to "La Mattchiche." It is no surprise that when *The Parisian Model* opened at the Broadway Theatre on November 27, after nearly two months on the road, the number was labeled "the most disgusting exhibition seen on Broadway this season." Though the *Dramatic Mirror* (December 8, 1906) was emphatic in its complaint that "Real merit the concoction has none, the music being reminiscent, the humor bewiskered and hoary, and the plot imperceptible," all the critics seemed to agree that the show would be popular because of its very salaciousness. And it was, remaining at the Broadway Theatre for 179 sold-out performances, followed by a yearlong tour.

To be fair, there was some "art" involved with *The Parisian Model.* Julian Mitchell's staging was highly praised, Gertrude Hoffman's impersonation of Anna Held in "A Lesson in Kissing" was found to be the "big hit" of the evening, and Smith's lyrics were singled out as having "raised the plane of his work a notch or two." Hoffman's husband Max was the composer of record, although the most often cited song by the critics for praise was an interpolation, "I Just Can't Make My Eyes Behave," with lyrics by Smith and Will D. Cobb and music by Gus Edwards.

While *The Parisian Model* was selling out and raising eyebrows on the path to New York City, another Smith musical opened on Broadway. This was *The Rich Mr. Hoggenheimer*, with music mostly by Ludwig

Gertrude Hoffman, Max Hoffman, Anna Held, and her daughter Liane Carrera

Englander, opening at Wallack's Theatre on October 22, 1906. Smith's story began at Hoggenheimer's London home during a typical afternoon tea, where an actress, Flora Fair (Georgia Caine), and her sweetheart, Hon. Percy Vere (Percy Ames), "an impecunious idiotic Englishman" who owes Hoggenheimer money, are in attendance. Hoggenheimer (Sam Bernard) receives word that his son, Guy (Edwin Nicander), living in New York, has broken off his engagement with Lady Mildred Vane

(Kathryn Hutchinson) and plans to marry Amy Leigh (Marion Garson), a poor shop girl instead. Hoggenheimer and Vere decide to go to America, telling Mrs. Hoggenheimer (Josephine Kirkwood) that her husband has been chosen as a diplomatic courier, sent to New York to avert a war. When the wife learns that Flora Fair has agreed to accompany the men on the voyage, she goes along as well to spy on her husband. When the boat docks in Hoboken, New Jersey, Hoggenheimer meets Guy's fiancée and expresses his disapproval, even though he is informed that Lady Vane is in love with Ned Brandon (Ivar Anderson), a Harvard athlete, and no longer interested in his son. Finally, at a charity bazaar in Great Neck, Long Island, Amy manages to melt Hoggenheimer's objections, and Mrs. Hoggenheimer catches up with her husband, just as he is raising a glass of champagne to toast Flora Fair. To escape what could be construed as a "comprising situation," he offers to forgive Vere of his financial obligations if he would immediately announce his engagement to the actress.

Smith felt that Sam Bernard was "one of those gifted creatures who could not help being funny," and critics and audiences agreed. All Smith and Englander had to provide was a stable framework to showcase the comedian's talents. The *Dramatic Mirror* (November 3, 1906)

Sam Bernard and Georgia Caine in *The Rich Mr. Hoggenheimer*

explained that Bernard "really needs little more than a stage and a few complications, and whatever singing and dancing may be provided to embellish the play are welcome though unnecessary." Some of the Smith-Englander songs were cited as notable, although more because of their presentation than their composition: "Cupid's Auctioneer," sung by Kathryn Hutchinson; "Little Old America for Me" (evoking "Little Old New York Is Good Enough for Me" from *Hurly Burly*), sung by Ivar Anderson; and "This World Is a Toy Shop" (recalling "Life Is a Toy Shop" from *The Casino Girl*), performed by Georgia Caine. Two songs added by the young Jerome Kern were also singled out, "Poker Love," with lyrics by Paul West, and "The Bagpipe Serenade," but the runaway hit of the show was "Any Old Time at All," an interpolation composed by Jean Schwartz, with lyrics by William Jerome.

The Rich Mr. Hoggenheimer remained at Wallack's Theatre for 187 performances, and once again Smith was in the ascendancy with two hits in a row. A month after *Hoggenheimer* opened and just as *The Parisian Model* was about to debut in New York, Harry married Irene Bentley in Boston on November 23, 1906. She had been hired for the American debut of *The Belle of Mayfair*, the recent London success by Charles H. E. Brookfield and Cosmo Hamilton, whose *Romeo and Juliet*–like plot was anonymously adapted by Smith for producer Thomas W. Ryley, one of the triad of managers who brought *Florodora* to the Casino Theatre in 1900. Following its American premiere at the Lyceum Theatre in Rochester, New York, on October 29, *The Belle of Mayfair* (with music by Leslie Stuart) opened in Boston on November 19 for a two-week run. The Smiths spent their honeymoon preparing for the New York City opening at Daly's Theatre on December 3, when the critic for the *New York Herald* (December 4, 1906) unwittingly complimented Smith's uncredited contribution: "While 'The Belle of Mayfair' is 'quite English, you know,' it is not so awfully English but that New Yorkers can enjoy and appreciate it. It might well have all happened on Murray Hill as in Mayfair, and the private park might as well have been at Newport as on the Thames." The *New York Clipper* (December 8, 1906) agreed, noting that "bright lines and good comedy situations are well spread through the work." The leading ladies, Christie MacDonald and Irene Bentley (Smith), judged outstanding in their performances, attractive songs and settings, and dialogue that was "always interesting, frequently brilliant" propelled *The Belle of Mayfair* through 140 performances.

Frank Daniels in *The Tattooed Man*

After a year's delay, on February 11, 1907, Charles Dillingham produced *Omar, Jr.*, under a new title, *The Tattooed Man*, at the Academy of Music in Baltimore, and a week later moved the show to the Criterion Theatre in New York City. The book by Smith and A. N. C. Fowler is set in Persia, where Omar Khayam, [*sic*] Jr. (Frank Daniels), an alcoholic who believes he is a descendant of the poet Omar Khayyam, is taking care of the country in the Shah's absence. He is engaged to Leila (Sallie Fisher), but her affections are directed toward Abdallah (William P. Carleton), a Bedouin chief, with whom she plans to elope. A "wall flower," Fatima (May Vokes), overhears their plans and tells Omar, who has just discovered that his own daughter, Alma (Gertie Carlisle), supposed to be betrothed to the Shah, has affianced herself to Algy Cuffs (Harry Clarke), an American matinee idol. Enraged, Omar orders both men arrested and beheaded. Omar was born with a birthmark on his neck that resembles a beetle, and he believes that if he encounters any man with a similar birthmark, he will share that person's fate. Fatima tattoos beetles on the necks of the prisoners, and, as a result, when they bare their necks to the executioner, Omar sets them free. He permits them to marry the women of their choice, and having incurred the Shah's displeasure by allowing Alma to marry the American, Omar is punished by having to marry Fatima.

The Tattooed Man reunited Smith with Herbert and Frank Daniels, and it was Daniels who, once again, walked away with the reviews. Most of the critics carped about the book, emphasizing its reliance on comic opera formulas without capitalizing on the strengths of the performers. Still, Daniels's first appearance in a sedan chair, designed like a berth in a sleeping car with all the modern conveniences, provided the star with another spectacular entrance, while his monologue at the end of the first act (a technique borrowed from *The Office Boy*) and the few clever and funny songs noted by the critics at least provided the opportunity of showcasing his idiosyncratic talents.

Although the reviews had predicted that it would be a popular success, *The Tattooed Man* was scheduled to close two months after it opened, on April 20, 1907. However, a fire in the New York Theatre next door on the morning of April 16 caused heavy water damage at the Criterion Theatre, and the show was forced to close four days early, after fifty-nine performances. Typically, Daniels and company headed for the road, where *The Tattooed Man* found a thriving second life for the next year and a half.

Chapter 7

Follies of the Year

In the spring of 1907, while *The Parisian Model* continued its lucrative run at the Broadway Theatre, Florenz Ziegfeld Jr., approached Harry B. Smith with a novel idea. Ziegfeld had been hired by Klaw and Erlanger to produce vaudeville entertainment at the roof garden atop the New York Theatre, and Anna Held suggested that a Parisian-style revue—a satire of politics, society, popular fads, and the entertainment industry using a *compère* and *commère* (a master and mistress of ceremonies), beautiful girls, music, and spectacle—might be an attractive conclusion to the vaudeville bill. Ziegfeld wanted Smith to come up with about an hour's worth of material in the Parisian style, and since the author's earlier experiences with the revue form had been in the burlesque of contemporary plays with Weber and Fields, he welcomed the opportunity to experiment with the genre. Because the Jamestown Centenary Exposition was being held in 1907, Smith decided to use Captain John Smith and Pocahontas as *compère* and *commère* of the revue he titled *The Follies of the Year*, evoking a column he regularly contributed to

The Rambler in the 1880s called "Follies of the Day." Florenz Ziegfeld did not like the title because it did not contain thirteen letters. His lucky number was thirteen, and his successful productions—*Little Duchess* and *Parisian Model*—had thirteen letters in the title. Accordingly, Smith's title was altered to *Follies of 1907*.

Ziegfeld convinced Klaw and Erlanger to fashion the roof garden into the "Jardin de Paris," resembling an outdoor Parisian café filled with exotic plants and brightly colored awnings. As the workmen were busy refurbishing the space, Smith's speedily assembled collection of gags, sketches, and songs was put into rehearsal under the able guidance of Herbert Gresham, director, and Julian Mitchell, choreographer. As rehearsals progressed, it was discovered that the librettist had produced closer to three hours' worth of material, and the opening vaudeville entertainment was omitted from the program. Ziegfeld did not appear bothered by the scope of Smith's libretto, provided it did not have a traditional story. As Ziegfeld explained in the *Green Book Album* (January 12, 1912):

> For over a generation, librettists have stuck to the same old stories, in which a tenor makes love to a soprano, while there is a low comedian to inject necessary humor. It makes no difference whether the scene is on a mythical island, in some strange kingdom, or amid what surroundings the librettist may choose—the plots are always the same. For this reason I boldly discarded every pretense of plot.

So adamant was the producer about a lack of plot that he began a publicity campaign threatening to sue Smith if "by some mistake a plot was unearthed." He need not have worried. Smith's libretto opens with John Smith and Pocahontas miraculously alive once again after three hundred years. Determined to experience what they missed in all that time, they go to the Weary Railroad Station to buy tickets to New York City. At the station, they encounter Tony Cornstock, a burlesque of Anthony Comstock, New York's self-appointed crusader against vice, and Topsy Toolite, the quintessential soubrette, who offer to guide the visitors through the city.

Some of the sights they see are Teddy Roosevelt in his Rough Rider uniform, Andrew Carnegie and John D. Rockefeller trying to run the country, Enrico Caruso being tried by a jury of chorus girls (satirizing his conviction for disorderly behavior with three women in the monkey house of the Central Park Zoo), and Bandstand Jimmy (John Philip Sousa) and Mickey Herbertheimer (Victor Herbert) in a boxing match where the loser has to compose an opera for Oscar Hammerstein. During the tour, Captain John Smith flirts with a chorus of bathing beauties, and Pocahontas threatens to avenge his apparent infidelity by marrying a carved "Yankee Doodle Indian Boy" (a nod to George M. Cohan) standing in front of a cigar store. Topsy is arrested for indecent exposure for wearing the latest fashions and appearing as Salome in a burlesque production of Richard Strauss's opera.

On July 3, four days after *The Parisian Model* closed on Broadway, the *Follies of 1907* gave its world premiere at the Savoy Theatre in Atlantic City, New Jersey, moving to the Jardin de Paris on the 8th. The opening night was hot and humid, made even more uncomfortable by the glass dome that caused the space to feel more like a hothouse than a theater. Because the stage was cramped and shallow, the use of elaborate scenery was impossible, and much of the action had to spill over into the audience. In the finale, sixty-four girls, dressed as drummer boys, appeared onstage beating snare drums. On cue, they marched down a flight of steps and paraded through the audience up the right aisle of the theater and returned to the stage down the left aisle, to the great delight of the crowd. In addition, a "Dance of the Seven Veils" spoof of *Salome* added to the steamy temperature on the roof, as the dancer, Mlle. Dazie, removed the veils, one at a time, until policemen rushed to the stage. The dancer trembled appropriately at the prospect of being arrested, as the audience gasped nervously at the thought of a police raid. Fear turned to delight when the policemen jumped onstage and joined the dancer in a spirited can can, as the audience expressed their relief in tumultuous applause.

Many of the critics found the entertainment in "poor taste" and "coarse and vulgar," and Smith's book "feeble and emaciated" even though they were warned not to expect a plot of any kind. Few of the songs created by fourteen composers and lyricists made any lasting impression, and Ziegfeld advertised weekly alterations to the bill, dropping and adding songs—and performers—as he saw fit. Because the weekly receipts were about $20,000 for a show that cost $13,000 to mount and less than $4,000 a week to run, *Follies of 1907* managed to remain atop the New York Theatre for the rest of the summer. On August 24, the entertainment moved to the Liberty Theatre in an attempt to run through the regular season, but attendance dropped severely. Hoping to cash in on the show's summer success, Ziegfeld, Klaw, and Erlanger booked engagements in Washington D.C., Baltimore, Philadelphia, and Chicago, and increased their profits to $120,000.

While the *Follies* was earning Smith considerable royalties during the summer and fall, he was working on an adaptation of *Le paradis de Mahomet*, by Henri Blondeau (music by Robert Planquette and Louis Ganne), in collaboration with his brother, and continued to produced new plays and musicals on his own: *An Amateur Sport*, *The Happiest Man in New York*, *The Happiest Man in Town*, and *The Hero of the Day*. He had also discovered a plot that would satisfy his latest commission from Ziegfeld, Klaw, and Erlanger, who had signed a contract with Danish dancer Adeline Genée to feature her in a Broadway musical. Smith was assigned the task of creating a vehicle for a dancer who could neither act nor sing. He was first attracted to the pantomimic ballets caricatured in Thackeray's 1836 drawing, "Flore et Zephyr," but after reading an interview in the *New York Evening World* with a psychic woman who claimed to have invented a phenomenon called "The Soul Kiss," in which a non-corporeal exchange of souls leads to "a billowy ecstasy," Smith knew he had a subject and a title for a musical comedy.

The rest of the year was spent accumulating royalties from the tours of *The Parisian Model* and *Follies of 1907*, and collaborating with composer Maurice Levi on *The Soul Kiss* and with Reginald de Koven on *Nearly a Hero*, a vehicle for Sam Bernard, optioned by the Shubert

Adeline Genée

Brothers. After the holidays, Adeline Genée was imported directly from the Empire Theatre in London to join the American cast of *The Soul Kiss*, who had already begun rehearsals. Because Genée had no dialogue and traveled with her own dance music (by English composer Cuthbert Clarke) and choreography (by her uncle, Alexander Genée), working her into the production was relatively easy, as Smith's book made every effort to maximize the star's abilities. The story begins in Paris in the studio of Maurice (W. H. Weldon), a sculptor who is in love with his model, Suzette (Florence Holbrook). She loves him as well, but refuses to allow him to kiss her until he agrees to marry her. Believing that humans are more inclined to physical rather than spiritual love, J. Lucifer Mephisto (R. C. Herz) bets $1 million, against the possession of their souls, that Suzette cannot keep Maurice faithful for one year. Because Maurice longs for the experience of "the soul kiss," Mephisto tempts him with Carmen (Billy Norton), Marguerite (Grace Rankin) from *Faust*, Cleopatra (Clara De Beers), a Gibson Bathing Girl (Jane Hall), and a French cabaret girl (Elphye Snowden), none of whom can provide the proper "soul kiss." In desperation, Mephisto summons the Dancer (Adeline Genée), who permits the sculptor to kiss her hand, and he becomes enthralled with her. Meanwhile, Suzette has met an American millionaire, Ketchum Short (Cecil Lean), and the couple fall in love. Although Mephisto has won the wager, he, too, has fallen in love—with Cleo (Stella Tracey), the "belle of the Tabarin"—so he renounces his claim on Maurice and Suzette's souls, and each of the happy couples gets married.

Genée performed four ballets during the evening: "The Soul Kiss," on New Year's Eve, when she wins the kissing competition; the "Money Ballet," at a gambling casino in Monte Carlo; "Sir Roger de Coverly," a folklike *divertissement* in her dressing room showing her in a lace-trimmed negligee; and the "Hunt Meadowbrooke," permitting the star to dress in a riding habit and high boots and make an entrance riding a horse against a backdrop of autumn foliage. On January 20, American audiences saw the celebrated dancer for the first time at the Chestnut Street Opera House in Philadelphia. Smith felt that the opening night was "unpromising," and he spent the rest of the week rewriting the show around the star whose four ballets could not be altered. By the Saturday matinee, the revisions had been rehearsed and integrated into the show, and *The Soul Kiss* was ready to debut in New York City.

In the midst of his rewriting, Harry and his brother stopped in at the nearby Lyric Theatre on January 24 to attend a single copyright performance of *The Paradise of Mahomet* they had Americanized for the Shubert Brothers. In their version, Bengaline (Grace Van Studdiford), a beautiful Turkish girl, becomes a wife and widow almost immediately when her husband runs from the wedding off to war and never returns. She is engaged, in turn, to Baskir (Arthur P. Ripple), a marriage broker, who broke with his sweetheart, Vaninka (Bernice Mershon), to marry the widow for her money. Prince Cassim (George Leon Moore), who is in love with Bengaline, does everything in his power to prevent her marrying Baskir, but without success. Vaninka and Noah Vale (Robert G. Pitkin), an American chauffeur, decide to drug the wine on the day of wedding and put everyone to sleep so that Bengaline, her aunt Clarisse (Maud Odell), and Maboul (Harry MacDonough), Clarisse's second husband, can be taken to Cassim's palace while they are unconscious. When the guests awaken, they are led to believe that they have died and gone to "the paradise of Mahomet," a ruse that succeeds only until Alphonse (Karl Stall), Clarisse's supposedly dead first husband, appears. Because his being alive deprives Bengaline of her fortune, Baskir is no longer interested in her and returns to Vaninka, allowing Bengaline to marry the Prince, the man she really loves. The *Dramatic Mirror* (February 1, 1908) questioned whether the opera would suit the popular taste because of the lack of catchy tunes in the score. The producers evidently shared the critic's concern, and three years were allowed to pass before the show was considered ready for Broadway.

On January 28, Harry was back in New York for the opening night of *The Soul Kiss* at the New York Theatre. The critics were at a rare loss for words to describe their fascination with the star. "What qualifying adjectives ought one to use to describe a ball of thistledown dancing in the breeze?" asked the *New York Times* (January 29, 1908). "That is Adeline Genée." The *Dramatic Mirror* (February 8, 1908) added:

> Some humor, some vulgarity, many girls, ten sets of scenery, drummy, horny music, and a few comedians, make up *The Soul Kiss*.
>
> And Genée! But Genée is a thing apart; a spirit untouched by her all too earthly surroundings; an elf, an angel, a bird, an incarnation of Terpsichore; indescribable in words, impossible of analysis; as intangible as sunbeams, as vapory as moonlight.

> *The Matinee Girl,* being a woman and observing, can tell how she looks and what she wears. The reviewer can do no more than say she dances. She dances with her eyes, her mouth, in every expression of her face; with her hands and body; her costumes dance; and her feet touch only the air. She is pure rhythm personified. What matters it if once she dances for the delectation of a "Hebrew comedian"—Ariel pleasing Caliban. When she dances the stage vanishes and there is only Genée.

As far as the play was concerned, it was judged "no better and not much worse" than the rest of the musicals on the boards that season, and several of the Smith-Levi songs were cited as effective: "I Wonder Where They'll Go," "There Were Actors Then," "I'm the Human Night Key of New York," and "Any Old Place in the World with You." Various individual performances were singled out, particularly R. C. Herz, and the chorus of girls dressed as French poodles was found to be amusing. Of course, Genée was considered "absolutely superior to the quality of her surroundings," but not a single critic complained that her imported, prefabricated ballets were improperly motivated into the fabric of the story. It was Smith's clever integration of a nonspeaking, nonsinging character into a musical that allowed the dancer's talents to shine for the rest of the season.

As soon as *The Soul Kiss* had settled into New York, Smith was back in Philadelphia where his next production for the Shuberts, *Nearly a Hero,* was scheduled to open on February 3 at the Adelphi Theatre. A "farce with music" designed for Sam Bernard, the plot involves the mysterious rescue of a drowning man. To explain to his wife (Zelda Sears) why he was not home on a particular night, Jabez Doolittle (Sam Edwards) claims to be the rescuer, and tailor Ludwig Knoedler (Bernard), a tenant of Doolittle, pretends to be the person rescued, hoping his landlord will repay the favor. The real victim was Harold Percy Montague (Edgar Norton), a matinee idol who was robbed of a large sum of money during the rescue. He believes that the tailor was the man who rescued him, and has Ludwig arrested for theft. Farcical complications are provided by Angeline De Vere (Ethel Levey), a musical comedy queen, Gwendolyn Doolittle (Ada Lewis), the landlord's stagestruck daughter trying to look like Ethel Barrymore, Moreau (Robert Paton Gibbs), a French dressmaker, and Wade Waters (Franklyn Roberts), a bathing master, while a romantic interest develops between

Fred Doolittle (Burrell Barbaretto) and Marie (Daisy Greene), the cashier in Moreau's shop.

In Philadelphia, the book was attributed to George Grant (another of Smith's pseudonyms) and the music to Reginald de Koven. By the time the show opened at the Casino Theatre in New York on February 24, the book was blamed on Smith and no composer was listed, though subsequently Edward B. Claypoole, Will Heelan, and Seymour Furth admitted to providing the music and lyrics. After the critics dubbed the book "inane" and judged none of the tunes catchy or original, producer Lee Shubert suggested that the musical should have been called *Nearly a Zero,* though the performances of Sam Bernard, Ethel Levey, Zelda Sears, and Ada Lewis seemed to please. *Nearly a Hero* held on for 116 performances, even though Levey and Sears abandoned ship during the run.

New York did not have to wait for the next Harry B. Smith libretto, because as soon as Bernard and company wound up their stay at the Casino Theatre, Ziegfield opened the next edition of the *Follies*, with book and lyrics by Smith and music by Maurice Levi. First produced at the Apollo Theatre in Atlantic City on June 8, the *Follies of 1908* opened at the Jardin de Paris a week later. The self-consciously plotless entertainment begins in the Garden of Eden, where Eve (Lucy Weston) is quarreling with Adam (Barney Bernard). The only thing preventing Eve from "going home to mother" is the fact that she has no mother. Satanette (Nora Bayes) appears and, prompting Eve to leave her husband, offers to show her the world. Among the sights Eve marvels at are the acrobatic stunts of a burlesque prizefight, the choice of a presidential nominee at the Republican Convention in Chicago, caricatures of recent hit musicals such as *The Soul Kiss*, *The Merry Widow*, and *A Waltz Dream*, and the site of a tunnel being dug from New York to New Jersey, where a swarm of chorus girls dressed in mosquito costumes fills the stage. In addition to this satirical commentary on New Yorkers' fears of being connected by a tunnel to New Jersey, and a subtle jibe against two of Theodore Roosevelt's "leading and substantial citizens," party boss and banker Tom Platt, and senator and railroad counsel Chauncey Depew, the audience is treated to a chorus of living pictures accompanying the "Nell Brinkley Girl," based on the famous cartoon, and a costume parade spoofing the "big hat" craze, with one chorus girl wearing an inverted flower pot so huge that only her legs are visible.

Predictably, the most successful songs of the evening were interpolations. Nora Bayes's performance of "You Will Have to Sing an Irish

Song," by Albert Von Tilzer and Jack Norworth, was considered the hit of the production, although "Shine On, Harvest Moon," written by Bayes and Norworth, certainly became the most popular and indelibly associated with the performer. "Take Me 'Round in a Taxicab," by Melville Gideon and Edgar Selden, was also singled out because of the clever staging by Julian Mitchell in which a dozen girls were costumed as taxis, wearing meters and "For Hire" signs on their hats. At one point in the number, the houselights were dimmed, and the girls turned on the battery-powered "headlights" attached to their shoulder pads and paraded like nighttime drivers on the highway. Although the *New York Times* (June 16, 1908) noted that the "comedy element of the show is not always up to the standard of the pictorial," the *Dramatic Mirror* (June 27, 1908) concluded that "the entertainment taken as a whole is one of the best of its kind ever given on a roof-garden." The *Follies of 1908* played 120 performances in New York before setting out on a lucrative national tour.

During the run of the revue, Smith had been working with Ludwig Englander on a new vehicle for Anna Held. Anna's first husband, Maximo Carrera, had died in April 1908, causing Anna to spend the summer in Paris with Liane, the teenage daughter she tried to hide from her public and the press. Ziegfeld planned to travel to Europe in August to visit them, and he wanted to take along the script of the new show so that Anna could begin learning her lines. In addition, Smith was working again with Reginald de Koven on *The Golden Butterfly*, scheduled to open in New York in October, and with Victor Herbert on a musical treatment of a series of cartoons drawn by Winsor McCay for the *New York Herald*, called *Little Nemo*. That project had begun a year earlier when popular librettist George V. Hobart was signed to provide the book. He was quickly replaced by Henry Blossom, one of Herbert's frequent collaborators, but Blossom subsequently withdrew from the show. Because the producers, Klaw and Erlanger, were looking for someone dependable who could turn out a clever lyric and an amusing situation quickly, Smith was finally brought on board.

Advertised as "the largest musical production ever attempted in this country," and costing $86,000 to mount, *Little Nemo* received its world premiere at the Forrest Theatre in Philadelphia on September 28, playing there for three weeks to excellent business. Described as a "massively spectacular production with wonderful scenic effects [and] a very expensive cast," *Little Nemo* begins in the playroom of the Little Princess of Slumberland (Aimee Ehrlich), who, dissatisfied with the characters in fairy stories, wants a playmate. King Morpheus (W. W. Black), her father, has employed a Missionary (Harry Kelly) to provide a faith cure for his backache. The Missionary, however, steals the "elixir of youth" from the court physician, Dr. Pill (Joseph Cawthorn), and the only way to recover the tonic is to have a human child search for it. Little Nemo (Master Gabriel), who has just defeated Flip (Billy B. Van) in becoming "captain of the boys," is chosen for the task. In revenge, Flip causes a rainstorm, but Dr. Pill (who turns into a policeman) stops the rain and carries Nemo, who had fallen asleep inside a hollow tree, home to bed. Flip tries to take Nemo's place on the journey to Slumberland, but because he is prevented by Gladys the cat (Dave Abrams), he goes to the Weather Factory in Cloudland to create storms designed to wreck the little ship conveying Nemo on his journey. After dealing with cannibals, a series of Olympian games, and a Fourth of July celebration, Nemo is safely brought to Slumberland, where he becomes the new playmate of the Princess.

On October 20, *Little Nemo* moved to the New Amsterdam Theatre in New York, where it was enthusiastically received by critics and audiences alike. Smith's book was judged "adequate to all needs," and "as bright as a silver dollar in its comedy." Critics predicted immediate popularity for Herbert's music, and noted a number of effective numbers in the course of the evening: the memorably tuneful "Won't You Be My Playmate?"; the waltz finale, "Won't You Be My Valentine?"; the lilting topical song, "Read the Papers Every Day"; and the bright polka patter, "I Guess I Talk Too Much." For Dr. Pill, Smith provided a very clever patter lyric entitled, "I Wouldn't Take a Case Like That":

A lady came to me one day and said, "Oh, doctor, dear
A good night's rest my husband ne'er enjoys
He lies awake all night and is a nervous wreck all day,
The cats in our backyard make so much noise[."]
I gave to her a powder but she hurried back next day
Said my husband's dead 'round at the flats
I gave him your powder[,] Doc—Now he's dead, 'twas such a shock
"Gott" I said "I gave you that to give the cats[."]
Oh! I wouldn't take a case like that
If they offered me a fee so fat
She did not care which one was cured and cats don't have their lives insured
I wouldn't—no I couldn't—take a case like that.

Voicing the consensus of reviewers, the *New York Times* (October 21, 1908) emphasized that the entertainment was designed for adults as well as children, and concluded that "New York has seen nothing bigger or better in extravaganza than 'Little Nemo.' It has been a long time, in fact, since it has seen anything nearly as good of its kind." After 111 performances in New York, *Little Nemo* joined the touring circuit, ending the season with a long run in Chicago.

A week before the Smith-Herbert collaboration opened in New York, the Smith–de Koven opera, *The Golden Butterfly*, opened at the Broadway Theatre. With a plot borrowed from *The Second Fiddle*, the opera centers on the romance between Ilma Walden (Grace Van Studdiford), an opera chorus girl, and Franz (Walter Percival), a young composer. Franz has gone to Paris to make his fortune, and Ilma has been "discovered" by Baron Von Affenkoff (Louis Harrison), who tries to convince her to marry him by telling her that Franz has become famous and forgotten her. He discovers that his leading lady, Tina Korbay (Gene Luneska), is ill and cannot sing the opening of his new opera, "The Golden Butterfly." Ilma offers to take her place, and the Baron agrees, provided that she will marry him if his opera is a success. As in the earlier play, Franz turns out to be the composer of "The Golden Butterfly," and after the Baron confesses his theft, Ilma and Franz are reunited.

Hussars and Society Girls in *The Golden Butterfly*

The critics of *The Second Fiddle*, complaining about the excessive comic business added by the star, had expressed a desire to see the piece "played straight." *The Golden Butterfly* provided such an opportunity, and the critics responded enthusiastically to Smith's libretto. The *Dramatic Mirror* (October 24, 1908) was exceptionally complimentary:

> Whether the book or the score should receive first praise is hard to decide, both are so good. Anyhow, the combination will serve to keep the theatre full for a long time. The librettist has let his plot carry the opera and has not had to resort to any tricks of the musical comedy writer to keep things going. He has been humorous without being witty, and he has retained an evidence of more than the average amount of logic displayed by musical book makers.

All the performances were considered first-rate, the staging was found handsome, and the costumes "in the best possible taste." The production, part of the Grace Van Studdiford Opera Company's touring repertoire, remained in New York for forty-eight performances and went out on the road, often crossing paths with Adeline Genée on tour with *The Soul Kiss*.

Ziegfeld had returned to New York with Anna Held and her daughter on September 1, 1908, and by the time *Little Nemo* and *The Golden Butterfly* had opened, Ludwig Englander, Harry B. Smith, and Julian Mitchell were back at work, rehearsing Held's new vehicle, *Miss Innocence*, scheduled for a Philadelphia premiere at the end of November. Originally conceived as a three-act musical comedy called *Miss Innocence Abroad*, by the time rehearsals began, the show had lost an act and a word from the title. What it did not lose was the kind of fairytale tone that Smith had borrowed from his work on *Little Nemo*. As the name suggests, *Miss Innocence* was designed to be less overtly naughty than *The Parisian Model*, and the childlike atmosphere of the piece allowed Smith to be suggestive without actually appearing dirty. The plot centered on Anna (Anna Held), a student at the "School of Innocence," run by Miss Sniffins (Emma Janvier), a lady with several "pasts," on the Isle of Innocence. Another student, Claire (Edith St. Clair), is secretly married, and her husband, Pierre de Brissac (Leo Mars), a Lieutenant in the French Navy, comes looking for her. He is accompanied by his friend, Roland Fitzmaurice Mountjoy (Lawrance D'Orsay), Captain of the First Life Guards, who falls in love with Anna. They all go to Paris, where the "greatest detective in the world," Ezra Pettingill (Charles Bigelow), hopes to collect the reward for reuniting Anna with her missing parents. Although the detective only manages to confuse the situation, Mountjoy ends up uniting Anna with her parents and himself in the "Land of Peach Blossoms."

Held and a company of 150 performers gave the world premiere of *Miss Innocence* at the Chestnut Street Opera House in Philadelphia on November 23, 1908. The Philadelphia critics, undoubtedly pleased that the new show had less offensive material than her previous vehicle, praised it as "a big hit . . . sure to attract immense returns for at least two seasons." A week later, Anna was back at the New York Theatre, where Ziegfeld had arranged to hang a huge electric advertisement over the marquee. Advertised as eighty feet long and forty-five feet high, containing 32,000 square feet of glass, 2,300 light bulbs, and eleven miles of wire, the sign announced the production in letters surrounded by bolts of lightning. The hyperbolic energy expressed in Ziegfeld's sign was reflected in the reception New Yorkers gave the show on opening night. The *New York Times* (December 1, 1908) reported that a larger audience had never been counted in the New York Theatre and that the demands for encores extended to virtually every song. The *Dramatic Mirror* (December 12, 1908) called it "a lavish merry-go-round of laughter, lights and music," and even admitted that "some of its repartee lives up to the flaming sign on the front of the theatre." Of the songs, Anna's ocular ditty, "I Wonder What's the Matter with My Eyes," by Egbert Van Alstyne and Harry Williams, and Ella Lee's "Oh! That Yankiana Rag," by Melville Gideon and E. Ray Goetz, were the most often cited, while "Shine On, Harvest Moon" was borrowed from the *Follies of 1908* as a song for Angele (Lillian Lorraine) and the schoolgirls.

Ziegfeld appreciated the way Harry B. Smith constructed librettos, because it allowed him the flexibility of adding and subtracting numbers during the run of a show—a practice he enjoyed because it guaranteed repeat business. In December, Smith and Englander created "We Two in an Aeroplane," a number designed to feature Anna and Pierre de Brissac (Leo Mars) suspended in a life-size biplane in front of a backdrop depicting Paris at night. By the spring of 1909, an extra performance had been added to the weekly run of the show. A program dated April 12, 1909, notes: "As seven performances a week are not enough to accommodate the crowds wanting to see Miss Anna Held in 'Miss Innocence' she has been induced to add Wednesday matinees. The prices at these special performances will range from 25 cents to $1.50."

A month earlier, Abraham Erlanger and Florenz Ziegfeld left for Europe in search of new projects to produce for American audiences. R. Richard Anderson, Klaw and Erlanger's art director, was invited along to explore new techniques in stage costuming, and Harry B. Smith was asked to join the party to help discover new jokes for the next edition of the *Follies*. Smith was not anxious to accompany his associates. The prospect of spending a month in Europe was certainly appealing, but he had been married only a short time to Irene Bentley, and none of the men's wives were permitted on the expedition. Besides, Smith did not believe in the possibility of discovering new jokes, certain that any innovation he might consider would be immediately traceable to the Greeks.

Like it or not, Smith was persuaded to cross the Atlantic for a sixteen-day excursion through Europe, spending four days each in London, Vienna, Berlin, and Paris, and learning how to live on virtually no sleep. Though everyone agreed to see as much theater as possible, Erlanger wanted to visit museums and other places of historical significance during the day, while Ziegfeld was the night owl, preferring cabarets and nightclubs. Because Harry was expected to accompany both in his quest for new jokes, he barely got to bed. The group's highly publicized "invasion" of Austria began and ended with border searches effected by polite, but surly, customs officials. Leaving the country, Harry was caught smuggling a small box of chocolates in his trunk, leading to hours of questioning from the Reichswehr, the Tugendbund, and the Wehmgericht. To avoid escalating an oversight into an international incident, Smith told his accusers in perfect German that he was happy to pay whatever fine was levied on such crimes, and to demonstrate his goodwill, he made a present of the chocolates to the chief inspector. Erlanger was similarly questioned about his belongings, and all of the cigars his European theatrical associates had presented to him during the trip were confiscated at the Austrian border.

Paris exhibited few charms in the way of theatrical activity. The musical plays had little interest for Smith, and the revues and cabarets seemed designed to show women in as little clothing as possible, and even that was unalluring. Smith discovered that the women so exposed were mainly middle-aged Englishwomen who would not have been hired for a low-budget Broadway chorus. The hit in London was a nationalistic play by Major Guy du Maurier called *An Englishman's Home*, which had opened at Wyndham's Theatre on January 27, 1909. The play discussed the possibility of war between England and Germany because of the

Kaiser's rampant imperialism, and was extremely popular because it reflected the fears of the English audience. In Berlin, however, Smith experienced very little suggestion of the eminence of war in the daily behavior of the people. He attributed the calmness to a subtle confidence shared by the German people that if war should come, Germany was ready for it.

In Berlin, the travelers requested an audience with the Kaiser, but even though they were American celebrities, they were not the royalty that Wilhelm was accustomed to meeting, and their request was denied. They did manage to hire a chauffeur who had been in the service of the Kaiser as their tour guide through the city. He painted his automobile the same color as the Kaiser's, and "tooted the same kind of horn" that was heard on the imperial limousine. Consequently, as the representatives of an American theatrical empire traveled around the city, they were often mistaken for officials of the German Empire. It was also the Kaiser's Imperial Palace in Berlin that inspired a piece of business used in the *Follies of 1909:* the throne room was reproduced, and the Kaiser, dressed as a Rough Rider, threw a reception for Theodore Roosevelt, wearing the Kaiser's army uniform. That was the only useful idea that emerged from the European expedition.

Back in New York, the quartet began work on the next *Follies*, scheduled to open on June 10 at the Apollo Theatre in Atlantic City. As in the previous year, the music was mainly by Maurice Levi, and the production was directed and choreographed by Herbert Gresham and Julian Mitchell. The *compère* and *commère* of this edition were Monty Van Swagger (William Bonelli), a man about town, and the goddess Venus (Annabelle Whitford), who begin the evening in the goddess's court at Olympus. The scene changes to the lobby of the Metropolitan Opera House, where Venus and Monty find managers, Herr "Got a Cazzaza" and Herr Dimpel, arguing over a preference for Italian or German operas. At Oscar Hammerstein's office in the Manhattan Opera House, they watch Carmen La Tosca (Nora Bayes) sing "Mad House Opera," spoofing prima donnas. Later, the "Pipe Dream Girl" (Lillian Lorraine), entering in front of a backdrop that suggests a Maxfield Parrish painting, and costumed to resemble the girl blowing bubbles on the cover of *Life* magazine, sings "Nothing but a Bubble," while real bubbles float across the stage. The scene changes to the African jungle, where Teddy Roosevelt (Harry Kelly) is discovered on safari, introducing Sophie Tucker as the Jungle Queen.

For this edition of the *Follies*, Marc Klaw had hired a twenty-four-year-old performer named Sophie Tucker on the strength of a blackface number she performed in Holyoke, Massachusetts, during the tour of *Gay Masqueraders*. Ziegfeld did not like the looks of this rather large and unattractive woman, so he found little for her to do in the show. Just as the show was about to open in Atlantic City, Ziegfeld ordered Nat D. Ayer and A. Seymour Brown to come up with a comic number for Tucker based on Roosevelt's well-publicized excursion to Africa. The following day, the team appeared with "It's Moving Day Down in Jungle Town," a song about the animals fleeing their native habitats as Roosevelt stomps through the jungle. Singing the number dressed in a leopard costume, Tucker managed to become one of the most applauded acts in the revue.

The end of the first act displayed "nearly half a hundred girls, one for each state in the union," each wearing a hat designed to look like a battleship. Described by the *Dramatic Mirror* (June 26, 1909), the entrance is followed by "a changing of lights, the lowering of a drop, the girls press buttons attached to their costumes, and nearly fifty battleships, all illuminated, are seen riding up and down against the waves of New York Harbor, against a skyline of tall buildings and docks lit with countless lights." The second act featured a parade of chorus girls dressed like Howard Chandler Christy's illustrations, and an "Aeroplane" number featuring Lillian Lorraine soaring above the audience in a flying machine, and the act ends at the Polo Grounds, where two teams made up of chorus girls play baseball with the audience.

On June 14, 1909, one of the hottest days on record in New York City, the *Follies of 1909* opened at the Jardin de Paris to a stellar audience that not only included old standbys like Lillian Russell, Diamond Jim Brady, and Charles Dillingham, but also Teddy Roosevelt, who attended to see himself impersonated on stage. Harry B. Smith knew Diamond Jim from the card games at the Ziegfeld residence. Irene Bentley was a close friend of Anna Held, and after her marriage to Smith, the couple became regular members of the Ziegfeld coterie. Because the producer was an inveterate gambler, dinners and parties invariably included games of chance. Brady was not a drinker—orangeade was his vice—but he was an avid card player, and a habitual first-nighter at the theater, where he was fond of displaying his wealth by accessorizing himself with huge gems. Smith recalled that Diamond Jim was highly opinionated in matters of dress and argued that no man should wear more than twenty-eight rings at one time, or should have more than seventeen colors in a vest.

Most important was his advice that diamonds "larger than door knobs should never be worn except in the evening."

The critics were highly enthusiastic about the new *Follies*, even avoiding the usual complaints against Smith's libretto, and the revue continued to be a hot ticket throughout the summer as Ziegfeld continued to add and subtract material. Eva Tanguay joined the company on July 12, and with her came her signature tune, "I Don't Care." On September 11, after sixty-four virtually sold-out performances, the *Follies of 1909* left New York to begin a national tour. Two weeks later, Anna Held was back with *Miss Innocence* for two weeks before heading off for a season on the road.

A month later, on November 1, Adeline Genée returned to the New Amsterdam Theatre in a new Harry B. Smith vehicle, *The Silver Star*, with music by Robert Hood Bowers, Raymond Hubbell, Karl Hoschna, Jean Schwartz, Albert Gumble, Herbert Ingraham, Al Piantadosi, and C. J. M. Glaser. *The Silver Star* centers on Viola (Genée), who, years before, had been discovered by two street musicians, Professor Alonzo Dingelblats (George Bickel) and Doctor Algernon Hornblower (Harry Watson). Because the girl had no identification except for a silver star hanging around her neck, the search for her parents has been a long and arduous one. Just as they are about to connect their girl with a rich man seeking his long-lost daughter, an impostor appears with another girl whom he claims is the man's child. Viola is finally embraced as the heiress, but not until she has the opportunity of dancing a "march militaire," becoming the "Spirit of Champagne," and behaving as "an exquisite sprite of youth and Spring."

Like *The Soul Kiss*, *The Silver Star* was designed to feature Genée's exceptional dancing but limited acting abilities, so the emphasis was on spectacle not text, even though she had spoken lines in the new vehicle. The critics appreciated the visual elements in the show, calling it "a whirlwind of color and delightful motion, furnishing palatial surroundings for the winsome and blonde personality of the dainty Genée." Once again, Smith's book was judged "slender" and unfunny, even though *Theatre Magazine* (December 1909) found it "a practicable three-act machine." The *Dramatic Mirror* (November 13, 1909) predicted that with an injection of real comedy, the show "will rank as one of the most satisfactory and pleasing productions the Messrs. Klaw and Erlanger have made for some seasons, and it promises to be profitable." After eighty performances in New York, *The Silver Star* joined *Miss Innocence* on the touring circuit.

On November 22, Harry found himself back in his hometown, Buffalo, New York, where *The Air King*, a collaboration with composer Raymond Hubbell, received its world premiere at the Star Theatre. Hubbell had written several musicals with Harry's brother, Robert, and some of the *Follies'* interpolated songs, but this was his first effort with Harry by himself. A vehicle for comedian John Slavin, *The Air King* tells the story of Willie Ketcham (Slavin), a bellboy, who impersonates an aviator to impress his sweetheart, Polly Hart (Ann Tasker). He soon realizes that he is expected to make a transatlantic voyage, which he does hanging by his toes from the trapeze of a balloon. When he reaches his destination, Toulon, France, he and Polly get married. To this slim plotline, designed to feature the spectacle of airplanes on stage, is added the comic antics of Minerva Shine (Josephine Hall), a manicurist working at the Sea View Hotel in Oceanport, New Jersey, trying to climb the ladder of high society.

The Buffalo reviews called the show "a decided success," so when *The Air King* opened at the Colonial Theatre in Chicago the following week, the company was unprepared for the less-than-enthusiastic reaction from both the public and the press. To be fair, the critics liked many of the performances and even some of the songs. "Farewell Prosperity" was even singled out as "one of Mr. Hubbell's prettiest songs," and performed effectively by the star:

Have you ever had that feeling stealing over you
That is commonly described as "Indigo or blue"
Some folks get it when they lose a sweetheart or a friend,
But I only get it when I've no more coin to spend.
Farewell Prosperity!
Goodbye success!
My pipe is going out
I'm all in I guess.
Here comes Misfortune now
[S]he's after me
And that is why I sadly sigh,
Farewell Prosperity!

Although designed for the out-of-luck bellboy, Smith's lyrics appeared to anticipate his vivisection by the Chicago critics. The correspondent for the *Dramatic Mirror* (December 11, 1909) diplomatically noted that "the idea is not well worked out," but Hammond in the *Chicago Tribune* (November 30, 1909) was less subtle. Calling Smith "the death's head at the feast," he argued that the star, the composer, producers Klaw and Erlanger, and the rest of the company "deserve more than the thing which Mr. Smith has dashed off for them." He felt that the lyrics were hackneyed and the topical references missed their mark, suggesting that the line "Chatfield-Taylors look like sailors" was about as successful "as a damp devil chaser on a rainy Fourth of July." In addition, he complained that only one line in the entire show could be called "bright," and that occurred in the second act when Willie Ketcham is about to fly the airplane. Saying goodbye, his sweetheart remarks, "You look so cool and collected." Ketcham replies, "They always look cool at the start and they are usually collected at the finish." That exchange got the single big laugh of the evening. Word of mouth was no better than the press, so Klaw and Erlanger decided to ground *The Air King* in Chicago, adding it to the small but growing list of Smith's shows that closed out of town.

After the holidays, Harry was back at work on a three-act play called *The Divorced Bride*, and the next installment of the *Follies*, designed much along the same lines as the three previous editions. The revue begins at a dress rehearsal where choreographer Julian Mitchell (Harry Watson) and musical director Maurice Levi (George Bickel) are putting the cast through their paces. Iona Carr (Grace Tyson), a chorus girl, is discovered complaining to her sweetheart, Towne Duer (John Reinhardt), that she wants a principal role in the revue, much to his dissatisfaction. The scene shifts to the office of the Get Poor Quick Syndicate, run by famous American capitalists, where Iona and Towne have gone to get the money to go out on the town. A street scene set in Reno, Nevada, is next for a satirical sketch on divorce, followed by a motion-picture display of Halley's Comet, with Anna Held depicted as the comet, and Harry Watson as the earth. Lillian Lorraine rode a pony from the back of the auditorium to the stage, and the act ended with a water tank onstage, providing an excuse for the chorus girls to disrobe and take a plunge. The second act introduced "Swing Me High, Swing Me Low," by Victor Hollander and Ballard Macdonald, during which Lillian Lorraine and chorus swung out over the audience on a latticework of swings. Choreographer Julian Mitchell made one of his infrequent appearances as a performer, dancing a pantomimic satire of Porter Emerson Browne's play *A Fool There Was*, with Louise Alexander, and the evening closed with the chorus dressed as West Point cadets in a burlesque of the hero's welcome Teddy Roosevelt received on his return from Africa.

Although the critics and audiences continued to be highly enthusiastic in their receptions, the major focus of their applause was hardly on the text or performances. Instead, what most pleased and excited about the *Follies of 1910* was the way in which the revue was staged, and the introduction of two new stars to the Ziegfeld fold. The staging was a development of the earlier technique of allowing the spectacle to spill from the stage into the audience. The *Dramatic Mirror* (July 2, 1910) reported:

> What did more than anything else to keep the performance from dying in its tracks was the introduction of several novel methods of presenting the players, from principals to chorus. One never knew from where or just when one might expect to see an artist spring up in any part of the house. Boxes were utilized by members of the company and groups of girls and men were paraded up and down the aisles, over the stage and down stairs in the auditorium with bewildering rapidity.

Even more important than the staging, however, was the introduction of two new stars: Fanny Brice and Bert Williams. Neither beautiful nor high class, Fanny Brice was not a typical Ziegfeld star attraction. According to Ziegfeld, she had been discovered in the chorus of a cheap burlesque company performing at the Columbia Theatre, where she was earning eighteen dollars a week. Julian Mitchell was set against her, arguing, "She's a lemon. How can you pick a burlesque girl and expect her to make good in a $2 show?" Never one to take anyone else's advice, Ziegfeld hired Brice at the princely sum of forty dollars a week and gave her "Lovie Joe," a coon song by Joe Jordan and Will Marion Cook. At rehearsals preceding the traditional opening in Atlantic City, Abe Erlanger heard Fanny sing the song, and he complained that her diction was unacceptable, sounding more like a low-class vaudeville act than a *Follies* headliner. When he demanded that she sing the word "more," instead of "mo" in the lyric, she refused, unaware that Erlanger was always used to getting his way, and she was fired. Ziegfeld subsequently rehired her, and when Brice sang the number her own way, she scored (in the words of the critics) "one of the biggest hits of the performance."

Bert Williams had already been a star with his comedy partner, George Walker, appearing in a number of significant African American musicals, including *In Dahomey* (1903) and *Bandana Land* (1908), both with music by Smith's infrequent collaborator Will Marion Cook. When Ziegfeld discovered in the spring of 1910 that David Belasco was planning to employ Williams in an otherwise all-white show, he became determined to have the comedian in the *Follies*. Bert Williams was inclined toward the Ziegfeld camp even before the impresario outbid Belasco. He already knew Smith from his collaboration with Will Marion Cook on *The Southerners* and other musicals. He felt secure in Smith's work, knowing that the author was sensitive to the needs of his performers, and always willing to listen to their ideas.

Williams's debut in the *Follies of 1910* marked the first time an African American performer was a headliner in an otherwise white Broadway show. This did not necessarily imply an integrated atmosphere within the company. In the contract negotiations, Williams stipulated that he would not have to appear onstage with any female cast member, and Ziegfeld agreed to book the tours only above the Mason-Dixon Line (because Williams did not perform in the southern states). Members of the company even refused to act onstage with Williams in the sketches that Smith wrote, working the comedian into the fabric of the show, and much of the material had to be scrapped—that is, until the cast realized that Williams was an artist. As the *New York Times* (June 21, 1910) suggested:

> There is no more clever low comedian on our stage today than Bert Williams, and few, indeed, who deserve to be considered in his class. Last night he was warmly welcomed, and deservedly so, though he has occasionally had better songs. In fact, without Williams to sing them, there would be little to any of these particular numbers, with the possible exception of "Constantly," [one of his own compositions, with lyrics by James Henry Burris and Chris Smith] in which he scored his best success.

Following the usual tryout in Atlantic City, the *Follies of 1910* opened at the Jardin de Paris on June 20 and remained there throughout the summer for eighty-eight performances. Reviewers appeared to be getting weary of the formula, with the *Dramatic Mirror* (July 2, 1910) regretting that "with such an outlay of money, time and talent a more consistently entertaining performance could not be devised." Harry B. Smith had become disenchanted with the series as well, and he decided to take the next year off from both the *Follies* and its producer. Ziegfeld's highly publicized infidelities with Lillian Lorraine had become a continued source of strain in Harry's relationship with Flo, because his wife, Irene, was one of Anna Held's closest friends. And what made matters even worse, while Ziegfeld was wining and dining his showgirl, he was continually behind in his royalty payments to the author.

Chapter 8

German Imports

On October 3, 1910, a month after the *Follies of 1910* closed, Harry B. Smith's adaptation of *Die geschiedene Frau*, by Victor Léon (music by Leo Fall), opened at the Globe Theatre bearing the title *The Girl in the Train*. Many of Smith's earliest works had been adaptations of foreign comic operas, usually from the "golden age" of Viennese operettas. As his career matured, he turned to French *opérettes* and vaudevilles to supply source material for summer entertainments at the Casino Theatre, or Ziegfeld's extravaganzas for Anna Held. With *The Girl in the Train*, an adaptation commissioned by producer Charles Dillingham, Smith began a series of translations and Americanizations of more recent German musical theater works that would occupy him for the next twenty years. *Die geschiedene Frau* (literally, "The Divorced Wife") originally opened at the Carltheater in Vienna on December 23, 1908. An English version had been prepared by Adrian Ross and produced by George Edwardes in London in 1910, and Dillingham sought Smith's help in providing American audiences with a more idiomatic translation.

The story begins in a courtroom in Amsterdam where Jana (Vera Michelena) is suing her husband, Karel (Melville Stewart), for divorce because of his alleged infidelities. On a recent business trip, Karel had persuaded his wife to remain at home, and aboard the train, he innocently turned over his wife's sleeping berth to an actress, Gonda Van der Loo (June Grey), unintentionally creating the appearance of a compromising situation. After the divorce is granted, Karel finds himself attracted to Gonda, who does not share his impulse to get married again. In the British version, Adrian Ross provided the following lyric for Gonda to sing during the couple's sprightly waltz duet:

Oh, well! your intentions are good, and conventions
Of course we can't forget,
But I don't care for you much, and therefore
We won't be married yet!
Still, no handle to leave for scandal,
And make your wife enraged,
I should like to suggest
That it would be best,
To stop any doubt
If we gave it out
That we are engaged.
Karel, charming little Karel,
Let us get engaged a little,
Really that appears quite our best plan!
Karel, charming little Karel,
Happiness awaits us yonder,
If you will but meet me just half way!

While sustaining a similar rhyme scheme, and maintaining the sense of the lyric, Smith produced a sharper and livelier tone in his adaptation:

My friend, tho' you please me,
I beg you don't tease me,
With notions out of date.
A love as pleasant
As ours at present
Should shun the marriage state.
Fondest lovers
A girl discovers

Are rarely husbands true.
When I weary of you, my dearie,
I'll marry you, maybe, just to get rid of you.
As many girls *do*.
That is why some girls will marry
Any old Tom, Dick and Harry.
Just to have two beaux upon one string.
In true love I'll never falter,
But the altar means the *halter*.
So no wedding bells for me shall ring.

Invariably, the husband's flirtation with the actress causes his wife to want him back and inspires the Judge (Claude Gillingwater) to attempt an affair with the actress as well. By the final curtain, the chorus celebrates a double wedding: the Judge is united with Gonda, and Jana and Karel get married again.

Critics found Smith's Americanization "commendable" in its ability to maintain most of the humor of the German original, and, judging Leo Fall's music to be first-rate, they predicted the show would be a hit. Oddly, the public did not agree, and after forty performances, *The Girl in the Train* headed out on tour, replaced at the Globe Theatre by Smith's next show of the season, *The Bachelor Belles*, a musical comedy with music by Raymond Hubbell. Produced by Klaw and Erlanger as another vehicle for Adeline Genée, *The Bachelor Belles* took its title from a women's organization whose members vow never to marry. Daphne Brooks (Eva Fallon) is about to be inducted into the group when Charley Van Renssalaer (John Park) appears to disrupt the proceedings. Daphne can resist any temptation but Charley, and she agrees to become his wife. When she announces to the group that she is, in fact, engaged, the rest of the members reveal their secret betrothals as well, and the society is disbanded.

Once again, Genée had a mute role—her spoken lines in *The Silver Star* were not appreciated by her fans—and her three dances were only tangential to the story: a classical ballet solo; a ballet called "Roses and Butterflies," accompanied by Sherer Beckefi, a Russian dancer, and eight chorus girls; and a Hungarian dance, a *pas de deux* with Beckefi. Again, the dancer was considered better than her surroundings, with the *Dramatic Mirror* (November 16, 1910) complaining, "Harry Smith's book and Raymond Hubbell's music lack the elements of dignity and color which one would expect of a composition intended to exploit an artist like Genée. Rag tunes and Spanish fandangos do not compare favorably with classic dances and seem all the cheaper in the comparison." The *New York Times* (November 8, 1910) called the production the weakest of Genée's vehicles, arguing that the libretto "was not funny and the score contained nothing worth whistling."

In contrast to the artistic portion of the evening (Genée and company), Smith and Hubbell's "Give Us a Ragtime Tune" proposed the aesthetic philosophy of *The Bachelor Belles:* "Just fun! that is what we're after,/ Girls and a lot of laughter;/ Shakespeare? not for us!/ He's too hot for us!/ Give us a Ragtime tune!" Even though the show was filled with spectacular chorus numbers staged by Julian Mitchell, it was obvious that it presented the wrong environment for its star—a fact emphasized by the critics. It was even suggested that if Genée were excused from the production, with some tightening *The Bachelor Belles* "could be worked over into a presentable musical play." As far as the producers were concerned, however, the star was the play, so, after thirty-two performances, it joined the rest of Smith's fleet of touring shows.

When Genée was leaving New York, Smith was at the Tremont Theatre in Boston for the December 5 opening of *The Spring Maid*, an adaptation of *Die Sprudelfee*, by Julius Wilhelm and Alfred Maria Willner (music by Heinrich Reinhardt), commissioned by producers Louis F. Werba and Mark A. Luescher. Former employes of Klaw and Erlanger, Werba and Luescher had decided to try their hand at producing and, liking Reinhardt's score, hired Harry and his brother Robert to provide the adaptation for their first production. The story that unfolds is strikingly similar to that of Oliver Goldsmith's *She Stoops to Conquer*. At the Carlsbad Springs in 1830, Prince Aladar (Lawrence Rea) has an aversion to women of his class, preferring to flirt with Annamirl (Elgie Bowen), a "Spring Maid" who works at the water fountains in the public square. Princess Bozena (Christie MacDonald), visiting the spa with her father, Prince Nepomuk (William Burress), feels compelled to teach Aladar a lesson that will humble him. Disguising herself as a Spring Maid, with her father masquerading as her "aunt" as chaperon, Bozena causes the Prince to fall madly in love with her. Once he admits his feelings, the Princess reveals her true identity, and, having overcome his aversion to women of his own rank, Aladar marries Bozena.

Adding to the entertainment is Roland (Tom McNaughton), a famous English tragedian who directs the yearly pageant commemorating the discovery of the Carlsbad Springs. Smith recalled that during

"Two Little Love Bees" in *The Spring Maid*

rehearsals, the actor asked permission to interpolate into the text a recitation that he had performed successfully in London. Entitled, "The Three Trees," the monologue had nothing to do with the plot of the show, but Smith promised to find a way of integrating it into the musical:

> When it was rehearsed, accompanied by eccentric orchestral noises, the effect was so decidedly vaudevillian, that in order to

account for its introduction in the operetta, a note was printed on the program stating that the fable of "The Three Trees" was the legend of the original discovery of Carlsbad Springs, and the authority given for this ingenious invention was "Richter's Folk Lore of Germany," of which, paraphrasing *Sara Gamp's* friend *Betsy*, I may say that "I don't believe there's no sich a book." However, my old friend, Mr. Krehbiel, referred to the note in his review and seemed to know all about the mythical historical work. Mr. Krehbiel was a good fellow, famous for his erudition in all things musical; but of course he could not be expected to know about things that did not exist.

Following its successful out-of-town tryout, *The Spring Maid* opened at the Liberty Theatre in New York on December 26, 1910. Both audiences and critics enjoyed the production, especially the spectacle of a real running-water fountain on stage. "Day Dreams," "The Fountain Fay," and "Two Little Love Bees" were judged the hits, although most of the critics found all the music as pretty as anything thus far imported from Germany. Werba and Luescher were applauded for beginning their producing career with a hit, and money continued to flow into their box-office accounts well into the new year, as *The Spring Maid* accumulated 194 performances in New York before going out on tour.

Three years after it first appeared in Philadelphia, the Smith Brothers' adaptation of *The Paradise of Mahomet* finally made its way to the Herald Square Theatre in New York on January 17, 1911, with Grace Van Studdiford still in the leading role, but produced by Daniel V. Arthur instead of the Shuberts. The critics were more than enthusiastic about the performers, the music, and the book. The *Dramatic Mirror* (January 25, 1911) exclaimed:

Wine, women and song; light, color and melody; mirth, beauty and youth, everything necessary for the delight of three senses, are offered in abundance in *The Paradise of Mahomet*. If Broadway doesn't accept the opera, then one must be convinced that Broadway doesn't know what it wants. There is a story for the logical, melodious numbers for the musical and vigorous comedy for the lover of ingenuous fun. . . . Altogether *The Paradise of Mahomet* is a delightful entertainment. One is surprised that it did not reach New York earlier.

Grace Van Studdiford (center) and female ensemble in *The Paradise of Mahomet*

Unfortunately, Broadway did not know what it wanted, and the opera closed after twenty-three performances.

While *The Spring Maid* was still in tryouts, Harry B. Smith had been collaborating with the popular performer, writer, and director Joseph Herbert on the lyrics for *Mlle. Rosita*, Victor Herbert's newest vehicle for Fritzi Scheff. A contract drawn between the Shuberts and Victor Herbert required the libretto and lyrics to be delivered to the composer by December 15, 1910, with the completed piano score due by the middle of February 1911. By the end of the month, the show was in rehearsal in preparation for a mid-March opening at the Shubert Theatre in Boston, but the need for additional rehearsal and illness in the company postponed the premiere until the end of the month. Although some of the critics determined that *Mlle. Rosita* was Scheff's best vehicle since the 1905 Victor Herbert–Henry Blossom collaboration, *Mlle. Modiste* (even to imitating the name), many found the music inferior to Herbert's usual standard, and once again, most hated the book (this time by Joseph Herbert).

The plot involves the courtship between a florist's daughter, Rose (Scheff), and Adolphe, Comte de Paravant (Joseph Herbert), who has been forbidden by his "octogenarian" parent from marrying anyone below the rank of a Marquise. To remedy the situation, Rose agrees to marry Philippe, Marquis de Montreville (Eugene O'Brien), who is going away to Algiers, sight unseen, with the understanding that the marriage will be

Fritzi Scheff and Eugene O'Brien in *Mlle. Rosita*

dissolved after three months, permitting her, as a Marquise, to marry Adolphe. Philippe and Rose, however, have already met and fallen in love, neither knowing who the other really is. When the three months have passed and husband and wife meet face to face to get a divorce as planned, they realize that they are in love and remain married, much to the disappointment of Comte de Paravant.

After the opening performance in Boston, the star became ill, forcing the cancellation of several shows; later in the run, the leading comedian, Walter Jones, collapsed and had to be replaced by his understudy. Before continuing on its pre-Broadway tryout tour, *Mlle. Rosita* was severely reworked, though without the presence of co-lyricist Smith, who was busy with other projects.

On April 3, *Little Miss Fix-It*, for which Smith collaborated on the book with William J. Hurlburt, opened at the Globe Theatre in New York, with music and lyrics by Nora Bayes, her husband Jack Norworth, and a half-dozen other songwriters, including African Americans J. Rosamond Johnson and his brother, James Weldon Johnson, and a relative newcomer, Jerome Kern. The "play with songs" was produced as a vehicle for Bayes by Werba and Luescher, attempting to move from operetta into the musical comedy idiom. The slight story (anticipating *Leave It to Jane* without the college environment) detailed the abilities of Mrs. Della Wendell (Bayes) to fix everyone else's problems but her own. Attempting to play matchmaker, she generally caused more problems than not, but by the end of the play, she manages to unite Ethel Morgan (Oza Waldrop) with Harold Watson (James C. Lane), and Bella Ketcham (Eleanor Stuart) with Percy Paget (Lionel Walsh), while effecting a reconciliation between Marjorie Arnold (Grace Field) and her husband, Buddy (Jack Norworth).

As usual, the critics found the cast superior to the material, but the seven-week run provided Bayes and her husband a forum in New York City for a number of new songs and routines before *Little Miss Fix-It* left for the touring circuit. Before Bayes and company had left the city, however, on April 27, 1911, Smith was at another premiere, all the more significant since it marked the opening of a new theater in New York: the Folies-Bergère Theatre on Forty-sixth Street, built by Jesse Lasky and William Harris as a kind of supper club where audiences could have dinner and drinks, and see a show. The opening bill comprised three one-act entertainments: *Hell*, a profane burlesque by Rennold Wolf, featuring Otis Harlan as the Devil and Ada Lewis as Maude Adams; *Temptation*, a ballet by Alfredo Curtis, with music by Edmond Diet; and *Gaby*, a satirical "revuette" by Harry and Robert B. Smith, with music by Robert Hood Bowers, depicting the notorious affair between French dancer Gaby Deslys and Manuel II, King of Portugal, and starring Ethel Levey as Gaby.

For six weeks, a large company rehearsed the triple bill under the able direction of George Marion while the theater—terraced with tables on the orchestra level and equipped with theater seats in the balcony—was being finished by workmen working around the clock to meet the opening night deadline. Like Ziegfeld's *Follies*, the show was hauled out to Atlantic City a week before the New York premiere to fine-tune the performances and material before a paying audience. The first night in New Jersey was less than successful, but the producers, having invested no less than $100,000 in the enterprise, remained positive, sure that with the appropriate tightening and rewriting the show would be a hit in New York. One of the writers, however, was nowhere to be found. In an interview with the *Green Book Magazine* (September 1912), Rennold Wolf notes that Harry B. Smith, committed to six other shows at the time, was unable to attend a single rehearsal of his revuette. What's more, he even neglected to attend the Atlantic City premiere. Wolf explains:

A telegram sent to him after the performance and requesting his presence was not answered. After the Tuesday rehearsal a second telegram—almost a cry for help—was dispatched. He replied that his engagements would not permit the three hours' journey. At midnight, Tuesday, a frantic manager called Mr. Smith on the long distance telephone and extracted from him a promise to witness the Wednesday matinee.

True to his word, he was on hand. Immediately following the performance he asked the management to assemble the company on the stage. When this had been accomplished, he arose and said very quietly: "'Hell' is all right. My piece, 'Gaby' is rotten. Do anything with it you like." And then he dashed to the railway station.

The reviewers agreed with Smith's assessment of his work, but the problem with the evening was not essentially the material but the concept of the theater. Many critics tried to support the endeavor by emphasizing the lavishness of the production (certainly offering Ziegfeld competition, and opening nearly two months earlier than his annual summer revue) and the well-appointed surroundings. Others were more impressed by the idea of eating, smoking, and seeing a show—all for the modest price of four dollars a ticket. But, soon after the Folies-Bergère opened, the producers discovered that, even with the income from a capacity audience, the running costs of a first-class entertainment *plus* a first-class meal were too high for them to make a profit, and the theater closed after ninety-two performances, only to reopen as a traditional Broadway house. As Abe Erlanger summarized the failed experiment, "How can you expect people to applaud a show when everyone has a knife in one hand and a fork in the other?"

While *Gaby* was playing to satisfied diners in Manhattan, *The Spring Maid* was in London, imported by one of Smith's most devoted advocates, Fred C. Whitney. Having established himself as a producer of musical imports with Oscar Straus's *The Chocolate Soldier*, Whitney was determined to repeat his success with other continental operettas, and the Smith Brothers' adaptation was high on his list. Smith was unable to cross the ocean for the production, because he and his brother were still fine-tuning the libretto of *The Red Rose*, a musical comedy with music by Robert Hood Bowers, scheduled to open at the Garrick Theatre in Philadelphia on May 2, 1911. Bowers was no stranger to the author, even though *The Red Rose* marked his first full-length score with Smith (he had previously provided additional music for *The Spring Maid*, and a score for the revuette *Gaby*).

The story opens at an art school in Paris where Lola (Valeska Suratt), a model, is in love with Dick Lorimer (Wallace McCutcheon), an American art student. Dick's millionaire father, Alonzo Lorimer (Alexander Clark), objects to his son having a relationship with the "daughter of a concierge," preferring him to marry Daisy Plant (Lilian Graham), the daughter of another millionaire, Silas Plant (John Daly Murphy). Trying to avenge himself on his enemy, Maxime Dupont (Henry Bergman), Baron Leblanc (Louis Casavant) pretends that Lola is his daughter so that Maxime can be caught wanting to marry her for her money. Dupont discovers the ruse early enough to escape the trap, but Alonzo Lorimer, thinking his son's sweetheart is really an heiress, suddenly supports the match and works to break off Dick's relationship with Daisy, who does not truly mind since her heart truly belongs to Lionel Talboys (Ernest Lambart), an English Peer. By the end, Lola is discovered to be the real daughter of the Baron, so everything works out happily for everyone.

On June 22, when the show opened at the Globe Theatre in New York, the patrons enjoyed each being given a rose at the entrance to the auditorium, and they welcomed the production with huge rounds of applause and many calls for encores. Critics liked the music and the spectacle best, noting that the star, Valeska Suratt, never made an entrance twice in the same dress, but before long, the costuming overwhelmed the libretto and, according to the *Dramatic Mirror* (June 28, 1911), "the narrative shriveled up like a mushroom before the morning sun." The melodically expansive "Bohemia" and the topical patter song "The Queen of Vanity Fair" (both with lyrics by Smith) were singled out by the critics, although the runaway hit of the performance was a song by Nat D. Ayer and Seymour Brown interpolated during the run: "Oh, You Beautiful Doll."

After seventy-six performances, the cast of *The Red Rose* was due for a vacation, and Harry was ready for the New York premiere of his latest adaptation for producer Charles Frohman. This was *The Siren*, originally written by the prolific librettists Leo Stein and A. M. Willner, with music by the celebrated Austrian composer Leo Fall. Advertised as a "musical play in three acts," *The Siren* opened at the Knickerbocker Theatre on August 28, with Julia Sanderson (a popular musical theater ingenue) and

Donald Brian (Prince Danilo in the American premiere of *The Merry Widow* in 1907) leading a strong supporting cast. The plot finds amateur poet and professional heartbreaker Marquis de Ravaillac (Donald Brian) chased by the police because of poems he had supposedly written satirizing the Kaiser. To prove that the Marquis actually wrote the scurrilous verse, the Minister of Police in Vienna, Baron Siegfried Bazilos (Frank Moulan), dispatched a variety of charming women to get a specimen of Ravaillac's handwriting, but sensing a trap, the Marquis refused to sign anything. He has fallen in love, however, with a country girl named Lolotte (Julia Sanderson), who is persuaded by the Baron to ask the poet to write something for her. Ravaillac replies with a love song, "Wallflowers," claiming to have composed it especially for her. Lolotte soon discovers that the poet wrote the song years earlier for the Baron's wife and, in a fit of jealousy, turns the lyric over to Bazilos. The Marquis is subsequently banished, but because this was a "first offense," he is quickly pardoned. When he realizes that Lolotte had no idea of the Baron's intentions in asking for a sample of the poet's handwriting, he forgives her indiscretion, and the couple ride off together into the Austrian sunset.

The critics found the work "agreeable and pretty," but lacking the "vivacity and resourcefulness of the genuine big hit." While Smith's translation was considered unfunny, with lyrics bristling "with unsingable words and phrases," his "The One Girl" was singled out as one of the "most delightful" moments of the evening, where music and lyrics seemed perfectly united to express the inner thoughts of the character while he continued his normal daily activities. The runaway comedy hit of the evening, however, was an interpolated number, a parody of grand opera called "I Want to Sing in Opera," by Worton David and George Arthurs (with slight alterations by Jerome Kern), performed by Will West in the character of Hanibal Beckmesser, a veterinary doctor. *Theatre Magazine* (October 1911) concluded, "Taken for all in all, 'The Siren' is a refined and innocuous musical play de luxe, in which Broadway may take pride as a probable season-through attraction." Audiences evidently agreed, and the show remained at the Knickerbocker for seventeen weeks.

In September, the Brothers Smith completed the text of a musical review, *Playing the Game*, and *Mlle. Rosita*, now called *The Duchess*, continued its pre-Broadway tryout tour at the Opera House in Providence, Rhode Island, after a short summer vacation. Another Victor Herbert work, featuring English actress Kitty Gordon, *The Enchantress*, gave its world premiere at the National Theatre in Washington, D.C., on October 9, 1911. Advertised as a "new opera comique," with book by Fred de Grésac (Fredérique de Grésac, wife of operatic baritone Victor Maurel) and lyrics by Harry B. Smith, *The Enchantress* centered on Vivien Savary (Kitty Gordon), a prima donna hired by Ozir (Arthur Forrest), the Minister of War, to "enchant" Prince Ivan of Zergovia (Harold H. Forde) so that he would abdicate his throne in order to marry her. When Vivien realizes the price the Prince had to pay for loving her, she refuses to marry him, even though she loves him as well. In the end, Troute (Ralph Riggs), the Head of the Secret Service, discovers that the prima donna is descended from royal ancestry, allowing the Prince to marry her without losing his title.

The Enchantress was said to have cost $60,000 to mount, and the Washington critics felt it was worth every penny, finding Herbert's score among his best work. A week later, Anna Held was at the Forrest Theatre in Philadelphia ready to begin the almost yearlong national tour of *Miss Innocence* (now called *M'lle. Innocence*, with Raymond Hubbell cited as composer) that would travel as far south as New Orleans and as far west as San Francisco. On October 16, the same day the tour began, *The Duchess* (with George Anderson in the role of the Marquis and John E. Hazzard as the Comte), finally opened in New York at the Lyric Theatre, where both audiences and critics were disappointed with what they saw. Victor Herbert's music was judged well below par, and Joseph Herbert's book was simply called "bad." As *Theatre Magazine* (December 1911) complained, "The first act is slow, but fair; the second picturesque and spirited; the third atrociously puerile and stupid." On opening night, the star, Fritzi Scheff, gave a speech after the second act pleading for the audience's enthusiastic support for the work: "If you only knew how hard we have worked—Mr. Herbert and the actors and orchestra and every one else. Mr. Herbert is such a good man that he deserves some encouragement. Please give it to him." Perhaps if Scheff had been in better voice and the score had been up to standard, the audience would have been generous in its approbation. As it was, New York was willing to support *The Duchess* for only twenty-four performances before sending her back out on the road where she disappeared before the end of the year.

The very next day, October 17, saw the opening of *Gypsy Love*, Harry and Robert B. Smith's adaptation of A. M. Willner and Robert Rodansky's *Zeigeunerliebe* (music by Franz Lehár), at the Globe Theatre, following a successful run in Philadelphia. The slender plot was set in

Romania, and traced the infatuation of Zorika (Marguerita Sylva) for Jossi (Arthur Albro), a gypsy musician. She drinks a magic potion that enables her to see the future, and discovers that the musician will soon tire of her and turn his attentions to Ilma (Frances Demarest), a young widow. Encouraged by her father, Niklas (Harry McDonough), she decides to relinquish her infatuations and accept Fedor (Carl Haydn) as a husband, while her father pairs off with the young widow, leaving Jossi to wonder about the reliability of fortune-telling.

On opening night, Marguerita Sylva lost her voice in the middle of the first act and announced that she could not continue. Her understudy, Phyllis Partington, completed the performance, winning immediate popularity with the critics and the crowd, neither of which seemed disappointed with the change. Although Lehar's music fell short when compared with his score for *The Merry Widow*, it was judged "in a decidedly superior class," behaving occasionally like grand opera, and better than any other light opera on Broadway. Forgiven for any awkwardness in the translation, the Smiths were complimented for writing intelligent lyrics that were appropriately graceful in the romantic parts and humorous when they needed to be. But the genuinely funny comedy in the book seemed "pitifully beneath the level of the opera" and better suited to musical comedies. Audiences left the theater humming "The Melody of Love," the hit of the evening, for thirty-one performances, after which the production joined the other Smith shows on tour.

On October 19, *The Enchantress* found its way to the New York Theatre, where the critics and audiences embraced it wholeheartedly. The book was found to be "consistently interesting and engaging," the lyrics were clever, and Herbert's score was judged "the best he has furnished since 'Mlle. Modiste.'" The cast was praised from Kitty Gordon, whose "stately carriage and languid gestures" more than made up for her limitations as a singer, on down to the soloists in the ensemble, and the scenery and costumes were found to be "gorgeous," "striking," and "in good taste." After seventy-two performances in New York, *The Enchantress* left for the touring circuit, where it remained a hit for the next three seasons.

While Smith and de Grésac were working with Victor Herbert, they began a similar project with Reginald de Koven called *The Wedding Trip*, scheduled to be produced by the Shubert Brothers at the Broadway Theatre on Christmas Day. Set in Dalmatia, the story concerns Felix (John McCloskey), who has just married Fritzi (Christine Nielsen). Their wedding reception is interrupted by the appearance of Captain

Josef (Arthur Cunningham), who announces that Felix must leave immediately to take the place of his twin brother, François, who has been chosen to lead an expedition against a band of men who were abducting young women and holding them for ransom. François, a ladies' man, has left his post to follow his latest attraction, and should he not return by morning, he will be shot as a traitor. To save his brother's life, Felix agrees to take his place at the frontier, forcing him to deal with kidnapping brigands while discouraging the advances of François's wife, Basilie (Gwen Dubarry), Aza (Dorothy Jardon), a gypsy, and Lotta (Fritzi von Busing), an innkeeper. His natural aversion to carousing and fighting is aggravated by the presence of his entire family and brand new bride, who have all accompanied him on his assignment.

On its pre-Broadway tour, *The Wedding Trip* was found to be lacking in comedy. By the time it appeared in New York, attempts to bolster the laughs had provided the show with a driving energy that critics called a "constant and vain effort to be vivacious." De Koven's score was appreciated for its integration with the plot, but only Aza's "Soldier's Song" was singled out by critics as having been encored on opening night. The *Dramatic Mirror* (December 27, 1911) called the dialogue "ordinary" and the chorus below par on looks, but the observation that best summarized the production was: "The male contingency as brigands and soldiers looked like a woman's college performance of a battle scene." Early in the run, the Shuberts announced the formation of the De Koven Opera Company, devoted exclusively to the performance of light opera, and employing the principal performers from *The Wedding Trip*. Modeled after The Bostonians, the company was planning to offer special matinees of Offenbach's *The Tales of Hoffmann* during the run of *The Wedding Trip*, and Smith was engaged to adapt Jules Barbier's original French text. A possible revival of *Robin Hood* was also advertised, but when de Koven's latest effort closed after forty-eight performances, plans for the development of the light opera company were postponed.

Harry B. Smith had no time to concern himself with the fate of his work with de Koven, because his next libretto was scheduled to be shown to New York audiences at the Liberty Theatre on New Year's Day. This was an American version of *Modest Suzanne*, adapted from the German megahit, *Die keusche Suzanne*, by Georg Okonkowsky and Alfred Schönfeld, with music by Jean Gilbert, commissioned by Peoria-born producer Harry Frazee and his partner, A. H. Woods. Working again with his brother Robert, Harry recast the story of a girl whose modesty was reversible into easily accessible, idiomatic verse that removed much of the naughtiness of the original and maintained most of the fun. Suzanne (Sallie Fisher) had been awarded a medal for "modesty," but there was more to her than meets the eye. When she meets up with Baron Dauvray (Stanley G. Forde), a respected member of the Academy, at the Moulin Rouge, they renew their old association and exchange their sober sides for fun and frivolity. On opening night, the critics and audiences enjoyed what they saw, but because the music was considered "gay" without being memorable and the potentially "tiresome" story "old and harmless," *Modest Suzanne* failed to stay a month and expired after twenty-four performances.

Barely two months later, on March 16, 1912, Smith signed a contract with Ziegfeld to adapt Charles H. Hoyt's popular musical farce, *A Trip to Chinatown*, into a musical comedy entitled *A Winsome Widow*. Smith was to provide the producer with a complete libretto, including lyrics for songs, and Ziegfeld agreed to pay the author a royalty of $150 per week for the run of the production. Smith was permitted to engage his brother to assist in the writing of lyrics at no expense to the producer—Harry paid Robert out of his own royalties—and, most importantly, it was agreed that Harry's name appear nowhere on the programs or in any advertisements as the author or adapter of the musical. In a week, Raymond Hubbell was setting Smith's lyrics to music, and before the end of March, the musical was in rehearsal, under the direction of Julian Mitchell.

On April 11, 1912, the show was welcomed at the New York Theatre (renamed the "Moulin Rouge" by the producer) by an audience that applauded everything and everyone so enthusiastically that the performance lasted until nearly midnight. What they saw was the familiar story. Rashleigh Gay (Charles J. Ross) and his sister, Tony (Ida Adams), have been forbidden by their puritanical uncle, Ben Gay (Leon Errol), from going to a restaurant called the "Poodle Dog." They decide to go anyway with their friends Wilder Daly (Charles King), Tony's sweetheart, and Isabel (Elizabeth Brice), in love with Rashleigh. They had invited a widow, Mrs. Guyer (Emmy Wehlen), along as a chaperon, but her reply had been mistakenly received by Uncle Ben, who thinks she is inviting him to meet her at the restaurant. All of the principals, including a hypochondriac named Welland Strong (Harry Conor) end up at the Poodle Dog and try to stay out of one another's way, until Ben Gay ruins his suit and is forced to assume the attire of a chef. Welland Strong empties Ben's suit pockets of all his identification, and in the ensuing police raid, unable to prove who he is, Ben Gay gets himself arrested while the others escape. During the proceedings, Rosie and Jenny, played by the Dolly Twins (later known as the Dolly Sisters), provided dance *divertissements,* and the chorus danced on ice skates in a spectacular "ice carnival" sequence in which the stage was covered with real ice. Among the featured performers was eighteen-year-old Mae West appearing as a "baby vamp," La Petite Daffy, who, according to the *Dramatic Mirror* (April 17, 1912), "assaults the welkin vigorously."

Critics complained that the plot appeared to be a vehicle for spectacular scenery, costumes, and choreography, and that Hubbell's music was full of "dash" but empty of hits. An interpolation, "Be My Little Baby Bumble Bee" with music by Henry Marshall and lyrics by Stanley Murphy, proved to be the most durable song of the evening. Still, the consensus was that *A Winsome Widow* was "a real novelty" and "as good or better than a lot," and the show went on paying Harry B. Smith $150 a week until September 7.

April 22 saw another Smith book in New York when *The Rose Maid* opened at the Globe Theatre. Producers Werba and Luescher were anxious to mount Bruno Granichstaedten's successful 1908 Viennese operetta, *Bub oder Mädel?* and commissioned Smith to translate and adapt the original libretto by Adolf Altmann and Felix Dörmann. Harry subsequently enlisted the help of his brother to provide lyrics, and author Raymond Peck to assist with the book and provide lyrics to Robert Hood Bowers's interpolated melodies. The complicated plot centers on the Duke of Barchester (J. H. Duffey), whose uncle, Sir John Portman (R. E. Graham), arrives for a surprise visit on the very day the Duke announces his engagement to Princess Hilda von Lahn (Edith Decker). Discovering his nephew to be extravagant and severely in debt, Sir John pretends to have a wife and child, thus leaving the Duke without his anticipated inheritance. Discovering her fiancé to be penniless, the Princess leaves him in favor of the Honorable Bertie Walpole (Burrell Barbaretto), a naval cadet, and at the insistence of his creditors, Dennis (Ed Gallagher), Schmuke (Al Shean), and Chumley (Arthur Laceby), the Duke agrees to marry one of the American millionairesses being chaperoned through Europe by Countess Bertrand (Juliette Dika). Daphne (Adrienne Augarde), a housekeeper's daughter, is palmed off as one of the millionaire ladies, and the Duke falls in love with her. Because she really loves him as well, Daphne reveals that she has no money, so that marrying her would in no way help the Duke pay off his creditors. However, when Sir John discovers that her father served under him in the army, he insists that his nephew and Daphne get married, confessing that he is yet a bachelor, and that the Duke is still his heir.

Critics enjoyed Granichstaedten's music, and predicted that most of the songs would be "resounding presently in all the cafes on Broadway." Smith's translation was found less effective, blamed once again for the presence of antique jokes, as the *Dramatic Mirror* (April 24, 1912) complained:

> This light but agreeable narrative is not developed for all it is worth because the adapters have wandered far afield in their search for suitable comic episodes. They have dragged in an almost interminable horde of tired jokes for the business man, but apparently there were enough business men in the audience, for laughter increased with the inanity of the humor. A modicum of genuine wit was injected into the book, and, had all other lines been eliminated, there would still have been enough left.

But most of the critics seemed to agree with the businessmen, calling *The Rose Maid* the best of Werba and Luescher's productions, and correctly anticipating that it would bloom throughout the summer, remaining at the Globe Theatre for 176 performances.

The spring was another hectic one for Harry B. Smith. He had just completed a three-act farce, *The Black Cat*, in April, and he was busy collaborating with his brother on an adaptation of *Das Mädel von Montmartre* for producer Charles Frohman, and working on a script for the *Ziegfeld Follies of 1912*, scheduled to open not as a summer entertainment at a roof-garden theater, but as a legitimate theatrical entry in the fall. Four months after it had been originally announced, the revival of *Robin Hood* took place on May 6, 1912, at the New Amsterdam Theater with a stellar company. Harry did not attend the opening. He had sold the rights to the show to Reginald de Koven a number of years earlier, and was wary of revisiting his twenty-two-year-old creation. He was finally persuaded to attend a performance late in the run; in spite of the excellent cast, he was only able to tolerate two scenes before leaving the theater exclaiming, "I couldn't stand it. Judged by contemporary standards, the dialogue and lyrics were distressing to me."

Even though New Yorkers had been visited by the show almost yearly since 1891, Daniel V. Arthur's production was sufficiently popular to remain until the beginning of July, when Harry and his brother were in rehearsal with *The Girl from Montmartre*, their American adaptation of *Das Mädel von Montmartre* by Rudolf Schanzer with music by Hungarian composer Henrik Berény. The story, originally based on Georges Feydeau's farce *La dame de chez Maxim*, centers on Praline (Hattie Williams), who is taken home from the Café Montmartre by a mature physician, Dr. Petypon (Richard Carle). He puts her in his bedroom, and he ends up falling asleep on the sofa in his living room, the next day forgetting all about the girl in his bed. His wife, Gabrielle (Marion Abbott), discovers the girl and thinks she is a "spirit," and General Petypon (Al Hart), the doctor's wealthy uncle, believes her to be his niece and invites her to Touraine for the wedding of another niece, Clementine (Moya Mannering), to Lieutenant Corignon (George Lydecker), the man Praline really loves. In Touraine, Praline teaches high society how to have fun "Montmartre style," and manages to win back the Lieutenant in the bargain.

When *The Girl from Montmartre* opened at the Criterion Theatre on August 5, Smith's libretto was once again attacked for having too many old jokes. Even still, the critics found the show "a pleasing mixture of the Continental materials" with catchy songs and engaging performances. Especially noteworthy were a song, "Don't Turn My Picture to the Wall," composed by Jerome Kern to Robert B. Smith's lyrics, and a "Kinemacolor" motion picture in the third act depicting various characters chasing Praline, an innovation that helped the farce accumulate sixty-four performances in New York before heading out on tour.

No sooner was *The Girl from Montmartre* open when Harry found himself back in rehearsal with Ziegfeld on the 1912 edition of the *Follies*. His libretto was full of the usual social, theatrical, and political satire, with references to Ivan Caryll's *The Pink Lady* (the popular British import that had opened in New York on March 13, 1912), Teddy Roosevelt, income taxes, and dozens of other current issues. He wrote a prologue, designed to be performed before the curtain rose, depicting members of the audience quarreling about the kind of entertainment they expected to see. Harry Watson Jr. played a "Gallery Boy" shouting about his fondness for the "bring-on-the-girls" kind of musicals, while Charles Judels, as a very French Monsieur Poulet, vociferously complained about American entertainments. Since these performers were planted in the auditorium, they created the illusion of a real argument, to the surprise and ultimate delight of the real audience, who understood this as a development of Ziegfeld's traditional practice of letting the entertainment spill over into the crowd.

Although he knew no French, Judels had made a career of playing eccentric Frenchmen speaking a lot of nonsense words using a French accent and delivery. During rehearsals, Ziegfeld asked Harry to teach the lyrics of Rouget de Lisle's "Marseillaise" to the actor so that he could sing it at the end of a scene that needed a better punch. Vainly Harry protested that Judels could neither read nor speak the language, but he obediently wrote down the French words for the actor and listened as Judels sang the song using his usual nonsense vocabulary. When the show opened at the Moulin Rouge on October 21, Judels's performance of the number was so realistically "patriotic" that the critic for the *New York Times* (October 22, 1912) complimented the performer for bringing "lots of spirit to his part."

Typically, spectacle was the most important feature of the entertainment, and "The Palace of Beauty," marking the first time Ziegfeld and his director, Julian Mitchell, employed the fashion-show device of sending out the girls one at a time, was repeatedly singled out by the critics. To the music of "Beautiful, Beautiful Girl," composed by Raymond Hubbell with lyrics by John E. Hazzard, chorus girls paraded across stage, dressed as famous characters: Harlequin (Evelyn Hart), Venus (Elise Hamilton), Carmen (Eleanor Christie), Joan of Arc (Beatrice Allen), Pocahontas (May Leslie), Salome (Ida Adams), and other celebrated beauties. The funniest sketch of the evening was the "Hansom Cab" routine, in which Bert Williams (as a taxi driver) takes Leon Errol (his drunken fare) all over the city to get to Seventh Avenue, right where they began. And the hit song, sung by Lillian Lorraine, was James V. Monaco and William Jerome's "Row, Row, Row."

After the *Ziegfeld Follies of 1912*, Smith broke off his long association with Ziegfeld. There were a lot of reasons for the parting, not the least of which was the producer's habit of neglecting to pay authors their royalties, but in one of the drafts of his essay "Ziegfeld of the Follies," Smith offers his own explanation:

> My own association with these reviews ceased abruptly, owing to an incident characteristic of their promoter. I had signed a contract with a manager to adapt a French play for him. This

manager happened to meet Mr. Ziegfeld on a train and informed him that I was to write the play. On his arrival in Chicago, Flo sent me one of his famous long telegrams, saying that if I wrote for any other manager, I would be neglecting the *Follies* and would be allowed to write no more of them. Perhaps there were other reasons. The *Follies* from having a small plot, had come to have none at all; a series of vaudeville acts. This caused one newspaper critic to inquire why my name was programmed as the author, and what, if anything, I did to earn a royalty. The critic graciously printed my reply in which I said that Mr. Ziegfeld's kind heart was well known and that he sent me royalty checks out of pure benevolence.

The *Ziegfeld Follies of 1912* remained at the Moulin Rouge for eighty-eight performances, closing on January 4, 1913.

A month later, *The Sunshine Girl*, by Paul Rubens and Cecil Raleigh, with lyrics by Rubens and Arthur Wimperis, and music by Rubens, appeared at the Knickerbocker Theatre. The show had been a success in London, playing nearly a year at the Gaiety Theatre, but when Charles Frohman purchased the American rights, he hired Smith to revise the libretto and adapt the roles to the personalities of Julia Sanderson, Joseph Cawthorn, and the rest of the American cast—much like the author used to do in his early work for Colonel McCaull. Smith agreed, so long as his name did not appear on the program, because he believed that critics always objected to revisions and interpolations whenever English musicals were performed in New York. Smith added American slang to the text, and altered the names and personalities of some of the characters: Foot, for example, the ex-cabby played by Edmund Payne at the Gaiety, became Schlump, a German American word twister played by Joseph Cawthorn. The basic plot, however, remained the same. Under the stipulation of his uncle's will, Vernon Blundell (Alan Mudie) must work for five years at the Sunshine Soap Factory without getting married before he can inherit the plant. Dora Dale (Julia Sanderson), who works with him in the factory, is in love with him. The day arrives when he can shed his anonymity, but to make sure that he is loved for himself and not his inheritance, he convinces his friend, "Bingo," Lord Bicester (Vernon Castle), to pretend to be the heir. Bingo enjoys playing the role until he is recognized by his ex-cabby, Schlump, and his fiancée, Lady Rosabelle Merrydew (Eileen Kearney), but the ensuing complications are resolved when Blundell finally acknowledges his inheritance and proposes to Dora.

The critics found *The Sunshine Girl* "bright" and "handsomely staged," with just enough plot to support the music and dancing. Even though Smith gave actor Tom Lewis the role of an American from Pittsburgh who hated the British, the critics made no complaint about the adaptation. One even exclaimed, "Here is one beautiful English piece that has not been tampered with by an American adapter." "Honeymoon Lane," an interpolated song by Jerome Kern with lyrics by M. E. Rourke, was singled out as a hit, and the dances by Vernon and Irene Castle managed to propel the show to a twenty-week run.

At the end of March, a new Harry B. Smith and Fred de Grésac operetta was on the boards in Baltimore, with music by Victor Herbert, lyrics by Robert B. Smith, and produced by Louis Werba and Mark Luescher. Originally titled *The Tulip Girl*, *Sweethearts* gave its world premiere at the Academy of Music on March 24, 1913, with the composer conducting, and starring Christie MacDonald. Back in July 1910, the *Dramatic Mirror* announced that Herbert intended to compose an opera for MacDonald, but it was only after hearing her sing the lead in *The Spring Maid* during the fall of 1912 that the composer began work in earnest, promising to complete the score by January 1913.

The Cinderella story concocted by Smith and de Grésac is explained in the program:

> The story of the opera is founded on the adventures of Princess Jeanne, daughter of King Rene of Naples, who reigned in the fifteenth century. Time has been changed to the present, and the locale to the ancient city of Bruges, to which the little Princess is carried for safety in time of war, and is given the name of Sylvia (Christie MacDonald). As an infant she is found in a tulip garden one morning by Dame Paula (Ethel Du Fre Houston), who conducts the Laundry of the White Geese, and who is known as "Mother Goose." Sylvia is brought up as the daughter of Paula, although the latter has six daughters of her own . . . known as the White Geese. To the laundry comes Mikel Mikeloviz (Tom McNaughton) who, disguised as a monk, left Sylvia when an infant in Dame Paula's care. Knowing that Sylvia is the Crown Princess of the little Kingdom of Zilania, Mikel is conspiring to restore her to the

> throne, which is about to be offered to Franz, the heir presumptive (Thomas Conkey) who, in traveling incognito, has fallen in love with Sylvia, and who finds a rival in Lieutenant Karl (Edwin Wilson), a military Lothario, betrothed to Sylvia. Mikel's plans are endangered by the schemes of Hon. Percy Algernon Slingsby (Lionel Walsh), Petrus Van Tromp (Frank Belcher), [and] Aristide Caniche (Robert O'Connor), who wish to purchase, for their own purposes, Prince Franz's estates in Zilania. Liane, a milliner [originally Ruth Lincoln, replaced by Hazel Kirke], has sought temporary employment in the Laundry of the White Geese, and is mistaken by Mikel and Slingsby for the lost Princess.

The tryout week in Baltimore was nerve-racking for Smith and his collaborators. On opening night, the critics complained about the length of the show, and they also found fault with Herbert's music. Such an untypical reaction led to desperate measures, and by Saturday evening, the entire show had been overhauled, ready for its five-week engagement in Philadelphia, where the response was much more enthusiastic. Another five weeks in Boston, where the response was best of all, led to a summer vacation, allowing the cast to recuperate before the New York opening scheduled for September 8 at the New Amsterdam Theatre.

While *Sweethearts* was in Boston, Smith's American adaptation of *Der kleine Freunden*, by Leo Stein and A. M. Willner, with music by Oscar Straus, opened as *My Little Friend* on May 19, 1913, at the New Amsterdam Theatre. In an arrangement with producer Fred C. Whitney, Harry once again engaged his brother Robert as lyricist. The well-worn plot details the attempts of impoverished Count Henry Artois (Fred Walton) to marry his son, Fernand (Craufurd Kent), to Claire (Maud Gray), the daughter of a self-made millionaire, Barbasson (William Pruette). As guests arrive at the millionaire's home for the wedding, the groom sends a telegram from Paris, refusing to marry a girl he has never met, a situation welcomed by the bride, who is really in love with Dr. La Fleur (Lionel Hogarth), an Egyptologist. The two parents go to Paris, arriving on the day Fernand has secretly married his "little friend," a florist named Philine (Leila Hughes). Thinking that he is romantically involved with Louison (Reba Dale), Philine's friend, the fathers pay Fernand to go away with Philine for six months, in an attempt to cure him of his infatuation. Six months pass, during which both fathers find themselves enraptured by Louison, who, having tolerated their attentions, finally admits that she has been secretly married to a poet, Saturin (Charles Angelo). Fernand and Philine return from their subsidized honeymoon and reveal that they are married at the same time Claire announces her marriage to La Fleur, and the fathers give up trying to unite their two families.

Although Straus's score was applauded greatly and Smith's book was found "not entirely without a suggestion of humor," providing "enough variety in character and incident to serve as a background for the music," *My Little Friend*, boasting a cast of nearly one hundred, remained only until the first week of June. In July, Smith registered another play for copyright, *September Morn*, named for the 1913 painting by Paul Chabas that had been the subject of the first nude pinup calendar and censored by the New York Society for the Suppression of Vice. Also in July, Smith was announced as the author selected to provide the book and lyrics for *The Coquette*, Victor Herbert's newest comic opera, but the project never materialized. At the end of August, still waiting for *Sweethearts* to come to New York, Smith saw the premiere of *The Doll Girl*, his adaptation for Charles Frohman of A. M. Willner and Leo Stein's *Das Puppenmädel*, with music by Leo Fall.

Opening on August 25 at the Globe Theatre, *The Doll Girl* tells the frothy story of Yvette (Dorothy Webb), an eighteen-year-old girl still addicted to playing with dolls, who works at her mother's tobacco and news stand in Picardy. She is courted by Tiborius (Robert Evett), nephew to the Marquis De la Tourelle (Richard Carle), an old roué who brought the girl to Paris to wine and dine her. Rosalilla (Hattie Williams), a Spanish actress, shows up in a variety of disguises to test the fidelity of the flirtatious Marquis, and in the end, Tiborius wins Yvette's affections.

The critics found it a "clean wholesome show" with a fine cast, lilting music, and "comedy that does not need a subtle sense of humor." Smith's songs, "Come on Over Here," with music by Walter Kollo, and additional lyrics by Jerome Kern, "If We Were on Our Honeymoon," composed by Jerome Kern, and "You're So Fascinating," composed by Leo Fall, were cited as the standouts of the evening. The last-named song, performed by Rosalilla, also provided some of the best comedy of the production, causing the Marquis to respond to her almost gymnastic amorous embraces: "This isn't love, it's massage!" Although opening night was a rousing success and critics predicted a long run, *The Doll Girl* lasted an unimpressive eighty-eight performances in New York before going out on tour.

Nearly six months after its premiere in Baltimore, *Sweethearts* arrived at the New Amsterdam Theatre on September 8, 1913. As usual, Herbert's score was highly regarded and the libretto considered the weakest element of the production. The *Dramatic Mirror* (September 10, 1913) noted the Cinderella-like plot and complained, "The transition of time and locale has not lifted it above the genre of the commonplace, and the story lacks intrinsically the humor which Mr. Smith as the collaborator has sought to supply in trimmings in the shape of a trio of eccentric comiques, headed by Mr. McNaughton, who made the best of their opportunities." Still, on the strength of Herbert's "bewitching" music, Frederick G. Latham's attractive staging, and Christie's MacDonald's "engaging" and "alluring" performance, *Sweethearts* managed a run of 136 performances in New York before continuing on tour.

Daniel V. Arthur put *Rob Roy* back on the boards at the Liberty Theatre for twenty-four performances beginning September 15, 1913. On this occasion, Smith was actively involved, producing the lyrics for "Love-Land," a waltz song interpolated into the second act for the character of Janet, the Mayor's daughter who is secretly married to Rob Roy. Smith spent the rest of the month completing the adaptation of another Victor Léon libretto, *Der fidele Bauer*, which had premiered at the Hoftheater in Mannheim on July 27, 1907, with music by Leo Fall. The story involved a peasant farmer set in his ways, whose son, the doctor, hesitates to reveal his engagement to the daughter of an aristocratic family, fearing that his family would not get along with hers. Smith called his version *The Jolly Peasant*, and engaged his brother to provide lyrics. The work was registered for copyright on October 29, 1913, but plans for production were never realized.

Chapter 9

Jerome Kern and Irving Berlin

The Doll Girl provided Harry B. Smith with his first real collaboration with Jerome Kern, the young composer who had written some of the music interpolated into *The Rich Mr. Hoggenheimer*, *Little Miss Fix-It*, *The Siren*, *A Winsome Widow*, and *The Girl from Montmartre*. Smith enjoyed working with Kern. Not only was he as rhapsodically melodic as the European composers of operetta, he was as harmonically up to date and syncopated as the best of the popular Tin Pan Alley crowd. What's more, he was quick and, best of all, like Smith, he was a book collector who enjoyed acquiring manuscripts and autographs as much as the lyricist. Early on in their association, Smith took the composer to an auction house, where Kern acquired a copy of *Endymion* by John Keats by bidding $100; he later discovered a copy of Keats's own signature, apparently unnoticed by the auctioneers, inside the book. The joy of that discovery was as valuable to both of them as the best of reviews about their work.

The Doll Girl was still running when their second collaboration opened in Albany, New York, at the end of September. The show was *Oh,*

I Say!, and was produced by the Shubert Brothers, with a book by Sidney Blow and Douglas Hoare, adapted from a French farce, *Une nuit de noces*, by Henri Keroul and Albert Barré. Sidonie de Mornay (Cecil Cunningham), a vaudeville actress, is supposed to be away on tour, so her maid, Claudine (Clara Palmer), rents out her apartment to a newlywed couple. The bride's father, Jules Portal (Walter Jones), soon appears at the house because he has hired Sidonie and her entire company to perform for the wedding party, and Madam Portal (Jeffreys Lewis), concerned about her daughter, shows up as well. Needless to say, when Sidonie arrives, she is not only shocked to find people in her home, she is overwhelmed by the fact that her ex-lover is the bridegroom.

After a month on the road, *Oh, I Say!* opened at the Casino Theatre on October 30, and the critics applauded the cast, the spectacle, and most especially Kern's music, finding it "tuneful and bright and also less hackneyed" than the standard musical fare on Broadway. Smith's lyrics were praised for their cleverness, and the critics predicted the show would last the season. It remained until Christmas and then continued touring until spring, with its name changed to *Their Wedding Night* in the vain hope that the innuendo would induce people to buy tickets.

The new year saw Smith and Kern in Rochester, where *The Laughing Husband* received its American premiere at the Lyceum Theatre. Producer Charles Frohman commissioned Smith to revise, albeit anonymously, Arthur Wimperis's adaptation of *Der lachende Ehemann*, by Julius Brammer and Alfred Grünwald, with music by Edmund Eysler. Additional music was added by Jerome Kern, and the lyrics to all of Kern's songs were supplied by Smith. The plot involves a rich, retired confectioner, Ottokar Bruckner (Courtice Pounds), who has married Hella (Betty Callish), a beautiful young Baroness and novelist. To do research for her novel, "The Laughing Husband," she allows Count Selztal (Gustave Werner) to court her actively. When Bruckner hears the couple frolicking behind a screen with a bottle of champagne, he breaks down and hires Mr. Rosenrot (William Norris), a famous divorce lawyer. After the publication of her book, however, Hella has no interest in the Count, and she and her husband are easily reconciled.

The Laughing Husband moved to the Knickerbocker Theatre in New York City on February 2. Perhaps because the critics did not realize that Smith had revised the book, they gave it a fine review, praising its ability to modulate "gracefully from farce to drama, and back again into farce." Eysler's score was applauded as "tuneful," even though the songs cited as hits by the *Dramatic Mirror* (February 4, 1914) were both by Kern: "Take a Step with Me" and "You're Here and I'm Here." Harry B. Smith recalled the spontaneous creation of the second song:

> [*The Laughing Husband*] was produced in Rochester and it was found that, among many other things, it needed a popular tune. Jerome Kern, who had contributed numbers to the opera, received a managerial mandate to try to "dig up" a song. Mr. Kern climbed into the orchestra pit and rattled off something on the piano. "That sounds all right," said Frohman. The composer wrote out the melody on the back of a discarded orchestra part and handed it to me. I took it to a theatre dressing room and wrote the lyric. This song, "You're Here and I'm Here," was a popular hit and was afterward sung in most of the English pantomimes of the year. Mr. Frohman's comment on the prompt filling of his order was[,] "You boys make your money too easily."

Kern recalled that the entire process took less than an hour. While *The Laughing Husband* managed to accumulate only forty-eight performances, the writers pumping it full of popular tunes were able to achieve a long-standing hit song.

As the spring progressed, Harry had his work cut out for him. He needed to complete the book for Victor Herbert's newest comic opera before he left for Europe to visit composer Ivan Caryll in his castle in Normandy to collaborate on a new musical comedy for Klaw and Erlanger. Charles Dillingham had given him an old French play that Augustin Daly had adapted as *Round the Clock*, and wanted him to transform it into the book for a musical; and former manager of the Metropolitan Opera House, Andreas Dippel, having discovered Charles Cuvillier's melodious score to *Der lila Domino*, was anxious to produce an adaptation in New York. In the midst of all of this activity, Smith noticed that Ziegfeld had neglected to pay him $4,330 in royalties. Divorced from Anna Held, and no longer infatuated with Lillian Lorraine, Ziegfeld was currently attached to actress Billie Burke and scarcely interested in the mundane business of fulfilling contracts. After the couple married on April 11, 1914, they went to Long Beach, New Jersey, for a two-day honeymoon. On April 12, Smith sent a process server to the honeymoon suite to hand the impresario a writ giving him notice that the royalties were due. Smith still did not receive his money, and it was only months later, when a judge threatened to send the producer to jail, that Ziegfeld told his lawyer, Leon Laski, to send a check to the author. Communications had finally ceased between Florenz Ziegfeld Jr. and Harry B. Smith.

Belgian-born composer Ivan Caryll had settled in England after his studies at the Paris Conservatoire, rising to international prominence through his work at the Gaiety Theatre in London. Smith was impressed both by his musicianship and by his ability to convince producers to back his shows. Caryll sometimes purchased the American rights to French farces, and while he was telling the producer the story of the farce, his hearty laugh would become so infectious that the producer invariably signed a contract then and there. Caryll had related the story of Grenet d'Ancourt and Maurice Vaucaire's *Le fils surnaturel* to Klaw and Erlanger with such hilarity that they immediately contracted Harry B. Smith to adapt it, necessitating a meeting between the author and composer at Caryll's castle in Normandy.

When Harry arrived in Paris, however, he received a telegram from the composer changing the meeting place from Normandy to Cap Ferrat, on the Mediterranean near Monte Carlo. Evidently, something had gone wrong with the plumbing in the castle, and the composer felt that his villa at Cap Ferrat would be more comfortable. At the villa, Smith and Caryll maintained a fairly rigid schedule. Work would begin at dawn and continue until noon, after which the author and composer would drive into the Alps in Caryll's small American car, and dine in a mountain restaurant as a kind of relaxation from what Smith called "the nervous strain of writing a musical comedy." On June 28, the collaborators were recuperating from their morning work at a table in front of a small café in Nice. The little band inside was playing an excerpt from Rossini's opera *William Tell*, and Caryll was jovially beating in time when a newsboy ran past them excitedly heralding the latest headlines. They bought a paper and discovered that the Austrian Archduke Franz Ferdinand had been assassinated at Sarajevo, and instantly Smith recalled the rumblings of war he had experienced on his excursion to Europe five years before. The imminence of a European conflict cut short the author's stay at Cap Ferrat. A few days later, the libretto for the musical having been completed, he said goodbye to Ivan Caryll and traveled first to Paris and then to London, where, on July 28, he learned that Austria had declared war on Serbia, and that Russia was mobilizing its forces. On August 3, while Smith was browsing through a treasure trove of Dickens first editions in a bookstore on Charing Cross Road, he learned that Germany, having already declared war on Russia, was now at war with France. The men in the bookstore seemed to agree that if Germany attacked Belgium, England would have to enter the conflict. On the night of August 3, Germany entered Belgium, so the following day, Harry B. Smith booked himself on a boat leaving for New York.

As soon as he arrived home, he was back to work. The first show to open was his Americanization for Charles Frohman of *The Girl from Utah*, originally produced at the Adelphi Theatre in London on October 18, 1913, with a book by James T. Tanner (and Paul A. Rubens), music by Rubens and Sidney Jones, and lyrics by Rubens, Percy Greenbank, and Adrian Ross. Scheduled to give its pre-Broadway premiere on August 17 at the Apollo Theatre in Atlantic City, and designed to fit the talents of Julia Sanderson, Donald Brian, and Joseph Cawthorn, Smith's version traced the adventures of Una Trance (Julia Sanderson), the Utah girl, escaping the Mormon lifestyle in London, where she meets Sandy Blair (Donald Brian), a handsome young actor. Trimpel (Joseph Cawthorn), the proprietor of a ham and beef shop in Brixton, is mistaken for one of the Mormons pursuing her, and a merry chase ensues, leading, of course, to a union between Una and Sandy. A week after the Atlantic City opening, *The Girl from Utah* moved to the Knickerbocker Theatre in New York City, where it remained for 120 performances.

Smith and Kern produced six songs for the show (a seventh, the celebrated "They Didn't Believe Me," had lyrics by M. E. Rourke, using the pseudonym Herbert Reynolds): "The Land of Let's Pretend," a wistful ballad used as prologue and epilogue to the piece; "Same Sort of Girl," "You Never Can Tell," "Why Don't They Dance the Polka Anymore?" all rousing, syncopated dance tunes; "We'll Take Care of You All," a march inviting European refugees to find safety in America; and "Alice in Wonderland," a wistful barcarolle, the lyric of which was a particular favorite of James M. Barrie, the English playwright and author.

Barely a month after *The Girl from Utah* opened in Manhattan, *The Debutante*, with music by Victor Herbert, and lyrics by Robert B. Smith, premiered at the New Nixon Theatre in Atlantic City. The plot centers on Elaine (Hazel Dawn), daughter of Sir Francis Vane, engaged to Philip (Wilmuth Merkyl), son of Godfrey Frazer, a wealthy American industrialist. When Philip returns from Paris infatuated with Irma (Zoe Barnett), a Russian dancer, Elaine engages the help of Armand, Marquis de Frontenac (Stewart Baird), to make him jealous. When that only partially succeeds, Elaine goes to Paris and plays the role of the dashing debutante so well that all thoughts of Irma are driven from her fiancé's head. Reviews were only lukewarm in Atlantic City, and *The Debutante* continued to tour for two months before trying its luck in New York City.

A month later, on October 28, *The Lilac Domino*, Harry and Robert B. Smith's adaptation of Béla Jenbach and Emmerich von Gatti's *Der lila Domino,* appeared at the Forty-fourth Street Theatre in New York, with music by Charles Cuvillier, and Eleanor Painter, prima donna of the Metropolitan Opera House, in the leading role. The story involves three young men, Count Andre (Wilfrid Douthitt), Prosper (John E. Hazzard), and Casimir (Robert O'Connor), who meet at a ball and throw dice to determine which of them shall marry a rich heiress and save them all from bankruptcy. Andre is chosen, and he falls in love with Georgine (Eleanor Painter), the girl in the lilac domino and daughter of the rich Vicomte de Brissac (George Curzon). As the romance develops, Istvan (Harry Hermsen), a Hungarian bandmaster, reveals to Georgine that Andre was chosen by lot to marry a rich girl, and she breaks off the relationship. When Andre is finally permitted to explain, however, she realizes that he really loves her as much as she loves him, and the couple head for the altar.

Opening night was a splendid affair attended by the wealthy supporters of the Metropolitan Opera, in addition to the usually enthusiastic musical theater audience. As the *Dramatic Mirror* (November 4, 1914) noted, "they applauded to the echo. It was a perfect ovation, unlike any premiere since premieres became things of almost nightly recurrence. And most of it was deserved." The reviews were generally good, even for the libretto, and two songs actually written for the show were singled out by the critics as hits: "What Is Done You Never Can Undo" and "What Every Woman Knows." In spite of good press, an excellent first night, and a "Kinemacolor" motion picture display of carnival scenes and flowers between the second and third acts, business was slow, and the show folded after 109 performances.

Less successful was Smith's collaboration with Ivan Caryll, opening on November 2, 1914, at the New Amsterdam Theatre. Produced by Klaw and Erlanger, and staged by Julian Mitchell, *Papa's Darling* told the story of one Achille Petipas (Frank Lalor), a teacher at a girls' school, who makes people believe that he has a child ("papa's darling") so that he has an excuse to travel to Paris to carry on an affair with a cabaret singer named Zozo (Dorothy Jardon). Believed by his students to be the "monopolist of virtue," Petipas is ultimately discovered to be something of a roué, as he explains in "The Popular Pop":

I'm in clover, look me over,
I'm the rollicking boy . . .
Chief promoter of joy
On the level, I'm a devil
Sport is my middle name . . .
Game for any old game
I start but never know when to stop
To all the girls I am known as Pop
My fav'rite saying is "Bring a Quart
And Pop is Papa for short."
I Pop up ev'ry ev'ning,
I Pop a cocktail down
I Pop into a taxicab,
I Pop around the town,
I Pop into a gay café,
And hop until I drop
I lose control of the old bank roll,
So I'm a popular Pop!

Critics judged the work acceptable, finding Caryll's music "delectable," though inferior to his earlier score for *The Pink Lady*, a comparable adaptation of another French play. "The Land of the Midnight Sun," "Who Cares," and "Oh, This Is Love" were among the several songs noted as potential hits, destined "to be whistled up and down the highways." Still, closing after forty performances, *Papa's Darling* was a failure simply because the audiences did not find the material funny. Smith regretted that Caryll laughed more in telling the plot to the producers than did any audience in the theater: "If we could have had him in the audience instead of in the conductor's chair, we might have had a success."

A month later, on December 7, *The Debutante* finally arrived at the Knickerbocker Theatre, where Herbert's music was reviewed as "lively, brilliant, and popular," without attempting "anything ambitious," and Smith's book was considered "better than harmless," though not "convulsingly funny." The *Dramatic Mirror* (December 16, 1914) blamed the show's deficiencies on the genre of musical theater it represented: "If you find fault with 'The Debutante' you must find fault with the whole species of musical comedies and not with this specimen. It does not soar above the level of a Smith libretto, and does not fall below it." The real star of the evening was Hazel Dawn, the Salt Lake City actress, who sang, spoke, and even played the violin three years earlier in *The Pink Lady*. Although the *Dramatic Mirror* judged her "as pretty and dainty as the prima donna of a musical comedy should be," Dawn was not enough to keep *The Debutante* singing for more than forty-eight performances.

On December 8, *Watch Your Step*, Smith's adaptation of *Round the Clock* for Charles Dillingham, opened at the New Amsterdam Theatre following a tryout at the Empire Theatre in Syracuse, New York (where W. C. Fields was fired from the company because he took too much focus away from the stars). Designed to feature dancers Vernon and Irene Castle, and the highly danceable, syncopated music of Irving Berlin, who also supplied his own lyrics, the show had only a bare thread of a plot. At the "Law Office de Danse," a group of people have assembled to hear the reading of a will that leaves $2 million to the heir who can avoid falling in love. Joseph Lilyburn (Vernon Castle), a dance teacher, and Ernesta Hardachre (Sallie Fisher), a simple country girl "too good to be true," lay claim to the inheritance. The scene changes to the "Old Stage Door," where Algy Cuffs (Charles King), a matinee idol and claimant to the will, complains about being chased by fans, and the act ends at the "Palais de Fox-Trot," where Algy serenades his sweetheart, Stella Spark (Elizabeth Brice), and Mrs. Vernon Castle, playing herself, teaches students how to do the fox-trot.

The second act takes place at the Metropolitan Opera House, where the ghost of Verdi appears to complain about performers syncopating his music in a long concerted number that juxtaposes motifs from Verdi operas with ragtime riffs. The third act is set in a "Fifth Avenue Cabaret" where Algy and Ernesta sing about their contrasting lifestyles in a counterpoint duet, "Play a Simple Melody," juxtaposing her simple, lyrical melody with his snappy, ragtime tune. The Castles lead the company in a dance, and the curtain falls. Smith had few pretensions about his libretto. In fact, he did not even use the word "libretto" in the program. His credit simply reads: "Plot (if any) by H. B. Smith."

The librettist had great respect for the twenty-six-year-old Irving Berlin, particularly his ingenuity at creating unexpected rhymes. In Algy Cuff's song, "They Follow Me Around," for example, Berlin produced a plausible rhyme for "Wednesday": "There's a matinee on Wednesday, /I call it my old hens' day." The first complete score for Berlin on Broadway, *Watch Your Step* was judged a hit by the critics, the *New York Times*

(December 9, 1914) calling it "hilarious fun," and attributing most of the success to Berlin's score. The *Dramatic Mirror* (December 16, 1914) called the show a "rag-time riot and dancing delirium," and argued that the Castles and comedian Frank Tinney contributed more than Berlin to the "phenomenal success of the entertainment." Either way, the opening night crowd that vociferously greeted every funny line and musical number with thunderous applause became the typical audience throughout the show's twenty-two-week run. After closing in New York, *Watch Your Step* moved to London, where the show played 275 performances with a revised book by Harry Grattan.

While Smith was working with Irving Berlin, he continued to write songs with Jerome Kern, and on December 31, *Ninety in the Shade,* with a full Smith-Kern score, appeared at the Empire Theatre in Syracuse, New York. The book by Guy Bolton, an Anglo American architect who had begun writing plays in 1911, was the first of his many collaborations with Jerome Kern. Produced by Daniel V. Arthur as a vehicle for Marie Cahill (Mrs. Arthur) and Richard Carle, the plot was set in the Philippines, where Willoughby Parker (Richard Carle), agent for the Manila Hemp Company, is carrying on with native women when his fiancée, Polly Bainbridge (Marie Cahill), appears unexpectedly. She ends up with Bob Mandrake (Ed Martindel), a sea captain, and Willoughby is left to his natives.

Syracuse critics found the musical comedy original with "a distinct flavor of its own." When *Ninety in the Shade* opened at the Knickerbocker Theatre in New York on January 25, 1915, however, the critics felt the show was overly conventional in plot and characterization, albeit a pleasant alternative to the "ragtime and patter species" of musical entertainment then prevalent on Broadway. Of the Smith-Kern songs, critics singled out "Peter Pan," "Whistling Dan," "I've Been About a Bit," and "Where's the Girl for Me?" as especially effective. Although the reviewers had much good to say about the production, it never managed to be as hot as its name, and *Ninety in the Shade* closed after forty performances.

In the winter of 1915, Smith completed the libretto for *All Over Town*, commissioned by dancer Joseph Santley to showcase his terpsichorean talents. It was a Faust-like tale, recalling *The Black Crook* (1866) and anticipating shows like *Damn Yankees* (1955). The curtain rises on the green room of the Cosmopolitan Opera House, where the evening's performance has been changed from Puccini's *La bohème* to Gounod's *Faust*. In attendance are Reggie Faust, his sweetheart, Marguerite, her brother, Val, and Doris Doolittle, Val's fiancée. While Martha, the Musetta in *La bohème*, complains to Marble Dome, a publicity agent and amateur detective, about the change, he invents the robbery of the leading lady's jewels as a publicity stunt, and engages Faust's apartment for his scheme. The performance of the opera begins and everyone goes to their seats in the auditorium, Faust falling asleep soon after the music starts. The scene changes to Reggie's apartment, where Marble Dome is entertaining a group of showgirls. Reggie suddenly appears as an old man—his "grandfather," Reginald Faust—and Howitt Burns enters from the fireplace, offering to restore his youth if he would agree to seduce Burns's wife, Lizzie. A contract is signed, and old Reginald becomes young Reggie. Marble, who has witnessed Burns with both the old and young Faust, is convinced that Reggie has killed his grandfather, and begins to shadow his every move.

In order to fulfill his commitment to Burns, Reggie finds himself breaking dates with Marguerite, causing her brother, Val, to want to avenge the insult. Burns, in turn, hires Marble Dome, as a private detective, to document his wife's infidelities with young Faust, hoping to trap her into a divorce. When Reggie has too little success on his own, Burns even coaches him in ways to compromise his wife, but as the deadline of midnight approaches, Mrs. Burns remains faithful to her husband. Reggie is turned back into an old man, and the scene changes to the Cosmopolitan Opera House, where the performance of *Faust* is ending, and young Reggie Faust awakens from his very strange dream.

Although Smith registered the libretto for copyright under his name only, Joseph Santley took credit for the book when the show opened at the Shubert Theatre in New Haven on April 26, 1915. Silvio Hein, a composer with whom Santley had worked in the past, was engaged to write the tunes, and Smith was kept on as lyricist. Three numbers—all Santley's dance routines—were singled out by the New Haven critics: "The Parisian Fox Trot," "The Temptation Waltz," and "Le Danse Pierette." The show moved to the Garrick Theatre in Chicago at the end of May and received good notices, enjoying a lucrative thirteen-week run.

While *All Over Town* was in rehearsal, Smith collaborated with Schuyler Greene on the lyrics for "Any Old Night Is a Wonderful Night," sung by Adele Rowland in the character of "Tony" Miller, the prima donna of the Winter Garden Theatre, in *Nobody Home*, an Americanization of *Mr. Popple (of Ippleton)* by Paul Rubens, with a book by Guy Bolton, and music mostly by Jerome Kern. Capitalized at a mere

Sheet music cover from *All Over Town*. The song, "Some Little Bug Is Going to Find You," with lyrics by Benjamin Hapgood Burt and Roy Atwell, was one of many added during the run of the show.

$7,500, the show opened on April 20, 1915, the first of a series of musicals produced by F. Ray Comstock and Elizabeth ("Bessie") Marbury at the new 299-seat Princess Theatre. The Smith-Greene lyrics (set to music by Kern and Otto Motzan) were also interpolated into Paul Rubens's *Tonight's the Night* which began a 460-performance run at the Gaiety Theatre in London on April 28, 1915. Later in the run of *Nobody*

Home, Smith provided the lyric to another interpolated song, "Wedding Bells Are Calling Me," with music by Jerome Kern. On May 3, *A Modern Eve*, adapted by Will M. Hough and Benjamin Hapgood Burt from *Die moderne Eva* by Georg Okonkowski and Alfred Schönfeld, opened at the Casino Theatre. Jean Gilbert and Victor Hollander's score was complemented by two songs from Smith and Kern: "I'd Love to Dance through Life with You," and "I've Just Been Waiting for You," a march described as "captivating" by the critics.

Harry spent the summer working on a revue with Ned Wayburn, collaborating on a new musical comedy with Irving Berlin, and creating an American version of Miksa Brody and Ferenc Martos's 1914 operetta, *Szibill*, with music by Hungarian composer Victor Jacobi. Another collaboration with Jerome Kern, advertised to open at the Princess Theatre in the fall, appears never to have materialized. The Wayburn piece, a lavish dance-heavy revue, was the first to appear in New York, on September 23 at the Century Music Hall. Titled *Ned Wayburn's Town Topics*, a "Musical Revue, on the Continental Order," it claimed to have been "conceived, developed and rehearsed by Ned Wayburn," with book and lyrics by Harry B. Smith, Robert B. Smith, and Thomas Gray, and music by Harold Orlob, the composer of the popular hit, "I Wonder Who's Kissing Her Now." The librettists provided Wayburn with too much material, and the dress rehearsal on Wednesday, September 22, took five hours to complete. A run-through the next afternoon managed to tighten the performance so that the opening night spectators were permitted to leave their seats by 11:45.

The production opens at the "Hotel de Gink," with guests arriving to see the famous—and notorious—sights in New York City. They ride a subway during rush hour, visit Mme. Flair's, a fashionable dress shop, and watch a baseball game at the Polo Grounds between the girls (dressed in pink) and the boys (in gray). Borrowing from the *Follies* device, the girls in the outfield are placed in the auditorium, allowing the audience to experience their athletic abilities firsthand. The backstage of the Century Theatre is the scene of a "benefit performance," during which performers engage in vaudeville specialties ending with "tone pictures" of the four seasons presented in music and pantomime. Blossom Seeley played Molly R. Motion, "a café canary" and ragtime shouter, Will Rogers played himself and spouted homespun philosophy while maneuvering his lasso, Clifton Webb played David Dansant, "who trips the light fantastic," Eileen Molyneux was Constance Spinner, assistant to a dance instructor, and Trixie Friganza appeared as Mrs. Albany Dayline, an actress with ambition.

Critics found much to praise in the production. Some scenes were considered "diverting," others, "genuinely beautiful," and the *New York Times* (September 24, 1915) noted that the show marked "the transition between the old lithographic spectacles and such gay decoration as Mr. Ziegfeld has made the fashion for revues." The use of a revolving stage in the dances was called "spectacular and novel," and the production looked expensive from beginning to end. However, critics less impressed with the extravagance argued that "were less gold devoted to costuming and scenic effects and more to securing principals of undisputed cleverness and skill the results would have proved more satisfactory." All the reviewers agreed that there was still too much material in the show. The *Times* quipped: "Suffice it to say that one rises from 'Town Topics' with the faint impression of having attended five musical comedies in rapid succession, all of them written by Harry B. Smith."

As *Town Topics* was concluding its sixty-eight performances at the Century Music Hall, Smith was in rehearsal with *Stop! Look! Listen!* his latest project with Irving Berlin. Charles Dillingham had approached Smith late in the summer about writing the book to feature the somewhat elusive talents of the French dancer Gaby Deslys, whom the author had lampooned years earlier in *Gaby*. Familiar with the eccentricities of dancers who are neither singers nor actors, Smith produced a backstage plot involving a chorus girl who offers to replace the leading lady when the diva decides to get married and retire from the stage. Typical of a Smithian plot, the chorine has to disguise herself as a seasoned melodramatic actress before she is accepted for her own abilities. While the *dramatis personae* featured burlesque-style names such as Iona Carr, Nora Marks, Gladys Canby, Helen Winter, Carrie Waite, and Van Courtland Parke, Gaby Deslys appeared simply as Gaby, playing herself in elaborately decorated headgear as she wandered through the proceedings, singing (in a thick French accent) and dancing, virtually independent of the plot.

Stop! Look! Listen! opened in Philadelphia on December 1 to highly enthusiastic reviews, arriving at New York's Globe Theatre on Christmas Day. Even though the opening night was packed to the rafters with well-wishers, including John Philip Sousa, who marched over from the Hippodrome Theatre with his band to join in the finale, the reviewers found the show less impressive than *Watch Your Step*. All agreed that *Stop!*

Look! Listen! was the work of master craftsmen: Berlin was called "clever" and "Professor Meritus in syncopation," and Smith "indefatigable," the "dispenser of one of the choicest assortments of reliable jokes in this country." A number of the songs were cited as potential hits, especially "Everything in America Is Ragtime" and "I Love a Piano," and the cast, including Blossom Seeley and Joseph Santley, recently in other Smith shows, were generally praised. But the view of the *Dramatic Mirror* (January 1, 1916) seemed to prevail that there was "no glowing, sensuous, extravagant appeal" about *Stop! Look! Listen!* It was "wholly ragtime, noisy, overdone ragtime, from the opening chorus to the final number."

In spite of the critics' misgivings, the show was a box-office sensation, selling out at every performance, but Dillingham had made the mistake of hiring Harry Pilcer in the role of Anthony St. Anthony, one of Gaby's dancing partners in the show. Pilcer had been Gaby's lover, and he was still proprietary over her affairs, claiming a percentage of her salary, and complaining to the producers when changes were made in the size of Gaby's role. Overly sensitive to begin with, Gaby was unable to tolerate Pilcer's constant interference, and the show became the arena for their shouting matches. Her performance suffered as a result, and attendance began to drop off considerably. Dillingham responded by closing the show after 105 performances.

As Gaby began missing cues and going up on lines in *Stop! Look! Listen!* Harry was looking forward to the New York premiere of *Sybil*, his adaptation of Victor Jacobi's operetta *Szibill*, scheduled to open at the Liberty Theatre on January 10, 1916. Produced by the Charles Frohman Company, and starring the popular trio Julia Sanderson, Donald Brian, and Joseph Cawthorn, *Sybil* is set in Russia and tells the story of a prima donna, Sybil Renaud (Julia Sanderson), who is compelled by circumstances to assume the identity of the Grand Duchess Pavlovna (Josephine Whittell) at a ball in Bomsk, in order to effect the escape of her lover, Captain Paul Petrow (Stewart Baird), and her manager, the impresario Otto Spreckles (Joseph Cawthorn). Knowing that his wife has been delayed in coming to the ball, Grand Duke Constantine (Donald Brian) is determined to trap the imposter, but when he meets Sybil, he is so charmed by her that he joins in the deception. Later in the evening, the Grand Duchess arrives, disguised as Sybil, and monopolizes the attentions of Captain Petrow, to the immediate dismay of the real Sybil and the Grand Duke. Eventually the roles are reversed, and Sybil is united with her captain.

The large opening night crowd greeted the show exuberantly, and the critics were equally as cordial with their views of Smith's book, finding that his American revision managed to sustain the "unusually coherent, continuous, and entertaining story" of the original. For once, the libretto received higher marks than the score, with the *New York Times* (January 11, 1916) suggesting, "The book as it stands really invites rather more distinctive, colorful, and melodious music than Composer Jacobi has been inspired to provide." Typically, the author filled the text with well-worn "Smithisms." When the Grand Duke appears in full military uniform, Otto Spreckles remarks, "Funny clothes for a soldier." The Duke replies, "Hussar," to which Otto retorts, "Why, yours are." Although the *Times* reported that there was "More Fun Than Melody or Beauty" in the show, the *Dramatic Mirror* (January 15, 1916) noted that *Sybil* "appears to be good for a stay." And stay it did, for the rest of the season.

On February 7, following an engagement in Atlantic City, the Gloria Opera Company opened at the New National Theatre in Washington, D.C., with *The Masked Model*, book and lyrics by Harry and Robert B. Smith, and music by Carl Woess. Inspired by Boccaccio's *Decameron*, the plot deals with a nobleman, Count Walter von Walden (Frank Doane), who marries Molly O'Malley (Katherine Galloway), an American heiress. Believing himself to have been a "purchased" groom, the Count flees fashionable Newport society, finding solace in Vienna at an art students' ball, where, at an art auction, he successfully bids $20,000 for the masked model who posed for a painting. Molly, who has been traveling in disguise searching for her husband, exchanges places with the masked model, and the husband, who felt purchased, realizes that he has just bought his bride.

The Washington critics were enthusiastic, calling it "a presentation of downright artistic merit, brilliant with real music, scintillating with enjoyable clean-cut comedy, and conspicuous for elaborate beauty of production and perfection of detail." The company, including Texas Guinan (before her career as a nightclub hostess), singing "Aesop Was a Very Moral Man," was lavishly applauded, and the score was found "exceptionally good, melodious, graceful, and catchy." When the show moved to the Academy of Music in Baltimore, however, attendance was so bad that, on February 20, unable to pay actors' salaries, the producers closed down the production. The *New York Clipper* (February 26, 1916) reported that, because the company was stranded in Baltimore, $180 was collected "and divided among the chorus for transportation," but the principals had to pay their own way back to New York.

When the show finally appeared in New York, the name was changed to *Molly O'* and John Cort took over the producing duties, opening it at the Cort Theatre on May 17, 1916, with only Katherine Galloway remaining from the original cast. The New York critics were impressed with Woess's Viennese-like score, finding it much superior to the Smiths' book, filled with "relics from the old jokes home." As the *Dramatic Mirror* (May 27, 1916) complained: "It seems to us at times that these indefatigable Smiths have a low opinion of the intelligence of the average New York audience else they would not permit specimens of the Joe Miller school of humor to assail our ears continually in their musical comedies. Perhaps, being excellent showmen, they have a keen box-office eye upon the profits of a tour, conscious that the judgment of New York and the 'road' are two quite different things." *Molly O'* remained at the Cort for forty-five performances and then disappeared. Cort attempted to revive it on tour as *The Masked Model* in the spring of 1917, with the Smith Brothers' lyrics, but with new music by Harold Orlob and a new book by composer-librettist Fred Herendeen. It is a mystery why Cort chose to jettison Woess's score, the only element of the original show that consistently earned good reviews.

In June, Harry completed the manuscript of a two-act comedy, *A Carnival Wedding*, and started a new project for the Shubert Brothers, adapted from *Was tut man nicht alles aus Liebe* by Felix Dörmann (music by Leo Ascher). Designed as a vehicle for Anna Held to return to Broadway, *Follow Me* told the story of Claire La Tour, star of the Théâtre Variétés in Paris, who reconciles a philandering husband, Hector, Marquis de Lunay (William P. Carleton), with his wife, Laura (Letty Yorke). Smith knew that Anna always wanted to learn her roles at a leisurely pace, so he dashed off the adaptation, letting his brother Robert fill in the lyrics to be set to music by Sigmund Romberg, the Shuberts' resident tunesmith. Meanwhile, in July, Harry produced another libretto for Victor Herbert, *The Garden of Eden*, but the composer completed only a few numbers before the project was discarded.

When *Follow Me* opened at the Casino Theatre on November 29, Harry was not credited with the adaptation; only the original writers were listed. Romberg's original score was supplemented by tunes written by a dozen other composers, and Robert B. Smith's lyrics were augmented by the work of ten different lyricists, including Anna Held. The most popular songs were all interpolations: Anna Held's "I Want to Be Good but My Eyes Won't Let Me" was composed by Harry Tierney, with lyrics by

Alfred Bryan and Held, and Henry Lewis's "Oh, Johnny, Oh, Johnny, Oh!" was written by Abe Olman and Ed Rose.

Even though she continued to charm audiences with her magnetic eyes and was supported by an exceptional cast that included Edith Day in one of her earliest roles on the New York stage, the legendary Anna Held could only keep the attraction open for seventy-eight performances at the Casino. The usual tour followed immediately, taking the show to Baltimore and Washington before *Follow Me* returned to New York City, playing a short engagement at the Standard Theatre in May 1917.

While Harry was working on Held's vehicle, his son, Sydney, began a collaboration with Augustus Thomas Jr., son of the author of *Arizona*, *Colorado*, *Soldiers of Fortune*, and many other plays. Both serving in the National Guard, and stationed at the Mexican border, the boys produced *Strike the Lyre*, the first "National Guard musical comedy," between hikes on the banks of the Rio Grande, with their backs against a cactus, in a temperature of 115 degrees. Smith wrote most of the jokes, and Thomas provided the romantic scenes. When the manuscript arrived in New York, Harry read it and found it sound enough to put on stage. He agreed to write lyrics if Jerome Kern would provide the music, and convinced Bessie Marbury and the Shubert Organization to back the show. As soon as they were on board, one of the first things the Shuberts did was change the title from *Strike the Lyre*, an appropriate name because the plot dealt with a liar, to *Girls Will Be Girls*, a name designed to do nothing but sell tickets.

The first performance took place at the Lyric Theatre in Philadelphia on November 20, 1916. The critics were unexcited about the piece and the audience was reserved in their applause, so, after two weeks, believing that the show was deficient in comedy, the producers brought it back to New York for an overhaul. A way was discovered to compress two low-comedy roles into one—a neat trick, because one of the roles was a "sentimental burglar" and the other was the detective hunting him down—and comedian George Hassell was engaged to play the hybrid part, now a butler and "moving picture fan," Bif Jackson. On January 15, the musical, retitled *Love o' Mike* (because Michael was the leading character), opened at the Shubert Theatre in New York, following a critically successful engagement in New Haven. The story involved a British ex–army officer, Captain Lord Michael Kildare (Lawrence Grossmith), who is the houseguest of Mrs. Alison Marvin (Allison McBain). When he begins to charm all the local ladies with his tales of valor, their boyfriends enlist the help of Bif Jackson, the butler, to expose him as a fraud. However, the butler, a former thief, cannot be trusted, and he reveals the plot to Michael and the girls, who, sufficiently impressed with Michael's accomplishments, return to their original boyfriends.

The critics praised the young librettists (who used the pseudonym Thomas Sydney) for having escaped many (although not all) of the clichés of musical comedy plots, but found that in writing about youth and a "life of sweetmeats," they "added too much of the sweets and too little of the meat" in their plot. Kern's music was judged "in that tinkly and melodious vein," and Smith's lyrics were considered "excellent," with "Don't Tempt Me" and "I Wonder Why" singled out as particularly effective numbers. While *Love o' Mike* was in the midst of its six-month run in New York, the young librettists were in Plattsburgh, New York, training to be army officers. Harry's son joined the Second Cavalry and went to France in command of Troop A, eventually becoming aide-de-camp to General Harry A. Smith, stationed in the occupied territory in Germany.

Back in New York, the Shuberts produced a critically acclaimed revival of *The Highwayman* at the Forty-fourth Street Theatre on May 2 that held on for the rest of the month. Typical of the Shuberts and the direction that the musical was taking, the producers cut down the size of the orchestra so that they could afford to maintain a large chorus of beautiful girls. The role of Dick was transposed from a tenor to a baritone, Constance's coloratura "Moonlight Song," considered by many of the original critics of the show to be a "tawdry, florid song," was replaced with a much simpler song, "For This," and Foxy Quiller's "Gipsy Song," omitted from earlier productions, was reinstated in the score.

In the spring of 1917, the Charles Frohman Company engaged Harry to adapt Michael Morton's 1911 comedy, *The Runaway* (based on a play by Pierre Veber and Henri De Gorsse), as a musical play. Smith spent the summer working with composer Victor Jacobi on the well-worn story of an American boarding-school girl, Rosamond Lee, who falls in love with Gerald Morton, an artist in Paris. She, in turn, is loved by Joseph Guppy, who will be disinherited if he does not get married before his next birthday. He follows Rosamond to Paris, hoping to impress her by creating and selling a masterpiece. The statue, actually the work of Gerald's friend, Marcel Petipas, is purchased by Guppy's rich uncle, who also manages to charm Gerald's former sweetheart, clearing the field for Gerald to pursue Rosamond, the girl he really loves.

Inspired by the name of the heroine, the show was titled *Rambler Rose*, and it opened at the Empire Theatre in New York City on September 10, 1917, with additional music and lyrics by Irving Berlin, Charles N. Grant, and Schuyler Greene, and featuring Julia Sanderson as Rosamond Lee, Joseph Cawthorn as Joseph Guppy, and John Goldsworth as Gerald Morton. The *New York Times* (September 11, 1917) found much to praise in Smith's libretto, suggesting that Cawthorn's success was due in no small part to the author's work:

> [T]hanks to Mr. Smith, he has an abundance of neat verbal turns, and shrewd observations, which never failed to give fresh delight to the audience. Really, one forgets from time to time how racy and authentic Mr. Smith's persiflage can be. And from time to time perhaps Mr. Smith also forgets it. Or perhaps the occasional fault lies in the fact that no comedian is at hand as finished in method and as breezy in personality as Mr. Cawthorn.

While Jacobi's music was found to be Viennese in character, "appropriately sentimental" and often "delightfully whimsical," the hit of the performance was "Poor Little Rich Girl's Dog," an interpolated song by Irving Berlin.

The *Dramatic Mirror* (September 22, 1917), however, voiced the disappointment of the majority of critics, who were weary of old plots continually being remade into musicals and hopeful of new trends on the horizon:

> While not directly occasioned by the war, the new forces which are being exerted today in all branches of theatrical art have in the main had their birth since the beginning of hostilities on that fateful August day in 1914. In the presentation of musical plays a new path has been blazed most conspicuously, for in this special activity we have passed from the supremely preposterous and laboriously silly concoction to a style which attempts to appeal to imagination, appreciation of youth and artistic sense as well as convey some truthfulness to life. No longer do we tolerate conventionality and unreasonableness in our musical plays, even though their musical embellishments may be ambitiously Danubesque.

In spite of an exceptionally popular and critically acclaimed cast, *Rambler Rose* could sustain only seventy-two performances in New York. Change was clearly in the wind.

In spite of the cry for novelty and realism, the Smith Brothers finished out the 1917–18 season with one of their old adaptations, dusted off and refurbished for British consumption. This was *The Lilac Domino*, a show that failed to turn a profit in New York in 1914. English producer Joseph L. Sacks had seen the American production, and he thought the show might succeed in England. Because the authors were convinced that in a time of war, few people would want to attend so light and frothy a show, they offered to sell their interest in the show for a flat fee. Luckily, the English producer was unwilling to take the risk, and Harry and Robert were forced to retain their royalty agreement. With three new songs, "For Your Love I'm Waiting," "Carnival Night," and "All Line Up in a Queue," added by Englishmen Howard Carr and D. S. Parsons, *The Lilac Domino* opened at the Empire Theatre in London on February 21, 1918. It remained there for over a year and a half, accumulating 747 performances, becoming the biggest new musical hit of the year. After seasons peppered with flops and near misses, Harry B. Smith was again a success.

Chapter 10

"Harry-B-Smithing"

Harry B. Smith began the 1918–19 season in the company of old friends. *The Soul Kiss* was once again touring the country, and a new vehicle for Nora Bayes, commissioned by producer Harry H. Frazee, was scheduled for an October 24 opening at the Broadhurst Theatre. The composer was A. Baldwin Sloane, who had provided songs for *The Liberty Belles* and *A Girl from Dixie*, the two shows Harry had a hand in producing. The result was *Ladies First*, an adaptation of Charles H. Hoyt's farce *A Contented Woman*, brought "up to the minute" by Smith's book and lyrics. The plot traded on the suffragette movement that had won a recent victory when the state legislature of New York adopted a constitutional amendment extending equal voting rights to women in November 1917. While *Ladies First* was on its pre-Broadway tour, the U.S. Senate was debating a women's suffrage amendment, but by the time the show opened in New York, the bill had been rejected.

The political environment surrounding the show would seem to have made the story of Betty Burt (Nora Bayes), who runs against her fiancé, Benton Holmes (Irving Fisher), for Mayor of their village, especially timely. She does not succeed in getting elected, but is satisfied with being the Mayor's wife. Florence Morrison played the role of Aunt Jim, an aging suffragette who convinces Betty to run for office, and William Kent acted the low comic role of Uncle Tody, her browbeaten husband. The critics complained that Smith's updating only served to demonstrate more clearly "the corrosion of time and the political tide," and that the most successful moments were those when Hoyt's original text managed to shine through the "Harry-B-Smithing."

After forty years as a writer, many of them as the critics' favorite whipping boy, Harry had acquired an international reputation—and notoriety—that earned him over $2 million in royalties. But he had not realized how familiar his name was to the general public until it became a verb form, conjuring up the specific image of his playwriting style. To the critics, "Harry-B-Smithing" meant filling a play with tired jokes, colloquialisms, hackneyed plots, improbable characterizations, and overripe puns. To audiences, it meant a well-constructed, easily accessible, often funny, and usually clever entertainment. Perhaps that is why Harry-B-Smithing was always more acceptable on the road than in New York City.

Because the majority of critics applauded the performances by Bayes and company in *Ladies First*, the show enjoyed a two-month engagement at the Broadhurst Theatre before moving to the Nora Bayes Theatre on December 30, where it remained through the spring of 1919. During the run, the Smith-Sloane score was embellished with interpolated songs that changed with regularity. Notable among them were "Spanish," by Harry Clark, "What a Girl Can Do," by Bert Kalmar and Harry Ruby, and "Some Wonderful Sort of Someone," composed by George Gershwin with a lyric by Schuyler Greene. After the Broadway run, the show joined the touring circuit, calling itself *Look Who's Here*. On the road, "Just Like a Gypsy," by Seymour B. Simons and Bayes, and "The Real American Folk Song Is a Rag," by George and Ira Gershwin, were among the songs added to the score.

During the tryout tour of *Ladies First*, *The Canary*, Harry B. Smith's musicalization of a farce by Georges Barr and Louis Verneuil, opened at the Nixon Theatre in Pittsburgh with Julia Sanderson and Joseph Cawthorn in the leads. The principal composer, Ivan Caryll, had purchased the rights to the French play, and convinced Charles Dillingham to produce it as a musical. Smith did not think much of the material, but as he was never one to refuse a commission, he set to work on a libretto. What emerged was the story of Timothy (Joseph Cawthorn), a worker in an antique shop, who inadvertently swallows the "Canary Diamond," scheduled for auction. Two crooks after the gem, Dodge (James Doyle) and Fleece (Harold Dixon), join in the chase to recover the stone, leading to a sanitarium where Timothy gets X-rayed and falls in love with Julie (Julia Sanderson), a "sentimental slavey."

The premiere in Pittsburgh was enthusiastically received, with the audience sitting merrily in their seats until 12:35 A.M., when the performance finally came to an end. Two songs were particularly noted as effective, "It's the Little Bit of Irish" and "I Wouldn't Give That for a Man Who Couldn't Dance." Both were interpolations, sung by Julia Sanderson, and written by Irving Berlin, who composed five songs for the show. By the time *The Canary* opened at the Globe Theatre in New York on November 4, 1918, lyricists Anne Caldwell, P. G. Wodehouse, and a half-dozen others contributed words to music by Jerome Kern, Harry Tierney, and others. Songs came and went with regularity; Berlin's "It's the Little Bit of Irish," so popular in Pittsburgh, was dropped in New York.

Critics found the plot anemic, but as the *Dramatic Mirror* (November 30, 1918) advised: "Take an idea from the French, embroider it with American jokes, color it with comely coryphées and picturesque settings, drape it with generally melodious tunes and assign it to a cast headed by the graceful Sanderson and the amusing Cawthorn and you are pretty sure to attract a large public." Perhaps because Smith was not openly credited with the adaptation, the critics were more congenial to the show, some even dubbing it a "hit." Noting the anonymous adapter, the *New York Clipper* (November 13, 1918) gushed: "whoever is responsible . . . has done good work. Its adaptation has not robbed it of its Gaelic [*sic*] flavor, and whatever American has been injected into it has been so deftly done that it can not be detected." Although *The Canary* played nineteen weeks in New York, Smith viewed it as a failure, and he felt that he Ivan Caryll resented his version because it stripped the farce of much of its humor. In his defense, Harry claimed that most of the comedy in the farce was off-color, and had he let it remain in the script, "we all would have been arrested." Smith and Caryll never collaborated on another show.

After the demise of *The Canary*, Smith repaid Anne Caldwell for her work on the show by interpolating a song he had written with Jerome Kern, "Where's the Girl for Me," into the score of her new musical, *The Lady in Red*, opening May 12, 1919, at the Lyric Theatre. That show had barely begun its six-week run when *A Lonely Romeo*, a collaboration between Smith and Lew Fields, moved into the Globe Theatre in Atlantic City. Conceived as a vehicle for the comedian, *A Lonely Romeo* traced the adventures of Augustus Tripp (Fields), a henpecked hatmaker by day and "cabaret fiend" by night, who pretends to be his own son in order to pass himself off as a younger man to the women he meets in nightspots. The scheme works until he brings his dance partner, Mazie Gay (Frances Cameron), back to his office in the early hours of the morning, both of them innocently trying to stay out of the rain. When his wife and family come to the shop the next day, Tripp's daytime identity collides with his nighttime disguise, and not only must he keep his wife from seeing Mazie, he must also appear as two completely different men to the women. After two acts of quick changes, Tripp decides to kill off his "son" and admits the imposture to Mazie.

A Lonely Romeo had music by Malvin M. Franklin and Robert Hood Bowers, the musical director for the production, and lyrics by Robert B. Smith. It opened at the Shubert Theatre on June 10, drawing excellent reviews for the dancing and Fields's performance, but poor notices for the book. The *New York Times* (June 11, 1919) vindictively took the Smiths to task, purposely omitting Fields's name among the writers: "To turn momentarily to less pleasant subjects, the book of the Messrs. Smith et al. is merely another of those things. Its complications are maladroit, and it asks an audience to believe that a wife will not recognize her husband if by chance he dons a wig." Theatrical conventions aside, one wonders why the complaint was not lodged against Fields as well. He had improvised much of his own material during rehearsals, and even changed some of the locations indicated in Smith's original draft. What the critics saw was as much his doing as either of the Smith Brothers. The *Dramatic Mirror* (June 24, 1919) took a similar attack, also neglecting to mention Fields as the author: "While the book by Harry B. Smith was obvious and uninspiring it did not interfere with the aim of Mr. Fields to extract laughter from the audience."

In spite of the diatribes against the book, the critics considered *A Lonely Romeo* "a good show" that was staged "with speed and artistic finish." The musical moved to the Casino Theatre on July 28, and before the actors' strike of 1919 closed the show after only eighty-seven performances, two songs were interpolated into the entertainment. "I Guess I'm More Like Mother than Like Father," composed by Richard A. Whiting with lyrics by Raymond B. Egan, was added shortly after the show opened, and "Any Old Place with You," composed by Richard Rodgers with lyrics by Lorenz Hart—their first song in a Broadway show—appeared late in August.

While Harry and his brother were engaged in dress rehearsals for *A Lonely Romeo*, their libretto for *Angel Face*, Victor Herbert's latest musical comedy, was produced by George Lederer at the Colonial Theatre in Chicago, beginning June 8, 1919. The Smiths had signed on to do the show in February, and had delivered the text to the composer early in the spring. Originally called *Little Miss Wise*, the plot turned on the recent discoveries of Dr. Serge Voronoff, head of the physiological laboratories of the Collège de France, involving the use of monkey glands on humans to curtail the aging process. An eccentric scientist, Professor Barlow (George Schiller), believing that he has perfected Voronoff's experiments and developed an elixir of life, unwittingly leaves the formula on a table in a bachelor apartment shared by Arthur Griffin (Tyler Brooke), a sculptor, and Tom Larkins (John E. Young), a wealthy composer of musicals. Arthur is in the midst of an unhappy relationship with Vera Wise (Minerva Grey); her younger sister, Betty (Marguerite Zender), the "little Miss Wise" or "Angel Face" of the title, tries to break it up, while Tom spends much of his time trying to convince his fiancée, Tessie Blythe (Emilie Lea), that all the attention he gets from women means nothing to him. Tessie drinks Barlow's elixir, and when a baby happens to appear in her place, the Professor believes that his formula has rejuvenated her back to infancy. Through the clever sleuthing of Slooch (Jack Donahue), a correspondence-school detective, the baby is discovered to have been kidnapped from the hotel across the street. No longer believed to be a child, Tessie is reunited with Tom, and Arthur realizes that he loves Betty.

After an extensive pre-Broadway tour, *Angel Face* arrived at the Knickerbocker Theatre on December 29, 1919, and was welcomed with open arms by the critics, who seemed to forgive the improbabilities of the plot because of their fondness for Herbert's melodies. The *Dramatic Mirror* (January 8, 1920) embraced the show as a relic of the "good old days of musical comedy, the Victor Herbert–Harry B. Smith days when sweet and lilting waltzes went hand in hand with mistaken identity jests," and the *New York Times* (December 30, 1919) noted that "as though stung by taunts at the feebleness of his books in recent seasons, Harry Smith has worked out this time a plot almost too complicated for the musical comedy mind, and the proceedings are fairly amusing." Of the cast, Jack Donahue was singled out for his dancing, and from the score, "I Might Be Your Once in a While" was chosen as the potential hit by first night critics. Although the Smith Brothers received some of their most positive reviews in several seasons, the musical comedy lasted a mere fifty-seven performances on Broadway and returned to the road.

In December, while *Angel Face* was working its way into New York City, Smith's collaboration with popular musical director Hugo Reisenfeld, *Betty Be Good*, opened at the Wilbur Theatre in Boston on its pre-Broadway tour. Resorting to his old device of attributing an overused plot to a famous source, Smith claimed to have based the musical on an unspecific vaudeville by Scribe. The plot involved a comic opera queen, Betty Lee (Josephine Whittell), who finds an ex-sweetheart, Sam Kirby (Frank Crumit), about to get married in Lenox, Massachusetts. To keep her from realizing that he is the groom, he pretends to be the best man. The real best man, however, has rented Betty's apartment in New York for the newlyweds, and the wedding party arrives just as Marion Love (Vivienne Oakland), the daughter of the fortune-teller who leased the apartment to Betty, is rehearsing a new cabaret act with her chorus-girl chums.

The Boston audiences loved the show, demanding encores of virtually every song in the score. The critics were charmed as well, finding it a "good evening's entertainment," even though the standards of comedy established in the first act quickly degenerated into farce. As *Betty Be Good* continued winning friends along the touring circuit, another Victor Herbert work was in production. *Oui, Madame* was a family affair for the Smiths: Robert wrote the lyrics, Marguerite Wright, his wife since 1913, produced the libretto, and Harry anonymously contributed one-liners. The project was designed to be the first in a series of intimate musicals appealing to "discriminating audiences" at the Little Theatre (newly christened the Philadelphia Theatre), a three-hundred-seat house in Philadelphia. Years earlier, when Marbury and Comstock were considering composers to inaugurate their series of musicals at the Princess Theatre, they had ruled out Herbert because they believed he would be too expensive and uninterested in working on a smaller scale. Neither Smith nor Herbert had written a Princess show; this was their opportunity.

The complicated mistaken-identity plot turned on Dick Sheldon (Vinton Freedley) and his wife, Polly (Dorothy Maynard), and their attempts to get ahead in the world of art and entertainment. Just as they are throwing a party in a borrowed apartment, attended by ten beautiful and ambitious girls, Dick's mother (Catherine Calhoun Doucet) and sister (Marguerite Fritts) arrive unexpectedly. Dick has led them to believe that he owns the comfortable abode, so, to prevent them from spending the night, he enlists the janitor of the building, Steve (Harry Kelly), to masquerade as Colonel Hutt, a houseguest occupying the spare room. Pansy (Georgia O'Ramey), a cook, believes the Colonel to be the man who jilted her years ago, and a maze of mistaken identities follows, accompanied by the usual Smithian complications and resolutions.

Oui, Madame was a success in Philadelphia, taking in $8,150 in its first week, extraordinary receipts for a theater seating no more than three hundred, with ticket prices ranging from $5.00 on opening night to $3.50 for the rest of the week. The show moved on to engagements in Atlantic City and Boston, where the music was found acceptable but the book was considered unfunny. Attempts to rework and revitalize the production in preparation for a New York opening continued through the summer months, and in September 1920, given a new title, *Some Colonel*, it opened in Springfield, Massachusetts, where the critics were even less impressed than they had been in Boston. After a stop in Stamford, Connecticut, where the show was reworked again, it moved on to Richmond, Virginia, where the producers ended the run. Although neither an artistic or financial success for the Smiths, *Oui, Madame* was significant in the canon of their work not only because of its intimate size, but because it introduced the Smith Brothers to Max Steiner, the Vienna-born musical director, with whom they would later collaborate.

On March 24, 1920, while the Smiths' intimate musical was on the road, the Shubert Brothers revived *Florodora* at the Globe Theatre in Atlantic City, followed by an April 5 opening at the Century Theatre in New York. Harry B. Smith revised and updated the libretto, and he provided lyrics for an interpolated song, "Caramba," with music by Milan Roder. A special feature of the revival involved the celebrated sextet, "Tell Me, Pretty Maiden." The number was first performed in contemporary costumes, then encored by another group of performers dressed in the costumes of the original production. Delighting audiences and critics, who called it a "perfect" and "scintillating" performance, the revival remained at the Century Theatre for sixty-four performances.

As *Florodora* was beginning its second month, *Betty Be Good* wandered into town, stopping at the Casino Theatre on May 4, 1920, for the first of thirty-one performances. Noting that *Betty Be Good* was closer to French farce than musical comedy sentimentality, the *New York Times* (May 5, 1920) concluded that "Mr. Smith has found many good lines for his French plot," and that "the tiredest business man this coming

Summer will not be embarrassed to follow it." The *New York Clipper* (May 12, 1920) was less impressed with the humor in the show, but felt that the strongest element in *Betty Be Good* was the score. Reisenfeld's music was universally applauded as tuneful and catchy, providing a good half dozen of "captivating songs and dances" that appealed to even the most discerning tastes. "Keep the Love Lamp Burning" was acclaimed as the hit of the show, with "I'd Like to Take You Away," "You Must Be Good Girls," and "Tell Me, Daisy" also singled out for success. Additionally considered praiseworthy was the staging by David Bennett, a dance teacher from Albany who would be applauded again in 1924 for his innovative choreography for *Rose Marie*.

On July 3, 1920, the *Dramatic Mirror* announced the Chicago opening of *The Miracle Maid*, a new Victor Herbert musical, produced and directed by George Lederer, with book and lyrics by Richard Bruce—a hitherto unused pseudonym of Harry and Robert B. Smith. A musicians' strike forced the show back to the East Coast for its premiere, taking place in Stamford, Connecticut, on July 7, 1920, five days before the scheduled opening in New York City. When the show arrived at the Knickerbocker Theatre on July 12, it was called *The Girl in the Spotlight*, a backstage musical about Molly Shannon (Mary Milburn), a maid at the boardinghouse where composer Frank Marvin (Ben Forbes) resides. From hearing him play his music all day long, Molly is able to learn all of the numbers in his new show. When Nina Romaine (June Elvidge), the temperamental prima donna of the show, refuses to perform, Molly is ready to take her place at a moment's notice, impressing Watchem Tripp (Hal Skelly), the choreographer, and Max Preiss (James B. Carson), a former Jewish fur dealer turned theater manager. Not untypically, the composer falls in love with the girl who has saved his show and marries her.

Even though the backstage Cinderella story was ancient even in 1920 and Herbert's music was not his best, the critics applauded the show, the *New York Clipper* (July 21, 1920) calling it a winner with "a pleasant tang" in the book and lyrics, and "a distinctive tunefulness about the score." Apologizing for the libretto, the *Dramatic Mirror* (July 17, 1920) noted, "The book mattered not at all. It had the familiar imprint of the Harry B. Smith factory upon it. . . . Incoherent, naive, laboriously-contrived and seldom bright, it served merely as a framework for the luscious Herbert tunes." Three songs were identified as destined to be "whistled, bought and sung, by the populi": "I Cannot Sleep without

Dreaming of You," "There's a Tender Look in Your Eyes," and "Dancing Lesson."

After seven weeks, the show left New York and headed out on tour, changing its name to *Mollie Darling* in January 1921. As *The Girl in the Spotlight* began to fade at the Knickerbocker Theatre, Harry was looking for something to occupy his time. The bad press he had been receiving had discouraged producers, seeking bright and novel librettos, from engaging his services, so the usual flow of commissions had suddenly begun to dry up. He continued to write daily, however, if only because of his "constitutional aversion to idleness." He joined the music publishing firm of Waterson, Berlin and Snyder as a lyricist, and learned how to write simple, unornamented lyrics to popular songs. One of his early efforts, written with composer Ted Snyder, was "Kathleen," popularized by Walter Scanlan and published, advertising E. E. Rose's comedy with songs, *Irish Eyes*, the main character of which is named Kathleen. Simplicity, however, had little effect on Smith's love of wordplay and sense of humor. The end of the chorus is typically Harry B. Smith: "The blue of Killarney's skies, / You stole for your Irish eyes. / If we must part, / 'Twill make my heart, / More blue than your eyes, Kathleen." Smith produced a number of songs with Snyder, often writing the lyric in collaboration with Francis Wheeler. Among the more familiar titles are "I Wonder If You Still Care for Me," "By the Sapphire Sea," "Dancing Fool," and the very popular "The Sheik of Araby," performed by Eddie Cantor in *Make It Snappy*, a 1922 revue at Winter Garden Theatre.

Smith also collaborated with Ted Snyder on a musical adaptation of Sinclair Lewis's first play, *Hobohemia*, performed at the Greenwich Village Theatre in 1919. After securing the rights from the author, Harry produced a full libretto that opens at the "Violette et Cie," a fashionable dress shop owned by Oliver Jasselby, a poet, and his wife, Jamesina, a former dancer, in South Washington Square where various Greenwich Village Bohemian artists congregate. Ysetta Jones, originally Bessie Jones from Northapolis, comes to New York with stars in her eyes, dreaming of becoming a writer, followed by her sweetheart, Donald Brown, a "hustling young business man." When he does not succeed in getting her to return to Northapolis with him, he decides to stay in New York to keep an eye on her, and convinces the local artists who have little business sense to unite under his leadership to form the Pan American Talent Company.

Two months pass and Ysetta's play, "A Woman's Wrongs," has opened in Washington, D.C., to devastating reviews. When Ysetta learns that Donald has been the anonymous financial backer of the play, she thinks that he did it all expecting her to fail and return with him to Northapolis. Feeling betrayed, she falls into the arms of Ciro Malavici, an Italian painter "whose genius is recognized only by himself," and announces their engagement. Meanwhile, the only artist in the firm who has managed to attain any kind of commercial popularity is Donald himself, who, writing as Zinzinoff, the bogus Russian author of "Frozen Souls," is in constant demand. To trick the rest of the artists posing as intellectuals, aesthetes, and socialists, Donald disguises Mischa Krakowsky, a dealer in second-hand clothing, as the great Russian novelist, and throws a reception for him at a farm in Nutley, New Jersey. The farm belongs to Jandorf Fish, "author of novels designed to reform the universe," and Nona Barnes, a sculptress, who pretend to be poor and living in sin but are really affluent and married. At the reception, the hypocrisy of the various Bohemians is unmasked, and Ysetta realizes that she really loves Donald, who admits to being Zinzinoff.

The show abounds with chorus girls who keep appearing to try on dresses at Violette et Cie, or to sing the latest ragtime tune by Ben Tyson, a hobohemian composer. The ubiquitous presence of a press agent always looking for a marketing gimmick (usually involving leggy girls) also keeps the proceedings bright and sassy. His entrance number, "Bring on the Girls," suggests the tone and style of the libretto, on the one hand, designed to give the lie to the artistic pretensions of the characters, and on the other, a statement of Smith's own theatrical inclinations:

Some may lament the "palmy days"
  That will not come again,
  When plays that had a pull were
  By Shakespeare or by Bulwer.
But now we see that lingerie
  Is mightier than the pen,
  Though supercilious high-brows
  May elevate their eyebrows.
And now if Hamlet starts to bark—
  "To be or not to be,"
One hears the average man remark:
  "This is no place for me."

Please bring on the girls,
The merry dancing prancing girls,
You might as well as not
Cut out the darned old plot
But ev'ry lively little stepper
Gives the show a dash of pepper
Start the dancing whirls
With lots of girls with smiles and curls.
We think the play's a bore.
We've heard the tunes before.
We'll all go home if you don't bring on the girls.

From London, on August 5, 1921, Sinclair Lewis wrote to his agent, Richard Madden of The American Play Company, asking, among other things, what was being done with *Hobohemia*, "the musical comedy Harry Smith made out of my play." Smith had passed the show on to the agency via Bessie Marbury, with whom he had recently worked on *Love o' Mike*. "Can't something be done with this?" Lewis complained. "It's been the very devil of a time selling." When Madden did not reply, Lewis wrote again, on October 19, restating his query about *Hobohemia*. If the agent responded, his letter has not survived. All that is known about the progress of the show comes from Harry B. Smith, who quipped that "the few managers who have read it have jumped the other way." By January 1923, the prospect of mounting the show as a musical was dropped, and a road show of the original play, produced by Max Ferguson, was announced.

Smith had only one show open in New York City in 1922, an uncredited American adaptation of Rudolf Bernauer and Rudolf Schanzer's *Sterne, die wieder leuchtet* (music by Walter Kollo). Produced by the Shuberts, Smith's version, *Springtime of Youth*, had lyrics by Matthew C. Woodward and Cyrus Wood, and music by Walter Kollo and Sigmund Romberg. Taking place in Portsmouth, New Hampshire, in 1812, the plot involved a sailor named Roger Hathaway (George MacFarlane), who returns after a long absence only to find that he is believed to be dead. By not revealing his true identity, he learns that his ward, Priscilla Alden (Olga Steck), who used to love him, has formed an attachment to the youthful Richard Stokes (J. Harold Murray), a ship's officer. So that Priscilla can marry her young man, Roger decides to remain dead to the people of Portsmouth.

Opening on October 26 at the Broadhurst Theatre in New York, *Springtime of Youth* was roundly applauded by the critics as a "lively and tuneful" musical, with a book that is a "find blend of high and low comedy" and a score "of more than usual persuasiveness and insinuating charm." Audiences were less enthusiastic, supporting the show for a lukewarm run of sixty-eight performances. Although he was underrepresented on Broadway in 1922, Smith did manage to publish a "picture play" about the life and music of Richard Wagner called *A Chained Eagle*. He had originally offered the project to film producers, but was told that there was no interest in the German composer at that time. Perhaps ten years later the response would have been different, but Smith was satisfied that the New York–based Chauncey Holt Company found sufficient merit in the work to print it.

The next year opened with a collaboration between the Smith Brothers and Max Steiner. Commissioned by producer George Lederer, *Peaches* was advertised as an adaptation "from the Hungarian of M. Martos," though no specific Martos work was named—most likely because the plot does not resemble any of his major plays. The story involved Vivian Grey (Marguerite Zender), a society girl masquerading as a maid in the home of her prospective husband, Bobby Trainor (Bradford Kirkbride), so that she can learn about him and his family at close range before the wedding. Rosey Jane Walker (Ada Mae Weeks), a real maid, appears and, mistaken for the prospective bride, is wined and dined by the family while, Cinderella-like, Vivian suffers their abuse long enough to find her real Prince Charming.

Produced for the first time on January 22, 1923, at the Garrick Theatre in Philadelphia, *Peaches* was not favorably received by all the critics. Harry B. Smith's book was called "trite" and "inexpert," with a "flimsy narrative" that wandered in all directions. The *Philadelphia Inquirer* (January 23, 1923) complained that the jokes and situations recalled "that sort of humor which was on its last legs during McKinley's Administration. In fact, as the evening progressed, one felt that Millard Fillmore will have been quite at home in the house. Or even Thomas Jefferson." The presence of money and talent in the production was duly noted, but the critics felt that it was mostly wasted on inferior material that was severely underrehearsed, although "nicely, if casually staged" by Lederer and choreographer Sammy Lee (who would go on to stage *No, No, Nanette* and *Show Boat*). Max Steiner's music (with lyrics by Robert B. Smith) was found "attractive, though routine," and the show was considered salvageable with "a quickened pace, more assurance of 'points,' and completely new dialogue."

A three-week, break-even engagement in Philadelphia led to a week's run in Baltimore, where the show closed, the producers unable to meet expenses. Lederer still intended to open the show in New York in March—under a new title, *I'm a Good Girl*—but the mismanagement of funds resulting in thousands of dollars in unpaid salaries placed his name on the Actors' Equity Association prohibited list, requiring him to pay off the outstanding claims before he could proceed further with the show.

A week after *Peaches* opened in Philadelphia, the Shubert Brothers' production of *Caroline* opened at the Ambassador Theatre in New York. Adapted from *Der Vetter aus Dingsda*, by Herman Haller and Rideamus (Fritz Oliven), *Caroline* had book and lyrics by Harry B. Smith and Edward Delaney Dunn, and music by Edward Künneke, the composer of the original work. Transplanted to the American South after the Civil War, the story concerns Caroline Lee (Tessa Kosta), an heiress who is attached to the memory of Roderick Gray (John Adair), her childhood sweetheart. Her guardian, General Randolph Calhoun (Harrison Brockbank), wants her to marry Captain Robert Langdon (J. Harold Murray), whom no one has seen in many years. Realizing that Caroline is still in love with Gray, the Captain pretends to be her childhood sweetheart and wins her heart. When he realizes that he loves her too much to carry on the deception, he reveals his true identity, only to find that Caroline is in love with him as well.

On opening night, Künneke's score was warmly applauded by both audience and critics, who called it "fully the equal of any musical comedy of recent years . . . too beautiful to suffer in competition with the text of the show." While the libretto was accused of having stripped most of the comedy from the German original, the *New York Clipper* (February 7, 1923) noted that to be the only weak point in the play and easily overlooked, and the *New York Times* (February 1, 1923) admitted that "the Smith and Dunn book is really not so bad as to interfere with the enjoyment of the rest of the show." With interpolated songs composed by Al Goodman and Ralph Benatzky and additional lyrics by Adrian Ross, *Caroline* continued for nineteen weeks before heading out on tour.

In July, Harry B. Smith and Ted Snyder were the principal songwriters for the first revue to play New York's Lyceum Theatre. With a cast that included comedian Jimmy Hussey and Carlotta Monterey, who would become the third Mrs. Eugene O'Neill, *Fashions of 1924* opened on July 18, 1923, to good notices, the *New York Times* (July 19, 1923) boasting that "it contains more good material than any of the other revues in town." Without a lot of lavish scenery, the entertainment relied on the display of sartorial fashion for its spectacle. Among "morning gowns, afternoon gowns and evening gowns" made of silks, taffetas, and lace, Smith and Snyder sprinkled a variety of songs and sketches, including a recycled "Bring on the Girls" from *Hobohemia* and a great many songs about love and dancing. Jimmy Hussey was praised for making the most of his comedy material, and Snyder's tunes were labeled "catchy in the extreme." However, audiences were unused to going to the Lyceum during summer weather, and the show closed after only thirteen performances. Smith also wrote a prologue for *Artists and Models*, the Shubert Brothers' revue opening on August 20, 1923, at the Shubert Theatre, but his material was uncredited in the production.

In 1924, Harry published a number of songs and magazine stories, including "Whisper to the Rose," with Francis Wheeler and Ted Snyder; "Mamie," with Jack Shilkret; "Lost World," with Rudolph Friml; "How Charles Dickens Wrote His Books," in *Harper's Monthly Magazine* (December); "Canned Music and the Composer," in the *American Mercury* (August); and "Sherlock Holmes Solves the Mystery of Edwin Drood," in the December issue of *Munsey's Magazine*.

In April 1924, Smith was a member of a delegation of songwriters, which included Victor Herbert, John Philip Sousa, Jerome Kern, and Irving Berlin, sent to Washington, D.C., by the American Society of Composers, Authors, and Publishers (ASCAP) to try to discourage Congress from passing legislation that would exempt radio broadcasters from having to pay for the use of copyrighted music. On April 17, the group attended the hearings on the bill, introduced by Senator Clarence Dill, designed to change the copyright laws in favor of the broadcasters. At one point in the proceedings, Sousa blurted out: "The Radio Corporation of America gets money, doesn't it? If they get money out of my tunes, I want some of it, that's all." Because of the efforts of the delegation of composers and lyricists that went to Washington in the spring of 1924, songwriters were granted royalties for the radio transmission of their compositions.

Harry spent the rest of the year working on two old-fashioned operettas. The first to appear in Manhattan was *The Love Song*, an adaptation commissioned by J. J. Shubert from Jenó Faragó's Hungarian musical, *Offenbach* (music arranged from Offenbach by Mihály Nádor),

Harry B. Smith and friends in Washington, D.C. Front row, left to right: E. C. Mills, Silvio Hein, Harry von Tilzer, Irving Berlin, Victor Herbert, Gene Buck, Jerome Kern, John Philip Sousa, Augustus Thomas, Raymond Hubbell. Back row: Con Conrad, Nathan Burkan, Charles K. Harris, Otto Harbach, Harry B. Smith, Irving Caesar, Max Dreyfus, Joseph Meyer.

that told of a love affair between the composer and Eugenie de Montijo, soon to become the wife of Napoleon III. Even though all of Smith's research into the Second Empire disclosed not even a hint of an affair between the two, Smith accepted the commission, hoping to divert the audience from any expectation of historical accuracy by portraying the rather comic-looking Offenbach as a handsome romantic leading man. For Smith's version, Edward Künneke borrowed from a variety of Offenbach's scores—*La belle Hélène, Orphée aux enfers, La vie parisienne, La Grande-Duchesse de Gérolstein, Les contes d'Hoffmann*—and wove entire melodies, motifs, and even original material into an organic musical composition. The attempt was clearly to re-create *Blossom Time*, the enormously popular 1921 musical produced by the Shubert Brothers that offered a musical biography of composer Franz Schubert, with a score derived from his compositions.

The Love Song opened on January 13 at the Century Theatre, and the opening night crowd gave the show a "more than cordial" welcome. The *New York Times* (January 14, 1925) began its review with superlatives: "The most stupendous of the musical plays came to town last night. It is called 'The Love Song,' and to at least one observer in the enthusiastic audience . . . it seemed by all odds the best thing of its kind since 'The

Merry Widow.' To which must be added mention of a production that at times dazzled the beholder with the extravagance of its investiture."

While Offenbach was settling into a healthy five-month run at the Century Theatre, the music of Russian composer Pyotr Ilyich Tchaikovsky appeared at the Knickerbocker Theatre in *Natja*, produced by Fred C. Whitney and his brother Bertram, with lyrics by Harry B. Smith and Tchaikovsky's music adapted by Karl Hajos. Perhaps wisely, Smith was uncredited for the book that tells of Natja Narishkin (Madeline Collins), who cross-dresses as a handsome young man to win the attention of Catherine the Great (Mary Mellish), Czarina of Russia. Once in Catherine's confidence, Natja weakens the influence of Prince Potemkin (George Reimherr), Governor of Crimea, relieves the conditions of her oppressed neighbors, and manages to find love with Lieutenant Vladimir Strogonoff (Warren Proctor).

Critics praised Hajos's "skillful adaptation" of material from familiar Tchaikovsky symphonies and the *1812 Overture*, but found the book even more old-fashioned than the set. One of problems was that the cast was composed of singers, not actors, so that the deficiencies of the text were magnified. But for the critics, the real question was "why no real attempt was made to supply the story of 'Natja' with even the elements of plausibility and coherence." *The Love Song* was still running strong when *Natja* expired after thirty-two performances.

Smith spent the spring and early summer completing another adaptation for the Shuberts, this time a musicalization of Anthony Hope's famous novel, *The Prisoner of Zenda*, into *Princess Flavia*, with a score by Sigmund Romberg. Faithful to the novel, the plot involved Rudolph Rassendyl passing through the Forest of Zenda and being mistaken for Crown Prince Rudolph of Ruritania. When Rudolph cannot attend the coronation the following day, Rassendyl is persuaded to take his place. Returning from a tour of the continent, Princess Flavia falls in love at first sight with the imposter, and he returns her affections, but at the end, they both accept the fact that they can have no future together, and Rassendyl returns home to London.

Princess Flavia opened at the Century Theatre on November 2, 1925, with Smith credited as author of both book and lyrics. Harry Weichman played the roles of both Rassendyl and Crown Prince Rudolph, and Evelyn Herbert was Princess Flavia. A crowded house found the production even more lavish than *The Love Song* and Romberg's previous success, *The Student Prince*. The male chorus of fifty voices and the female chorus of young, beautiful women so astounded the reviewers that the critic for the *New York Times* (November 3, 1925) gushed, "Beautiful, tuneful, majestic and splendid in all its appointments, 'Princess Flavia' makes the conscientious reporter regret the superlatives he wasted on even the gorgeous 'Student Prince.'"

A week later, on November 9, *Leave It to Me*, with book by Smith, lyrics by Ballard MacDonald, and music by Walter Donaldson, opened at the Majestic Theatre in Brooklyn. Based on the William Collier farce *Never Say Die*, the plot centers on Dion Woodbury (Eddie Buzzell), a nervous millionaire who believes he has only a short time to live. He arrives at the Stevenson family estate to discover that Stevenson's daughter, Violet (Mary Milburn), is about to marry Lord Hector Raybrook (Fred Leslie) for his money. Madly in love with Violet, Dion offers to marry and then desert her, knowing that in a short time he would be dead, making her a wealthy widow, able to marry anyone she chooses. The Stevensons accept Dion's offer, the couple get married, and time passes. When Violet discovers that Dion's condition was not life threatening after all, she rejoices in the fact that her husband is still alive, because he is the man she truly loves.

By the time *Leave It to Me* appeared in New York, Ballard MacDonald was sharing credit for lyrics with Irving Caesar, Walter Donaldson was dividing the composing chores with Joseph Meyer, and the name of the show was changed to *Sweetheart Time*. Opening at the Imperial Theatre on January 19, 1926, the musical was greeted with mixed notices. The reviewer in *Theatre Magazine* (April 1926), finding it "snappy entertainment," with "several catchy numbers of the type that will be radioed, whistled and phonographed," was balanced by the critic from the *New York Times* (January 20, 1926), who argued, "all the speed and bang of the performance, . . . all the amazing energy displayed by the young ladies of the chorus and the dizzy-footed young men who assisted them, did not accomplish the feat of creating a satisfactory evening in the theatre." Though the gag-ridden book was generally considered dispensable, the entertainment managed to stay alive for eighteen weeks, one week shorter than the critically acclaimed *Princess Flavia*.

In December, before *Sweetheart Time* opened in Manhattan, another of Harry B. Smith's adaptations for the Shuberts was in production in Baltimore. Designed as a vehicle for diminutive star "Mitzi" (Hajos), *Naughty Riquette* had book and lyrics adapted by Smith from *Riquette*, by Rudolf Schanzer and Ernst Welisch, and a score by Oscar Straus, the composer of the German original. The musical told the story of Riquette Duval (Mitzi), a telephone operator who needs money in a hurry so she can send her sickly brother to the seashore. Gaston Riviere (Alexander Gray) engages her to appear as his companion in Monte Carlo so that no one will suspect he is having an affair with a married woman, Clarisse La Fleur (Audrey Maple). After they all settle in at Monte Carlo, however, Gaston realizes that he loves Riquette more than the married woman, and she finds herself attracted to him as well.

After a long pre-Broadway tryout tour, *Naughty Riquette* opened at the Cosmopolitan Theatre in New York on September 13, and remained there for eleven weeks. Critics found the score enchanting and the performers delightful, particularly Mitzi and comedian Stanley Lupino, who played Theophile Michu, the office boy at the telephone exchange. Brooks Atkinson, however, did not appreciate Smith's book or lyrics. He felt that the text indulged "in all the stuffy ineptitudes of old-time musical comedy, with lines both musty and flat; and few of his lyrics could endure transcription into remorseless type." Less than a week later, Atkinson would give Smith a more benevolent nod when *Countess Maritza* opened at the Shubert Theatre on September 18.

Gräfin Mariza, by Julius Brammer and Alfred Grünwald, with music by Austro-Hungarian composer Emmerich Kálmán, premiered on February 28, 1924, at the Theater an der Wien in Vienna. Seeking to be the first to produce it in the English language, the Shuberts immediately tied up the rights and acquired the German text for Harry-B-Smithing. The plot concerns Count Tassilo Endrody (Walter Woolf), a down-on-his-luck nobleman, who takes a job as caretaker on the estate of Countess Maritza (Yvonne D'Arle). The two immediately fall in love, but she becomes suspicious of the handsome caretaker's real intentions, and sends him packing. When she realizes who he really is and understands that he loves her for herself, not her money, the Countess proposes to Tassilo by mail, and welcomes him back with open arms.

The first performance of the operetta in America occurred on March 29, 1926, at the Apollo Theatre in Atlantic City. It was greeted with warm applause and sent off on a long national tour before arriving in New York at the Shubert Theatre on September 18 with a cast of sixteen principals and a chorus of sixty-four voices. *Countess Maritza* was Smith's 115th show to open on Broadway and his last big hit, running 321 performances, the longest uninterrupted run of any of his productions in New York City. It helped certainly that the Shuberts assembled an extraordinary cast that could appreciate and perform his style of comedy, ever remaining perilously close to burlesque. When the comedy succeeds, the critics praise the performer; when it fails, they blame the author. So went the notices for *Countess Maritza*. In the *New York Times* (September 20, 1926), Brooks Atkinson, for example, was lavish in his praise of George Hassell in the role of Prince Populescu, citing fragments of lines and pieces of character business in the script as if the actor had invented it all himself. After applauding Kálmán's score as "quite superior to the thin conventionalized scores usual to routine musical comedy," and noting that, although operettas of this class "are never brilliant, never spiced with daring originality, they are all continuously enjoyable, perhaps because of their simplicity," Atkinson ends his comments: "With 'The Student Prince,' and to a certain extent with 'Princess Flavia,' the producers have discovered the popularity of this type of musical drama. 'Countess Maritza' is worthy of its predecessors." With two of the shows mentioned written by Harry B. Smith, Atkinson could not disregard Smith's contribution to the popularity of the form.

The new year began in reverse for Smith. Instead of his working on an adaptation, Daniel Kusell and Alfred Jackson adapted Smith's book for *The Rich Mr. Hoggenheimer* into *Piggy*, with music by Cliff Friend, and lyrics by Lew Brown. Originally called *That's My Baby* in tryouts, the show inaugurated the Royale Theatre on January 11, 1927, after which the title was changed again, to *I Told You So*. With Sam Bernard reprising the role of Piggy Hoggenheimer, the show kept the Royale Theatre occupied for ten weeks, and just as it closed, Harry B. Smith and Sigmund Romberg had a new musical ready for the Shuberts to move into the Forty-fourth Street Theatre.

Cherry Blossoms was adapted from *The Willow Tree*, a 1917 "Fantasy of Japan in three acts" by Joseph H. Benrimo and Harrison Rhodes. Ned Hamilton (Howard Marsh) is an American on a world tour, trying to recover from an unhappy love affair. In Japan, he happens upon a curio shop, where he buys a statue of a girl carved "out of the heart of a willow tree." Having heard the legend that the statue will come to life if the soul of a woman captured in a mirror is placed above her heart, Ned places a mirror as the legend instructs. The shrewd shop owner, George Washington Goto (Bernard Gorcey), seeing a gullible American, exchanges the statue with Yo-San (Desiree Ellinger), a real Japanese girl, and not untypically, the pair fall in love. All is well until Yo-San realizes that Ned has a girlfriend back home. Believing that he would be happier with his own kind of people, she misbehaves in public so that he will leave her. Many years later, after Yo-San has died, Ned returns to Japan and becomes acquainted with his daughter, the very image of her mother.

Recalling the drama of *Madama Butterfly*, and anticipating the racial issues embedded in *South Pacific*, as well as the ending of *Show Boat*, *Cherry Blossoms*, "a musical play," opened at the Forty-fourth Street Theatre on March 28, 1927. Reviewers found Romberg's music "tuneful," although devoid of hits, and complained that the composer's attempt to combine popular music with authentic Japanese motifs was "shoddy and unnecessary," suggesting a cross between Puccini's "Italian orientalism" and Gilbert and Sullivan's *The Mikado*. The *New York Times* (March 29, 1927) noted that, while Smith and Romberg's musical bore little relation to the original play, "it is more ambitious in scenery, costumes and musically, than the average Broadway productions and may mark the beginning of the end of the 'sure-fire' technique of musical comedy." A true hybrid between operetta and musical comedy was still eight months away—*Show Boat* did not open until December 27, 1927—but the Shubert production was praised as an "ambitious and fairly satisfactory attempt." As is often the case with transitional works, audiences did not know how to respond to the show, and after beginning better than expected with a $16,000 first week, *Cherry Blossoms* closed after fifty-six performances, leaving Howard Marsh, the original Prince in *The Student Prince*, free to become Ravenal in *Show Boat*.

A month after *Cherry Blossoms* opened, Smith was back with book and lyrics for an adaptation of another three-act Emmerich Kálmán operetta. Commissioned by the Shuberts, *Die Zirkusprinzessin*, by Julius Brammer and Alfred Grünwald, was transformed into *The Circus Princess*, the story of Prince Alexis Orloff (Guy Robertson), who joins the circus as the "Mysterious Mr. X" after his uncle has disinherited him. He meets his uncle's young widow, Princess Fedora Palinska (Desirée Tabor), and successfully courts her using his princely title. When she discovers that Prince Alexis is also the masked marvel in "Stanislavsky's Combined Wonder Shows," she leaves him, only to return when she learns that "Mr. X" is a bona fide prince. After an exceptionally successful tryout tour, *The Circus Princess* opened in New York at the Winter Garden Theatre on April 25, 1927, and lived up to its highly favorable advance publicity. The typically large and enthusiastic audience greeted the show with "violent manifestations of approval," particularly at the end of the second act when the lovers part, and the critics agreed that *The Circus Princess* had everything necessary to appeal to most theatergoers, including a circus.

While his latest adaptation was settling in for a six-month run at the Winter Garden, Harry completed a collaboration with Frank Dupree on the book and lyrics for *Half a Widow*, a "musical play of the World War," with music by performer Shep Camp (composer of the "Milkman's Rag"), and produced by newcomer Wally Gluck. Babette (Gertrude Lang), daughter of Pierre Lafarge (Albert Froom), an innkeeper, is about to marry Jean Marie Alphonse Bettingcourt (Paul Doucet) when his wealthy father forbids the marriage. Jean's rich friend, Captain Bob Everett (Halfred Young), offers to marry her the night before his army unit goes to the front line in France. Expecting to die in battle, he signs a will leaving all of his money to his new wife so that she will be able to marry Jean after his death. Time passes and, as expected, Babette receives news that her husband was killed in battle. Just as she is about to marry Jean, however, Bob returns unexpectedly, and Babette realizes that she really loves her husband.

With a plot borrowed from Smith's own *Sweetheart Time*, *Half a Widow* opened at the Waldorf Theatre on Monday, September 12, 1927, and closed after the Saturday evening performance. The critics found the show obviously underrehearsed and completely conventional in its depiction of war, a "pale image of the real thing," full of antique jokes and stereotypical situations. Benny Rubin, playing a Jewish soldier named Izzy Preiss, made the most of Smith's one-liners, but even a fine comedian could not keep the show afloat for more than a week. The experience was an important one for Smith, however, because a performer and composer named Geoffrey O'Hara was in the company. O'Hara had established a reputation as an arranger of barbershop quartets and the composer of the World War I hit "K-K-K-Katy," as well as the more ambitious anthem "There Is No Death." Not only did O'Hara provide an additional song for the score, he also began a collaboration with Harry B. Smith that would last until Harry died.

Soon after the demise of *Half a Widow*, Smith's lyrics for *Bonita*, Edward Locke's adaptation of Augustus Thomas's play *Arizona*, were heard on tour, set to music by Sigmund Romberg, and produced by the Shuberts. Locke's libretto is set in the old West in 1869, and it trades on the conflict between the Indians led by Black Hawk (Stanley Jessup) and a white settlement under the command of Colonel Bonham (William T.

Carleton). A renegade captain (John Rutherford) stirs up the Indians, but Lieutenant Denton (John Barker) heroically manages to penetrate enemy lines in time to save the Canby ranch and fall in love with the rancher's daughter, Bonita (Berna Deane).

By the time *Bonita* reached Broadway, it was titled *The Love Call*, opening at the Majestic Theatre on October 24 with an army of "cow rangers, cow girls, Mexican dancing maidens, Federal army scouts and scurvy, treacherous Indians." The critics found the entertainment "average" and "tasteless," but noted a tuneful and diversified score by Romberg that "does as well by the tom-tom Indians as the passionate Mexicans." Inspired perhaps by the template they helped to create, Romberg and Smith produced the requisite number of waltzes, and love songs, and the obligatory virile expression of bravado, "Ranger's Song," recalling "The Rangers' Song" in *Rio Rita* and anticipating "Stout-Hearted Men" in *The New Moon*. Again Smith and Romberg attempted to create a hybrid form between operetta and musical comedy by setting whole scenes to music in which individual numbers are connected through underscored dialogue, or arioso-like recitative. In the opening number, for example, exposition is accomplished through the development of four or five different melodies: "Hi There! . . . Hurry Up That Soap," "You May Drink to My Wedding Day," "You Leave My Girl Alone," "Tony! Tony! Tony!" and "'Tis Love," and the whole score is unified through a recurring waltz song, "Eyes That Love," recalling a similar use of "Deep in My Heart" in *The Student Prince*. The juxtaposition of operatic devices with more easily accessible songs was central to Smith's work with Romberg.

The Love Call closed after eighty-eight performances, barely making it through the new year. *Countess Maritza* was back in the spring for two weeks at the Century Theatre, and Harry was hard at work on the libretto for yet another bio-musical for the Shuberts, still seeking another *Blossom Time*. Derived from *Chopin*, a Hungarian musical play by Jenó Faragó and István Bertha, *White Lilacs* was a musicalization of the romance between composer Frederick Chopin (Guy Robertson) and author George Sand (Odette Myrtil). Because Myrtil was a violinist, Smith found justification for Sand to play the instrument from a comment the author made in her autobiography: "I was born to the sound of the violin." As a result, the cigar-smoking Sand of history became the violin-playing author of musical romance. For the music, Karl Hajos was engaged to fashion a score out of Chopin's melodies, one of which had already been adapted by Harry Carroll as "I'm Always Chasing Rainbows" in 1918.

When *White Lilacs* opened at the Shubert Theatre on September 10, 1928, audiences and critics embraced the show, and Smith was reunited with comic De Wolf Hopper, whose portrayal of Dubusson, Sand's publisher, won acclaim from the critics and hearty applause from the opening night crowd. The *New York Times* (September 11, 1928) argued that the show was done "in the best traditions" of operetta, "a stylized form, emphasizing song and story," not dancing and comedy, and the book was found "florid and high-sounding, as probably befits such an unabashedly theatricalized 'romance.'" Smith managed to restrain his predilection for puns, slang, and burlesque humor, and transformed language and situations that critics had earlier called "stodgy" and "contrived" into the accepted conventions of operetta. Where critics before had complained of improbabilities in Smith's plotting, they now forgave historical inaccuracies, arguing that the alterations of fact "have been made better to fit the subject to its medium of projection."

The seventeen-week run of *White Lilacs* at the Shubert Theatre was followed, on Christmas Day, by the opening of *The Red Robe*, adapted by Smith and Edward Delaney Dunn from Stanley Weyman's novel *Under the Red Robe*, and *Das Weib im Purpur*, by Leopold Jacobson and Rudolf Österreicher with music by Jean Gilbert. Set in seventeenth-century France, the plot deals with the enmity between Cardinal Richelieu (Jose Ruben) and Henri, Count De Cocheforet (S. Herbert Bragiotti). As a gesture of gratitude to the Cardinal who released him from serving a prison sentence, Gil De Berault (Walter Woolf) takes it upon himself to capture Cocheforet. When he sees Renee De Cocheforet (Helen Gilliland), the Count's daughter, however, he realizes that love is stronger than gratitude, and he allows her father to escape.

The critics noted the similarities in period and plot to the 1925 hit operetta *The Vagabond King*, even to imitating the earlier show's love song, "Only a Rose," with its romantic ballad, "Only a Smile." But unlike earlier days when such obvious borrowing was reprimanded in harsh tones, the critics found *The Red Robe* "a very tolerable entertainment of its kind," enjoying the fun, even though it was "of unblushing slap-stick quality." The show continued for 167 performances, during which the Smith-Gilbert score was interpolated with songs by Arthur Schwartz, Alberta Nichols, Maurie Rubens, and Robert Stolz.

When not involved in projects for the Shubert Organization, Harry continued to produce librettos for his own amusement and gratification. *The Happiest Man*, *The White Fox*, and *The Runaway* all date from this period when the dearth of steady commissions incited him to look for other work to occupy his time. With the emergence of "talking pictures" at the end of the 1920s, Smith got a job at Warner Brothers, evaluating more than sixty-seven plays and stories that were being considered for adaptation into motion pictures.

In the fall of 1929, the Jolson Theatre Musical Comedy Company produced a series of revivals of "classic" operettas and comic operas, each scheduled to run for two weeks at the Jolson Theatre in New York. *Sweethearts*, Smith's collaboration with Fred de Grésac and Victor Herbert, opened on September 21, *The Fortune Teller* appeared on November 4, and finally, *Robin Hood* on November 18. It had been seventeen years since Smith walked out of a production of his earliest success in New York, and he and his wife were resolved to attend the opening night, if only because de Koven had died in 1920 and the creative team needed to be represented. After the performance, the author was exuberantly applauded by both the audience and the critics for his work. Except for the odd presence of the Albertina Rasch Dance Company playing wood nymphs in Sherwood Forest, the *New York Times* (November 20, 1929) noted that the production was "pretty much 'Robin Hood' as it ever was." What was most remarkable to the reviewer was not the music or individual performances, but that Smith's libretto still worked: "the book stands up under what are sometimes known as the ravages of time better than most other thirty-eight-year-old comic opera librettos that you could name. That it does so must have been a source of satisfaction last night to its author."

Chapter 11

"A Long Walk Uphill against the Wind"

Harry's triumph carried him through the new year. He felt that if he must be remembered for something, *Robin Hood* was as good an example of his work as anything else, and for the three or four weeks it took him to create it, the return in commissions, royalties, and reputation was staggering. Smith never really understood why the show was so very popular and had always preferred his libretto to *The Serenade*, but when that show was revived in March 1930 as part of the Jolson Theatre series, it was clear to the author that he was in the minority. Critics called it a "fairly melodious but prodigiously unfunny" work with a book that is "no match on any count for the libretto of 'Robin Hood.'" Smith's text was considerably revised, with the leading character's name changed from Yvonne to Inez, and the monastery and adjoining convent altered to a military barracks and a girls' boarding school so that the audience would not be scandalized by the promise of fun between nuns and monks. However they chose to do it, it was fine with Harry, so long as they paid him his royalties. Unlike Reginald de Koven and Victor Herbert, he was still alive to enjoy these revivals: alive and working.

A week after *The Serenade* closed at the Jolson Theatre, Smith's newest assignment for the Shuberts premiered in Newark, New Jersey. Based on *Drei arme kleine Mädels* (libretto by Bruno Hardt-Warden and Herman Feiner, music by Walter Kollo), *Three Little Girls* had a book by Gertrude Purcell and Marie Armstrong Hecht, lyrics by Smith, and music by the original composer. The story was quite similar to *Maytime*, a 1917 Shubert production, adapted by Rida Johnson Young with music by Sigmund Romberg. In 1846, Beate-Marie (Natalie Hall) and Hendrik Norgard (Charles Hedley) are in love, but in order to keep her family from financial ruin, Beate-Marie marries Count Von Rambow (John Goldsworthy). Twenty years later, their three daughters, Beate (Natalie Hall), Marie (Bettina Hall), and Annette (Martha Lorber), learn of their mother's emotional sacrifice, and when Beate falls in love with Hendrik's son, Karl (Charles Hedley), necessity forces them to separate as well. The younger generation is more fortunate than their parents, and the lovers are eventually united. The production opened at the Shubert Theatre on April 14, 1930, and was judged "a melodious, treacly exhibit which theatergoers, who like their musical shows sugared with an abundant plot should find greatly to their liking." Critics noted the waltz "Love's Happy Dream" and the "Letter Song" as the outstanding numbers of the score, and the physical production, particularly the use of the turntable, was also greeted with vigorous applause.

The following month, while *Three Little Girls* was accumulating its 104 performances, *Rogues and Vagabonds*, with book and lyrics by Harry B. Smith and music by Geoffrey O'Hara, was presented at the Waldorf Theatre by the Garden Players of Forest Hills, Long Island, on May 7, the third day of the Eighth Annual National Little Theatre Tournament. If Smith's professional opportunities had begun to wane, he was certainly not opposed to having his work performed by amateurs. *Rogues and Vagabonds* was the fourth of four shows (the three others were psychological problem plays) competing that night for the National Little Theatre award, and by the time it began, all of the critics and much of the audience had left. The judges remained, however, and what they saw was an adaptation of Smith's earlier play *Will Shakespeare*, displaying life in the theater during the Elizabethan era.

During the summer, Harry and his brother completed *The Night Owl*, "a play with music adapted from *Das Gespensterschiff* by Lothar and Ritter," for producer George Lederer. Designed as an intimate musical, the show takes place on the deck of the freighter Aurora, bound for New

York City. Captain Burton (Mark Smith), a "gruff sea dog," was persuaded to take passengers aboard for a fee, so, in addition to the usual crew, the ship is crowded with newlyweds, Ted (Dick Keene) and Polly (Bobbie Perkins), Martha Miggs (Alice Hegeman), a spinster novelist, Professor Updike (Robert Capron), a psychologist and hypnotist, Daisy (Barbara Newberry), his niece, a trio of showgirls, and a stowaway pair of blackface comedians, Bunker (Tom Fant) and Flam (Billy Lytel). In between the scramble for staterooms among the passengers, we discover that the first mate, John Larned (John Barker), who is engaged to Daisy, is also scheduled to marry the captain's daughter, Flossie (Marian Warring-Manly), who just happens to be aboard the ship. Just as that situation appears to create complications, an even greater conflict arises when a ghost ship, the Night Owl, docks alongside the Aurora. Like the "Flying Dutchman" of legend, "The Unknown" (Al Ochs), the spectral captain of the Night Owl, comes aboard looking for a maiden "pure of heart," who will sail away with him.

George Lederer presented the musical under the title *The Pajama Lady* (the girl chosen by the ghostly captain is in her pajamas), changing the name of the professor's niece from Daisy to Barbara, and tightening up much of the dialogue. Philip Charig and Richard Myers, the composers of the 1927 revue *Allez-Oop*, were engaged to provide the music, and Johnny Mercer was hired to help Robert B. Smith with the lyrics. With dances by Albertina Rasch, and stage direction by Lederer, *The Pajama Lady* opened at the National Theatre in Washington, D.C., on October 6, 1930, to excellent reviews. The critics found the music tuneful, the story interesting, and the performances engaging. As the *Washington Post* (October 7, 1930) noted:

> A long time since patrons have left the playhouse mulling over memories of what went on during the acts. If for no other reason this should mark "The Pajama Lady" out of the ordinary. There were other reasons, to wit: It was the best first night Washington theatergoers have seen, in the musical line, for y'ars and y'ars. "The Pajama Lady" is totally different from the current musical fanfare. It has a story and it sticks to it. Not only that, it has music that measures to a standard slightly higher than the modern classics.
>
> With the theater in the doldrums these past several seasons, "The Pajama Lady" has the stuff to awaken it out of its

apathy. . . . The triumph of this musical comedy is the rejuvenation, not to say the reincarnation, of George Lederer, a showman of the old school—which, after all is said and done, knew its theater.

The same day *The Pajama Lady* opened in Washington, *Prince Chu Chang*, an American version of *Das Land des Lächelns*, by Edgar Smith and Harry Clarke, with music by Franz Lehár and lyrics by Harry B. Smith, opened in Newark, New Jersey. While it was advertised that the writers based their work on an earlier version of the piece, Victor Léon's *Die gelbe Jacke*, instead of the more familiar text by Ludwig Herzer and Fritz Löhner-Beda, the plot of the American edition differed from both German texts, in which Prince Sou-Chong actually marries the Viennese girl. Here, Lisa Lichtenfels (Gladys Baxter), who is engaged to Lieutenant Gustave von Poppenstein (Gerry Goff), falls in love with Prince Chu Chang (Clifford Newdahl), heir to the throne of China. She drinks a cup of drugged tea, and dreams about what life would be like as the wife of a polygamous Chinese prince. Realizing that even the deepest love cannot conquer the monumental differences in their cultures, Lisa awakes from her dream and decides to stay in Vienna and marry von Poppenstein.

Prince Chu Chang gave Smith the opportunity to create the lyric for the last great song of his career, "Yours Is My Heart Alone," an adaptation of the most famous song in Lehár's score, "Dein ist mein ganzes Herz." But that song and a few kind words from the *Newark Evening News* were insufficient to keep the show on the boards. It was an expensive project, and the Shuberts as producers did not like to lose money, so they closed it in New Haven on October 18.

A month later, Harry Clarke and Harry B. Smith were in Philadelphia, where their adaptation of *Hotel Stadt-Lemberg*, by Ernst Neubach with music by Jean Gilbert, was about to open under the title *Arms and the Maid*. Produced by the Shubert Brothers at the Walnut Street Theatre on November 25, with lyrics by Smith written to Gilbert's original music, the story involves the efforts of Countess Anna Von Hatfield (Emmy Kosary) to hide her soldier-lover, Lieutenant Franz Almasy (Halfred Young), from the Russians when they march into Austria in 1915 and occupy the Imperial Hotel of Lemberg. In an attempt to outwit a Russian spy, Anna permits Russian Colonel Petroff (Edward Neil Jr.) to lavish his attentions upon her, much to the discomfort of Franz, masquerading as a waiter. In the end, important documents are intercepted, and Franz and Anna find safety in one another's arms.

Audiences and critics were disappointed in the show, the *Philadelphia Inquirer* (November 26, 1930) finding it a "hackneyed story," devoid of humor and freshness, with only "desultory snatches of pleasing music." The leading lady, Emmy Kosary, was considered a letdown as well, and the rest of the cast "seemed to sense the hopelessness of the task in hand, and while the individual members simulated an enthusiasm they evidently did not feel, it had a hollow ring." Three songs were cited as effective, "To Have, to Hold and to Love," "I Like You," and "I Gotta Keep My Eye on You," but they were insufficient to propel the show beyond Philadelphia.

To fill the gap between theater projects, Harry continued to evaluate scripts and stories for Warner Brothers, making extensive notes and comments that attest to his appreciation of nineteenth-century literature and dramatic structure. Reliving his days as a newspaperman, he was as quick, perceptive, and witty as he had been fifty years earlier. As well as editing the work of others, he reviewed his own as he prepared his memoirs for publication by the Boston firm of Little, Brown, and Company in 1931.

Late in November 1931, a substantially rewritten *Arms and the Maid*, with its title changed to *Marching By*, was attempted again in Newark, New Jersey, in the hopes of bringing the show to Broadway. After more revisions, the musical opened on March 3, 1932, at Chanin's Forty-sixth Street Theatre, with Mack Gordon and Harry Revel credited with additional music and lyrics. Desirée Tabor played Countess Anna, Guy Robertson was her lover Franz, and Leonard Ceeley was the libidinous Colonel Petroff. Once again it was less than acceptable to audiences and critics, with Brooks Atkinson, in the *New York Times* (March 4, 1932), explaining why: "As a production it is shoddy. As a musical play it is dull. Now that taste in musical entertainment has been considerably elevated everywhere by the application of art to the staging and intelligence to the playmaking, it is difficult to know why producers cling to the worn-out patterns. . . . Especially during the last year the musical stage has marched swiftly by every department of 'Marching By' and left it far to the rear." After thirty-two performances, the show ceased to march for good.

Following an outdoor summer production by the St. Louis Municipal Opera Company, *Prince Chu Chang*, renamed *The Land of Smiles*, appeared in Boston the day after Christmas 1932. This time, advertisements for the libretto credited Ludwig Herzer and Fritz Löhner's text, Harry Graham's

English version, and an American version by Edgar Smith and Harry B. Smith. Produced by the Shuberts and directed by (Joseph H.) Benrimo, the production featured Charles Hackett as Prince Chu Chang, Nancy McCord as Lisa Lichtenfels, and John McCauley as Gustave von Poppenstein. The Boston critics were mixed on the virtues of the script and individual performances, but all agreed that "Yours Is My Heart Alone" was outstanding and destined to be as popular in America as "Dein ist mein ganzes Herz" had been in Europe. A week in Boston led to a week in Philadelphia, where the critics again praised the score but found the libretto filled with "ineptitudes and absurdities," made "even duller and more muddled" by the adapters than the original German text.

When *The Land of Smiles* closed in Philadelphia on January 14, 1933, Harry B. Smith's professional career came to an end. The commissions finally having ceased and forced into retirement, Harry spent the rest of his days finishing old scripts, jotting down ideas for new ones, and collaborating with composer Geoffrey O'Hara. The pair produced two comic operas, both published by Samuel French, between which Smith managed to complete another play, entitled *The Star Witness*. Appearing in 1934, Smith and O'Hara's *Harmony Hall* involved General Earnest Work, a millionaire manufacturer of musical toys, who agrees to endow a college as long as every student learns how to sing or play an instrument. Because his son, Doolittle Work, is hopelessly unmusical, the General pays McTavish, a Scotch globetrotter, to keep the boy out of the United States, and adopts Mlle. Rosalie, a young prima donna, as his heir. He arranges a marriage between her and Felix Brownini, a famous tenor, and both are engaged to sing the premiere of his opera, but when the day of the wedding arrives, the two singers get into a fight over who has the better voice, and they break off the engagement. The General's pianist, Mr. Hammersley Keys, suggests that Brownini's ego is so great that if Rosalie gets engaged to someone else, he will again want to marry her. The General engages Smith, the business manager for the Glee Club, to act as a substitute groom, a situation that pleases all of the parties, because Rosalie and Smith are really in love. Having fallen in love with Maritana, Rosalie's maid, Brownini fails to become jealous, and Rosalie marries Smith, who turns out to be the long-hidden General's son, and not unmusical after all.

The work is filled with the improbable fun of Harry's old burlesques, and it even offered O'Hara the opportunity of capitalizing on his popular "K-K-K-Katy," in a stuttering song, "How Hap-Hap-Happy Life

Would Be." The following year, Samuel French published *The Princess Runs Away*, borrowing its plot from *The Free Lance*, this time dealing with the kingdoms of Amnesia and Montebello where the battle is won not by Sigmund's super strength, but by a new explosive designed to "exterminate the enemy," created by the court jester, Aleck Smart, disguised as a scientist. Since he sells his invention to both kingdoms, neither wants to go to war. Trading on the popularity of motion pictures, in this version the runaway Prince and Princess disguise themselves as a war correspondent and newsreel photographer.

In the fall of 1935, Harry began to feel old. Throughout his long career, he had faced the deaths of his friends and associates with a kind of stoic resignation, always finding in the next writing assignment or rare book an antidote to sadness, a prescription for a healthy life. But when De Wolf Hopper died in September 1935, followed in October by Francis Wilson, Harry felt sure that he would be next. He became quite ill, the pressures of an overly active, stress-filled life finally taking their toll. Two days after Christmas 1935, Harry felt well enough to accompany his wife to the Marlborough-Blenheim Hotel in Atlantic City for their traditional holiday vacation, joined by Spencer Bentley, Irene's twenty-six-year-old nephew. New Year's Eve was especially festive, with fireworks and champagne, and food that seemed to give Harry indigestion. He did not complain. He went to sleep thinking about beginning a new play with the coming year, but the play was never begun. At 6:30 on Wednesday morning, January 1, 1936, Harry B. Smith died of a heart attack, his wife of nearly thirty years by his side. Smith's body was returned to his home at 319 West 107th Street in Manhattan, just off Riverside Drive, where the funeral took place at 11 A.M. on Saturday, followed by a private burial in Greenwood Cemetery.

Smith left an estate worth $79,956, of which the most valuable single asset was his literary collection of first editions, autograph letters, manuscripts, and Napoleonic memorabilia, appraised at $31,179; at the time of his death, he was owed royalties in the amount of $30,800. When Smith's will was offered for probate in Surrogates' Court on January 8, his wife Irene was named chief beneficiary, receiving all of her husband's jewelry, all income from Smith's ASCAP contract (due to expire on December 31, 1940), three-fourths of all bank deposits, lyrics, plays, motion pictures, books, copyrights, magazine articles, and scenarios, and 60 percent of the sale of his literary collection. Harry's son, Sydney Reed Smith, a former army captain residing in Canaan, New York, was left real estate property and a one-quarter share, along with Robert, Mary, and Bessie Smith, Harry's brother and sisters, of one-fourth of all bank deposits, and of 40 percent of the proceeds from the sale of his collection. Robert, Mary, and Bessie also inherited joint interests in the house at 166 St. Mark's Avenue, Brooklyn, where they all currently resided. Lena Reed, Harry's former wife, then residing in Pittsfield, Massachusetts, was not named in the will, a matter of bitter contention between her and the designated heirs.

On the 8th and 9th of April, 1936, Harry B. Smith's literary collection was put on the auction block at the American Art Association Anderson Galleries at 30 East 57th Street. Four sessions of trading brought $29,231, the highest sums going for the presentation copy from Dickens to Hans Christian Andersen of *The Cricket on the Hearth*, bought by Walter M. Hill for $1,450, and Robert Louis Stevenson's autograph manuscript of *In the South Seas*, also purchased by Hill, for $1,150.

During his lifetime, Harry B. Smith had been praised and criticized by many. To some, he was little more than a hack, mass-producing librettos with no concern for art or literary value. And in many ways, that is a valid assessment. Harry wrote quickly and not always carefully. He wrote on demand, giving stars and producers exactly what they paid for, and he never turned down a commission because he had too little time to write the libretto. As a result, Dillingham, Frohman, Klaw and Erlanger, Lederer, the Shubert Brothers, and Ziegfeld all relied repeatedly on his work—even after seasons of bad reviews. Smith was never a favorite with the critics. He wrote to make a living, and because critics do not pay royalties or buy tickets or sheet music, he wrote to please the people who do, and that often meant preparing shows suitable for touring and unsophisticated audiences. Perhaps because he was less concerned with creating art than with making a living, he was not overprotective of his work, and producers, stars, directors, and composers all readily altered his libretti, and not always for the better. He was often honestly amused by the irony of being severely reprimanded by critics for jokes he did not write and improbable situations against which he fought with producers and composers.

After his death, many collaborators and friends wrote lines of remembrance to honor the most prolific librettist in American history, but no one summed up his life better than Harry B. Smith, who ends his autobiography with these words:

Often my life seems all of the theatre, a Chinese play lasting not through many nights but through many years. In other moods, I feel that the theatre has been just a shop where I worked at a trade, and that my real life has belonged to my own people and my friends. Life is for most of us a long walk uphill against the wind, with now and then a pleasant place to rest, perhaps to laugh a little before plodding on. Still, the reflections of men on the slope toward the sunset are not without comedy. Hazlitt, generally perturbed in mind and sickly in body, said on his deathbed, "After all, I have had a happy life," while Goethe, conqueror of the hearts of women and the minds of men, and who lived to be eighty-three, declared that he remembered "only fourteen days of happiness." It would be instructive to have a diary of that fortnight. It might give a hint to some of us how to make the best use of our time.

Appendix

The Museum of the City of New York and the Harry Ransom Humanities Research Center at the University of Texas at Austin possess the following undated, unproduced, and unpublished manuscripts by Harry B. Smith not mentioned in the text.

Administration
Adventures of a Bell Boy
After the Girl
A La Paree
Alias Pittsburg Sadie
Alice in Wonderland
Alienation, a legal episode in one act
The Ambassador, scenario
An American Sport
Anna-Liza
Artists Must Love, synopsis of a story for a screen play
Aztec, an opera

Babette, a picture play with music
Bachelor from Conviction
Beau Brocade
Beggars on Horseback, scenario
Bianca, synopsis of an opera
The Black Pierrot
Bohemia Limited
The Butterfly
"Chinese Radio Sketch"
Code Widows
Colonel Chabert
The Dance of Cairo
Dance Waiter, a scenario
The Dancin' Fool
The Dancing Mistress
The Devil Skirts
The Divorce Trip
Dolly Dollars, a musical photoplay
A Dresden Doll
The Duchess of Chicago
The Duchess of the Follies-Bergère [*sic*]
The Duck with Three Beaks
Eight Monkeys and a Catspaw
Find Me a Girl
Find the Girl
The First Treasury Clerk
Five To
The Flirt
The Forbidden Dance, an opera in two acts
Fraſtiana (Love a la Mode)
French as She Is Spoken
A Friendly Call, a farce in one act
"The Funny Mooners," a radio continuity in two parts
Galahad, Jr.
The Gay Gordons
Get Rich Quick Sadie
The Ghost Show
The Girl and the Canary
The Girl on the Beach

Girl Wanted
Give Me a Ring
The Golf Widow
Go to Bed Papa
Grafitana
Gypsy Blood
"Harry and Harriet, the Record of a Wedding Trip," a radio continuity
Held for Ransom
Hello
Her Majesty Mimi
Der Herr Professor
High Finance
The Highwayman, a musical picture play
The Hold Up
The Honeymooners, synopsis
The House in the Mist, by Katherine Green and H. B. Smith
The Idol's Eye, a photoplay with music
The Impresairio [*sic*], *scenario of*
The Joys of Life
Just Another Blonde, and synopsis of a picture comedy
Keeping His Wife at Home
Key to Room No. 10
King Reme
Kiss the Bride, a comedy in three acts
Kitty
Kommando
The Lady of the Cinema
Lafitte
Das Land Der Liebe (The Land of Love)
Lieutenant Cupid
Little Dorrit, synopsis
The Little King
"Long View Scene"
Look After Amelie
Love Is All
Loveland (The Golden Girl)
The Love Pirate
The Loves of Casanova
The Love Syndicate

The Love Trap
Madame Flirt
The Maid of Honor
Masculine, Feminine and Neuter
The Mermaid Tavern
Miquette
The Miracle Maid
The Money Burner
La Montansie
Morgan
Mr. Audacious
The Music School
My Cousin from Nowhere
My Sister and I
My Six Wives
The Name and the Game
Napoleonette
The New Girl
New Plays for Old
Night Birds
Night of the Ball
Nuts and Dates
The Opera Girl
The Original Photographer
The Other Leg
Our Friend the Baron
A Pantomime Rehearsal
Papa's Boy
Patpachou
The Pettibone
The Picture Girl
The Play Actress
Polly in Politics
Polly's Gone to Paris
The Prince of Good Fellows
The Princess Olivia
A Queen of Society
The Radio Whirl
The Road to the Spotlight

Rome Was Right
Rosy Posy
Le Rouie
A Russian Idiot
Sally Smith (or, *Dr. Juci Saxbo,* or, *Good Morning Sally)*
Seen but Not Heard
The Serenade, *a musical photoplay*
The Seven Darlings
The Sex Appeal A.D. *1950*
The Sham Aristocrat
The Sheik
The Siren's Song
Spanish Love
The Spanish Nightingale
Stage Door Johnny
Stephen Foster, *a story for an operetta*
Sweet Pansy
Swift and Stella
Sylvia Steps Out
The Thousandth and Second Night
Tiger Girl
To Whom Does Helen Belong
The Trombonist
The Troubadours
The Twins
Uncle Sam's Motel
Undress Parade
The Vagabond
The Wades Move North
The Waltz King
Where the Lark Sings
The White Vest
You Know Me Alice
Zizi

INDEX

Aarons, Alfred E., 142, 165, 167
Abbey, Henry, 79
Aborn, Milton, 75
Accooe, William, 142
Adams, Ida, 220, 224
Ade, George, 145
Adonis, 11
Air King, The, 200–201
Algerian, The, 76
Ali Baba Jr., 64–68, 73, 74, 83
Ali, George, 67, 118
Allez-Oop, 277
All Over Town, 239–240, 241
Amateur Sport, An, 186
Amaryllis, 15–17, 19, 26, 175
American Extravaganza Company, 54, 55, 63
American Girl, 169
Anderson, Ivar, 179, 180
Angel Face, 255–256
"Any Old Night Is a Wonderful Night," 240
"Any Old Place with You," 254
Arabian Nights, The, 36–38
Arms and the Maid, 278–279
Arthur, Daniel V., 210, 223, 229, 239
Artists and Models, 264
Ascher, Leo, 246
"As the Sunflower Turns to the Sun," 160–161
Ayer, Nat D., 198, 215

Babette, 158–159
Bach, Elizabeth, 4. *See also* Smith, Elizabeth (mother)
Bach, James Brown (grandfather), 4
Bachelor Belles, The, 207–208
Baird, Stewart, 235, 244
Bambo, the King of the Tramps, 35
Barbara Fidgety, 125
Barbara Frietchie, 125
Barbaretto, Burrell, 190, 221
Barbier, Jules, 219
Barker, Richard, 90–91, 108
Barnabee, Henry Clay, 46, 48, 50–53, 61, 63, 72, 89, 95, 125, 126, 144
Barr, Georges, 252
Barr, Albert, 232
Bartlett, Jessie. *See* Daves, Jessie Bartlett
Bartlett, Josephine, 46
Batchelor, W.H., 54, 59, 82
Bayes, Nora, 120, 190, 191, 197, 212, 213, 251, 252

Beaumont, Rose, 105, 110, 150
Begum, The, 26–33, 46, 92
Belasco, David, 122, 203
Bell, Digby, 30, 31, 33, 34, 43, 48, 54, 56, 58, 63–65, 68, 69
"Belle of Avenue A, The," 174
Belle of Bohemia, The, 129–132, 134, 135
Belle of Hong Kong, The, 169
Belle of Mayfair, The, 180
Belle of New York, The, 114, 128, 146
Belle of the Beach, The, 130
Belle of the Halls, The, 130
Belle of the West, The, 170–171
Belles and Beaux, 130
Bellman, 28, 29
"Be My Little Baby Bumble Bee," 221
Benatzky, Ralph, 263
Bennett, David, 258
Benrimo, Joseph H., 269, 280
Bentley, Irene, 115, 116, 120, 127, 131, 137, 145, 152, 180, 196, 198, 204, 281
Bentley, Spencer, 281
Bently, Wilmer H., 152
Bereny, Henrik, 223
Bergen, Nella, 172, 173
Bergman, Henry, 122, 215
Berlin, Irving, 238, 239, 242–244, 249, 253, 264, 265
Bernard, Dick, 130–131
Bernard, Sam, 104, 127, 130, 176, 178–180, 186, 189, 190, 269
Bernauer, Rudolf, 261
Berthald, Barron, 77, 79
Bertram, Helen, 125, 128
Betty Be Good, 256, 257–258
"Bid Me Good Bye and Go," 47
Bickel, George, 199, 201
Bigelow, Charles A., 122, 176, 194
Billionaire, The, 146–148, 163
Black Cat, The, 222
Blake, Gordon, 167
Blizzard; or, *Families Supplied, The*, 35
Blondeau, Henri, 186
Blonde in Black, The, 149–150, 160, 162
Blossom, Henry, 191, 211
Blossom Time, 265, 272
Bluebeard, Jr., 44–45
Boccaccio, 28, 34, 40, 165, 169
Bolton, Guy, 239, 240
Boneface, George C., Jr., 94, 165
Bonita, 271, 272. *See also Love Call, The*
Booth, Edwin, 5
Bostonians, The, 46, 48–51, 53, 55, 60–63, 72, 73, 78, 85, 86, 89, 95, 97, 106, 125, 128, 144, 219
Boston Ideals, 45–45
Boucicault, Dion, 42–43
Boullard, Marius, 143
Bowers, Charles H., 150, 152
Bowers, Robert Hood, 199, 213–215, 221, 254
Brady, Diamond Jim, 198–199
Braham, David, 9
Brammer, Julius, 232, 268, 270
Brian, Donald, 216, 235, 244
Bric-a-Brac, 171
Brice, Elizabeth, 220, 238
Brice, Fanny, 202
"Bring on the Girls," 260–261, 264
Brody, Miksa, 242
Brown, A. Seymour, 198, 215
Bruce, Richard, 258
Bryan, Alfred, 247
Bub oder, 221
Burke, Billie, 233
Burt, Benjamin Hapgood, 241, 242
Busy Woman, A, 113

Cadet Girl, The, 129–131
Caesar, Irving, 265, 267
Cahill, Marie, 145, 146, 152, 239
Caine, Georgia, 178–180
Caldwell, Anne, 253
Caliph, The, 75, 90–91
Cameron, Grace, 125, 132
Camp, Shep, 271
Canary, The, 252–253
Captain Fracassa, 47
Captain Kidd, 75
Carle, Richard, 223, 228, 239
Carleton, W.T., 26,
Carleton, William P., 182, 246
Carleton, William T., 271–272
Carnival Wedding, A, 246
Caroline, 263
Carrera, Liane, 176, 191
Carrera, Maximo, 191
Carter, Mrs. Leslie, 113
Caryll, Ivan, 176, 223, 233, 234, 236, 237, 252, 253
Casavant, Louis, 132, 215
Casino Boy, The, 130
Casino Girl, The, 128–130, 135, 180
Castle, Irene (Mrs. Vernon), 238, 239
Castle, Vernon, 225, 238, 239
Catherine, 110–11, 113
Cawthorn, Joseph, 118, 172, 173, 192, 225, 235, 244, 249, 252, 253
Chained Eagle, A, 262
Chamberlyn, A.H., 129, 131, 135
Charig, Philip, 277
Charles Frohman Company, 244, 248
Charley's Aunt, 142
chatte blanche, La, 171
Cherry Blossoms, 269–270
Chicago Church Choir Opera Company, 11
Chicago Dramatic Club, The, 10
Chimes of Normandy, The, 11

China Doll, A, 149, 159, 163, 165–167
Chivot, Henri, 135
Chocolate Soldier, The, 214
Chopin, 272
Christian, The, 109
Circus Princess, The, 270–271
Clark, Arthur, 85, 86
Clark, Hilda, 97, 102, 103
Clarke, Cuthbert, 187
Clarke, Harry, 182
Clarke, William H., 111
Clayton, Bessie, 127
Cleopatra, 106
Clover, 42–44
Cobb, Will D., 137, 177
Coffin, C. Hayden, 56
Cohan, George M., 172, 185
Cole, Bob, 149
Collyer, Dan, 124
Comstock, F. Ray, 241, 256
Conor, Harry, 150, 220
Contented Woman, A, 251
Cook, Will Marion, 127, 146, 153, 159, 160, 202, 203
Coquette, The, 228
Cort, John, 246
Cottrelly, Mathilde, 27, 30
Countess Maritza, 268–269, 272
Court Singer, The, 80
Cowles, Eugene, 46, 72, 95, 107, 118, 135, 158
Crawford, Clifton, 142, 146, 148, 149, 153
Crystal Slipper, The, 36, 38–41, 44, 54
Cunningham, Arthur, 165, 219
Cupid, Hymen and Company, 13–14, 23
Current, The, 167
Cushman, Charlotte, 5
Cuvillier, Charles, 233, 236
Cyrano de Bergerac (musical), 115, 117
Cyrano de Bergerac (play), 109
Cyranose de Brecabrac, 109–110
Czibulka, Alfons, 41

Dailey, Peter F., 104, 105, 113, 118, 119, 125
Daly, Augustin, 75
Daly, Dan, 115, 129, 130
Dalziel, Davison, 9, 15
dame de chez Maxim, La, 223
Daniels, Frank, 83, 85–87, 89, 99, 100–102, 104, 153–155, 181, 182
D'Ancourt, Grenet, 234
D'Arville, Camille, 72, 100, 120
D'Auban, Ernest, 172
Davenport, Eva, 122
Davenport, Fanny, 106
Davenport, Harry, 114, 142
Davis, Jessie Bartlett, 11–13, 46, 50, 60–61, 72, 95, 120
Davis, William J., 11, 13
Dawn, Hazel, 235, 238
Day, Edith, 247
de Angeles, Jefferson, 30–31, 43, 90
Debutante, The, 235–238
Decker, Edith, 221
de Cottens, Victor, 129
De Gorsse, Henri, 248
de Grésac, Fred, 217, 218, 226, 274
"Dein ist mein ganzes Herz," 278, 280
de Koven, Anna, 23, 27, 51, 61
de Koven, Reginald, 13–14, 21, 23–26, 30, 32–34, 36, 45, 46, 48, 49, 51, 53–58, 60, 61, 69–73, 76–80, 86, 89, 92, 94, 99, 102–104, 111, 112, 122, 124, 125, 132, 143, 144, 148, 157, 158, 165, 186, 190, 191, 193, 218, 219, 222, 274, 275
Dellinger, Rudolph, 47
demoiselles de Saint-Cyriens, Les, 129
de Najac, 143
Deslys, Gaby, 213, 243, 244
Dey, The, 58, 69–70, 72, 79
Dickie Lingard Company, 9, 11
Dillingham, Charles, 89, 153–154, 157–158, 162, 165, 167, 169, 170, 172, 182, 198, 205, 233, 238, 243, 244, 252, 282
Dippel, Andreas, 233
Divorced Bride, The, 201
Dixey, Henry E., 11, 68, 99
"Dixie," 150–151
Doll Girl, The, 228–229, 231
Donaldson, Walter, 267
Don Quixote, 33, 34, 45–51, 54
D'formann, Felix, 221, 246
Dorothy, 70
D'Orsay, Lawrance, 194
Drei arme kleine Mädels, 276
Dressler, Marie, 82–83
Duchess, The, 216, 217. *See also* Mlle. Rosita
Duchess of Dantzig, The, 158
Duff, James C., 21, 28, 63, 64, 221
Dungan, Charles W., 43–44
Dunn, Arthur, 68
Dunn, Edward Delaney, 263, 273
Dunne, Peter, 145
Dunning, Alice, 9

Earle, Virginia, 127, 129, 130
Easy Street, 55
Edwardes, George, 205
Edwards, Gus, 137, 177
Edwards, Julian, 63–64, 69
Eine Nacht in Venedig, 21
Ellinger, Desiree, 269
Enchantress, The, 216–218
Englander, Ludwig, 75, 90, 91, 97, 104, 107, 114, 127, 129–131, 137, 142, 145, 148, 149, 153, 155, 161, 171, 176–178, 179, 194

Erlanger, Abraham, 132, 134, 141, 146, 171, 172, 183, 184, 186, 191, 196, 199, 201, 202, 207, 208, 214, 233, 234, 236, 282
Erminie, 80, 174, 175
Errol, Leon, 220, 224
Eysler, Edmund, 232

Fall, Leo, 205, 207, 215, 228, 229
"Farewell Prosperity," 200
Farnie, Henry B., 9
Farag, Jen, 264, 272
Farrington, Adele, 82
Farrington, Frank, 174
Fashions of 1924, 263–264
Fatinitza, 11, 34, 41, 165, 169
Faversham, William, 113
Feiner, Herman, 276
femme à papa, La, 122
Fencing Master, The, 58, 61, 69–72, 75, 103
Fenton, Mabel, 110, 113, 115, 120, 125
Fétards, Les, 113–114
Feydeau, Georges, 118, 223
fidele Bauer, Der, 229
Field, Eugene, 35
Fields, Lew, 105, 109, 110, 115, 116, 119, 254
Fields, W.C., 238
fils surnaturel, Le, 234
First Nights and First Editions, 5, 13, 17, 29, 33, 48, 63, 71 115, 168, 279, 282
Fisher, Sallie, 182, 220, 238
Fist, Marguerite, 40, 41
Florence, W.J., 5
Florodora, 139, 143, 180, 257
Follies of 1907, 184–186
Follies of 1908, 190–191, 195
Follies of 1909, 197–199
Follies of 1910, 201–205
Follow Me, 246–247
Fort Caramel, 26
Fortune Teller, The, 103, 106–109, 119, 135, 274
Fowler, A.N.C., 182
Foxy Quiller, 132–134, 141, 146
Foy, Edwin (Eddie), 41, 45, 68, 73–75, 82–83, 145
Franklin, Malvin M., 254
Frazee, Harry H., 219, 251
Freedley, Vinton, 256
Free Lance, The, 172–176, 281
Freeman, Max, 150
Friganza, Trixie, 174, 243
Friml, Rudolph, 264
Frohman, Charles, 153, 176, 215, 222, 225, 228, 232, 233, 235, 282
Frothingham, George B., 46, 48, 51, 144
Furth, Seymour, 190

Gaby, 213–215, 243
Galloway, Katherine, 245, 246
Gandillot, Leon, 106
Ganne, Louis, 186
Garden of Eden, The, 246
Gatti, Emmerich von, 236
Gavault, Paul, 129, 153
Gayest Manhattan, 97, 99, 103–104
gelbe Jacke, Die, 278
Genée, Adeline, 186–189, 194, 199, 207–208
Genée, Alexander, 187
Genée, Richard, 21, 28, 33, 96
Gershwin, George, 252
Gershwin, Ira, 252
geschiedene Frau, Die, 205
Gespensterschiff, Das, 276
Gibson Girl, The, 149
Gideon, Melville, 191, 195
Gilbert, Jean, 219, 242, 273, 278
Gilbert, William Schwenck, 15, 17, 24, 30, 32, 58, 101, 112, 129
Gilbert and Sullivan, 11, 13, 16, 18, 26, 30, 45, 54, 270
Gilfoil, Harry, 137, 142
Gillman, Mabel (Mabelle Gilman), 114, 127, 135
Girl from Dixie, A, 150–153, 251
Girl from Kay's, The, 176
Girl from Martin's, The, 118, 119
Girl from Maxim' s, The, 118
Girl from Montmartre, The, 223, 231
Girl in the Spotlight, The, 258–259
Girl in the Train, The, 205–207
Girl from Utah, The, 235
Girls Will Be Girls, 247. *See also Love o' Mike*
Giroflé-Girofla, 165, 169
"Give Us a Ragtime Time," 208
Glaser, Lulu, 91–93, 107, 117, 120, 129, 135, 152, 161–162, 169–170
Gluck, Wally, 271
Goetz, E. Ray, 195
Golden Butterfly, The, 191, 193–194
Goldoni, Carlo, 96
Gondoliers, The , 112
Goodman, Al, 263
Goodwin, J. Cheever, 69, 70, 101, 129, 130
Gorcey, Bernard, 269
Gordon, Kitty, 216–218
Gordon, Mack, 279
Gräfin Mariza, 268
Graham, Harry, 279
Graham, Robert E., 99, 221
Granichstaedten, Bruno, 221, 222
Grant, Richard, 159
Grau, Maurice, 79
Gray, Maud, 227
Greenback, Percy, 235
Greene, Clay M., 44–45
Greene, Schuyler, 240, 241, 249, 252
Gresham, Herbert, 142, 172, 184, 197
Grossmith, Lawrence, 247

Grünwald, Alfred, 232, 268, 270
Guinan, Texas, 245
Gunning, Louise, 154, 155
Gypsy Love, 217–218

Hajos, Karl, 266, 272
Half a King, 91–92, 95
Half a Widow, 271
Hall, Owen, 176
Hammerstein, Oscar, 104–105, 185
Happiest Man, The, 274
Happiest Man in New York, The, 186
Happiest Man in Town, The, 186
Harbach, Otto, 265
Hardt-Warden, Bruno, 276
Harlan, Otis, 213
Harmony Hall, 280–281
Hart, Albert, 100, 127, 145, 165, 172, 223
Hart, Lorenz, 255
Hassell, George, 247, 269
Haverly, J.H., 11
Hawley, Ida, 158
Hazzard, John E., 217, 224, 236
Heathen, The, 109
Hein, Silvio, 240, 241, 265
Held, Anna, 120–125, 136–137, 143, 169, 176–178, 183, 191, 194, 195, 198, 199, 201, 204, 205, 217, 233, 246–247
Hell, 213, 214
Helter Skelter, 113
Henderson, David, 36, 44–45, 54–55, 68, 171
Hennequin, Alfred, 122
Hennequin, Maurice, 114
Herbert, Joseph, 106, 119, 211, 217
Herbert, Victor, 83, 86–87, 89–90, 92, 95–97, 99–102, 104, 106, 109, 115, 117, 125, 128, 135, 158, 165, 169–170, 176, 182, 191, 192, 211, 216–218, 226–229, 233, 235, 237, 246, 255, 256, 258, 264, 265, 274, 275
Hero of the Day, The, 186
Herz, R.C., 169, 187, 189
Herzer, Ludwig, 278, 279
Hess, C.D., 21, 28
Highwayman, The, 102–104, 109, 132, 248
Hill, James M., 61, 69, 70
H.M.S. Pinafore, 11, 13, 45
Hobart, George V., 146, 191
Hobohemia, 259–261, 264
Hoff, Edwin, 46, 50, 53, 61, 62, 72
Hoffman, Gertrude, 177, 178
Hoffman, Max, 177, 178
Holbrook, Florence, 187
Hollander, Victor, 201, 242
Hopper, De Wolf, 27–28, 30–31, 33–34, 43, 45, 47–48, 58, 69–70, 273, 281
Hopper, Edna Wallace, 175
Hoschna, Karl L., 170, 199
Hotel Stadt-Lemberg, 278
Houghteling, Laura, 5, 29
Hoyt, Charles H., 85, 111, 121, 220, 251–252
Hubbell, Raymond, 199–200, 207–208, 217, 220, 221, 223, 265
Hurlburt, William J., 212
Hurly Burly, 105–106, 109, 111, 119, 180
Hutchinson, Kathryn, 179–180

Idol's Eye, The, 99–103, 107, 129
"I Don't Care," 199
"If I Only Had a Theatre on Broadway," 163
"I Just Can' t Make My Eyes Behave," 177
I'm a Good Girl, 263. *See also Peaches*
Iolanthe, 54
Irwin, May, 75
I Told You So, 269. *See also Piggy*
"It' s Moving Day Down in Jungle Town," 198
Itzel, Adam, Jr., 58–59, 76
"I Want to Sing in Opera," 216
"I Wouldn' t Take a Case Like That," 192

Jacobi, Victor, 242, 244–245, 248–249
Janvier, Emma, 194
Japonica, 159
Jarbeau, Verona, 99
Jardon, Dorothy, 219, 236
Jerome, William, 137, 171, 180, 224
Jewel of Asia, The, 148–149, 159
jockey malgré lui, Le, 153
Johnson, James Weldon, 149, 212
Johnson, J. Rosamond, 212
Jolly Peasant, The, 229
Jones, Walter, 212, 232
Jordan, Joe, 202
Judels, Charles, 223–224
Judic, Anna, 122
Jupiter, 63–64, 68–69, 82, 92, 130–131

"K-K-K-Katy," 271, 280
Kálmán, Emmerich, 268, 269, 270
Kalmar, Bert, 252
Karl, Tom, 46, 61
"Kathleen," 259
"Keep Away from Emmeline," 110
Kelly, Harry, 192, 197
Kelly, John T., 105, 110–111, 113, 118–119
Kerker, Gustave, 146, 149–150, 161, 163
Kern, Jerome, 180, 212, 216, 223, 226, 228, 231–233, 235, 239–242, 247, 248, 253, 264, 265
Keroul, Henri, 232
keusche Suzanne, Die, 219
King, Charles, 220, 238
King for a Day, 172. *See also Free Lance, The*
Klaw, Marc, 132, 141, 146, 171–172, 183–184, 186, 191, 196, 198, 199, 201, 207, 208, 233, 234, 236, 282
kleine Freunden, Der, 227

Knickerbockers, The, 72–73, 100
Knights, The, 48
Kollo, Walter, 228, 261, 276
Kosary, Emmy, 278, 279
Krehbiel, Henry Edward, 96, 210
Künneke, Edward, 263, 265

Lachaume, Aimé, 135, 136, 142
lachende Ehemann, Der, 232
Ladies First, 251–252
Lady in Red, The, 253
Land des Lächelns, Das, 278
Land of Smiles, The, 279–280
Landstreicher, Die, 137
La Shelle, Kirke, 85, 86
Laughing Husband, The, 232–233
Leave It to Me, 267. *See also Sweetheart Time*
Lecocq, Charles, 125, 165, 169
Lederer, George, 114–115, 125, 128–129, 131, 137, 145, 148–149, 152, 255, 262, 276–278, 282
Lee, Sammy, 262
Lehár, Franz, 217, 278
Léon, Victor, 205, 229, 278
Leterrier, Eugène, 91, 165
Levey, Ethel, 189–190, 213
Levi, Maurice, 139–140, 186, 189–190, 197, 201
Lewis, Ada, 189–190, 213
Lewis, Ian, 23–24
Lewis, Sinclair, 259, 261
Liberty Belles, The, 140–143, 151, 153, 251
Lilac Domino, The, 236, 250
lila Domino, Der, 233, 236
Lindau, Carl, 137
Ling, Richie, 118, 158
Lingard, Dickie, 9, 15
Lingard, William Horace, 9
Litt, Jacob, 16–17
Little Corporal, The, 107–108
Little Duchess, The, 137, 143–144, 169, 184
"Little Gypsy Maid, The," 146–147
Little Miss Fix-It, 212–213, 231
Little Miss Wise, 255. *See also Angel Face*
Little Nemo, 191–194
"Little Old New York Is Good Enough for Me," 111
Little Robinson Crusoe, 82–83
Löhner-Beda, Fritz, 278, 279
Lonely Romeo, A, 253–255
Look Who's Here, 252. *See also Ladies First*
Lorraine, Lillian, 195, 197–198, 201, 204, 224, 233
Lost Twins, The, 55
Love Call, The, 272
"Love-Land," 229
Love o' Mike, 247–248
Love Song, The, 264–266
Lowrie, Jeanette, 172–173
Luders, Gustave, 82
Luescher, Mark A., 208, 210, 212, 221, 222, 226
Lydia Thompson Burlesque Company, 5
"Lydy Wot Is Studin' for the Stige, (The)," 111, 127
Lyrics and Sonnets, 78

McCaull, Colonel John, 27–28, 31–32, 36, 42–43, 45, 47, 225
McCaull' s Opera Company, 28–29, 33–34, 39, 41–43, 45, 47, 54–55, 63, 85, 90
MacConnell, Harry T., 127, 130, 142
McConnell, William A., 33, 35–36, 48
McCree, Junie, 145, 160
MacDonald, Ballard, 201, 267
MacDonald, Christie, 129–130, 180, 208, 226, 229
MacDonald, William H., 46, 51, 72, 89, 95, 128, 144
MacDonough, Glen, 76
MacDonough, Harry, 30–31, 102–103, 132, 188, 218
Mack, Cecil, 146
McNally, John J., 139, 172
McNaughton, Tom, 208, 226, 229
Maconda, Carlotta, 50, 53
McVicker, James H., 10
McVicker Stock Company, 9
McVicker's Theatre, 15, 44
Madame Sans-Géne, 158
Madcap Princess, A, 161–162
Mädel von Montmartre, Das, 222–223
Maid Marrian, 144–145
Mam'zelle Nitouche, 122
Mandarin, The, 92–95
Mandarin Zune, The, 94
Mann, Louis, 15, 167–168
Manola, Marion, 43, 56, 120
Mansfield, Richard, 109
Marbury, Elizabeth ("Bessie"), 241, 247, 256
Marching By, 279 *See also Arms and the Maid*
Marion, George, 122, 143, 213
Marlowe, Julia, 125
Mars, Antony, 114
Mars, Leo, 194–195
Marsh, Howard, 269–270
Martos, Ferenc, 242
Masked Model, The, 245–246
Masquerading Girl, 172
May Queen, The, 41–42
Maytime, 276
Meilhac, Henri, 122
Mercer, Johnny, 277
Mercer, Will, 159. *See also* Cook, Will Marion
Merry Widow, The, 190, 216, 218, 265–266
Mesmerist, The, 147
Mestayer, Louis, 5
Meyer, Joseph, 265, 267

Mikado, The, 16, 26, 92, 270
Milburn, Mary, 258, 267
Millaud, Albert, 122, 143
Millöcker, Karl, 54
Minute Men, The, 76
Miracle Maid, The, 258. *See also Girl in the Spotlight, The*
Miss Dolly Dollars, 169–171, 176
Miss Innocence, 194–195, 199, 217
Miss Innocence Abroad, 194. *See also Miss Innocence*
"Mister Dooley," 145
Mistletoe Bough, The, 5
Mitchell, Julian, 102, 111, 113, 177, 184, 191, 194, 197, 201, 202, 208, 220, 223, 236
Mitchell, Maggie, 102
Mitzi (Hajos), 267–268
M'lle Innocence, 217. *See also Miss Innocence*
Mlle. Modiste, 211, 218
Mlle. Rosita, 211–212, 216
moderne Eva, Die, 242
Modern Eve, A, 242
Modest Suzanne, 219–220
Mogul, The, 83. *See also Caliph, The*
Mollie Darling, 259. *See also Girl in the Spotlight, The*
Molly O', 246. *See also Masked Model, The*
Monaco, James V., 224
Monterey, Carlotta, 263
Moreau, Emile, 158
Morgan, Eloise, 148–149
Motzan, Otto, 241
Mr. Popple (of Ippleton), 240
Myers, Richard, 277
"My Josephine," 113
My Little Friend, 227–228
Myrtil, Odette, 272

Nancy Brown (musical), 146
"Nancy Brown" (song), 146
Nanon, 96
Natja, 266
"Naughty Little Clock, The," 127
Naughty Riquette, 267–268
Nearly a Hero, 186, 189–190
Ned Wayburn's Town Topics, 242–243
Nethersole, Olga, 127
Never Say Die, 267
Nichols, Alberta, 273
Nielsen, Alice, 95, 97–98, 104, 106, 108–109, 117–120, 135
Nielsen, Christine, 218
Night Owl, The, 276–277. *See also Pajama Lady, The*
Ninety in the Shade, 239
Niniche, 143
Nobody Home, 240–242
Norworth, Jack, 191, 212–213
"Nothing Is Like It Used to Be," 59
nuit de noces, Une, 232

O' Brien, Eugene, 211–212
O' Connor, Robert, 227, 236
O'Donnell, George, 102, 148
Offenbach, 264
Offenbach, Jacques, 7, 16, 18, 56, 80, 219, 264–266
Office Boy, The, 153–155, 176, 182
Ogden High School, 6, 14
O' Hara, Geoffrey, 75, 271, 276, 280
Oh, I Say!, 231–232
"Oh, Johnny, Oh, Johnny, Oh!," 247
"Oh, You Beautiful Doll," 215
Okonkowsky, Georg, 219, 242
Omar, Jr., 172, 176, 182
Omar, 169
O' Mara, Joseph, 102–103, 111
Only Way, The, 119
"O Promise Me," 56, 60–61
Ordonneau, Maurice, 153
Orlob, Harold, 242, 246
Österreicher, Rudolf, 273
O' Sullivan, Denis, 107
O'Thello, 9
Other Way, The, 119, 125
Ouden, Eugene, 43
Oui, Madame, 256–257
Our Friend the Baron, 160
Outlaw, The. See Robin Hood
Oxygen, 10

Painter, Eleanor, 236
Pajama Lady, The, 277–278
Papa' s Bride, 169
Papa's Darling, 236–237
Papa's Wife, 122, 124–125, 134, 136, 142
paradis de Mahomet, Le, 186, 188,
Paradise of Mahomet, The, 210–211
Paris Doll, The, 99, 106, 111–112, 127
Paris Model, 176
Parisian Model, The, 169, 176–177, 180, 183–185, 194
Parlor Match, A, 121
Patience, 11, 13, 16, 54
Peaches, 262–263
Peattie, Robert, 35–36
Peck, Raymond, 221
Peg Woffington, 100–101
Périchole, La, 18, 80
Perkins, Carrie E., 127, 145, 148–149
Perry, Irene, 118–119, 127
Piantadosi, Al, 199
Piggy, 269
Pink Lady, The 223, 237–238
Pirates of Penzance, The, 18
Planquette, Robert, 11, 186
Playing the Game, 216
Pluto, 9
Pompon, Le, 125

"Popularity," 113
"Popular Pop, The," 237
Power, James T., 148–149
Prima Donna, The, 135–136
Prince Ananias, 86
Prince Chow Chow, 17, 20, 26
Prince Chu Chang, 278, 279. *See also Land of Smiles, The*
Princess Flavia, 266–267, 269
Princess Runs Away, The, 281
Pruette, William, 68, 77, 162, 227
Pryor, Thomas W., 68–69, 82
Puppenmädel, Das, 228

"Quiller Has the Brain," 133–134

Rafter, Adele, 144, 154
Rag Baby, A, 85
Rambler, The, 23–24, 26, 184
Rambler Rose, 249–250
Ranken, Frederic, 146, 148
Rasch, Albertina, 274, 277
Rea, Lawrence, 208
"Real American Folk Song Is a Rag, The," 252
Red Feather, The, 158
Red Hussan, The, 70
Red Robe, The, 273
Red Rose, The, 214–215
Reed, Lena. *See* Smith, Lena Reed (wife)
Reed, Roland, 9
Rehan, Ada, 75, 113
Reinhardt, Heinrich, 208
Reisenfeld, Hugo, 256, 258
Revel, Harry, 279
Rich Mr. Hoggenheimer, The, 176–180, 231, 269
Ring, Blanche, 149–150, 152, 174
Riquette, 267
Rival Cantineers, The, 10–11
Robertson, Guy, 270, 272, 279
Robin Hood, 48–57, 60–64, 68–69, 71–73, 75, 78, 80, 89, 94–96, 103–104, 107, 112–113, 125, 128, 134, 144, 219, 222–223, 274, 275
Robinson Crusoe (burlesque), 10
Rob Roy, 76–79, 83, 86, 165, 229
Rodansky, Robert, 217
Rodgers, Richard, 254
Roger, Victor, 114, 153
Rogers, Gus, 139
Rogers, Max, 139
Rogers, Will, 242
Rogers Brothers in Washington, The, 139–141
Rogues and Vagabonds, 75, 276
roi de carreau, Le, 91
roi l' a dit, Le, 21
Roll of the Drum, The, 135
Romberg, Sigmund, 246, 261, 266, 269–272, 276
Rope Dancer, The, 63
Rose Maid, The, 221–222
Rosita; or, *Boston and Banditi*, 20
Rosita; or, *Cupid and Cupidity*, 18–20
Ross, Adrian, 205, 235, 263
Ross, Charles J., 105, 109–110, 113, 118, 125, 220
Rounders, The, 114–115, 128–129
Round the Clock, 233, 238. *See also Watch Your Step*
Rourke, M.E., 226, 235
"Row, Row, Row," 224
Rubens, Paul, A., 225, 235, 240, 241
Ruby, Harry, 252
Runaway, The (Morton), 248. *See also Rambler Rose*
Runaway, The (Smith), 274
Rushworth, Frank, 106, 144
Russell, Annie, 110
Russell, Lillian, 6, 76, 79–82, 115–120, 198

St. Clair, Edith, 171, 194
Salem Witch, The, 64
Sambo Girl, The, 160–164
Sanderson, Julia, 215–216, 225, 235, 244, 249, 252, 253
Santley, Joseph, 239, 240, 241, 244
Sapho, 125, 127
Sapolio, 125, 127
Sardou, Victorien, 106, 158
Scarecrow, The, 35–36, 48
Schanzer, Rudolph, 223, 261, 267
Scheff, Fritzi, 155, 157–159, 165, 169, 211–212, 217
Schleiffarth, George, 17–18, 20
Schönfeld, Alfred, 219, 242
Schwartz, Arthur, 273
Schwartz, Jean, 137, 171, 180, 199
Seabrooke, Thomas Q., 83, 90, 114
Sears, Zelda, 189–190
Second Fiddle, The, 15, 160, 167–169, 193–194
Seeing New York, 165
Seeley, Blossom, 242, 244
Selden, Edgar, 191
September Morn, 228
Serenade, The, 20, 89–90, 95–97, 104, 125, 128, 134–135, 144, 275, 276
Serenaders, The, 95. *See also Serenade, The*
Seven Suabians, The, 54
Shean, Al, 221
"Sheik of Araby, The," 259
Sheriff of Nottingham, The, 125
Shilkret, Jack, 264
"Shine on Harvest Moon," 191, 195
Show Boat, 262, 270
Shubert Brothers (J.J. and Lee), 188, 189, 210, 211, 218, 219, 232, 246–248, 257, 261, 263–266, 268–272, 274, 276, 278, 280, 282

Shubert, J.J., 264
Shubert, Lee, 190
Shubert, Sam S., 151
Siège de Grenade, Le, 135
Silver Star, The, 199, 207
Sinbad, 59–60, 63, 73, 75
Sindbad, 5
Singing Girl, The, 115, 117–119, 134
Siren, The, 215–216, 231
"66," Le, 16
Slaven, John C., 118, 142, 174, 200
Sleeping Beauty and the Beast, The, 171
Sloane, A. Baldwin, 125, 142, 251–252
Smith, Bessie (sister), 6, 282
Smith, Edgar, 104–105, 278, 280
Smith, Elihu H., 4
Smith, Elizabeth (mother), 3–4, 9
Smith, Gertrude (sister), 6
Smith, Henry Tisdale (uncle), 3
Smith, Josiah Bailey (father), 3–4, 6, 9
Smith, Lena Reed (wife), 29, 35, 75, 153, 282
Smith, Mary (sister), 6, 282
Smith, Robert B. (brother), 7, 130, 165, 200, 208, 213, 217, 219–223, 227, 229, 235, 236, 242, 245, 246, 250, 254–256, 258, 262, 276, 277, 282
Smith, Sydney Reed (son), 75, 247–248, 281
Snyder, Ted, 259, 263, 264
Soldier of Fortune, 76
Solomon, Edward, 70
Some Colonel, 257. *See also Oui, Madame*
"Some Little Bug Is Going to Find You," 241
Sorcerer, The, 11
Soul Kiss, The, 186–190, 194, 199, 251
Sousa, John Philip, 171–174, 185, 243, 264, 265
Southerners, The, 159–161, 203
Spring Maid, The, 208–211, 214–215, 226
Springtime of Youth, 261–262
Sprudelfee, Die, 208
Stage Lyrics, 134
Stange, Stanislaus, 118–119
Star Witness, The, 280
Stein, Leo, 215, 227–228
Steiner, Max, 257, 262
Sterne, die wieden leuchtet, 261
Stewart, Melville, 169, 206
Stolz, Robert, 273
Stop! Look! Listen!, 243–244
Straus, Oscar, 214, 227–228, 267
Strauss, Johann, II, 21, 33
Strike the Lyre, 247. *See also Love o' Mike*
Strollers, The, 137–139, 152
Stromberg, John, 104, 110–111, 113, 118, 125, 127
Stuart, Leslie, 139, 143, 180
Student Prince, The, 266–267, 269–270, 272
Sullivan, Arthur, 56, 58, 112
Sultan of Sulu, The, 145
Sunshine Girl, The, 225–226
Suppé, Franz von, 11, 28, 33–34, 42
Sweethearts, 226–229, 274
Sweetheart Time, 267, 271
Sybil, 244–245
Sykes, Jerome, 102–103, 132–133, 146, 148
Sylva, Marguerita, 218
Sylvia; or, *The May Queen*, 79
Szibill, 242, 244. *See also Sybil*

Tabor, Desirée, 270, 279
"Take Me 'Round in a Taxicab," 191
Tales of Hoffmann, The, 219
Tanguay, Eva, 120, 155, 162–165, 199
Tar and the Tartar, The, 56, 58–59, 63, 68, 75–77
Tattooed Man, The, 181–182
"Tell Me, Pretty Maiden," 139
Tempest, Maire, 58, 61, 69–71, 120
Templeton, Fay, 19–20, 29, 106, 109–111, 113, 115, 120
Templeton, John, 19–20
Temptation, 213
That's My Baby, 269. *See also Piggy*
"They Follow Me Around," 238
Their Wedding Night, 232. *See also Oh, I Say!*
Thiele, Henry, 15, 17, 26
Thomas, Augustus, 265, 271
Thomas, Augustus, Jr., 247–248
Thompson, Captain Alfred, 36–38, 44–45
Thompson, Lydia, 5–6, 10, 36
Three Dragons, The, 111–113, 127, 174–175
Three Little Girls, 276
Tierney, Harry, 246, 253
Tilbury, Zeffie, 6
Toler, Sydney, 154–155
Tonight's the Night, 241
Tortue, La, 106
Tréfeu, Étienne, 111
Trilby, 104
Trip to Chinatown, A, 111, 220
trois cadets de Gascoyne, Les, 111
Tucker, Sophie, 197–198
Tulip Girl, The, 226. *See also Sweethearts*
Turtle, The, 106
"Two Little Love Bees," 209
Tzigane, The, 76, 79–82, 88

Van Alstyne, Egbert, 195
Van Dresser, Marcia, 126
Vanloo, Albert, 91, 165
Van Nostrand, Mary (grandmother), 4
Van Studdiford, Grace, 120, 144, 188, 193–194, 210–211
Varney, Louis, 129
Vaucaire, Maurice, 234
Veber, Pierre, 248

Verneuil, Louis, 252
Vetter aus Dingsda, Derr, 263
Viceroy, The, 115, 125, 128
Von Tilzer, Albert, 191
Vokes, May, 182

Walker, George, 202
Walsh, Lionel, 213, 227
Waltz Dream, A, 190
Wang, 70
Warfield, David, 105–106, 110, 118–119
Was tut man nicht alles aus Liebe, 246
Watch Your Step, 238–239, 243
Watson, Harry, 199, 201
Watson, Harry, Jr., 223
Wayburn, Ned, 148, 172, 242
Wayhighman, The, 104
Webb, Clifton, 242
Weber, Joseph, 105, 109–110, 119
Weber and Fields, 104, 105, 106, 109, 111, 113, 115–116, 127, 183
"Wedding of the Reuben and the Maid, The," 139–140
Wedding Trap, The, 218–219
Weekly Scene, The, 7
Weib im Purpur, Das, 273
Werba, Louis F., 208, 210, 212, 221, 222, 226
West, Mae, 221
West, Paul, 155, 180
"We Two in an Aeroplane," 195
"What! Marry Dat Gal?" 111
Wheeler, Francis, 259, 264
Whelan, Alfred C., 68, 90
"When Chloe Sings," 120
"When Cupid Comes a-Tapping," 99, 112, 127
Whirl-i-Gig, 117–119, 125
White Cat, The, 171–172
White Fox, The, 274
White Lilacs, 272–273
Whiting, Richard A., 254
Whitney, Fred C., 76–77, 79, 165, 214, 227, 266
Whitney Opera Company, 75
Whittell, Josephine, 244, 256
"Who Will Buy My Roses Red," 17
Wild Oats, 113
Wild Rose, The, 145–146, 152
Williams, Bert, 202–203, 224
Williams, Hattie, 223, 228
Willner, Alfred Maria, 208, 215, 217, 227–228
Willow Tree, The, 269
Will Shakespeare, Player, 75, 276
Wilson, Francis, 80, 90–92, 104, 107–108, 117, 137, 162, 281
Wimperis, Arthur, 225, 232
Winsome Widow, A, 220–221, 231
Wizard of the Nile, The, 83, 86–89, 92, 95, 99–100, 104
Wodehouse, P.G., 253
Woess, Carl, 245–246
Wolf, Rennold, 213
Wood, J. Hickory, 171
Woodruff, Henry, 122
Woodward, Matthew C., 20, 261
Woolf, Walter, 268, 273

Yohe, May 40–41
Young, Halfred, 271, 278
Young, Rida Johnson, 276
"You're Here and I'm Here," 233
"Yours Is My Heart Alone," 278, 280

Zauberer vom Nil, Der, 92. *See also Wizard of the Nile, The*
Zeigeunerliebe, 217
Zell, Friedrich, 21, 28
Zenobia, 14
Ziegfeld, Dr. Florenz, 14
Ziegfeld, Florenz, Jr., 14, 26, 106, 121–122, 124, 136, 143, 158, 183–186, 190–191, 194–198, 202–204, 213–214, 220, 223–225, 233–234, 243, 282
Ziegfeld Follies of 1912, 222–225
"Ziegfeld of the Follies," 224–225
Ziehrer, Carl Michael, 137
Zirkusprinzessin, Die, 270